*The 25 Greatest Baseball Teams
of the 20th Century Ranked*

ALSO BY CHRIS HOLADAY

Professional Baseball in North Carolina:
An Illustrated City-by-City History, 1901–1996
(McFarland, 1998)

The 25 Greatest Baseball Teams of the 20th Century Ranked

by CHRIS HOLADAY *and*
MARSHALL ADESMAN

McFarland & Company, Inc., Publishers
Jefferson, North Carolina, and London

Front cover: *(clockwise from the left):* Frank "Home Run" Baker of the 1912 Athletics, the 1944 St. Louis Cardinals, Hall of Fame second baseman Johnny Evers of the 1906 Cubs, and the 1976 Cincinnati Reds *(all photographs courtesy of the authors).*

Library of Congress Cataloguing-in-Publication Data

Holaday, Chris, 1966–
    The 25 greatest baseball teams of the 20th century ranked / by Chris Holaday and Marshall Adesman.
        p.   cm.
    Includes bibliographical references and index.
    ISBN 0-7864-0925-8 (softcover : 50# alkaline paper)
    1. Baseball teams.   2. Baseball players — Rating of.
I. Title: Twenty-five greatest baseball teams of the twentieth century ranked.   II. Adesman, Marshall, 1949–   III. Title.
GV875.A1 H64   2000
796.357'0973'0904 — dc21   00-41828

British Library cataloguing data are available

Manufactured in the United States of America

McFarland & Company, Inc., Publishers
  Box 611, Jefferson, North Carolina 28640
  www.mcfarlandpub.com

To the Texas Rangers.
May they one day field a team
worthy of inclusion in this book.
JCH

To Susan,
who never complained,
and to Sidney, who was
looking over my shoulder.
MA

ACKNOWLEDGMENTS

The authors gratefully wish to thank several institutions for their kind assistance in the writing of this book. The libraries at Duke University, the Duke University Medical Center, the University of North Carolina at Chapel Hill and the County of Durham have been especially helpful in helping us find books, articles and little-known facts. We are also grateful to *The Sporting News* and to *Baseball America* for being such fountains of information over the years.

As always, a great many people gave us help along the way. William Donelan and Susan Clark, of the Duke University Health System, were indulgent employers. Eunice Adesman supplied a great many old books, photos and clippings that proved to be very helpful, especially for some of the New York teams. Mary Greenway turned up tons of newspaper clippings, plus a World Series video, on the 1995 Atlanta Braves. And Ruta Zemaitis Bloomfield willingly donated a book of photographs she took herself at the 1984 World Series. Hank Utley contributed photographs from his Detroit Tigers collection, while John Crabill shared his memories and knowledge of the Big Red Machine. Special thanks as well go to Dylan Jenkins for his technical expertise.

And of course we thank our wives, Sue and Susan, who learned when to leave us alone and when to lend a sympathetic ear over the months we were working on this book. While they didn't write a word, their contributions may have been the most important of all.

CONTENTS

PREFACE

Which was the greatest baseball team ever? That question will be argued for as long as the game is played.

Fans of the game are generally biased by numerous personal factors, including age and environment. We tend to over-romanticize the sports memories of our youth; in our minds, no one can possibly compare to our childhood heroes. We guarantee that if a survey were taken asking fans to select the greatest baseball team of all time, the vast majority would respond with a team from their youth. Personally, we may be biased toward the teams of the 1960s and 1970s, because those just happen to be the teams we went to see in person, watched on television, or listened to on the radio. At one time we could have probably recited the lineups and batting averages of the '61 Yankees, '74 Dodgers, '75 and '76 Reds, and the '77-'78 Yankees. For those of us in our formative years at that time, these teams epitomized greatness.

The other huge bias is environment, or where we grew up. What diehard Yankee fan is going to admit that a team of Dodgers or Red Sox is the greatest ever? To test this theory, we asked a friend, a native New Yorker and longtime Yankee fan, his opinion as to the greatest team ever. There was no surprise as to his choice of franchise, although we were a little startled by his selection of the late–1930s edition of the boys in pinstripes, rather than the more famous 1927 team. In asking another friend, a lifelong Detroit fan, the same question, we received this quick response: "Probably the '34 Tigers, or maybe even the '68 Tigers." Now these are all great teams in their own right and deserve to be considered, but the reasons behind their selection were just a little prejudiced.

Perhaps, then, we should first try to determine what makes a great team.

Though the objective of every team is to win ball games, is the team that wins the most automatically the best? If that is the case, then the 1998 Yankees, winners of 114 games in the regular season and another 11 in the postseason, would be the greatest team ever. Another case could be made for the 1954 Indians, winners of 111 games in the 154-game schedule. On the other hand, others might say that winning percentage is the best way to determine a great team. Using this criterion, the 1906 Cubs' .763 would easily prevail.

We admit to wondering whether teams from different eras can truly be compared. Was the brand of baseball played by Ty Cobb's Tigers or Christy Mathewson's Giants the same as that played by the Yankees of Joe DiMaggio, or the Dodgers of Jackie Robinson, or the Reds of Johnny Bench? No, there were some significant differences, but at least all teams played by the same set of rules at the same time; in other words, the ball was just as dead for Cobb as it was for all of his opponents. Therefore, in order to make our list, a team simply had to prove its greatness against its opponents and generally over a period of time.

Star quality must also be a factor, although a smaller one. You simply cannot have a great team without having at least one marquee player, and probably more. The Yankee squad that closed the 20th century with three World Series triumphs in four years liked to say they were a true 25-man aggregation, devoid of individual stars, but in truth they featured Derek Jeter, David Cone, Bernie Williams, and even future Hall of Famer Roger Clemens during the 1999 season. Compare them, please, to the 1928 Philadelphia Athletics, who were able to trot out eight players who later were enshrined in Cooperstown, but you will notice the A's did not even win the pennant that year and therefore did not make our list.

And certainly winning at least one World Series is a must for a great team; winning more than one ensures a club's lasting place in history. Those 1928 A's did not make our final cut for just that reason, while their 1929–31 successors did. Thus many of the teams listed in this book represent more than one year, because the bulk of the playing personnel remained the same for several seasons and brought glory to the team and their city for that entire period. Just one case in point: the Brooklyn Dodgers, 1949–1956.

One other criterion for a great team is how they are perceived over time. We have included the 1960 Pittsburgh Pirates and the 1969 New York Mets, which might raise a few eyebrows, but they are here for several reasons. They both won World Series and they both featured Hall of Fame–bound players (Clemente, Seaver). But over time they have achieved a unique, almost mythic status, not just in their communities but in baseball circles as well. They were dragon-slayers, achieving the ultimate triumph in the face of long odds. Their legend (if we may be so bold) has only grown through the decades, and this quality, we feel, elevates them to the status of greatness and lands them into this volume.

What we have done, then, is to use these criteria to present the teams we have determined to be the best of the 20th century, the so-called modern era of baseball. We are listing them in chronological order and telling you a little bit about them and who and what made them great. And then, when all is said and done, we stick our necks out a bit and make a very subjective rating of the clubs, understanding that they cannot possibly be rated except in some perverse, someone-has-to-be-number-one sort of way. At that point, though, we leave you to make your own decisions and your own lists, based as always on age and environment, as well as the facts presented here. But please remember how subjective this truly is, and that this debate can and will go on for as long as there are barrooms, as long as people have differing opinions, and as long as the great game of baseball is played. Let the arguments begin!

THE TEAMS

1906–08
Chicago Cubs

At the beginning of the 21st century, it is easy for us to forget, or to never have learned, what happened at the beginning of the 20th century. For fans of the Chicago Cubs, it's easy to assume the team has always been baseball's loveable losers. There have been no trips to the World Series since 1945, and in the 54 seasons since then the Cubs have lost more games than any other franchise — 4,534. They have made only three postseason appearances: in 1984, 1989 and 1998, and lost all three series. They have, in fact, finished the season at .500 or better only 15 times in those 54 seasons, a success ratio of just .278.

So it's easy to assume Cub history is simply one long tale of woe, with only occasional moments of brilliance and joyous memories. That assumption would be wrong. In the first four decades of the 20th century the Cubs were one of the National League's elite teams, a consistent pennant contender and home to a great many of the game's brightest stars. Three of those early stars were even immortalized in poem by journalist, poet and diehard New York Giant fan Franklin P. Adams:

> These are the saddest of possible words:
> Tinker to Evers to Chance.
> Trio of Bear-cubs, fleeter than birds,
> Tinker to Evers to Chance.
> Ruthlessly pricking our gonfalon bubble,
> Making a Giant hit into a double,
> Words that are weighty with nothing but trouble:
> Tinker to Evers to Chance.

Thus the first rhapsody to ballplayers was for shortstop Joe Tinker; Johnny Evers, the second baseman; and Frank Chance at first, the most famous double-play trio of its day, and names which are still linked together and associated with the twin killing. They were the stars for a Cubs team that dominated the first decade of the 20th century.

As the 1900s began, the face of baseball was radically different from today, and even different from how it had looked just a few short years before. The National League, established in 1876, had spent much of the last quarter of the 19th century fighting off challengers, most recently from the American Association, which gave up the battle following the 1891 season and allowed four of its clubs to join the NL (Baltimore, Louisville, St. Louis and Washington). Peace reigned for nearly a decade but it was not joined by prosperity, as a 12-team league proved to be unwieldy. Early in 1900, the league voted to buy out four franchises — Baltimore, Cleveland, Louisville and Washington — and go with their strongest eight. Thus the National League began the century with the Boston Bees, Brooklyn Dodgers, Chicago Cubs, Cincinnati Reds, New York Giants, Philadelphia Phillies, Pittsburgh Pirates and St. Louis Cardinals, an octet that would stay together unchanged for 53 years. The American League, at the time, was a minor league, having operated for years as the Western League, but this would change after the 1900 season. The AL asked to be recognized as a major league and was rejected by the haughty "senior circuit." Considering that a "state of war" existed, American League teams began to offer higher salaries to established NL stars and lured a great many of them over. The war lasted two years, at which time the two leagues agreed to peacefully coexist, which more or less describes the situation today.

Chicago's National League team (they were known by a couple of nicknames, most notably Orphans and Spuds) began their rise to the top in 1898, when a young catcher from California named Frank Chance joined the team. Two years later Johnny Kling, another catcher, was added to the roster. Kling was better than Chance with the glove but Chance could hit and run, and he was also establishing himself as a team leader. Chance moved to the outfield.

The next key addition was Frank Selee, a name even old-time Cub fans may not recognize. Selee had managed Boston for 12 years, winning five pennants and finishing in the first division nine times. He has been described as "taciturn and colorless," yet was recognized as a great judge of talent. In Boston he had discovered or developed such stars as Kid Nichols, Fred Tenney, Hugh Duffy, Bobby Lowe, Jimmy Collins and Chick Stahl. Though suffering from tuberculosis, which would eventually kill him, Selee was eager to leave Boston, which had lost a great many players to the American League in the war, and signed on to manage in Chicago after the 1901 season.

In judging talent Selee didn't just stop at determining whether or not they had the ability to play in the majors, he also had a skill for moving players to a position that better suited them. In Boston he had turned Tenney from a mediocre catcher to one of the best first basemen of his era. When he moved to Chicago, Selee saw similarities in Chance and wanted to make the same move, but Chance balked, even threatening to retire when Selee ordered him to first base. The manager then tried a different approach, offering Chance more money if he would switch; ballplayers being about the same then as they are now, Chance suddenly agreed.

Nineteen hundred and two proved to be a watershed year for Chicago's National League club. Selee brought with him three young players: infielder Joe Tinker, outfielder Jimmy Slagle and righthanded pitcher Carl Lundgren. Tinker had played third base in the minors but Selee liked his range and strong arm and saw him as a shortstop. Tinker, like Chance, was hesitant to change positions but eventually moved; no word on whether a more lucrative contract was also at the heart of his assent. Slagle had played briefly for Selee the year before in Boston and the man-

Hall of Fame second baseman Johnny Evers.

ager liked his speed and keen batting eye. Lundgren had been a star at the University of Illinois, whose baseball coach and athletic director, George Huff, proved also to be an excellent talent scout and began a pipeline to the big-league club. Huff would subsequently discover pitcher Ed Reulbach and outfielder Frank Schulte, two more key components for the Cubs. And in September of that year a wispy young infielder, Johnny Evers, also joined the team.

The team nickname proved to be another product of 1902. Two years earlier it had been used in a newspaper headline primarily because it fit. But by 1902 it was being used regularly by both writers and fans, so the team began using it, too. They have been the Cubs ever since.

Selee may have had many wonderful qualities but miracle worker was not one of them. His 1902 squad finished fifth, 34 games behind pennant-winning Pittsburgh. But they were just one game below .500, a considerable improvement over the 1901 club that produced a mere .381 winning percentage. The following year they made the leap to third place, winning 82 times and finishing just eight games out of first, the closest they had been in a dozen years.

Frank Chance was becoming both a star and a team leader. He admired the ability of a rookie pitcher in St. Louis, Mordecai Brown, and lobbied management to try and get him. They finally made a deal after the 1903 season, bringing to Chicago a future Hall of Famer.

The Cubs won 93 games in 1904 and 92 in 1905 but finished 13 games behind John McGraw's Giants both years. Reulbach became a part of the rotation in 1905, joining Brown and Lundgren, while Schulte claimed one of the outfield positions. But in mid-season the Cubs lost Selee, whose tuberculosis became too severe for him to continue as manager. In an unusual move, he allowed the players to select one of their own to succeed him, and in a clubhouse vote Frank Chance defeated third baseman Doc Casey and Jimmy Kling. When the season ended the team was sold to Charlie Murphy, who not only agreed to let Chance remain as manager but also listened to his skipper's suggestions. "Husk" (Chance's nickname) identified the Cubs' needs and also targeted specific players to fill them. He traded four players, including Casey, to Brooklyn for outfielder Jimmy Sheckard. He sent Jake Weimer, a lefthanded pitcher who had won 58 games in three years, to Cincinnati for third baseman Harry Steinfeldt, replacing Casey. He picked up pitcher Jack Pfiester and catcher Pat Moran in minor deals.

After back-to-back pennants and a spectacular victory in the 1905 World Series (in which they shut out Connie Mack's Philadelphia Athletics four times*), the New York Giants were favored to triumph again. They started off well but so did the Cubs, and a two-team race quickly developed. For several weeks they battled for the lead, but the Cubs began pulling away at the end of May. Shortly thereafter, probably on the theory that you can never have too much pitching, the Cubs picked up a pair of righthanders, bringing in Orval Overall from the Reds and reacquiring Jack Taylor from the Cardinals. The team won, and won, and won some more. They put together a 14-game winning streak, and their record in the month of August was 26–3. They left the Giants, the rest of the league and the baseball record book in the dust as they went on to win 116 games, still the all-time regular season mark, and fashion a winning percentage of .763. Their margin over the Giants was 20 games as they won their first pennant since 1886.

In this pre–Babe Ruth age, pitching always dominated, but these Cubs took it to an extreme. Their hurlers had a team ERA of 1.75, an unbelievable mark even in that dead-ball era, and they held opposing batters to an average of just 6.6 hits per game. Six pitchers won in double-figures, led by "Three Finger" Mordecai Brown's 26 wins (and all-time NL mark of 1.04 ERA) and Pfiester's 20. Ed Reulbach's .826 winning percentage led the league, the first of

---

*The A's won one game in the Series, 3–0. The three runs they scored were all unearned, so Giant pitchers logged a perfect 0.00 ERA. It is also the only World Series in history in which the losing team in every game was shut out.

three straight seasons he would do so. Even mid-season acquisitions Overall and Taylor won 12 games apiece in a Cub uniform. While it must be remembered that relief pitching was not the specialization at the beginning of the century that it would become in later years — in fact, being sent to the bullpen was considered a demotion for a pitcher — Cub pitchers tossed 125 complete games that season, which still was only third in the league (last-place Boston had 137).

The offense was pretty potent, too. They led the majors in runs scored and the NL in hits, and they stole 283 bases (second to the Giants), with every member of the lineup except catcher Johnny Kling chipping in with at least 25 steals (Kling, by the way, had 14). They even had 20 home runs, a goodly number for the time and second in the league to the Dodgers. Defensively they were perhaps the best team baseball had seen up to that point, making fewer than 200 errors for the year on the hard, poorly-kept ballfields of the day. They were able to accomplish this even though Tinker and Evers, the exalted double-play combo, hated each other. Formerly good friends, an argument the year before had escalated into a fistfight, and the two did not speak off the field for more than 30 years.

The World Series had begun in 1903 as part of the settlement to end the war between the American and National leagues. In 1904, however, an obstinate John McGraw had refused to play Boston in the postseason. He changed his mind the next year — or had it changed for him — and the World Series became baseball's annual showcase. The 1906 edition, then, was only the third one ever played, and the first one to feature just one city as the Chicago White Stockings (or White Sox, for short) came out on top of a great four-team battle in the American League. Like their crosstown rivals, the Sox had their own great month of August, winning 19 games in a row to move from fourth place to first in just ten days, then holding on for their first flag in five years. Like the Cubs, the White Sox featured great pitching, with righthanders Frank Owen and Ed Walsh and lefties Nick Altrock and Doc White all winning in double digits. Also like the Cubs, they featured excellent defense with their own sterling double-play combo of second baseman Frank Isbell and shortstop George Davis. The White Sox needed this pitching and defense to win because they had one of the poorer-hitting lineups in baseball. Their .230 team batting average and 1,132 hits trailed every team in the majors except for Boston of the National League. They hit just six home runs all season, a pitiful figure even in the dead-ball era. Only Isbell and Davis batted above .270 for the season. But they drew the most walks in the league, stole more than 200 bases and finished third in runs scored, which proved that they knew how to get around the bases and make the most of their opportunities. Still, having won 23 fewer games than the Cubs, the "Hitless Wonders" were decided underdogs going into the 1906 World Series.

It was cold and snowy when the two teams met before a capacity crowd. With Davis injured, third baseman Lee Tannehill (who had batted a robust

.183 for the season) moved to short and backup George Rohe started at third. Rohe broke up a scoreless tie in the fifth when he tripled off Brown and scored when, on an infield grounder, Kling could not hold onto the throw home. Kling, one of the best defensive catchers in baseball, committed a passed ball in the next inning that helped to set up the White Sox' second run, which proved to be the winner when the Cubs scored in their half of the sixth. Both Brown and Altrock were in top form, giving up just four hits apiece, but the White Sox shocked everyone with their 2–1 win.

The next day, though, it appeared as if sanity had been reestablished as the Cubs pounded out a 7–1 victory. Reulbach gave up just one hit and two White Sox errors resulted in five unearned runs as the Cubs evened the Series. But the American League champs rebounded for a key win in Game Three. There were only six hits in the entire ballgame, but the Cubs could only manage two off spitballing Ed Walsh. The big blow was once again delivered by the unheralded Rohe, who cleared the bases with yet another triple for the only scoring of the game in the Sox' 3–0 triumph.

George Davis returned to the Chisox lineup for Game Four, but he and his teammates faced a virtually-unhittable Brown. The "Miner" (Brown had a variety of nicknames) yielded just two hits and made the outstanding play of the day, knocking down a line drive in the ninth and converting it into the third out with the potential tying run on second base. It preserved the 1–0 lead and knotted the Series once again.

Ed Walsh came back with just one day's rest, and it looked like a bad move on the part of White Sox manager Fielder Jones as the Cubs scored three times in the first inning. But the Sox caught a break as neither Reulbach, the starter, nor Pfiester, his replacement, was sharp this day. Isbell cracked four doubles, driving in two runs and scoring three, while Rohe added three more hits and Davis contributed a pair. When the Cubs pulled to within two in the sixth inning, Jones decided Walsh had had enough and brought Doc White in for the seventh; he threw three shutout frames as the White Sox won, 8–6. They needed just one more win for the world championship.

And they got it, with the help of a local policeman. Chance, apparently oblivious to Walsh's problem the day before, asked Brown to pitch on just one day's rest. The Sox put two men on in the first inning but it looked like the threat was ended as right fielder Frank Schulte was tracking a routine fly ball. With almost 20,000 in attendance, the overflow was seated in the outfield, separated from the players by a rope (a common practice at that time). Before Schulte could make the catch, the unnamed officer kicked him in the pants, allowing the ball to drop. Both runners scored and the undeserving batter-runner came home, giving the White Sox the lead. Brown's arm gave out in the next inning as he yielded four more runs, effectively putting the game out of reach. White, the stopper the day before, pitched a complete game to cap off the White Sox' improbable six-game World Series triumph.

The White Sox won the Series the way they had won games all season, by scoring when they had the chance. They collected only 37 hits in the six games and batted just .198, but they scored 22 runs. The Cubs, certainly the better-hitting club, managed to bat a paltry .196 against White Sox pitching and could only score 18 runs. If you overlook the Cubs' 7–1 win in Game Two, then they scored just 11 runs in the other five games of the Series. For one week at least, the wrong Chicago team was labeled the "Hitless Wonders."

The 1906 World Series proved to be the prime motivator for the team the following season. Just to prove that the galling loss had not been forgotten, manager Chance called his troops "a fine bunch of stiffs" during the spring of 1907. But "Husk" knew he had a good team and made no major changes in the off-season. None were needed as the Cubs once again blew through the National League. While they didn't match the previous year's victory total, they still rung up 107 wins, the second-best in league history. The offense slumped a bit but pitching more than made up for it with an unmatched performance. Over-all and Brown both won 20, and Reulbach, Pfiester and Lundgren combined for another 50 victories. Pfiester, Lundgren and Brown finished 1-2-3 in the ERA race with eye-popping marks of 1.15, 1.17 and 1.39, while Overall and Reul-bach finished fifth and sixth with 1.68 and 1.69, respectively. (Pittsburgh's Sam Leever snuck into fourth place with his 1.66.) The staff, as a whole, wound up with a team ERA of 1.73, still the best in the history of modern major league baseball.

The Cubs won the pennant by a 17-game margin over Pittsburgh and prob-ably knew in July they would again be in the World Series. What they didn't know, however, was the identity of their opponent, as the American League staged another free-for-all. Four teams contended for the crown, and at the end of September the Detroit Tigers and Philadelphia A's found themselves in a vir-tual tie for first and scheduled to play a doubleheader in the City of Brotherly Love. Leading 7–1 after two innings and with Rube Waddell on the mound, Connie Mack had to be feeling confident. Even in the ninth inning his troops maintained an 8–6 advantage, but a 20-year-old outfielder named Ty Cobb walloped a two-run homer to tie the game. Both teams scored in the 11th, the A's lost a chance to score again on an interference call in the 14th, and the game was eventually called on account of darkness after 17 innings, still tied. Not winning after holding the big lead proved to be costly to the Philadelphians, as the Tigers won their first American League flag by just six-thousandths of a percentage point.

Managed by John McGraw's old Baltimore Oriole teammate Hughie Jennings, the Tigers were a young team, with no regular position player older than 27. They were led by Cobb, the brash "Georgia Peach" who had his break-out year in 1907, leading the league in batting average, hits, runs batted in, total bases, stolen bases and slugging percentage. He was part of a one-two punch that included fellow outfielder "Wahoo" Sam Crawford, who led the league in runs scored and was second in doubles, triples and most of the categories Cobb topped. Their pitching staff featured three 20-game winners in righthanders "Wild" Bill Donovan and George Mullin and lefty Ed Killian, while another southpaw, Ed Siever, just missed with his 19 victories.

History has shown that most World Series revolve around a crucial game, one that keys a team's ultimate victory. In 1907 this proved to be the very first game. The Tigers, behind Donovan, took a 3–1 lead into the ninth inning, but the Cubs loaded the bases. Frank Schulte grounded out, scoring a run but leaving the Cubs down to their final out. Pinch-hitter Del Howard then struck out, which should have ended the game, but Tiger catcher Charlie "Boss" Schmidt let it get away from him and the tying run scored.* Three more innings were played but no more runs crossed the plate, and since it would be another 28 years before major league ballparks had lights, the game was called after twelve, tied at three.

The Tigers did not seem to recover, or perhaps the Cubs, reminded of the dangers of taking an opponent too lightly, decided to turn up the heat. In any event, Cub pitching took control. Pfiester outdueled Mullin in Game Two, 3–1, then Reulbach spun a six-hitter for a 5–1 win. Donovan was brought back for Game Four but was no match for Overall in a 6–1 Chicago triumph. Chance finally started Brown in Game Five, and the Miner made two early-inning runs stand up as he defeated Detroit, 2–0, in less than two hours to give the Cubs their first World Series championship.

The Tigers scored just six runs in the five games, three of them in that first-game tie. Of their 36 hits, only three went for extra bases. Cobb batted just .200 and Crawford was only a bit better at .238. Moreover, the Tigers' defense betrayed them, as nine Detroit errors led to eight unearned Chicago runs. The Cubs, for their part, played smart, aggressive baseball, stealing 16 bases against three Detroit catchers. Chicago pitching was overpowering, compiling an ERA of 0.75 and tossing four straight complete games after the tie in the opener.

A somewhat-humorous footnote to the Series had to do with attendance. Weather had been bad in Detroit, and that, coupled with the team's poor performance, led to small crowds, punctuated by just 7,370 for the final game. During the off-season there was some talk, purportedly begun in Cleveland, of throwing the Tigers out of the league and replacing them with a Buffalo franchise. The AL eventually decided to maintain the status quo.

Basking in the glow of a world championship, Chance once again decided to keep his team intact. You can't argue with success, it is said, and the Cubs

---

Thirty four years later a similar play would occur, as Dodger pitcher Hugh Casey struck out the Yankees' Tommy Henrich. But catcher Mickey Owen couldn't hold the ball and Henrich reached first. Casey then could not get that elusive third out, four runs scored, and the Yankees went on to win the 1941 World Series.

had won 223 regular-season games over the previous two years and had made a shambles of National League pennant races. In fact, the senior circuit had not seen a nail-biting, down-to-the-wire battle for the title since 1897, while the American League had featured just that sort of excitement in each of the past four years. The 1908 season, however, would prove to be unique as both leagues kept fans on the edge of their chairs all summer long.

The Cubs, perhaps a bit overconfident, started slowly and found themselves trailing both the Pirates and Giants. An August slump, however, dropped Pittsburgh to third and the Cubs took dead aim at New York. In early September, trailing by just percentage points, Chicago went into Pittsburgh for a series and found themselves locked in a scoreless tie. With the bases loaded and two out in the bottom of the tenth, Pittsburgh's Chief Wilson lined a clean single to center to apparently end the game. Most players left the playing field, as did the two umpires. Tinker and Evers, however, did not. They had noticed that Doc Gill, the Pirates' runner on first, had not gone all the way down the baseline to touch second base. While it was a common practice of the day it was still clearly against the rules. They got the ball from the outfield and Evers tagged second, but to no avail. Umpire Hank O'Day ruled that the run would have scored before a force out could have occurred, and let the game end 1–0 in Pittsburgh's favor. While he was correct in assuming the run would have scored anyway, he was incorrect in allowing it to score since Gill never ran down to second.

Less than three weeks later the Giants played host to the Cubs in a crucial series. The Cubs won three of the first four, shaving the Giants' lead to 1½ games. For the finale, McGraw chose his ace, Christy Mathewson, as his starter while Chance countered with Jack Pfiester, who was known as "The Giant Killer" for his past successes against New York.

The score was tied at one going into the bottom of the ninth. With two out and a man on first, rookie Fred Merkle, playing because regular first baseman Fred Tenney was injured, delivered a base hit. Then shortstop Al Bridwell singled and the winning run ostensibly scored. Happy Giant fans poured out onto the field as the players retreated to safety. But the fun was just beginning.

Merkle had not touched second, and once again Tinker and Evers were aware of the gaffe. This time, so was someone else — Giants pitcher Joe McGinnity, who was coaching at third. The Cub infielders shouted for the ball but the throw from the outfield sailed over their heads, towards McGinnity. The three of them wrestled for the ball and eventually the old hurler was able to break free and heave the ball into the stands. Third baseman Harry Steinfeldt and a young Cub pitcher, Floyd Kroh, went into the stands for the ball, finally knocking it loose from the fan who had caught McGinnity's toss. The Cubs relayed the ball back to Evers at second, who tagged the bag. As luck would have it, one of the umpires for this game was the same Hank O'Day who had been in

Pittsburgh earlier that month. Perhaps he had realized he had erred in his previous call; perhaps he had simply reviewed the rule book. In any case, this time he called Merkle out, nullifying the run.

The problem was that by now the field was overrun with angry, fighting Giant fans, all of whom were attempting to kill the Cubs and O'Day. There was no chance to clear the field and resume play before dark, so the game was declared a tie. The Giants filed a formal protest of O'Day's decision while the Cubs filed their own protest, claiming that, because the field was full of fans and the game could not be continued, they should have been declared the winners via forfeit. National League President Harry Pulliam backed his umpires and ruled that the game was a tie. The Giants appealed to the league's board of directors, who listened to evidence for two days before finally upholding both O'Day and Pulliam. They also ruled that, if the Giants and Cubs ended the season in a tie, the game would have to be replayed. Actually, they offered the teams the option of playing a five-game playoff, but the Giants, knowing they had 37-game-winner Mathewson, opted for just one game, winner take all. Sure enough, several days later the National League season ended, for the first time in history, in a flat-footed tie between the Cubs and Giants.

On October 8, 1908, some 35,000 fans jammed the Polo Grounds in New York to see how this drama would play out. Even the pregame activity was intense: fans surrounded the Cubs' hotel the night before the game, blaring horns in an attempt to deprive the players of sufficient rest; umpire Bill Klem reported that the Giants' team physician tried to bribe him to give all close calls to New York; several fans fell either from the stands or outside vantage points, with at least three being killed; police outside the ballpark battled all day against fans who tried various methods of getting in, including an attempt to burn down the outfield fence; during warmups, Chance was struck by a beer bottle, causing his neck to bleed profusely.

Pfiester got the starting nod for the Cubs, and Mathewson took the hill for the Giants. Neither pitcher was very sharp. The Giants scored in the first inning and, threatening to break it open right away, forced Chance to summon Mordecai Brown out of the bullpen. Brown had won 29 games but might have been a little arm-weary, having appeared in 14 of the season's final 19 games. But he stopped the Giant rally, then watched his teammates touch Matty for four runs in the third. New York center fielder Cy Seymour misplayed a Joe Tinker drive into a triple, opening the floodgates. Brown, pitching on adrenaline, was touched for just one run as the Cubs won, 4–2, to take their third straight pennant. As soon as the game ended, a mob descended from the stands and chased the Cub players, some of whom were hurt in the melee. The police reportedly had to draw their guns to subdue the crowd, and the team had to be taken back to their hotel in patrol wagons.

The American League race, by comparison, was a piece of cake. The defending champion Tigers battled all season long against the Indians and

White Sox, and did not clinch their American League title until they defeated Chicago on the final day of the season. Their margin of victory was just .004 over Cleveland and .009 over the Sox.

The Series opener pitted Ed Reulbach and his 24 victories against Ed Killian, a 12-game winner. The Cubs jumped on Killian for four in the third, at which point Hughie Jennings summoned his leading winner, 23-year-old rookie knuckleballer Ed Summers, to quell the rally. Chicago had trouble with the dancing pitch; meanwhile, Detroit finally got to Reulbach in the seventh, pulling to within one run, then took a 6–5 lead against Overall in the eighth. With victory in sight Summers suddenly weakened and gave up six straight hits, good for five Cub runs and a come-from-behind victory.

Overall was back in Game Two, this time starting against "Wild" Bill Donovan, and the two righties were at the top of their game. After seven innings neither club had dented the plate, and the Cubs had been able to solve Donovan for just one hit. But in the eighth the roof caved in on Detroit. Joe Tinker hit a home run that was argued — to no avail, of course — by the Tigers. (It was the first home run in World Series play since 1903.) The debate with umpire Klem lasted for 15 minutes, after which a stiff-armed Donovan gave up four more runs. Overall held the Tigers to four hits for a 6–1 triumph.

Having lost six consecutive games to their midwestern rivals, Detroit finally broke through with a victory against Jack Pfiester. Cobb collected four hits as the Tigers, trailing in the sixth, scored five times to cement the win. Since they were heading back to Detroit, the Tigers had to feel as if the battle was finally joined.

Cub pitching, however, felt otherwise. Brown tossed a four-hitter in besting Summers, 3–0, and he was aided by his batterymate, Kling, who in the fourth inning picked off Sam Crawford at second and threw out Ty Cobb attempting to steal, ending the Tigers' only threat. The next day Overall needed just 85 minutes — the fastest World Series game on record — to close out the Series with a 2–0 win before just 6,210 fans, the smallest crowd in World Series history. He allowed just three hits as the Tigers extended their scoreless streak to 19 consecutive innings. In the five games Detroit scored only 15 runs, with 14 of them coming in two contests (Games One and Three). While Cobb had a much better Series than the year before, batting .368 with four RBI, none of his other teammates were able to contribute much as they combined for a .203 team batting average. Once again the Cubs scored more runs, had more hits and stolen bases, and committed fewer errors. Chicago's hurlers simply outpitched Detroit's as the Cubs became the first team to win back-to-back World Series. It would also prove to be the Cubs' last World Series triumph in the 20th century.

The Cubs didn't exactly collapse after the 1908 World Series. Despite losing catcher Johnny Kling to a season-long holdout, Chicago won 104 games in 1909, with the quartet of Brown, Overall, Reulbach and Pfiester winning 83 games. But Fred Clarke's Pittsburgh Pirates won 110 games to take the flag, and then whipped the Tigers in the World Series. The Cubs were back in 1910, however, winning 104 games and capturing their fourth pennant in five years by a margin of 13 games. But they went into the World Series without the injured Johnny Evers, and they were starting to show their age, especially on the mound, as Brown was the only member of the Big Four to win consistently. His 25 victories paced the club, and he received surprising help from righthander Leonard "King" Cole, who won 20 games in his rookie season and led the league with an .833 winning percentage. They had to take on the young Philadelphia Athletics, who featured the fabled "$100,000 infield" of Harry Davis, Eddie Collins, Jack Barry and Frank "Home Run" Baker. They also faced a pair of 27-year-old righthanders in Chief Bender and Jack Coombs. Bender had become one of Connie Mack's mainstays since his arrival in the majors at age 19, and in 1910 he won a career-high 23 games on his way to the Hall of Fame. Coombs, later the baseball coach at Duke, had been a .500 pitcher until 1910 when he suddenly blossomed, leading the majors with his 31 wins and 13 shutouts. Though Mack also had the reliable Eddie Plank and Cy Morgan on his staff, he chose to throw just Bender and Coombs against the Cubs, and his strategy worked as the duo turned in five complete games. Bender's three-hitter in the opening game set the tone as Philadelphia defeated the Cubs the way Chicago had defeated the Tigers a couple of years earlier, with pitching. Cub hurlers were battered for 56 hits and 35 runs in the five-game Series, and the Athletics' .316 team batting average was a record that stood for the next fifty years. Their team ERA was 4.70, as opposed to Philadelphia's 2.76. Coombs won three games, and the Cubs' only victory came in Game Four; on the verge of being swept, they rallied to tie the game in the ninth and win in the tenth.

The last gasp for this great Cub squad came the following year. Despite removing himself from the everyday lineup, Chance was able to keep his aging players in contention into August, when the Giants got hot and passed Chicago, which was running out of steam. The team began to be broken up through retirement, trades and dismissals — Chance himself was fired after the 1912 season — and the first heyday of the Chicago Cubs came to an end. With the exception of a fluke during the World War I season of 1918, the Cubs would not be serious pennant contenders again until 1928.

1910–14
Philadelphia Athletics

When Ban Johnson, founder and president of the American League, established a new club in Philadelphia in 1901, he chose former catcher Connie Mack to run it. Given 25 percent ownership in the club, Mack, whose real name was Cornelius McGillicuddy, began what would prove to be a fifty-year managerial stint with the club. Within that half century time span the Philadelphia Athletics fielded two of the greatest teams ever as well as some of the most completely inept.

Mack first tasted success when his team won the 1905 American League pennant. New York pitcher Christy Mathewson almost single-handedly destroyed the Athletics in the World Series, however, by winning three games and not allowing a single run as the Giants took the championship, four games to one. The Athletics went into decline after that season but in 1909 they made a remarkable improvement. Winning 98 games while losing only 58, they challenged Ty Cobb's Tigers for the pennant but fell 3½ games short.

In the so-called "dead ball" era, baseball games were won with pitching and defense. The Athletics excelled in both of these areas. Connie Mack assembled a pitching staff that, though not deep, was probably the most dominant in all of baseball at that time. His infield unit was perhaps as close to perfect as the game has ever seen. Of the four starters, each led the league in fielding at their position at least once between 1910 and 1914. In addition, all four had speed on the base paths and could hit for both power and average.

Mack also built his first great dynastic team around former college stars, a rarity in professional baseball at that time. Preferring intelligent players, his recruiting trips to college campuses led to the signings of many of his top stars: second baseman Eddie Collins, shortstop Jack Barry, and pitchers Eddie Plank, Charles "Chief" Bender, and Jack Coombs.

There was no doubting who was the American League's best team in 1910 as the Athletics ran away with the pennant. With a record of 102–48, they left the second-place New York Highlanders 14½ games back and finished 18 games in front of reigning league champs Detroit.

Mack had once stated "pitching is 75 percent of baseball" and he put together a pitching staff which nearly proved that to be true. The ace pitcher in 1910 was Jack Coombs, who had perhaps as great a season as any pitcher ever has. He finished with a record of 31–9, a 1.30 ERA, 35 complete games, 224 strikeouts, 13 shutouts, and 353 innings pitched. Though Coombs' performance was remarkable, even more amazing was the fact that the rest of the staff was nearly just as good. Chief Bender (23–5, 1.58 ERA), Cy Morgan (18–12, 1.55 ERA) and veteran lefthander Eddie Plank (16–10, 2.01 ERA) all had excellent seasons. Harry Krause, however, who had been one of the American League's best pitchers in 1909, lost some of his effectiveness and contributed only a 6–6 record. Still, the staff had an amazing 1.79 combined ERA.

The heart of the Athletics offense was Eddie Collins. Undeniably one of the greatest players to ever hold down the second base position, he was equally gifted with the bat and the glove. In 1910, the 23-year-old Collins batted a team-high .322, drove in 81 runs, scored the same number and equaled that total again in stolen bases (led league). At third base the Athletics had Frank Baker, also one of the game's all-time greats. He contributed a .283 batting average, 74 RBI, and 21 stolen bases. Rounding out the infield were shortstop Jack Barry (.250, 60 RBI), also a slick fielder, and first baseman Harry Davis (.248). In a back-up role, promising 19-year-old shortstop Stuffy McInnis appeared in 38 games and hit .301.

The Athletics outfield featured Rube Oldring (.308, 57 RBI) and veteran Danny Murphy, who hit an even .300 and drove in 64 runs. Both were exceptional fielders with good speed and they stole 18 and 17 bases, respectively. Bris Lord, who had been a rookie with the pennant-winning 1905 Athletics, returned to the Athletics at the end of June after a season and a half with Cleveland and hit .280 in 70 games. On the bench, Connie Mack had 35-year-old Topsy Hartsel, who hit only .221 in 90 games, and promising youngster Amos Strunk (.333 in 16 games).

The catching duties were shared by Ira Thomas (.278 in 60 games) and Jack Lapp (.234 in 71 games). Though both were strong defensively, neither was a great threat with the bat.

Surprisingly, it was bats and not the pitching of the Athletics that brought the team its first World Series title. Against the strong Chicago Cubs, a team playing in their fourth World Series in five years, Connie Mack's men were evenly matched. Behind a three-hit, one-run shutout from Chief Bender the Athletics took the opener, 4–1. The offense then erupted for 9–3 and 12–5 wins in the next two games. The Athletics almost took Game Four for a sweep but gave up a run in the bottom of the ninth and lost 4–3. Five runs in the top of the eighth made the difference in Game Five and Philadelphia pulled out a 7–2 win to take the Series. Incredibly, Coombs, who won three games, and Bender were the only pitchers Connie Mack used for the entire series; with Collins (.429) and Baker (.409) leading an offense that hit for a combined .316, two pitchers was all that was necessary.

In 1911 the Athletics (101–50) were nearly just as dominant as they had been the previous season. Though they trailed the Detroit Tigers for part of the summer the Athletics overtook them in August and then stretched the lead to 13½ games by season's end. Again, it was the bat of Eddie Collins and the arm of Jack Coombs that led the Athletics to victory. Collins hit .365 that season, drove in 73 runs and stole 38 bases while Coombs posted a 28–12 record (and even batted .319 with 23 runs driven in).

That season, Collins and his fellow infielders combined for a .323 average. Baker (.334, 115 RBI, 11 HR) and Barry (.265, 63 RBI, 30 stolen bases) both led the league in fielding at their positions. Stuffy McInnis, who had moved from shortstop and taken over the first base starting job, batted .321, drove in 77, and stole 23 bases. Collins, Baker, Barry and McInnis soon became known as the "$100,000 infield," since Connie Mack had declared he wouldn't part with the quartet for even that grand sum of money.

There were no real changes in the Athletics lineup. The outfield unit was again comprised of Oldring (.297, 59 RBI), who led the league in fielding, Lord (.310, 92 runs), and Murphy (.329, 66 RBI, 104 runs, 22 stolen bases), who had the best season of his 16-year career. Again backing up the starters were Strunk (.256 in 74 games) and Hartsel (.237 in 25 games). Likewise the catcher position saw no change with Thomas (.273) and Lapp (.353) again sharing the backstop duties.

The pitching staff also remained largely unchanged. Again joining Coombs in the starting rotation were Bender (17–5, 2.16 ERA), Plank (23–8, 2.10 ERA) and Morgan (15–7). Coming out of the bullpen, the Athletics had Harry Krause (11–8), who was used as an occasional starter, and rookie lefthander Dave Danforth, who finished with a 4–1 record.

Just as they had in 1905, the Athletics took on the New York Giants of John McGraw in the World Series. It was a classic confrontation between two of the game's greatest managers as well as the greatest pitchers. In their previous meeting the Giants — and Christy Mathewson — had totally dominated Connie Mack's team, but the Athletics were not to be denied in 1911.

In Game One, it appeared Mathewson would again get the best of the Athletics as he out-pitched Chief Bender for a 2–1 win. The A's, however, recovered from the loss to take three in a row. Thanks to a home run by Baker and brilliant pitching by Plank, they won Game Two, 3–1. Game Three saw Mathewson hold the Athletics scoreless through eight innings while his team held a 1–0 lead. In the top of the ninth, though, Baker hit his second home run of the series to tie the game and the Athletics took a 3–1 lead in the top of the eleventh. Only able to cut the margin by one run in the bottom of the inning, the Giants' rally fell short.

Several days of rain allowed Mathewson to rest his arm enough to take the mound again in Game Four. He pitched well but Bender was better and the Athletics won the game 4–2. Facing elimination at home, the Giants were down 3–0 in the eighth inning but they rallied to tie it up in the bottom of the ninth and then won it, 4–3, in the tenth. Back in Philadelphia for Game Six, the Athletics' offense seemed to have had enough of the pitching duels and they unleashed a 13-hit, 13-run bombardment upon the New York pitchers. Undeniably, the stars of the Series for the Athletics were the three pitchers used: Coombs, Plank, and Bender — who had a combined ERA of only 1.29. Offensively it was Frank Baker, who earned the nickname "Home Run" in the series with his two key round-trippers, and shortstop Jack Barry, who batted .368 with four doubles and two stolen bases.

In 1912, the Athletics' dynasty was interrupted as they slipped to third place in the American League. They still played well, finishing with a 90–62 record, but Boston took the pennant and Washington narrowly edged out Philadelphia for second. As before, Collins (.348), who scored a league-leading 137 runs and stole 63 bases, and Baker (.347, 10 HR, 116 runs), who drove in

Frank "Home Run" Baker

133 runs and stole a career-high 40 bases, led the Athletics' offense. The team still featured three of the game's best pitchers — Coombs (21–10), Bender (13–8) and Plank (26–6, 2.22 ERA) — but they could never catch the phenomenal Red Sox and eventually finished 15 games back.

First baseman McInnis (.327) had one of the best seasons of his career and drove in 101 runs while shortstop Barry (.261, 75 runs) also had a solid season. Among the outfielders, both Oldring and Murphy missed considerable time due to injury. It allowed Strunk, however, to become a regular starter and he played well, hitting .289, stealing 29 bases, and leading the league in fielding. Joining the Athletics' outfield late in the season were rookies Jimmy Walsh (.252 in 31 games) and Eddie Murphy (.317 in 33 games), who had just won the International League batting title with Baltimore. Both would be key members of the team in the following seasons.

In 1913, the Athletics re-established their dominance of the American League and returned to the top of the league standings. Despite several challenges by Washington during the season they held on and eventually took the pennant by 6½ games with a 96–57 record.

The "$100,000 infield" continued to produce runs and great defense. Third baseman Frank "Home Run" Baker batted .337, stole 34 bases, scored 116 runs and led the league in both home runs (12) and RBI (117). In the middle of the infield, Eddie Collins hit .345, stole 55 bases and led the league with 125 runs scored, while Jack Barry's .275 batting average and 85 runs batted in were both career highs. Stuffy McInnis, on his way to becoming the greatest defensive first baseman of his generation, excelled at the plate as well, batting .324 and driving in 90 runs. Harry Davis, the team's starting first baseman from 1901 to 1910, had left the team after the 1911 season for a chance to manage Cleveland but returned to the Athletics in 1913 as a coach and occasional player. Used primarily as a pinch hitter, he batted .353 in seven games.

Rube Oldring (.283, 71 RBI, 101 runs, 40 SB) and Eddie Murphy (.295, 105 runs) were the only two members of the outfield to start consistently for the entire season. Amos Strunk played well and hit .305 but only appeared in 94 games due to injury. That allowed Jimmy Walsh (.254) to see considerable playing time though his bat lacked the offensive punch of Strunk. Replacing Bris Lord, who had been sold to the Boston Braves, the Athletics brought up Tom Daley (.255 in 62 games) from the minor leagues. The final member of the unit was 37-year-old veteran Danny Murphy, who excelled in his role as a pinch hitter and outfield backup by hitting .322 in 40 games.

Though a platoon situation at any position might appear as a weakness, it seemed to work fairly well for the Athletics at catcher. Again Jack Lapp (.227 in 82 games) handled the bulk of the duties while Ira Thomas (.283) was limited to only 22 games. In May of that season, 23-year-old catcher Wally Schang made his big league debut with the Athletics. In his first of what would prove to be 19 seasons in the major leagues he hit .266 in 79 games.

Though Bender (21–10, 2.21 ERA) and Plank (18–10, 2.60 ERA) had great seasons yet again, the pitching suffered from the loss of Jack Coombs. The great righthander, who had won an amazing 80 games over the past three seasons, missed nearly the entire season due to injury and illness and forced Connie Mack to make some big changes in his strategy. One of the experiments Mack tried was to frequently use Bender in a relief role. The move paid off as Bender, who started 21 games and appeared in 27 as a reliever, wound up leading the league with 13 saves. Picking up a lot of the slack in the starting rotation were Carroll "Boardwalk" Brown (17–11), who had joined the team at the end of the 1911 season, and promising rookie Joe Bush, who won 15 games and lost only six. Rookies Bob Shawkey (6–5) and Weldon Wyckoff (2–4) were also pressed into action, as was Herb Pennock. A promising 19-year-old lefthander, Pennock, who had appeared in few games in 1912, won two games and lost one.

As in 1911, the Athletics met the New York Giants in the World Series. With Chief Bender taking the mound for Philadelphia and lefthander Rube Marquard getting the start for New York, Game One proved to be an even matchup. The great Christy Mathewson shut out the Athletics in Game Two as the Giants evened the Series with a 3–0 win. Thanks to three hits and three RBI by Collins and a home run by Schang, the Athletics easily won Game Three, 8–2. In Game Four, Philadelphia jumped out to a six-nothing lead and then survived a New York rally for a 6–5 win. Game Five saw Eddie Plank masterfully out-duel Mathewson. The veteran Giants ace gave up three early runs before settling down and pitching six straight shutout innings, but it was all Plank needed as he surrendered only two hits and took the game 3–1. The Giants' third World Series title in four years was so decisive that they only needed three pitchers (Bender, Bush, and Plank) and only used one substitute in the field (Lapp caught one game).

The Athletics continued their dominance of the American League in 1914 and their record of 99–53 gave them their fourth pennant in five years. As was the case since the beginning of the A's rise to prominence, the infielders were the heart of the team. Eddie Collins, who won the Chalmers Award as the league's Most Valuable Player, had an incredible season; he won the batting title with a .344 average, led the league with 122 runs, stole 58 bases and was the league's best fielder at his position. Stuffy McInnis (.314, 95 RBI, 24 SB), who led the league in fielding, and Frank Baker (.319, 89 RBI, 9 HR) also turned in exceptional performances, while the always reliable Jack Barry batted .242 and stole 22 bases.

In the outfield, Oldring (.277), Eddie Murphy (.272, 101 runs, 36 stolen bases) and Strunk (.275, 25 stolen bases), who led the league in fielding, were the starting three. Top reserve Danny Murphy had departed for the new Federal League before the season and Jimmy Walsh had been sold to the Yankees, leaving Tom Daley as the main backup. In mid-season, however, the Athletics got Walsh back from the Yankees in a move that sent Daley to New York instead.

Behind the plate, Wally Schang (.287) established himself as the team's starting backstop, though Jack Lapp still saw considerable action and batted .231 in 69 games. Ira Thomas essentially retired from active duty but remained with the team as a coach.

The pitching staff, still led by veterans Plank and Bender, remained largely unchanged from the previous season, but the young members had developed to give the Athletics a depth not had previously. In what would prove to be the last great season of his Hall of Fame career, Chief Bender won 17 games, lost only three and had an ERA of 2.26 while Plank, who would also be enshrined at Cooperstown, finished the season with a 15–7 record. Lefthander Herb Pennock (11–4, 2.79 ERA), whose great career was just beginning to blossom, would make it to the Hall of Fame as well — though he achieved most of his fame later with the Red Sox and Yankees. Rounding out the Athletics' 1914 rotation were second-year men Bush (16–12), Wyckoff (11–7), and Shawkey (16–8), each of whom would play a vital role in the team's success that season. Boardwalk Brown, whose career had looked so promising in 1913, was traded to the Yankees after starting the season with a 1–6 record.

In the 1914 World Series, the Athletics were clear favorites over the Boston Braves. Instead, the Braves swept the Series in four straight games. In the first game the Braves took an easy 7–1 win. Great pitching by Plank shut the Braves out for eight innings before giving up one run in the ninth. His opponent Bill James, however, gave up no runs. Game Three was also decided by one run while a close Game Four saw Boston's 3–1 win clinch the Series. Batting for a combined .172 average, the Athletics scored only six runs in the Series, four of those coming in the 5–4 Game Three loss.

After the 1914 season, Connie Mack decided to break up his team of stars. Famous for his stinginess, Mack began selling off his players and those he kept (some say it was because of the World Series sweep) were forced to take pay cuts. Baker decided to sit out the season instead and was sold to the Yankees. Collins was sold to the White Sox for $50,000. Barry began the 1915 season with the A's but was soon traded to the Red Sox. Eddie Murphy, who went to the White Sox, and Bob Shawkey, who joined the Yankees, were also sold in mid-season. Bender and Plank both left for the upstart Federal League while Coombs, who had hardly played during the 1913 and 1914 seasons, went to Brooklyn where he became a solid contributor for a few more seasons.

Since Mack was widely hailed as baseball's greatest teacher, he falsely believed he could turn anyone into a ballplayer. He proceeded to stock his team with "bargain basement" players — only to watch the Athletics drop to the American League cellar in 1915. They would remain there for an astonishing seven seasons (the 1916 team, which lost 117 games, is often regarded as the worst ever). The Athletics would not become serious contenders again until the mid–1920s.

1912
Boston Red Sox

Though they had won the very first World Series in 1903 and repeated as American League Champions the following season, the Boston Red Sox slipped into mediocrity shortly thereafter. In 1911 the best they could do was fifth place but the following season that changed in a big way. Under first year player-manager Jake Stahl, who had been a rookie backup catcher on the World Series–winning 1903 team, everything came together. Somehow the Red Sox of 1912 found that ever-elusive perfect combination of pitching and hitting. In addition, the team had a brand new ballpark (Fenway Park opened on April 20 of that season) and the veteran leaders meshed perfectly with the young talent to form a cohesive unit. Like any truly great team, the performance of the Red Sox' stars helped elevate the level of play for everyone; nearly every player had at least close to a career-best season. In early June the Red Sox rose to the top of the American League and by season's end had stretched their lead to 14 games. The 105–47 record of the 1912 Red Sox still stands as the franchise record.

Patrolling center field for the Red Sox that season was Tris Speaker, one of the greatest players to ever hold down that position. The 24-year-old Texan had broken in with the Red Sox back in 1907 and within a couple of seasons had established himself as one of the game's premier hitters and most skillful fielders. With incredible speed and a cannon for an arm, Speaker set the standard by which all other center fielders have been measured. He played shallow, had a knack for anticipating which direction the ball would go before it was even hit, and in 1912 tied his own major league record by gunning down 35 baserunners.

Joining Speaker in the outfield the Red Sox had Harry Hooper in right and Duffy Lewis in left. Together the three formed what is still considered by many to be the greatest defensive outfield ever. Hooper had made his debut in April of 1909 and would remain a fixture in the Boston outfield for more than a decade, while Lewis had broken into the Red Sox lineup in April of 1910 and became an instant starter.

The outfield unit also led the team's offense. Speaker — who hit .383, drove in 90 runs, scored 136, stole 52 bases, and led the league with 53 doubles and 10 home runs (tie) — won the Chalmers Award as the league's most valuable player. Harry Hooper (.242, 53 RBI) had only average power but his speed helped him to score 98 runs and steal 29 bases. Duffy Lewis had what would prove to be the best season of his 11-year career and batted .284, scored 85 runs and drove in 109. The team's fourth outfielder, Danish-born Olaf Henricksen, played his role well and hit .321 in 44 games.

Among the infielders, third baseman Larry Gardner carried the biggest bat. A rookie with the Red Sox since 1908, he had steadily improved and in 1912 Gardner hit .315, pushed 86 runs across the plate, scored 88 times and stole 25 bases. Playing to Gardner's left was shortstop Heinie Wagner, for whom 1912 was the best season of his career: he batted a respectable .274, drove in 68 runs and stole 21 bases. Second baseman Steve Yerkes (.252) was perhaps the weakest link in the offense but he contributed by scoring 73 runs and playing solid defense. At first base, skipper Jake Stahl, in what was really the final playing season of his career (he pinch hit twice in 1913) hit .301 with 60 RBI in 95 games.

Behind the plate the Red Sox' primary backstop was Bill Carrigan (.263 in 87 games). With the team since 1906, he was very strong defensively but had never really been an everyday player. Backing him up was rookie catcher Hick Cady who hit .259 in 47 games.

While the Red Sox offense featured a balanced attack that focused more on speed than slugging, the pitching staff was overpowering. Charley "Sea Lion" Hall only had a mediocre big league career (though he eventually became a legend in the high minor leagues where he won 284 games) but 1912 was his best season. He started 20 games, appeared in relief 14 times and finished with a 15–8 record and a 3.02 ERA. Lefthander Ray Collins (13–8, 2.53 ERA) was a reliable performer throughout his career. Thirty-year-old Thomas "Buck" O'Brien (20–13, 2.58 ERA) had made his big league debut near the end of the previous season and showed great promise with a 5–1 record and a minuscule ERA of only 0.38; in 1913, however, he was 4–11 and never appeared in the big leagues again. Rookie Hugh Bedient, who was just 22 years old, was the surprise of the staff. In what would prove by far to be the best season of his short career he won 20 games, lost only 9, and had an admirable 2.92 ERA.

Though the rest of the pitching staff was very strong, the ace was a fireballing righthander named "Smokey Joe" Wood. Purchased from Kansas City, he arrived in Boston at the end of the 1908 season and his talent was such that Wood was soon considered heir apparent to the great Cy Young. In 1911 he compiled a 23–17 record, pitched a no-hitter, and struck out a record 15 batters in one game. He followed that with an even more amazing performance; in 1912 Wood turned in what is arguably the greatest single season performance in the history of baseball. Thoroughly dominating the opposition he won 34 games, lost only five, struck out 258 batters, had an ERA of 1.91, and led the league with 35 complete games and 10 shutouts.

On September 6 of the 1912 season one of the most storied moments in Red Sox history took place. Though he wasn't scheduled to pitch that day, the Senators dared the Red Sox to throw Wood — who was riding a 13-game win streak — against their star Walter Johnson. In his sixth season and already established as the game's premier pitcher, Johnson had set a record earlier in the season by winning 16 straight games. The Red Sox accepted the challenge and the press went wild. Comparing it to a championship boxing match (with Johnson as the reigning champ and Wood as the challenger), one writer called it "Louis and Dempsey in spiked shoes." In traditional boxing fashion, the height, weight, biceps, and triceps of the two pitchers were all compared.

To accommodate the crowd, which had turned out in droves to witness the matchup, parts of the outfield foul territory at Fenway Park had to be roped off to allow more standing room. In the end, the duel lived up to all the hype as "Smokey Joe" beat the "Big Train" 1–0. Boston scored the game's only run with two outs in the sixth thanks to back-to-back doubles off Johnson by Tris Speaker and Duffy Lewis. Wood would go on to win two more games before losing, tying Johnson's 16-game record.

After winning the pennant, the Red Sox advanced to meet the New York Giants and their superb pitching duo of Christy Mathewson and Rube Marquard in the World Series. To this day, the 1912 Series rates as one of the most exciting ever; four games were decided by one run, and one game was declared a tie after 11 innings due to darkness. In the final game, the Red Sox came from behind in the bottom of the tenth inning to take the win and the trophy. Speaker hit .300 for the Series and scored four runs, but the team's real star was pitcher Hugh Bedient: he started two games, appeared in relief in two more and in 18 innings pitched gave up just two earned runs.

The Red Sox' reign as baseball's best team was a brief one. In 1913 the team got off to a poor start, Jake Stahl was replaced as manager by catcher Bill Carrigan at mid-season, and they could do no better than a fourth place finish with a record of 79–71. The Sox did return to the top of the American League in 1915, however, thanks to another strong performance by Smokey Joe Wood and an impressive showing by a young pitcher named Babe Ruth.

1921–23
New York Yankees

On December 26, 1919, the New York Yankees officially began their ascent into greatness. On that date, one the Red Sox fans would like to forget, the Yankees obtained the contract of Babe Ruth from the financially ailing Boston club for $125,000 plus a loan of approximately $300,000. Ruth, who began his career as a great pitcher before switching to the outfield, was fast becoming the game's most feared slugger and had blasted a record 29 homers the season before.

Though Ruth would prove to be the most important piece of the Yankee puzzle, the first was manager Miller Huggins. A former infielder for the Reds and the Cardinals, the diminutive Huggins took over the helm of the St. Louis club in 1913 while still a player. In five seasons guiding the Cardinals he never finished better than third but Col. Jacob Ruppert, owner of the Yankees, liked

Huggins' fiery spirit and lured him to New York after the 1917 season. Handed the reins of a club that had finished 28½ games out of first in 1917, Huggins faced a big challenge but his club improved steadily each season; in 1920 the Yankees finished only three games back.

Together with 26-game-winning ace pitcher Carl Mays, another former Red Sox star, Babe Ruth led the Yankees to a 95–59 record in 1920. He more than earned his $20,000 salary, an amount previously unheard of for a baseball player, by shattering his own home run record with 54 round-trippers (more than any other *team*), driving in 137 runs, scoring 158, and compiling a batting average of .376. The excitement that the Babe brought to New York baseball helped the Yankees set a major league attendance record of 1,289,422, more than twice what they had drawn in 1919.

At the end of the 1920 season Ruppert hired Ed Barrow as the Yankees' general manager. An experienced baseball executive, Barrow had been the field manager of the Boston Red Sox for the previous three seasons. Backed by the deep pockets of Ruppert, he was quick to assess the Yankees' needs and immediately set about building what would become the greatest dynasty American sports has ever known. Barrow had always been a great judge of talent (he had discovered Honus Wagner more than 20 years previously and had converted Babe Ruth from a pitcher to an outfielder) and he determined that the Yankees needed one more pitcher and a starting catcher to complete the lineup. Turning to two players with whom he was familiar, Barrow made a trade with the Red Sox in December of 1920 for young righthanded pitcher Waite Hoyt and veteran backstop Wally Schang.

It was in the 1921 season that George Herman Ruth brought the New York Yankees their first pennant. It wasn't an easy win, though, and the Yankees needed every one of the Babe's 59 home runs to hold off a strong challenge by the defending world champion Cleveland Indians. The two teams had emerged from the pack by the end of June and the lead went back and forth between them until mid–September. In the end, however, the Yankees pulled away and their record of 98–55 gave them the league title by 4½ games.

In the history of baseball, no one had ever put up numbers like Ruth did in 1921. In addition to his record number of home runs, he set new marks in runs scored (177), runs batted in (171) and total bases (457). Hitting for a .378 average, he had 204 hits, 44 doubles, 16 triples, and 144 bases on balls (at least 50 were intentional). Ruth wasn't just an offensive player, however, and the speed that allowed him to steal 17 bases also helped him make sensational catches in left field. A strong and accurate throwing arm, with which he threw out 17 baserunners from the outfield, made him the complete player.

Though Ruth was spectacular, he did not win the pennant by himself. His exceptional supporting cast included first baseman Wally Pipp (.296, 97 RBI), second baseman Aaron Ward (.306), and shortstop Roger Peckinpaugh (.288, 128 runs). Catcher Wally Schang batted .316 while future Hall of Famer Frank

Baker (.294, 71 RBI) and Mike McNally (.260) operated in an effective platoon at third.

Joining Ruth in the outfield was Bob Meusel, the team's other big slugger. In only his second big league season, the right fielder hit .318 with 40 doubles, 16 triples, 24 homers and 135 RBI. In addition, he had a cannon-like arm and tied for the league lead with 28 assists. Center field was shared by three players — Elmer Miller, Braggo Roth, and Chick Fewster — who combined to score 114 runs and drive in 65.

Carl Mays (27–9) was the best pitcher in the American League that season. The league leader in wins, games and innings pitched (336), he was also the top reliever with 7 saves. Waite Hoyt (19–13), Bob Shawkey (18–12), and Rip Collins (11–5) rounded out the regular rotation while veteran Jack Quinn, used as both a reliever and occasional starter, contributed eight wins.

The 1921 World Series turned out to be travel-free for the Yankees as their opponents were the New York Giants, a club with whom they shared the Polo Grounds stadium. The National League club had had a similar season to the Yankees and with a record of 94–59 had won the pennant by four games.

With back-to-back 3–0 shutouts by Mays and Hoyt to start the best-of-nine Series, things looked good for the Yankees. They got a rude awakening in Game Three, however, when the Giants' offense exploded for 20 hits and 13 runs. The score was actually tied at four until the end of the seventh, when eight hits and two walks scored eight runs.

Carl Mays got the start in Game Four. He pitched well and held a 1–0 lead after seven but the Giants scored three in the eighth. Hitting his first ever World Series home run, Babe Ruth tried to rally the Yankees in the bottom of the ninth but they were unable to score again and lost the game 4–2. With the Series tied at two, the Giants had the momentum but Waite Hoyt shut them down in Game Five. An error allowed the National Leaguers to score in the first but the Yankees scored in the third and twice more in the fourth. That was all Hoyt needed as he held them to only scattered hits for the remainder of the game.

Game Six saw the Yankees jump out to a 3–0 lead in the first. In the top of the second, however, home runs by Frank Snyder and Irish Meusel (brother of Yankees slugger Bob Meusel) tied the score up. The Yankees retook the lead when Chick Fewster homered in the bottom of the inning but lost it for good in the fourth when the Giants added four more runs. The Giants' Phil Douglas outdueled Carl Mays in Game Seven. The Yankees held a 1–0 after three but the Giants tied it up in the fourth and then added the game-winner in the seventh when a double by Frank Snyder pushed a run across the plate.

Waite Hoyt, who had two wins and an ERA of 0.00, was on the mound for the Yankees in Game Eight. He pitched brilliantly but so did Art Nehf, and the Yankee bats could only manage four scattered hits. In the end, it was a fielding error by Roger Peckinpaugh in the top of the first that allowed the Giants to score the game's only run. With the loss, the Yankees joined the 1905 Athletics as the only teams to lose a 1–0 World Series game on an unearned run (the 1986 Mets and 1996 Braves later joined this group).

Before the start of the 1922 season, several player changes were made by the Yankees. Continuing to decimate the Red Sox roster, they made trades that brought them righthanded pitchers Joe Bush and "Sad Sam" Jones, and short-stop Everett Scott. In return, the Yankees dealt pitchers Rip Collins and Jack Quinn to the Boston club. Scott, the leading fielder in the American League at his position for the previous six seasons, was acquired to replace Roger Peck-inpaugh, who had been sold to Washington. In the middle of the 1922 season the Yankees would make yet another deal with Boston, this for third baseman Joe Dugan.

The Yankees began the 1922 season with a setback: Ruth and Meusel each had to sit out a six-week suspension for violating a league rule that prohibited World Series participants from barnstorming in the off-season. The absence of the teams' two most powerful players hurt but the club survived the slow start and returned to the top of the American League standings. After holding off a strong late-season challenge by the St. Louis Browns, the Yankees repeated as pennant winners with a 94–60 record.

Again powering the team was Babe Ruth (.315, 99 RBI, 35 HR), but his numbers were down, due in large part to his suspension. The suspension hurt Bob Meusel as well but he still hit for a .319 average and drove in 84 runs. With the acquisition of Whitey Witt from the Philadelphia Athletics, the Yankees found the center fielder they had been lacking. In his first season wearing pin-stripes, Witt batted .297, scored 98 runs and led the league with 89 bases on balls.

The rest of the well-rounded offense included the bats of first baseman Wally Pipp (.329, 90 RBI, 96 runs), second baseman Aaron Ward (.267), short-stop Everett Scott (.269) and catcher Wally Schang (.319). Frank Baker (.278), in the final season of his long Hall of Fame career, continued to play well at third base though he shared the duties with Mike McNally (.252 in 52 games) and mid-season acquisition Joe Dugan (.286 in 60 games).

The trade the Yankees made with the Red Sox to acquire pitcher Joe Bush proved to be a wise one. With a career-best performance of 26–7 he led the league in winning percentage. Bob Shawkey (20–12) also reached the 20-win mark while Waite Hoyt (19–12) was close. Sam Jones, the other pitcher acquired from the Red Sox, finished with an even 13–13 record and led the league with eight saves. Carl Mays, on the other hand, the ace of the staff in 1921, could manage only a 12–14 mark.

In another all–Polo Grounds affair, the Yankees met the Giants in the World Series for a second straight year. Led by second baseman Frankie Frisch, John McGraw's club had won the National League by seven games with a 93–61 record and appeared to be evenly matched with their stadium-mates. It didn't turn out to be that way, however, as the Giants prevented the Yankees from winning a single game.

In Game One the Yankees held a 2–0 lead in the eighth but gave up three runs in the bottom of the inning. Down 3–0 in the first inning of Game Two, the Yankees fought back to even the score. Unfortunately, the game remained deadlocked after ten innings, and with darkness approaching, the umpires called it a tie. The following day, Giants pitcher Jack Scott tossed a masterful four-hit shutout for a 3–0 win. Aaron Ward homered for the Yankees in Game Four but the Giants pulled out a narrow 4–3 victory. Game Five was close and the Yankees held a 3–2 lead in the eighth but, just like Game One, they surrendered three runs in the bottom of the inning and then failed to answer in the ninth.

Though the Yankees were loaded with talent, any casual observer could see that Babe Ruth was the heart of the team. The Giants knew that the way to win the Series was to shut the great slugger down and they did just that, limiting him to just two hits in 17 at-bats (a .118 average). The ineffectiveness of Ruth seemed to demoralize the entire team and as a whole they batted only .203. The pitching staff wasn't much better and their combined ERA of 3.35 was considerably higher than the 1.76 of the Giants' mound corps.

In 1923, the Yankees moved into a new home directly across the river from the Polo Grounds in the Bronx. Named Yankee Stadium, the ballpark — the nation's first with triple-decks — was the perfect home for a franchise that was fast becoming one of baseball's greatest.

On April 18, the more than 74,000 fans packing the new stadium for Opening Day got to witness Babe Ruth set the tone for the whole season by blasting a home run in his first at bat. The towering shot seemed to signify that the Yankees were not about to be denied the world championship that had eluded them each of the previous two seasons. With a near perfect mix of brilliant defense, awesome power and an overwhelming pitching staff, the Yankees cruised to their third consecutive American League pennant. This time there was no close pennant race and by the season's closing day the Yankees (98–54) had opened up a 16-game lead over second place Detroit.

The Yankees infield that season combined incredible defense with consistent offense. At second and third bases as well as shortstop, the Yankees had the league's leading fielders. Aaron Ward hit .284 and drove in 82 runs while Joe Dugan (.283) scored 111 runs. Everett Scott (.246) was the league's best glove man at his position for the eighth consecutive season. First baseman Wally Pipp hit .304 and drove in 108 runs though he probably should have worried when the Yankees called up a promising young first baseman named Lou Gehrig from Hartford in the Eastern League. In a 13-game trial beginning in late June Gehrig batted .423 and drove in 9 runs; it was pretty apparent that he had the talent to make it in the big leagues after a little more seasoning in the minors.

Behind the plate, Wally Schang (.276) remained one of the game's best all-around catchers though injury limited him to 84 games. In his absence, backup

Fred Hofmann performed admirably and even challenged for the regular starting job by batting .290 in 72 games.

Right fielder Bob Meusel (.313, 91 RBI) remained one of the team's big threats at the plate while Whitey Witt, in addition to being the league's leading center fielder, batted .314 and scored 113 runs. Over in left, Babe Ruth (41 HR, 130 RBI, 151 runs) continued his assault on the record books with a .393 batting average, 151 runs scored, 45 doubles, 205 hits and 170 bases on balls — all of which were career highs. Needless to say, he won the league's Most Valuable Player Award.

In search of a lefthander to round out the Yankee pitching staff, Ed Barrow went to the Red Sox well one more time and came back with veteran Herb Pennock. Perhaps the final piece of the puzzle that would help the Yankees win the World Series, Pennock won 19 games and lost only six. He combined with four righthanders — Waite Hoyt (17–9), Bob Shawkey (16–11), Joe Bush (19–15) and Sam Jones (21–8) — each of whom won at least 16 games (the only other team to have ever had five starters win 16 games is the 1998 Atlanta Braves). Carl Mays, the former ace of the staff, lost his effectiveness and only contributed a 5–2 record with a 6.20 ERA (he would recover and have a 20–9 season for the Reds in 1924).

Once again, the Yankees faced the Giants in the World Series. Things got off to an inauspicious start when they lost Game One 5–4 after blowing an early 3–0 lead but Ruth's two home runs in Game Two and a strong pitching performance by Pennock gave the Yankees a 4–2 win and evened the Series at one.

Game Three was a pitching duel between Sam Jones and Art Nehf. Scattering six hits, the lefthanded Nehf got all of the run support he needed when Giants outfielder Casey Stengel hit a solo home run in the seventh. The Yankees came back in Game Four and jumped out to an early lead. They held off rallies by the Giants in the eighth and ninth to take the game, 8–4.

In Game Five, Joe Bush pitched a three-hit gem while Joe Dugan led the Yankee attack with four hits including a three-run inside-the-park homer. The 8–1 victory gave the Yankees a 3–2 lead in the Series and left them just one win away from their first world championship. Returning to the Polo Grounds, their old home, the Yankees overcame a 4–1 deficit in Game Six with five runs in the eighth to take the game and the title of world champion.

The following season saw Washington dethrone New York in the American League. With a lineup that included the league's best pitcher, Walter Johnson, and top RBI man Goose Goslin, the Senators were able to hold off the Yankees and win the pennant by two games.

Despite a great season by Yankee slugger Bob Meusel in 1925, the club disintegrated. Ruth missed more than 50 games, the pitching was less effective, and it became apparent that the club had some weaknesses at the infield positions. All of this resulted in a 69–85 record and seventh place, 28½ games behind the Senators. Fortunately for Yankee fans, the decline was a brief one and the team was back on top of the league in 1926. Building on a foundation of players like Ruth, Meusel, Hoyt and Pennock, Ed Barrow proceeded to make some key personnel moves and assemble an even better team — a team considered by many to have been nearly perfect.

1921–24
New York Giants

For 31 seasons John McGraw ruled the New York Giants with an iron fist. Nicknamed "Little Napoleon" for his autocratic style of rule, he was undoubtedly one of baseball's toughest managers ever, but also one of its greatest. Though cocky and often humorless, his unpleasant personality traits were easily overlooked if one could appreciate McGraw's true baseball genius. A master tactician, he is credited with developing the hit-and-run and his teams manufactured runs instead of relying on the long ball.

In the spirit of the original Napoleon, McGraw was a general on the baseball field and his troops obeyed his every order. He even went so far as to often call every pitch, particularly in big games. But much like his rival Connie Mack in the American League, McGraw was also a great teacher. His biggest strength, however, may have been his ability to assess talent. He traveled far and wide to check out new talent (McGraw found future Hall of Fame first baseman Bill Terry playing for an oil company team in Louisiana), his search often leading him to college campuses. Again like Connie Mack, McGraw preferred intelligent players and he tried to sign as many collegiate stars as possible.

McGraw's Giants had won the National League pennant in 1904, 1905, 1911, 1912, 1913, and 1917, with a World Series title in 1905. The franchise's greatest reign of supremacy, however, would begin in 1921. After back-to-back second place finishes (neither pennant race was particularly close) the Giants reascended to the league throne in 1921. With a powerful offense that featured seven regulars who hit over .300 and a solid pitching staff, they posted a 94–59 record and took the flag by four games over the Pittsburgh Pirates.

First baseman George Kelly had made his debut with the Giants in 1915, spent time in the minor leagues and even played a few games for the Pirates. He returned to the Giants in 1919 and finally showed he could hit big league pitching with a .290 average in 32 games. In 1920 Kelly became a full-time player and proceeded to lead the league with 94 RBI. The next season he improved to drive in 122 runs while batting .308 and slugging a league-leading 23 home runs. Kelly's development into one of the National League's top hitters, as well as one of the best fielding first basemen, played a big role in the Giants' rise to prominence.

The Giants' other big offensive threat was third baseman Frankie Frisch. Nicknamed "The Fordham Flash," Frisch had been an All-American football player in college. He joined the Giants in June of 1919 and by the next season had taken over as the starting third baseman. In 1921, only his second full season in the major leagues, the 22-year-old hit .341, drove in 100 runs, scored 121, and led the league with 49 stolen bases.

Even if opposing pitchers managed to get by Kelly and Frisch they still had to face outfielders Ross Youngs (.327, 102 RBI) and George Burns (.299, 111 runs), shortstop Dave Bancroft (.318, 121 runs) and platooning catchers Frank Snyder (.320) and Earl Smith (.336). Outfielder Emil "Irish" Meusel (.329) was acquired from the Philadelphia Phillies in mid-season, adding another potent bat to the lineup.

Not just an all-offense team, the Giants had the pitching to match. Jesse Barnes was the ace of the staff and had won 25 games in 1919, which he followed with a 20-win season. He was not quite as effective in 1921 but he still compiled a record of 15–9. Lefthander Art Nehf had also reached the 20-win mark the previous season and he did so again in 1921 with a 20–10 record. Completing the regular starting rotation were Phil Douglas (15–10) and Fred Toney (18–11), each an established veteran.

Though he had great starters, McGraw also had plenty of other strong arms to call upon when the need arose. Veteran Rube Benton was 5–2 with a 2.88 ERA as a reliever and spot starter. The same role was played by Rosy Ryan, who put together a 7–10 record in his first full season in the big leagues. The Giants' primary reliever, however, was veteran lefthander Slim Sallee; in the final season of a long career, he appeared in 37 games and won six of them.

The Giants rolled on to repeat as league champs in 1922 and with a record of 93–61 left the second-place Reds in their wake by seven games. George Kelly (.328, 107 RBI, 17 HR, 96 runs) and Irish Meusel (.331, 132 RBI, 100 runs) each had an outstanding season and again provided the power in the offense. Youngs hit .331; Bancroft's .321 average was the best of his career while the same was true of Snyder's .343 mark. Frisch, who moved over to second base to make way for veteran Heinie Groh, hit .327 and scored 101 runs. Taking over at third, the 32-year-old Groh, acquired from the Reds for outfielder George Burns before the season, hit .265. He brought to the team a strong bat but his real strength was with the glove; he would lead the National League in fielding for the next three seasons. Veteran outfielder Casey Stengel, who had joined the Giants near the end of the previous season from the Phillies, also had an outstanding season and hit .368 in 84 games as a backup player.

With a 19–13 record, Art Nehf assumed the role of the team's number one starter. Phil Douglas, though he wasn't nearly as durable as Nehf, won 11 games, lost four and led the league with a 2.64 ERA. Beyond those two, however, the starting rotation was a little more shaky and McGraw had to call upon his great tactical abilities to get the job done.

Former ace Jesse Barnes continued his decline but he managed a 13–8 record. Fred Toney had also been expected to play a key role for the team after his 18-win performance the previous season, but after only 12 starts (five of which were wins), he went down with an injury. To fill the void, the Giants picked up righthander Hugh McQuillan from the Boston Braves in a mid-season deal. Taking a turn in the starting rotation he won six games and lost five. Jack Scott was another starter McGraw picked up after the season began. Released by the Reds, the Giants signed him even though he had never had a winning season in the big leagues. Proving he was worth the risk, Scott responded with an 8–2 record.

The versatile Rosy Ryan was the savior of the pitching staff; he appeared in 46 games, started 20 of them and finished the season with a 17–12 record, a 3.01 ERA, and three saves. Claude Jonnard, who had made his big league debut on the final day of the 1921 season, took over as the Giants' number one reliever. He had an outstanding rookie season, finished with a 6–1 record and led the league with five saves.

McGraw had another pitching nightmare to deal with late in the season when Phil Douglas, who was unhappy over salary issues, suggested that he would leave the club to make the Giants lose the pennant. The statement resulted in Douglas being banned indefinitely by Commissioner of Baseball Landis, a judgment that ended his bright career.

The Giants seemed to have an even greater command of the National League in 1923 and they improved their record to 95–58. Again their closest challenger was the Reds but the Giants kept them at bay and took the pennant by four-and-a-half games.

The key players in the offense remained unchanged that season with Kelly (.307, 103 RBI) and Meusel (.297), who was tops in the league with 125 runs batted in, leading the way. Frisch was the league leader in hits with 223 and batted .348, drove in 111 runs and scored 116. Not far behind him was Youngs ("He was the greatest outfielder I ever saw," McGraw would later say), who hit .336 with 200 hits and 87 RBI. With 121 runs scored, he was also a league leader. The slick-fielding Groh contributed a .290 batting average while Stengel (.339) continued to excel in a reserve role. Catcher Frank Snyder's batting average dropped significantly to .256 but he led the league with a .990 fielding percentage. Shortstop Travis Jackson (.275), who had come up the previous September, showed great promise and platooned with Bancroft (.304).

Art Nehf (13–10, 4.50 ERA) didn't pitch up to his normal level but Jack Scott (16–7), Hugh McQuillan (15–14) and a couple of newcomers picked up the slack. Mule Watson, brought over during the season from the lowly Boston Braves, chipped in with an 8–5 record while lefthander Jack Bentley, after a decade of being shuffled back and forth from the minors, finally stuck in the big leagues and contributed a 13–8 record. Also a good hitter, Bentley had won the 1921 International League batting title while with Baltimore and in 1923 hit an amazing .427 in 89 at-bats. Rosy Ryan, used in both a relief role and as a spot starter, won 16 games and lost only five. Claude Jonnard remained the team's ace reliever; appearing in 45 games and saving five, he led the league in both categories.

The 1924 pennant race was extremely close as the Giants were chased by Brooklyn and Pittsburgh for the entire season. McGraw's club opened up a fairly big lead in August but a brief slump allowed their pursuers to close the gap. At one point Brooklyn actually held the lead for a day in September but the Giants (93–60) rallied and in the end took the league by 1½ games over Brooklyn with Pittsburgh three games back.

Once again, the Giants offense was probably the most well-rounded in the game. Kelly (.324) hit 21 home runs and drove in a league-best 136 runs and Frisch, who hit .328, tied Rogers Hornsby of St. Louis with the most runs scored (121). Youngs (.356) crossed the plate 112 times and had the team's highest batting average while Meusel (.310) drove in 102 runs. Still the league's best fielding third baseman at age 34, Heinie Groh hit .281.

The composition of the Giants offense began to change somewhat in 1924 as McGraw began to insert talented young players into the lineup more and more. Twenty-year-old shortstop Travis Jackson continued to improve and batted .302 with 76 RBI after inheriting the starting job (Bancroft was traded to the Braves). To his right, another youngster, 18-year-old third baseman Fred Lindstrom, also saw a fair amount of playing time and hit .253 in 52 games. Before the season Casey Stengel had been dealt to the Boston Braves and to replace him the Giants brought up a young outfielder named Lewis "Hack" Wilson. Though only 5'6", Wilson carried a powerful bat and had won the Triple Crown with Portsmouth of the Virginia League in 1923. He showed he could hit major league pitching as well by batting .295 with 10 home runs and 57 RBI in 107 games. Another rookie who played a significant role was first baseman Bill Terry. Promoted from the minors at the end of the 1923 season after batting .377 at Toledo, Terry backed up Frisch and hit .239 in 77 games.

The mainstays of the pitching staff in 1924 were Art Nehf, who had returned to form with a 14–4 record, Jack Bentley (16–5) and Hugh McQuillen (14–8). Joining them was Virgil Barnes who, after several brief trials with the team, finally won a spot in the starting rotation. With a 16–10 record and an ERA of 3.06 he pitched well and even saved three games when called on in relief. The bullpen consisted of Mule Watson (seven wins) and Rosy Ryan (8–6, five saves) among others but Claude Jonnard was the ace with five saves and an ERA of 2.41 in 34 games.

For three straight years, the Giants' opponent in the World Series would be the New York Yankees, a club that had established a dynasty of its own in the American League. While the matchup meant an exciting in-city rivalry, it also meant that no travel was involved since for two of those seasons both teams played at the Polo Grounds ballpark.

In the first meeting of the two great teams the Yankees came out strong and took a 2–0 lead in the best-of-nine series with a pair of 3–0 shutouts. Game Three was tied at four until the Giants erupted for eight hits and eight runs in the bottom of the seventh. They added one more in the eighth to take a 13–5 win. The Giants evened the Series the next day when they put four runs on the board in the final two innings after being down 1–0. Pitcher Phil Douglas, who only allowed seven hits total, surrendered a bottom-of-the-ninth homer to Babe Ruth but the Yankees failed to come up with any additional runs.

Game Five was a pitching battle between Art Nehf and the Yankees' Waite Hoyt. An error allowed the Giants to score in the first but the Yankees tallied runs in the third and twice more in the fourth. That was all Hoyt needed as the Giants could only get a few scattered hits for the remainder of the game. The Yankees jumped out to a 3–0 lead in the first inning of Game Six but in the top of the second, home runs by Frank Snyder and Irish Meusel (whose brother Bob played for the Yankees) tied it up. The Yankees retook the lead on a Chick Fewster home run in the bottom of the inning but the Giants came back with four more runs in the fourth. Jesse Barnes shut the Yankees out for the remainder of the game and the Series was even at three.

The final two games of the 1921 Series were classic pitching duels. In Game Seven the Giants' Phil Douglas took on Carl Mays. The Yankees held a 1–0 lead after three but the Giants tied it up in the fourth and then added the game-winner in the seventh when a double by catcher Frank Snyder scored Johnny Rawlings. Art Nehf and Waite Hoyt were matched up again in Game Eight. In the end, neither pitcher surrendered an earned run but a fielding error by Yankees shortstop Roger Peckinpaugh allowed the Giants to score the game's only run in the top of the first.

The 1922 World Series proved to be the apex of the Giants dynasty. Again they took on the Yankees of manager Miller Huggins, against whom they appeared to be very evenly matched (the Yankees had won just one game more than the Giants during the season). The Series, which had returned to a best-of-seven format, was close and two games were decided by one run, but in the end the Giants essentially swept their rivals (one game was declared a tie).

The Yankees jumped out to a 2–0 lead in Game One and held it into the eighth but gave up three runs in the bottom of the inning. It was the Giants who took an early lead in Game Two as they scored three runs in the top of the first thanks to a home run by Irish Meusel. The Yankees came back, though, with single runs in the first, fourth, and eighth innings to even the score. The game remained deadlocked after ten innings, and with darkness approaching, the umpires called it a tie. Pitcher Jack Scott was the hero of Game Three for the Giants when he tossed a brilliant four-hit shutout to take a 3–0 win. The Yankees got to Hugh McQuillan for two runs in the first inning of Game Four but he settled down and was saved by a big five-hit fourth inning that scored four runs. The Giants held on to the lead and pulled out a narrow 4–3 victory.

Game Five was also close and the Yankees appeared to have survived to play another day with a 3–2 lead in the eighth. Yankee pitcher Joe Bush tired in the bottom of the inning, however, and surrendered four hits and a walk, which led to three runs. When the Yankees failed to answer in the ninth the Giants were again world champions.

The two New York clubs squared off for the third time in 1923 (though the Yankees had moved out of the Polo Grounds and into their new home, Yankee Stadium, just across the river). Recovering from a 3–0 deficit in the first game to tie the score at four, the Giants went to take a 5–4 victory when Casey Stengel hit an inside-the-park home run in the ninth. With a pair of homers, the mighty "Sultan of Swat," Babe Ruth, was the undoing of the Giants in Game Two as he led the Yankees to a 4–2 win.

Art Nehf dueled Sam Jones in Game Three. Neither pitcher had surrendered a run through six innings, but the game's only run was scored in the seventh when Giants outfielder Casey Stengel hit a solo home run. Game Four was the highest scoring contest of the Series and the Yankees held an 8–0 lead after four innings. An inside-the-park home run by Ross Youngs highlighted the Giants' rallying attempts in the late innings but they fell short and lost the game 8–4.

In Game Five, Yankee pitcher Joe Bush was almost untouchable and he gave up only three hits (all to Irish Meusel) while the Yankee batters pounded Jack Bentley. The 8–1 victory gave the Yankees a 3–2 lead in the Series and left the Giants in a do-or-die situation. They had a chance to even the Series in Game Six but blew a 4–1 lead in the eighth inning and lost the game and their title, 6–4.

The 1924 World Series ranks as one of the most hotly contested ever. The Series went a full seven games, four of which were decided by one run and two of those after 12 innings. Game One saw Art Nehf take on the legendary Walter Johnson, and both went the distance in what turned out to be a classic 12-inning duel. Home runs from George Kelly and Bill Terry gave the Giants a 2–1 lead, but in the bottom of the ninth the Senators tied it up when Roger Peckinpaugh's double scored Ossie Bluege. In the 12th, the Giants loaded the bases for Ross Youngs, who came through with a single. That was followed by a run-scoring sacrifice fly from Kelly which put McGraw's team up by two. Mounting a rally, Washington scored in the bottom of the inning and had a runner on third but Kelly bare-handed a grounder from Goose Goslin to record the final out.

Game Two was another close one as Washington took a 3–0 lead. The Giants fought back and tied it up but Roger Peckinpaugh came up with another big, ninth-inning double for the Senators, this time to drive in the winning run. The Giants jumped out to a 3–0 lead in Game Three and never trailed on their way to a 6–4 victory. The next day, Washington evened the Series again with a 13-hit attack that produced seven runs and featured a three-run homer by Goslin. The Giants had scored first but were only able to scatter six hits, which resulted in four runs.

On the strength of a great performance from pitcher Jack Bentley, who hit a two-run homer off Walter Johnson in his own support, the Giants took Game Five, 6–2. That win gave them a 3–2 Series lead, and left Washington one loss away from elimination. In Game Six, however, the pitching of Tom Zachary denied the Giants their first chance to take a third world crown in four years. The lefthander surrendered a run in the top of the first but settled down to cruise the rest of the way. Though the Senators only managed four hits against Art Nehf, the two runs they scored were enough to even the Series.

Game Seven would become one of the most memorable in the history of the World Series. Washington scored first when second baseman/manager Bucky Harris hit a solo home run in the bottom of the fourth but New York claimed the lead with three runs in the sixth. In the bottom of the eighth inning the Giants still held a 3–1 lead and seemed to be headed toward another Series title. With one out in the inning, however, pinch-hitter Nemo Leibold doubled off Virgil Barnes, catcher Muddy Ruel was safe with an infield single which was followed by a walk from pinch-hitter Bennie Tate. The bases were loaded for outfielder Earl McNeely but he was out with a fly ball that wasn't deep enough for Liebold to tag-up on. Harris came to the plate and hit a grounder to third that bounded over the head of Lindstrom. Two runs scored and tied the game. McQuillan was brought in to take over for Barnes and was able to stop the damage by getting Sam Rice to ground out.

The Senators brought Walter Johnson on in relief in the ninth and, after retiring the first batter, he gave up a triple to Frank Frisch. With the winning run 90 feet from scoring, Johnson intentionally walked Youngs, struck out Kelly and got Irish Meusel to ground out. Withstanding the pressure, "The Big Train" showed the stuff that had made him one of baseball's all-time greatest pitchers.

Still deadlocked at three in the bottom of the 12th with one out, Jack Bentley, who had come on in the 11th, got Ruel to pop up in foul territory. It should have been an easy out but catcher Hank Gowdy tripped over his own mask going for the ball, allowing it to drop. Given a new lease on life, Ruel proceeded to double to left field. Walter Johnson was next up and managed to safely reach first when his grounder was bobbled by shortstop Jackson. He was followed by McNeely, who hit a possible double-play grounder to third. But just like four innings earlier, the ball took a bad hop and went over Lindstrom's head; Ruel took off from second and scored the Series-deciding run.

The Pittsburgh Pirates dethroned the Giants in 1925. McGraw's team still played well and finished in second place but, at 8½ games back, the pennant race wasn't really close. The slide down the National League standings continued in 1926 as the Giants could do no better than fifth place with a 74–77 record.

John McGraw would continue to manage for several more seasons and, though he came close a couple of times, never won another pennant. Handing over the reigns of the club to first baseman Bill Terry, he retired in the middle of the 1932 season. In 1937, McGraw was the first of the 1921–1924 Giants elected to the Hall of Fame. He was eventually joined there by his former players Frankie Frisch, George Kelly, Bill Terry, Hack Wilson, Dave Bancroft, Ross Youngs, and Travis Jackson. Casey Stengel also made it to Cooperstown, though primarily for his 25-year managerial career and seven World Series titles with the Yankees.

1926–28
New York Yankees

The New York Yankees of 1926–1928 were one of the most talented assemblages of baseball players the sport has ever seen. That team, particularly the 1927 version, is the one against which all others are measured. It was the team of Ruth and Gehrig, of Lazzeri and Combs, of Hoyt and Pennock. It was a team made up of many stars with many different personalities but for those three seasons, everything came together. They went to the World Series three times, won it in 1927 and 1928, and came extremely close in 1926. Great, dominating, amazing, incredible — the list of superlatives to describe their accomplishments as a team could just go on and on.

Coming off their remarkable season in 1923, the Yankees stumbled slightly the following year. They lost a close pennant race to Washington and their 89–63 record left them two games back. After a dismal season in 1925, at the end of which the Yankees stood 28½ games out of first with a record of 69–85, it became apparent to manager Miller Huggins that some changes needed to be made. The problems that season had been ineffective pitchers and weakness at a couple of infield positions. Also, Ruth hadn't been himself in 1925 and had only appeared in two-thirds of the team's games. Plagued by a stomach ailment which required surgery, he hit only .290 with 25 HR and 66 RBI in 98 games. Not a bad season by ordinary standards but for the mighty Babe it was quite a poor performance.

If the Yankees were to return to the top they needed Babe Ruth back at full strength. They need not have worried, though, because the mighty Sultan of Swat wasn't about to stay down for long. He stormed back in 1926 to hit .372 and lead the league in runs (139), home runs (47), RBI (146), and bases on balls (144). Again joining Ruth in the outfield was Bob Meusel, who, probably thanks to Ruth's slump in 1925, had led the league in home runs (33) and RBI (138) in 1925. The man with probably the greatest throwing arm in baseball ("He could hit a dime at 100 yards and flatten it against a wall," teammate Joe Dugan once said) saw a drop in his power in 1926 but his batting average rose from .290 to .315. Second year man Earle Combs, the Yankees' third starting outfielder, would develop into one of the game's all-time best leadoff hitters. In his phenomenal rookie season he had hit for a .342 average with 203 hits and 117 runs scored. He didn't quite live up to that in 1926 but he still batted a very respectable .299 and scored 113 runs. Ben Paschal, the team's top reserve outfielder, also saw considerable playing time and batted .287 in 96 games.

The 1925 season had seen the emergence of Lou Gehrig, and Miller Huggins decided to stick with the young first baseman after he hit .295 with 20 HR and 68 RBI in his first full big league season. The player whose job Gehrig had essentially taken, veteran Wally Pipp, was traded to Cincinnati before the start of the 1926 season after putting in 11 seasons with the Yankees. In 1926, Gehrig began his ascent into legend. He batted .313, drove in 112 runs, scored 135, hit 16 home runs, led the league with 20 triples, and played in every single game.

At second base, the Yankees had another young player: rookie Tony Lazzeri. In 1925 the San Francisco native had belted an amazing 60 home runs and driven in a prodigious 222 runs with Salt Lake City in the Pacific Coast League. The Yankees quickly moved to acquire him and paid $55,000 and gave up four players for his rights. Lazzeri immediately made an impact, and in his first of what would prove to be 12 seasons with the club, he hit .275 with 18 home runs and 118 RBI. Aaron Ward, the Yankees' starting second baseman for the previous six seasons, was relegated to the backup role. He only appeared in 22 games in 1926 and was traded to the White Sox after the season.

One of the Yankees' big problems in 1925 had been the lack of a strong shortstop but that situation was remedied by the arrival of Mark Koenig. The Yankees purchased him from St. Paul of the American Association for $50,000 and he joined the team in September of 1925. In his first full season in the big leagues, the 23 year old hit .271 with 62 RBI and scored 93 runs. Koenig's partner in the left side of the infield was veteran Joe Dugan. A great fielder, the third baseman hit a solid .288 and drove in 64 runs.

At the catcher position, Wally Schang's production had been steadily dropping off and he hit only .240 in 1925. The Yankees decided to make a change so they traded him for 29-year-old Pat Collins, who had been a part-time backstop with the St. Louis Browns. The move paid off and Collins became a solid contributor in 1926, hitting .286 in 102 games. At mid-season he was joined by longtime veteran Hank Severeid. A one-time great catcher for the St. Louis Browns, he closed out his career by appearing in 41 games for the Yankees after coming over from Washington.

Among the regular starting pitchers Waite Hoyt remained the ace of the staff. He had an off year in 1925 and finished with his first losing season (11–14) since joining the Yankees in 1921. In 1926, however, he returned somewhat to form and won 16 games while losing only 11. The improved offense in 1926 gave veteran lefthander Herb Pennock the run support he needed. In 1925, though his ERA had only been 2.96, his record was 16–17. He improved to 23–11 in 1926. Urban Shocker had made his major league debut with the Yankees back in 1917 and then been traded to the St. Louis Browns two years later. After several great seasons for that team, including a 27-win performance in 1921, he was reacquired by the Yankees during the winter of 1924–25. Only 12–12 for the Yankees his first season back, Shocker improved and finished the 1926 season with a 19–11 record and an ERA of 3.38. Sam Jones, 15–21 in 1925, was probably the starting rotation's weakest link. He finished the year with a winning record (9–8) but his ERA rose to a lofty 4.98.

The team's star reliever was lefthander Garland Braxton. He had joined the team at the end of the 1925 season after winning 24 games for Springfield of the Eastern League. Appearing in 37 games he compiled a 5–1 record with an ERA of only 2.67. Rookie Myles Thomas, a former Penn State University star, was obtained from Toronto of the International League. He appeared in 33 games, 13 of them as a starter, and finished the season with a 6–6 record and an ERA of 4.23. Bob Shawkey, who had joined the Yankees in 1915, was also used out of the bullpen. Four times he had won 20 games in a season but in 1925 his record had dropped to 6–14. He regained some of his effectiveness in 1926, when switched to primarily a relief role, and finished with an 8–7 record and three saves.

On August 27, the Yankees acquired pitcher Dutch Ruether, who had been put on waivers by the Senators. A lefthander who was nearly 33 years old, Ruether had been one of the National League's top pitchers from 1919 to 1922. He would start five games for the Yankees late in the 1926 season, winning two of them and losing three.

At season's end, the Yankees' record stood at 91–63, good enough for the league pennant and a three-game margin of victory over the Cleveland Indians. In the World Series, the Yankees faced the St. Louis Cardinals of player-manager Rogers Hornsby. In Game One the Yankees offense failed to ignite, but thanks to masterful three-hit pitching by Herb Pennock, they held on for a 2–1 win. Game Two saw the Yankees jump out to a 2–0 lead, but thanks to home runs by Billy Southworth and Tommy Thevenow, the Cardinals came back to score six unanswered runs and take the game. Cardinal pitcher Jesse Haines, who even hit a home run to help his own cause, completely shut down the Yankees in Game Three and won 4–0. Thanks to three home runs by Ruth in Game Four, the Yankees came from behind for a 10–5 victory. Game Five was a classic pitching duel between Pennock and the Cardinals' Bill Sherdell. Each pitcher gave up two runs over nine innings and the game went to the tenth. A sacrifice fly by Tony Lazzeri put the Yankees ahead in the top of the inning. Pennock held on to the lead in the bottom half to chalk up his second win of the series.

For the sixth game, the series moved back to New York and with the Yankees up three games to two, it appeared they would prevail. The Cardinals sent

39-year-old Grover Cleveland Alexander to the mound while the Yankees countered with Shawkey. The Cardinals jumped out to a three-run lead in the top of the first and never looked back. When the game ended the scoreboard read St. Louis 10, New York 2. In the deciding game, Hoyt got the start for the Yankees while Haines was on the mound for the Cardinals. Both pitched well but at the end of six innings, the Cardinals held a 3–2 lead. In the seventh inning, Cardinal manager Hornsby summoned Alexander to the mound, even though he had pitched a complete game the night before. The bases were loaded with two out, and 22-year-old rookie Tony Lazzeri was at the plate. On four pitches, Alexander struck him out. He retired the Yankees in order in the eighth and then in the ninth got the first two batters to ground out. Ruth, who could have tied the game with one swing of the bat, was the Yanks' last hope and he drew a walk. He then tried to steal and was thrown out, ending the game and the Yankees' hope for a World Series title.

While the 1926 Yankees were extremely good, the 1927 team was astounding. That season, the team unleashed a combination of devastating offense and overpowering pitching the likes of which baseball had never before seen. The Yankee juggernaut would roll on to enjoy an unprecedented record breaking year. They destroyed their opponents (at one point had beaten the hapless St. Louis Browns 21 consecutive times) and from the first day of the season to the last, the Yankees were in first place.

The stage was set for the Yankees' amazing season when Babe Ruth signed a three-year contract for $70,000 per year in early March. As had been proven in 1925, their performance as a team depended a lot upon their star.

Much of the team remained the same from the previous season but the Yankees did pick up seven new players, two of whom would figure prominently into the campaign. Pitcher George Pipgras had been with the Yankees in 1923 and 1924 but after some rather poor performances Miller Huggins shipped him off to the minors to work on his control. He spent the 1925 season in the Southern League with Atlanta and Nashville and then went to St. Paul in the American Association for 1926. After posting league-leading strikeout numbers in both of those seasons he was returned to the Yankee lineup. Fellow pitcher Wilcy Moore was a 29-year-old rookie who in 1926 had posted a 30–4 record with Greenville (S.C.) of the South Atlantic League. The Yankees promptly purchased him for $5,000 to fill the void left by the departure of Garland Braxton, who had been sold to Washington.

With the exception of infielder Julie Wera, who was a rookie and had been with Pipgras at St. Paul, the rest of the newcomers were acquired in deals with other big league clubs. Outfielder Cedric Durst and lefthander Joe Giard, both of whom had had mediocre seasons with the Browns, joined the team as part of a trade that sent Sam Jones to St. Louis. Catcher John Grabowski and second baseman Ray Morehart had each put in a couple of seasons in backup roles with the White Sox.

The 1926 New York Yankees

When all of the player moves had been made, little did Yankees owner Jacob Ruppert, general manager Ed Barrow and manager Miller Huggins realize that they had put together a near perfect team. Amazingly, after the roster was set, no changes had to be made and the team went the entire season using the same 25 players. Simply put, the 1927 Yankees were the most fearsome lineup ever assembled. They hit for power and average, they had speed and they had the pitching to match.

Babe Ruth continued to rewrite the record books in 1927 and broke his own home run record with 60 round-trippers. He alone hit more homers than the collective total of any other American League team. He batted .356 and drove in 164 runs. In addition, he led the league in runs scored (158) and bases on balls (144). Ruth's fellow outfielders, Earle Combs in center and Bob Meusel in left, hit .356 and .337, respectively. Combs, the Yankees' leadoff hitter, more than made up for his weak throwing arm with his bat and his speed. He led the league with 231 hits and 23 triples. Meusel also had speed and stole 24 bases to go with his 103 RBI. Together the three starting outfielders combined for 597 hits and a .350 average.

Though he played in Ruth's shadow in 1927 (and indeed, for a large part of his career) Lou Gehrig's performance in 1927 ranks as one of the most impressive single seasons in the history of baseball. The first baseman, who was named as the league's Most Valuable Player, batted .373 with 47 home runs,

218 hits, 149 runs scored, a league-leading 52 doubles, and a major league record 175 RBI. At second base Tony Lazzeri hit .309 and became the fourth Yankee to top the 100 RBI mark when he pushed 102 runners across the plate. His 18 home runs and 22 stolen bases both ranked third in the American League. At shortstop, Mark Koenig put in a very solid season with a .285 batting average and 99 runs scored. Third base was somewhat of a trouble spot for manager Huggins. Regular starter Joe Dugan (.269, 43 RBI) only appeared in 112 games due to injury and even then he wasn't particularly effective at the plate.

The position of catcher was the only position that could really be considered a weakness. Due to injuries, three different men shared the duties though none of them was a real threat offensively. Benny Bengough was scheduled to be the starting catcher in 1927 but hadn't recovered from an arm injury suffered the previous season. Instead, John Grabowski got the nod on Opening Day. Grabowski (.277, 25 RBI) caught 68 games during the season but missed several weeks due to injury. Bengough (.247) finally returned to the lineup in midseason but played in only 30 games. Pat Collins was probably the Yankees' best catcher. He caught the most games and was generally thought of as the team's number one backstop. In 89 games Collins hit .275 with seven home runs and 36 RBI.

Among the supporting players, outfielder Ben Paschal, Ray Morehart and Mike Gazella contributed the most. A good hitter who could have started for some teams, Paschal batted .317 in 50 games. In late June, Tony Lazzeri moved over to shortstop to fill in for injured Mark Koenig. Morehart (.256) was called on to take over second base and did a good job. By season's end he had appeared in 73 games, 18 of them as a pinch hitter. Gazella (.278) played in 54 games, most of them as a replacement for the injured Joe Dugan at third base.

The accomplishments of that offense are staggering. Their 975 runs set the major league record, as did their 158 home runs and 908 RBI. The team batting average of .307 was the best in the league and they averaged more than six runs and ten hits per game. Nicknamed "Murderers' Row," they were lethal to their opponents.

While the 1927 Yankees will be eternally famous for its hitting attack, the accomplishments of the pitching staff are equally as impressive. Four players won 18 or more games and they gave up so few runs that they probably could have been just as successful with only an average offense supporting them. That season's team is still the only major league team in history to have the top four pitchers in winning percentage and the top three in ERA in the same season.

Moore was undoubtedly the surprise success of the staff. Primarily a reliever he appeared in 50 games but started only 12 times. Finishing the season with a 19–7 record, Moore led the league with 13 saves and an ERA of 2.28. Among the regular starters, Waite Hoyt (22–7, 2.63 ERA) was the ace of the staff. He tied Ted Lyons of the White Sox for the league lead in wins and was second to Moore in earned-run average. Herb Pennock (19–8, 3.00 ERA) and

Urban Shocker (18–6, 2.84 ERA) both had outstanding seasons while Dutch Ruether (13–6) and George Pipgras (10–3) made great contributions. Even Bob Shawkey, whose great career was coming to an end, pitched well. Though his record was only 2–3, he had an ERA of just 2.89.

Even as that season wound to a close, the Yankees didn't let up. After clinching the pennant the team posted a 12–3 record, thanks in large part to the pitching staff's combined ERA of 2.48 for the month. From September 16 through the 21st, six Yankee pitchers (Moore, Shocker, Pennock, Pipgras, Hoyt and Ruether) turned in complete games. When all was said and done, the Yankees had won more games than any American League club in history, their final record stood at 110–44, and the Bronx Bombers had run away with the American League pennant by a league record margin of 19 games. New York led the league with a team ERA of 3.20, outscored its opponents by nearly 400 runs and hit .307 as a team. Never before had a baseball team so completely destroyed its opponents. With the exception of batting (Detroit's Harry Heilmann took the title) and strikeouts (Philadelphia's Lefty Grove), a Yankee led the league in every major statistical category.

When the 1927 World Series rolled around, the Yankees were ready. They faced a strong Pittsburgh Pirates team that had survived a tight pennant race and just edged out the Cardinals and Giants. Led by third baseman Pie Traynor (.342, 106 RBI) and the young Waner brothers, batting champ Paul (.380, 131 RBI) and his brother Lloyd (.355, 133 runs), the team won 94 games that season. They lacked the power of the Yankees, but the Pirates could hit and their .305 team average was the best in the league. Though it looked to be a good matchup on paper, the Yankees were not going to be denied after such an incredible season.

In the first game, they jumped out to an early lead and held on for a 5–4 victory. The second game saw them give up a first inning run to the Pirates, but George Pipgras settled down and the Yankees came back to win 6–2. Thanks to a masterful performance by Pennock, who had a perfect game going into the eighth, and a three-run homer by Ruth, the Yankees had an easy time in Game Three and won 8–1. The final game was close and the score was tied 3–3 in the bottom of the ninth but a wild pitch by the Pirates' Johnny Miljus allowed Combs to score the game-winner from third. It was the first time that an American League club had pulled off a sweep, just another in the long list of amazing accomplishments by the 1927 Yankees.

Surprisingly, the Yankees didn't even use their power to win the series. All four pitchers (Pipgras, Moore, Hoyt, and Pennock) put in great performances, particularly Moore. After relieving Hoyt in the first game and then pitching all nine innings of Game Four, his ERA was a minuscule 0.84. Shortstop Mark Koenig was the star of the offense, going 9–18, scoring five runs and driving in two. Combs also had a good series and hit .313 with six runs scored. And of course there was Ruth; the Yankees' larger-than-life outfielder batted .400 for the series, drove in seven runs and hit the only two home runs.

When the 1928 season began, the Yankees picked up right where they left off. They jumped out to an early lead and by July had opened up a 13 game lead over the second-place Philadelphia Athletics. Connie Mack's team didn't give up, however, and in early September the Athletics finally caught the Yankees and even briefly took the lead. In the end, however, the Yankees withstood the challenge and held on to take the pennant by two-and-a-half games.

The 1928 offensive unit remained unchanged for the most part. In the outfield Babe Ruth continued to add to his legend. He hit .323, and led the league in runs scored (163), home runs (54), RBI (142), and bases on balls (135). Center fielder Earle Combs' batting average dropped by 46 points, but he still hit .310 with 194 hits and a league-leading 21 triples. Bob Meusel's batting average also dropped considerably but his 113 RBI surpassed his 1927 total by ten. Ben Paschal (.316), who appeared in 65 games, continued to excel in his role of reserve outfielder and pinch hitter and almost exactly duplicated his performance of 1927. Cedric Durst also figured into the outfield equation and, playing in 74 games, he contributed a .252 average.

For the infield, Lou Gehrig was once again its foundation. Though he didn't equal his performance of 1927, he had another outstanding year. He tied with Ruth for the league lead with 142 runs batted in, hit 27 home runs, scored 139 times and batted for a .374 average. Tony Lazzeri also had another great season and he raised his batting average to .332, but his RBI, home runs, and runs scored all dropped. At third base, Joe Dugan had a season similar to the previous one, hitting .276 with 34 RBI in 94 games. For shortstop Mark Koenig, it would prove to be the best season of his career. He had 170 hits, scored 89 runs, drove in 63 and raised his batting average to .319. Utility infielder Mike Gazella was back for his third straight season with the team and hit .232 in 32 games.

The two main changes to the lineup were in the infield. Leo Durocher, who had played in two games for the Yankees back in 1925, replaced backup second baseman Ray Morehart. Filling in at second base and shortstop, he appeared in 102 games and hit .270 with 31 RBI. The other addition was third baseman Gene Robertson, who spent several seasons with the St. Louis Browns; appearing in 83 games he hit .291 with 36 RBI.

Behind the plate, Benny Bengough (.267), John Grabowski (.238) and Pat Collins (.221) all continued to share the catching duties. Another young catcher by the name of Bill Dickey made his big league debut with the Yankees that August and appeared in ten games. By the next season there was no more uncertainty as to who the Yankees' number one catcher was. Dickey would develop into one of the game's all-time greatest at his position.

The pitching staff saw the most changes for the 1928 season. Dutch Ruether and Bob Shawkey both decided to retire after the 1927 season (Shawkey would return to the Yankees in 1930 as manager). Urban Shocker, who won a combined 37 games over the previous two seasons, was forced to retire from the game at the beginning of the 1928 season due to a heart ailment. He would succumb to his illness that September and die at the age of only 38.

Once again, George Pipgras, Waite Hoyt, and Herb Pennock were the heart of the staff. All three actually had better seasons in 1928 than they had had in 1927. Pipgras improved to 24–13 and led the league in wins. Hoyt surpassed his 1927 total of 22 wins by one and lost only seven. Pennock finished his outstanding season with a 2.56 ERA and a 17–6 record.

For Wilcy Moore, his outstanding rookie season proved to be the best of his career. He pitched only 60 innings in 1928 (compared to 213 in 1927), his ERA rose by nearly two full runs to 4.18, and he finished the season with a 4–4 record. Myles Thomas, who had gone 7–4 in 1927, also contributed less and won only one game in 1928. Righthander Hank Johnson, who had been with the Yankees for trials in 1925 and 1926, was called up from the minor leagues. He pitched in 31 games (22 of them starts) and finished the season with a 14–9 record and a 4.30 ERA. The Yankees also brought in veteran lefthander Tom Zachary, who joined the team late in the season from Washington and posted a 3–3 record.

In the World Series the Yankees got revenge on the Cardinals for the heartbreaking loss in 1926 and easily swept them. None of the four games was closer than a three-run margin of victory as the Yankees basically put on a show of power. Gehrig alone drove in as many runs as the entire Cardinal offense. He slugged four home runs and hit for a .545 average over the four games. Not to be outdone, Ruth was an amazing 10 for 16 in the Series and capped it off with a three–home run performance in the fourth game. Grover Cleveland Alexander, the aging St. Louis veteran who had broken the Yankees in 1926, was shelled for 11 earned runs in the five innings he pitched.

But it wasn't just the Yankees' hitting that dominated; the pitching staff, which used only three pitchers for the entire Series, shut down Chick Hafey, Jim Bottomley and the rest of the Cardinal offense. With Pennock out due to an arm injury, Hoyt was forced to pitch both the first and fourth games. In 18 innings of work he only gave up four runs. Pipgras and newcomer Tom Zachary also tossed complete game victories, giving up only two and three runs, respectively.

In 1929, the Yankees just weren't the same team. Though a few players left the club, notably Joe Dugan and Pat Collins, many of the others including Ruth, Gehrig, and Hoyt returned. Still the team just didn't have the magic of the previous three seasons. With players like Jimmie Foxx, Lefty Grove, and Al Simmons, Connie Mack's Philadelphia Athletics soon rose to the top of the league. At season's end in 1929 they had dethroned the Yankees and taken the pennant by a surprising 18 games. For three seasons, the Athletics would rule the American League. It would be 1932 before the Yankees returned to power.

The final curtain came down on this era of the Yankee dynasty when manager Miller Huggins, who had taken a group of immensely talented players and

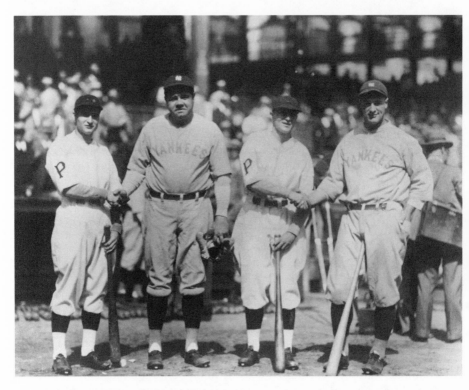

Ruth (second left) and Gehrig (right) pose with Pittsburgh stars Lloyd Waner (left) and Paul Waner (second right) during the 1927 World Series.

molded them into a unit, died near the end of the 1929 season. In September of that year, Huggins asked Coach Art Fletcher to take over for him so he could check into the hospital for treatment of a skin ailment. He never recovered and five days later was dead from a streptococcal infection at the age of 50. In Huggins' all-to-brief tenure with the club he had guided them to six pennants and three world championships in 12 seasons.

Certainly, the Yankees of 1926–28 would never have reached the heights that they did without Ruth and Gehrig. The names of these two players are among the most revered in all of American sports — if not all of American culture. But just as Ruth and Gehrig are icons, so is the entire Yankees team of that period. Every member contributed. The team will go down in history known as "Murderers' Row" for its fearsome offense but the pitching staff was just as formidable. In the end, seven members of the 1926–28 Yankees would go to be enshrined in the Hall of Fame: Babe Ruth, Lou Gehrig, Herb Pennock, Waite Hoyt, Earle Combs, Tony Lazzeri, and manager Miller Huggins. The man primarily responsible for assembling this legendary team, general manager Ed Barrow, has also been honored with a spot in Cooperstown.

1929–31
Philadelphia Athletics

From 1915 through 1921, Connie Mack's Philadelphia Athletics lived in the American League cellar. Slowly, by buying promising minor leaguers or, in the case of Jimmy Dykes, discovering them playing on the sandlots of Philadelphia, baseball's grand old man began to rebuild the dynasty he had enjoyed in the early 1910s. Slowly, one step at a time, the club rose back to the top. Seventh in 1922, sixth the next season, and fifth in 1924, they were ready to mount a challenge for the pennant by 1925. For the next four seasons, however, the A's were never quite able to catch the frontrunner; in both 1927 and 1928 they finished second to the Yankees.

The lineup of the 1928 Athletics read like a Who's Who of future Hall of Famers. In addition to his young stars like Jimmie Foxx and Mickey Cochrane, Mack had brought in 40-year-old Tris Speaker, 41-year-old Eddie Collins and 42-year-old Ty Cobb, three of the greatest players ever. (While the other two retired after that season, Collins stuck around and pinch hit a few times in 1929 and 1930.)

The youngsters on the team must have learned something from those legendary veterans because in 1929 they destroyed the competition and finished the season with a 104–46 record. Even the great Yankees and their "Murderers' Row" offense were swept aside by the A's, left in a distant second place, 18 games back. The 1930 season was another glorious one for Connie Mack and his 102–52 team. The second-place Senators made a valiant run at the pennant but they could not get closer than eight games. In 1931, the Athletics were at their greatest. Their offensive attack was virtually unstoppable and the pitching staff was the best in the game. With a 107–45 record they crushed the runner-up Yankees by 13½ games.

Though Mack had constructed a complete team that excelled in nearly every area of the game (they didn't exhibit particularly great speed on the base paths but, with such a powerful offense, there wasn't much need to steal bases), it was four players who made the Athletics what they were. Among the greatest ever seen in the game at their respective positions, each would have a career of almost mythological proportion.

Left fielder Al Simmons (whose real name was Aloysius Szymanski) turned pro with his hometown Milwaukee Brewers in 1922 at the age of 19. After quickly establishing himself as both a potentially great hitter and fielder, Simmons drew the attention of scouts for the Athletics. Connie Mack liked what he saw and he purchased the youngster after the 1923 season. Since Mack was the "Great Teacher," Simmons worried that he would try to change his unorthodox batting stance. Mack didn't even try, telling the young left fielder, "You can hold the bat in your teeth, provided you hit safely and often." Simmons did just that and in 1925, just his second season in the big leagues, he batted .387 and set a still-standing record for righthanded batters with 253 hits.

The 1929 season saw Simmons lead the league by driving in 157 runs; he also batted .365, slugged 34 homers and scored 114 times. An extremely intense player at the plate, he seemed to have a personal grudge against every pitcher he faced and that rage helped him win back-to-back American League batting titles in 1930 and 1931 with marks of .381 and .390. One of the rare players who could hit for power as well as average, Simmons drove in a total of 293 runs with 411 hits and 58 home runs over those two seasons. Simmons also led the league in 1930 with 152 runs scored and was the best fielder at his position.

With a nickname like "The Beast," first baseman Jimmie Foxx had a lot to live up to. Discovered by A's legend Frank "Home Run" Baker, who was managing a team in the low minor leagues, Foxx was originally a catcher. Baker recommended the young player to his old boss Connie Mack and the 17-year-old Foxx joined the Philadelphia club in 1925. Since Mack had the promising young Mickey Cochrane behind the plate he converted Foxx to a first baseman. Still, Foxx sat on the bench for much of his first three seasons with the Athletics.

In 1928, Foxx's first season as a full-time player, he performed well and batted .327 with 70 runs driven in. The following season the 21-year-old began to develop a true power swing. Over the three seasons of 1929–31, Foxx would drive in at least 118 runs in each, and average 33 home runs and 114 runs scored. Amazingly, despite those great performances, Foxx was still developing as a player. His best years were yet to come and he would win three American League MVP awards (1932, 1933, 1938).

Mickey "Black Mike" Cochrane was, without argument, one of the best catchers ever. To get him, Mack had to buy an entire minor league franchise. After he hit .333 in 1924, Portland of the Pacific Coast League agreed to sell their rising star but wanted $50,000 for him. Rather than spend that much for just one player, the ever-frugal Connie Mack just bought the whole ballclub for $200,000, sold the other players, and kept Cochrane for what worked out to be a fraction of the original price.

A former star quarterback at Boston University, Cochrane had natural leadership abilities which played a large role in the success of the A's. Though he never led the league in a major offensive category during his 13-year career, he developed into a consistent hitter capable of driving in runs. In 1929, his fifth big-league season, Cochrane batted .331, drove in 95 runs and scored 113. The next season he led the league in fielding percentage and hit .357 with 85 RBI and 110 runs scored. More of the same followed in 1931 as Cochrane drove in 89 runs with a .349 batting average.

Pitcher Robert "Lefty" Grove had been purchased from the Baltimore Orioles of the International League. Owner Jack Dunn knew the kind of potential

The 1930 Philadelphia Athletics

Grove had and he sold him to Connie Mack for $100,600. The price topped by $600 the amount Dunn had gotten when he sold another young pitcher, Babe Ruth, to the Red Sox several years earlier. Grove made his big league debut in 1925 but, with a 10–12 record and an ERA of 4.75, he had some trouble adapting to big league hitting. The following season Grove's ERA dropped to a league-leading 2.51 and he saw the first of eight 20-win seasons in 1927. With a 24–8 record in 1928, Grove firmly established himself as the premier pitcher in all of baseball.

In 1929, the first great season of the A's second dynasty, Grove was 20–6 with an ERA of 2.81 and a league-best 170 strikeouts. The following season, not only was he the league's winningest pitcher with 28 victories, Grove was also the top reliever with nine saves. In addition he struck out a career high 209 and had a 2.54 ERA. Amazingly, he topped that in 1931 by winning 31 games and losing only four. He led the league in complete games (27), strikeouts (175), and ERA (2.06); it was a performance worthy of consideration for best ever by a pitcher. At one point during that season he won 16 straight games, lost one, 1–0, on an unearned run, and then won eight more in a row. There was little disputing that Grove deserved the MVP award he won in 1931.

In addition to his three truly great position players, Mack had a supporting cast that would make any manager jealous. Leadoff hitter Max Bishop, one of the league's best second basemen, was an expert at getting on base. All three seasons he drew well over 100 walks. Veteran right fielder Bing Miller was a consistent .300 hitter and he averaged 90 RBI from 1929 to 1931. Joe Boley was an exceptional fielder at shortstop; he was backed up by the equally talented Dib Williams. Third baseman Jimmy Dykes was perhaps the most versatile player on the team since he could play every position except catcher. Also a good hitter, he batted .327 in 1929. Mule Haas, bought from the Atlanta Crackers of the Southern League, played center field like he owned it and could be counted on to hit .300 and score close to 100 runs.

Mack's stable of pitchers included a wide range of ages and levels of experience but they seemed to complement ace Lefty Grove perfectly. Like the leader of a great symphony, Mack flawlessly conducted his staff as only a manager of his experience could. It resulted in him being able to get big wins from supposedly washed up veterans and young rookies alike.

George Earnshaw, a 6'4" righthander out of Swarthmore College, was the A's number two starter. He won at least 21 games in each of the team's great seasons and led the league with 24 victories in 1929. Lefthanded Rube Walberg was often wild but he won 18 games in 1929 and 20 in 1931. Eddie Rommel, twice a 20-game winner for the Athletics in the early 1920s, became one of the team's premier relievers in the glory years; in 1929 he was 12–2, with a 2.85 ERA and four saves.

The ageless Jack Quinn, in the big leagues since 1909 and 46 years old by the end of the 1929 season, pitched well and won some big games as a reliever and sometime starter in 1929 and 1930. With an 11–6 record and seven saves, Bill Shores had a big rookie season in 1929; he went 12–4 in 1930. Roy Mahaffey was 9–5 in 1930 and even better in 1931 with a 15–4 record. Veteran Waite Hoyt, who had played such a large role for the great Yankee teams of the late 1920s, was purchased from Detroit in June of 1931. He made an immediate impact and finished with a 10–5 record.

In one of the most famous managerial moves of his long career, Mack named seldom-used Howard Ehmke as his starter in Game One of the 1929 World Series. A 14-year veteran at the end of his career, Ehmke had started only eight games that season. Still, Mack believed his sidearm delivery would be an effective weapon against the Chicago Cubs. Ehmke surprised everyone (except Mack perhaps) and he won the game, 3–1. In doing so he struck out 14 and set a Series record that stood for 23 years.

The Athletics went on to win the 1929 Series by defeating the Cubs four games to one. Simmons and Foxx homered in Game Two to drive in five runs, and the A's cruised to a 9–3 win, but the Cubs came back to take Game Three. Strong pitching from Guy Bush silenced the big bats of Connie Mack's men and Chicago took the game, 3–1. Game Four saw one of the greatest rallies in World Series history. Trailing 8–0 in the bottom of the seventh, the Athletics seemed to have little chance but Al Simmons led off the inning with a home run. What followed was a combination of seven singles, a double, a walk, a hit batsman, and an inside-the-park home run by Mule Haas. When the fireworks were over the A's had won the game 10–8 and taken a 3–1 Series advantage. Game Five was also a come-from-behind win; trailing 2–0, the A's scored three runs in the bottom of the ninth to win their first Series since 1913.

Meeting the St. Louis Cardinals in the 1930 World Series, it seemed the mighty Athletics would have little trouble repeating as world champs. Mickey Cochrane homered in both of the first two games and the A's took relatively easy wins by the scores of 5–2 and 6–1. However, the Cardinal pitching staff took over and allowed a total of just one run by the A's in the next two games. Suddenly the Series was even at two games apiece. The pitching by both teams was strong in Game Five but a two-run homer by Foxx in the top of the ninth ruined a shutout bid by the Cardinals' Burleigh Grimes. The A's pitchers, Earnshaw and Grove, combined on a three-hit shutout. On the strength of home runs by Dykes and Simmons, and more outstanding pitching from Earnshaw, the A's rolled to a 7–1 victory in Game Six and their second Series title in as many seasons.

The Cardinals were again the A's opposition in the 1931 Series. With 101 wins, the Cards were stronger than they had been the previous season but were easily the underdog. In Game One, the Cardinals scored two runs in the first but the Athletics, though outhit 12–11, came back for a 6–2 victory. Evening the Series with a three-hit, 2–0 shutout by Bill Hallahan in Game Two, the Cardinals took the advantage by winning Game Three. Burleigh Grimes gave up just two hits (though one was a ninth-inning home run by Simmons) while the Cardinal batters scored five runs on 12 hits.

In Game Four, it was strong pitching by the Athletics (and a home run by Foxx) that won the game as George Earnshaw tossed a two-hit shutout. Bill Hallahan started for the Cardinals in Game Five and he continued his mastery of the A's batters. With the support of two home runs by his teammates, he easily won the game, 5–1. (For the Series, Hallahan was 2–0 with an ERA of 0.49.)

Lefty Grove pitched a masterful five-hitter in Game Six and the A's evened the Series again with an easy 8–1 win. In the deciding Game Seven, however, Burleigh Grimes silenced the A's batters through eight innings. The Cardinals had jumped out to a 4–0 lead and the two ninth-inning runs the Athletics managed to score were not enough. Connie Mack's greatest team had fallen three runs short of becoming the first ever to take three consecutive World Series.

The A's dropped to second place in 1932 as the Yankees reclaimed the American League throne. Though league MVP Jimmie Foxx powered the team to 94 wins, Gehrig, Ruth, and company were 13 games better. After that season Mack proceeded to break up his team, just as he had with his first great team in 1914. Feeling the effects of the Great Depression (attendance in 1932 was less than half of what it had been in 1929), Mack began the fire sale — one of the more notable transactions being the off-loading of Mule Haas, Al Simmons, and Jimmy Dykes to the White Sox for $100,000. A year later he sold Lefty Grove to the Red Sox for $125,000.

By the 1935 season, the Athletics were back in the league cellar. Mack was never again able to find and develop the kind of young talent necessary to challenge for another pennant. Even if he did happen to have a promising player it seemed Mack would rather sell him than pay the wages top players were earning. In Mack's final 16 seasons at the helm of the Athletics (he retired after the 1950 campaign at age 87) his team finished dead last ten times.

The players at the heart of the Athletics' success — Foxx, Grove, Cochrane, and Simmons — as well as manager Mack all went on to be enshrined in the Hall of Fame. Waite Hoyt also made it to Cooperstown, though the 16 games he pitched in 1931 where his only ones in an A's uniform. Max Bishop later served 24 years as the baseball coach at the U.S. Naval Academy while Jimmy Dykes managed in the big leagues; after guiding the White Sox for 13 seasons he returned to Philadelphia to take over the reins of the Athletics upon Mack's retirement in 1950.

1934–35 Detroit Tigers

After the 1933 season it was apparent to Frank Navin, part-owner and general manager of the Detroit Tigers, that some changes needed to be made if his club was ever again going to be a pennant contender. From 1927 to 1933, the club had finished no higher than fourth place and in 1931 they wound up a dismal 47 games out and in seventh place.

The first move Navin made was to find a new manager. Bucky Harris had led the Senators to a World Series title in 1924 but was never able to equal that success in five seasons at the helm of the Tigers. Navin first attempted to hire Babe Ruth as manager in 1934 but, unable to lure him away from New York, turned to Mickey Cochrane. For the sum of $100,000 Navin purchased the contract of the star catcher from the Philadelphia Athletics and brought him to Detroit to be a playing manager.

A born leader who had the ability to inspire players, Cochrane was exactly what the Tigers needed. The club had plenty of young talent, particularly first baseman Hank Greenberg and pitcher Lynwood "Schoolboy" Rowe. Both had showed great promise as rookies during the 1933 season. Outfielder Joyner "Jo-Jo" White had been a rookie with the Tigers in 1932 while third baseman Marv Owen had made his debut with the club the season before. Curveball specialist Tommy Bridges broke in to the big leagues with the Tigers late in the 1930 season. Eldon Auker, a 6'2" righthander with a submarine delivery, came up with the Tigers in August of 1933. Perhaps the team's best all-around athlete, Auker had won nine varsity letters — three each in baseball, basketball and football — during his college career at Kansas State.

Veteran second baseman Charlie Gehringer was a career Tiger. He broke into the big leagues with Detroit as a 21-year-old at the end of the 1924 season and would remain with the team until his retirement in 1942. Nicknamed "The Mechanical Man" for his smooth and flawless play both in the field and at the plate, Gehringer was arguably baseball's most consistent performer for the entire decade of the 1930s. Quiet and unassuming, he never drew the attention that some of the day's other big stars did.

Pitcher Firpo Marberry had spent ten seasons with Washington before joining the Tigers in 1933. The 34-year-old Texan was near the end of his career but was one of the American League's most reliable pitchers, plus he had World Series experience. He won 16 games in his first season in Detroit and would play a large role in 1934.

To complete his roster for 1934, Navin brought in another seasoned veteran. Outfielder Leon "Goose" Goslin, who had spent more than a decade with Washington plus a couple of seasons with the Browns, was acquired to play left field. The 33-year-old Goslin was a solid performer throughout his career and could usually be counted to hit over .300 and drive in at least 100 runs.

The Tigers started the 1934 season out slowly but by mid–July had taken the American League lead from the Yankees. During August and September they extended their lead and at the end of the season the Tigers' record of 101–53 gave them the pennant by seven games. They batted .300 as a team and their winning percentage of .656 was the highest in Tiger history.

Young first baseman Hank Greenberg had the first great season of his stellar career and batted .339, drove in 139 runs, hit 26 home runs, scored 118 times, and led the league with 63 doubles. At second base, longtime Tiger Charlie Gehringer had one of the best seasons of his career: he hit .356, drove in 127 runs and led the league with 214 hits and 134 runs scored. Shortstop Billy Rogell (.296, 144 runs) also reached the 100 RBI mark while third baseman Marv Owen (.317, 96 RBI) came very close.

In addition to guiding the team as its manager, catcher Mickey Cochrane led with his bat, his defensive abilities and his determination. With a .320 batting average and 76 RBI, Cochrane was named as the American League's Most Valuable Player in 1934. Ray Hayworth, who had been the club's starting catcher for the previous couple of seasons, was relegated to a backup role by the arrival of Cochrane but he contributed with a .293 average and 27 RBI in 54 games.

Right fielder Pete Fox displayed very little power (only two home runs and 45 RBI in 516 at-bats) but he made up for it with speed (101 runs and 25 stolen bases) and strong defense. In his first season in Detroit, left fielder and former American League batting champ Goose Goslin hit .305, drove in 100 runs, and scored 106. In center field, Jo-Jo White had what would prove to be the best season of his career by hitting .313, scoring 97 runs and stealing 28 bases. Gee Walker, often platooning with White, hit an even .300 in 98 games as the reserve outfielder.

In his first season as a regular member of the starting rotation, 24-year-old Schoolboy Rowe (24–8, 3.45 ERA) had an outstanding season and at one point won 16 straight games. Tommy Bridges (22–11) also topped the 20-win mark while Firpo Marberry and Eldon Auker each won 15 games. Much of the relief duty went to lefthander Chief Hogsett, who appeared in 26 games and finished with a 3–2 record. Veteran righthander Alvin "General" Crowder, who had led the league in wins in 1932 and 1933 while with Washington, joined the Tigers in late 1934. He gave the pitching staff a boost down the stretch and in nine games compiled a 5–1 record.

In the World Series, the Tigers were matched against the fearsome "Gashouse Gang" of the St. Louis Cardinals. A team that led the National League in nearly every offensive and pitching category, the Cardinals' lineup featured such great players as Joe Medwick, Pepper Martin, Ripper Collins, and the Dean brothers, "Dizzy" and Paul. In Game One, General Crowder proved ineffective against the Cardinal offense and took the loss as the Tigers went down in defeat 8–3. After giving up two early runs in Game Two, Schoolboy Rowe shut the Cardinals out for nine straight innings and the Tigers rallied for a 3–2, 12-inning win. Paul Dean gave up only one ninth-inning run on his way to an easy 4–1 win in Game Three. The Tigers recovered to easily win Game Four, 10–3, while Game Five saw Tommy Bridges outpitch Dizzy Dean to give Detroit a three games to two lead in the series. With Game Six being played at home and staff· ace Rowe on the mound, things looked good for the Tigers. The game went back and forth and after six innings the score stood at 3–3. In the top of the seventh the Cardinals took a one-run lead which pitcher Paul Dean held by shutting out the Tigers for the remainder of the game. Game Seven proved to be a humiliating loss for Detroit. The game was scoreless after two innings but in the third the Cardinals erupted for seven runs. Dizzy Dean, working on only one day's rest, scattered six hits and St. Louis cruised to an 11–0 victory.

With a team that had won over 100 games the previous season there was really not much reason to make any major roster moves during the off-season. The Tigers entered the 1935 campaign as favorites to repeat as pennant winners, though they were expected to face a strong challenge from the Yankees. Much like the 1934 season they got off to a slow start but by August had opened up a wide lead in the American League race. A late season slump allowed the Yankees to make up some ground on the Tigers but when the season came to a close Detroit had won the pennant by three games with a record of 93–58.

First baseman Greenberg just continued to improve as a hitter; with 203 hits he batted for a .328 average, scored 121 runs, and led the league with 36 home runs and 170 RBI. Second baseman Gehringer (.330) put on an offensive show as well by driving in 108 runs, crossing the plate 123 times, and slugging 19 balls out of the park. Billy Rogell, the league's best fielding shortstop, hit a respectable .275 and drove in 71 runs. Third baseman Marv Owen batted .263 and equaled Rogell's RBI total while utility infielder Herman "Flea" Clifton

The infield of the 1934 Tigers: (l-r) Greenberg, Gehringer, Rogell, and Owen. (Courtesy of Hank Utley.)

contributed with a .255 average in 43 games. Overall, the starting infielders averaged 105 RBI each and helped the Tigers commit only 128 errors, the fewest in the major leagues that season.

Skipper Mickey Cochrane had another great season behind the plate, hitting .319 and scoring 93 runs, while Ray Hayworth (.309 in 51 games) continued to excel in the backup role.

In the outfield, right fielder Pete Fox was the leading run producer; with dramatically improved power he batted .321, drove in 73 runs, hit 15 home runs, and scored 116 runs. The batting average of speedy center fielder Jo-Jo White (.240) dropped considerably from the previous season but he still managed to score 82 runs and steal 19 bases. In left field, veteran Goose Goslin continued to excel and batted .292 with 109 RBI. Fourth outfielder Gee Walker turned in a performance nearly identical to the one he had in 1934 and batted .301 with 53 RBI in 98 games.

Led by Tommy Bridges (21–10 and a league-best 163 strikeouts), four members of the 1935 Tigers pitching staff won at least 16 games. Schoolboy Rowe (19–13) led the league with six shutouts while Eldon Auker chalked up 18 wins against only seven losses for the league's best winning percentage. Thirty-six-year-old General Crowder, in the last full season of his career, finished with a 16–10 record. Relief specialist Chief Hogsett appeared in 40 games, winning six and saving five.

For awhile late in the season it looked as if the Tigers might be rematched with the Cardinals in the 1935 World Series. The Chicago Cubs, however, had other ideas and swept in to take the National League pennant by winning 21 straight games in September. With such great momentum going into the World Series, many thought the Cubs would roll right over the Tigers. Lon Warneke, a 20-game winner that season for the Cubs, completely shut down the Tiger offense in Game One and cruised to a four-hit, 3–0 win. In Game Two, Greenberg hit a home run in the first inning as the Tigers took a 4–0 lead. They went on to win 8–3 though they lost Greenberg for the rest of the series due to a broken wrist. Game Three saw the Tigers go down 0–3 in the sixth inning but they rallied to take a 5–3 lead only to see the Cubs come back to tie it up in the bottom of the ninth. The Tigers went on to win in the 11th, however, on two singles and an error by Cubs third baseman Fred Lindstrom which allowed an unearned run. Game Four was a pitching duel between Crowder and the Cubs' Tex Carleton but the Tigers pulled out a 2–1 win; errors by the Cubs again allowed the winning run to score. Masterful pitching by Lon Warneke and a home run by Chuck Klein gave the Cubs a 3–1 win in Game Five and saved them from elimination. For Game Six, the Tigers sent Tommy Bridges to the mound while the Cubs countered with Larry French. The game went back and forth as each pitcher gave up 12 hits and the game was tied at three going into the ninth inning. Thanks to Goose Goslin's two-out single in the bottom of the inning, which scored Mickey Cochrane from second base, the Tigers took their first title in five trips to the World Series.

During the off-season it quickly became apparent that things would be different for the Tigers in 1936. In mid–November part-owner Frank Navin, who had run the club since 1908, suffered a heart attack and died at the age of 64. In April of 1936, Greenberg re-injured his wrist and missed nearly the entire season. With their slugging power gone the team struggled and went into a slump. The pressure on manager Cochrane led to a nervous breakdown — and an absence from the team of more than three weeks — but he recovered to guide a second-half resurgence. Still, the Tigers' second place finish left them 19½ games behind the Yankees. It was 1940 before the Detroit Tigers won another American League pennant.

1936–39
New York Yankees

The third great dynasty of the New York Yankees — and some say their finest — began in 1936.

After winning the World Series in 1932, the Yankees spent three seasons as runner-up in the American League. In both 1933 and 1934, they finished seven games out of first and in 1935 they came up but three games short. In 1936, however, they destroyed the opposition and finished a club-record 19½ games ahead of second place Detroit. The Yankees went on to take the World Series by defeating their old nemesis, the New York Giants, four games to two.

The spectacular 1936 season was followed by three more pennants and three more world championships. In 1937, the Yankees won the league by 13 games and then put nine-and-a-half games between themselves and second-place Boston in 1938. With a record of 106–45, the margin of victory in 1939 was 17 games. In the World Series that followed each of those three seasons, the Yankees totally outclassed their opponents and dropped a total of one game. Up three games to none in the 1937 Series against the Giants, the Yankees lost Game Four. They came back to take Game Five and the next eight postseason games they played by sweeping the Cubs in 1938 and the Reds in 1939.

Behind the Yankees' great success was manager Joe McCarthy. A former minor league player who had never made it into the big leagues, he worked his way up the managerial ranks and in 1929 led the Chicago Cubs to the National League pennant. Joining the Yankees in 1931, he took over a third place club that had finished 16 games out of first the previous season; by 1932 they were world champions once again. Considered by some to be the greatest manager of all time, McCarthy's greatest strength was his ability to pull a team together as a close-knit unit. (Babe Ruth did cause some dissension in McCarthy's first few years, however, since he was not afraid to express his belief that he should be manager of the club.) Thanks to his powers of observation and attention to detail, McCarthy was also a great teacher; once said Joe DiMaggio, "Never a day went by when you didn't learn something from McCarthy." The usually quiet McCarthy was a strict disciplinarian, but his players respected him immensely. By the time he left the Yankees in 1946, he had guided the club to a record seven world titles.

Though Lou Gehrig had been one of the game's best players for more than a decade, he had always played second chair to the larger-than-life Ruth. When the Bambino hung up his pinstripes at the end of the 1934 season, however, "The Iron Horse" (Gehrig hadn't missed a game since the 1925 season) took his rightful spot as the team's leader. The first baseman came out swinging in 1936 and put up numbers that won him his second American League MVP

The 1938 New York Yankees

Award. In addition to compiling a .354 batting average he drove in 152 runs, tied his career best with 49 home runs, and set a career mark with 167 runs scored.

Besides Gehrig, the only other member of the famed "Murderers' Row" lineup of the late 1920s remaining with the team was second baseman Tony Lazzeri. He continued to produce just as he had for the previous decade by hitting .287 with 109 runs batted in.

The rest of the Yankees offense, one that scored an average of seven runs per game during the 1936 season, included a mix of seasoned veterans and promising youngsters. Holding down third base was Red Rolfe (.319, 70 RBI, 116 runs). The 27-year-old New Hampshire native was an outstanding fielder and a reliable run producer. Gifted shortstop Frankie Crosetti (.288, 137 runs) had joined the Yankees in 1932 — he would go on to spend 17 seasons with the team. Catcher Bill Dickey (.362, 107 RBI, 22 HR) had developed into the best defensive catcher in all of baseball and one of its most consistent hitters.

The Yankees outfield had seen some changes. The legendary Ruth was gone and brilliant center fielder Earle Combs had retired after the 1935 season. Taking their places was a new crop of young stars including Canadian George Selkirk (.308, 107 RBI, 18 HR) and an exciting 21-year-old rookie from San Francisco named Joe DiMaggio (.323, 125 RBI, 29 HR, 132 runs). Joining those two was Jake Powell (.302), who had been acquired from Washington in mid-season.

Pitcher Lefty Gomez was 13–7 with a 4.39 ERA in 1936, an off-season by his lofty standards. The Yankees had purchased the future Hall of Famer from the San Francisco Seals for $35,000 after the 1929 season. He struggled in his rookie season and was sent down to the St. Paul Saints of the American Association but in 1931 was recalled to New York and responded with 21 victories.

In the 1920s, Red Ruffing had twice lost more than 20 games in a season with the Boston Red Sox. However, Yankee general manager Ed Barrow believed Ruffing could succeed with a powerful offense behind him, so in 1930 Barrow acquired him for backup outfielder Cedric Durst and $50,000. By 1936, Ruffing (20–12) had established himself as one of the best pitchers in baseball and joined with Gomez to form the core of the Yankees' legendary staff.

Like Ruffing, many of the pitchers on the Yankees roster had been acquired from other big league teams. Pat Malone, a veteran of two World Series with the Chicago Cubs, joined the Yankees in 1935. A starter for seven seasons he was moved to the bullpen and in 1936, his best season with New York, he was 12–4 with a league-leading nine saves. While with the Browns, righthander Bump Hadley had led the league in losses one season but things got better when he was traded to the Yankees. In 1936, Hadley's first season in Yankee pinstripes, he finished 14–4 and gave the team some quality starts as well as some strong relief innings. Monte Pearson, who had been with Cleveland the previous four years, was 19–7 in his first season in New York. Relief ace Johnny Murphy, a Yankee since 1932, was one of the few who had come up with the team; in 1936 he was 9–3 with five saves.

Despite having played every game of every season for more than a decade, Gehrig showed no signs of letting up in 1937 and batted .351 with 37 home runs and 159 RBI. The Yankees' other great veteran, Tony Lazzeri, was approaching the end of his career, however, and in his final season with the team hit .244 and drove in 70 runs. Third baseman Rolfe (.276) and shortstop Crosetti (.234) combined to score 280 runs while catcher Bill Dickey (.332, 133 RBI, 29 HR) continued his march toward the Hall of Fame.

The star of Joe DiMaggio continued to rise. On his way to becoming perhaps the greatest center fielder ever, he hit .346, drove in 167 runs, slugged 46 homers, and scored 151 runs. The other two outfield spots were shared by four players. Playing primarily in left was George Selkirk, a patient hitter who was skilled at drawing walks; he batted .328 with 68 RBI in 78 games. Rookie Tommy Henrich contributed a .320 batting average with 42 RBI in 67 games. A standout with New Orleans of the Southern Association, he had been signed by the Yankees for $25,000 after being declared a free agent. Completing the group were journeyman Myril Hoag (.301 in 106 games) and the impetuous Jake Powell (.263 in 97 games), who was always quick to start a fight.

Lefty Gomez returned to the form that had made him the American League's most feared pitcher in the early 1930s; with a 21–11 record he led the league in wins. He also was best in strikeouts (194), ERA (2.33), and shutouts (6). Not far behind him was Red Ruffing (20–7, 2.98 ERA), who equaled his win total of the previous season. Bump Hadley (11–8) and Monte Pearson (9–3, 3.17 ERA) were the other regular starters but neither performed even close to the level of Gomez and Ruffing. Lefthander Kemp Wicker, who had appeared in a few games in 1936, was used as an occasional starter and, with a 7–3 record, had the best season of his brief big-league career. Brilliant control pitcher Johnny Murphy (13–4, 10 saves) was well on his way to becoming the best reliever of his time. Joining him in the bullpen was veteran Ivy Andrews; acquired from the Indians at mid-season, he appeared in 11 games and won three.

Before the 1938 season, Tony Lazzeri joined the Chicago Cubs where he took a job as a coach and part-time player. Replacing him at second base was rookie Joe Gordon (.255, 25 HR, 97 RBI). A former University of Oregon star, he had been purchased by the Yankees after spending the 1936 season with Oakland in the PCL. Sent to the Yankees' top farm club in Newark, he did well and got the call to come to the other side of the Hudson River in 1938.

The departure of Lazzeri left Gehrig as the last member of the famed Murderers' Row still wearing a Yankees uniform. Gehrig, too, was beginning to slow down (.295, 29 HR, 114 RBI, 115 runs) but he still had a season that would have most players jealous. At third, Red Rolfe (.311, 80 RBI, 132 runs) continued to shine while shortstop Frankie Crosetti hit .263, scored 113 runs, and stole a league-leading 27 bases. Behind the plate, Bill Dickey (.313, 115 RBI, 27 HR) was as strong as ever.

By 1938 it was clear that DiMaggio (.324, 140 RBI, 32 home runs, 129 runs) was heir apparent to the throne once held by Ruth and currently occupied by Gehrig. Gracefully patrolling the vast expanse of the Yankee Stadium center field and able to hit as well — if not better than — anybody in the game, there seemed to be no limit to his abilities. Again playing on either side of DiMaggio were Tommy Henrich (.270, 91 RBI, 22 HR, 109 runs) and a platoon of Myril Hoag (.277 in 85 games) and George Selkirk (.254, 62 RBI in 99 games).

The one-two, left-right combination of Gomez and Ruffing continued to stun Yankee opponents in 1938. The smoking fastball of Gomez carried him to an 18–12 record while Ruffing posted a 21–7 mark that led the league in wins. The Yankees' number three and four starters also put up big numbers as Monte Pearson contributed a 16–7 record and Spud Chandler finished at 14–5. Wes Ferrell, who had six 20-win seasons between 1929 and 1936, joined the Yankees from the Senators late in the season. He took a turn in the starting rotation but wasn't particularly effective and contributed only a 2–2 record.

Though he wasn't forced to go to it as much as other managers, McCarthy had the security of knowing that he had a great bullpen. Johnny Murphy's curveball again made him the best reliever in baseball and he led the league with 11 saves. Also performing well was rookie righthander Steve Sundra, who appeared in 25 games and won six.

The 1939 season was one of the most glorious and yet one of the most tragic in Yankee history. In January, owner Jacob Ruppert, the man who had built his club into the greatest franchise in the history of sport, passed away. Eight games into the season, Lou Gehrig took himself out of the lineup, ending his streak of 2,130 consecutive games. Little did anyone at the time know that he had a fatal illness.

Even without the Iron Horse, the Yankees had a balanced attack in 1939 and they outscored their opponents by a total of 411 runs. Seven of the eight regular starters drove in 80 or more runs and the offense led the league in slugging for the fourth consecutive year. Not to be outdone, the Yankee pitchers compiled the league's lowest ERA (an amazing 1.31 below the league average) for the sixth straight campaign.

It must have been an almost impossible job filling in for Gehrig but Babe Dahlgren performed admirably and contributed to the offense with 89 RBI. Second baseman Gordon (.284, 111 RBI, 28 HR) continued to improve and Frankie Crosetti, though he only hit .233, scored 109 runs and was defensively brilliant at shortstop. Red Rolfe had by far the best season of his career. The third baseman hit .329, drove in 80 runs and led the league in runs scored (139), hits (213) and doubles (46).

The quiet and unassuming Bill Dickey (.302, 105 RBI, 24 HR) continued to handle the pitchers with unmatched skill, and at the plate he had another strong season. His backup, rookie Buddy Rosar, also showed great promise; the International League batting champ in 1938 while with Newark, he hit .276 in 43 games with the Yankees.

Despite missing much of the first month of the season with a leg injury, DiMaggio recovered to win the league MVP Award and have one of the greatest seasons of his career. His numbers for the month of August are impressive just by themselves: he hit .405, slugged 14 home runs and drove in 52 runs. When the season came to an end, DiMaggio had won the batting title with a .381 average, driven in 126 RBI, and hit 30 home runs. George Selkirk (.306, 101 RBI, 21 HR, 103 runs) recovered from his subpar 1938 season, led the league in fielding and earned a spot on the All-Star team. A newcomer in the Yankee outfield was rookie Charlie Keller (.334, 83 RBI). After two outstanding seasons at Newark he was finally promoted and won the starting right field job. Tommy Henrich (.277, 57 RBI in 99 games) became the primary backup and manager McCarthy's favorite pinch hitter.

Joe McCarthy liked to rotate his pitchers around and over the course of the 1939 season eight different pitchers on the Yankees staff made at least 11 starts. Still, they allowed nearly 150 runs fewer than any other team in the league. Future Hall of Famer Red Ruffing (21–7, 2.93 ERA) equaled his record of the previous season while Lefty Gomez, who struggled with some minor injuries, finished at 12–8. Bump Hadley (12–6, 2.98 ERA) and Monte Pearson (12–5) also won 12 games while veteran righthander Oral Hildebrand, who had been picked up from the St. Louis Browns, contributed a 10–4 record with a 3.06 ERA. Righthander Atley Donald had appeared in two games at the beginning of the 1938 season but was sent down to Newark. He rejoined the Yankees in 1939 and went 13–3 with a 3.71 ERA. Second-year-man Steve Sundra proved to be somewhat of a surprise as he compiled an 11–1 record with a 2.76 ERA as a reliever and sometimes starter. Lefthanded rookie Marius Russo served in the same capacity and won eight games with a 2.41 ERA as a starter/reliever. If any of the starters got into trouble fireman Johnny Murphy was called in; again the league's best reliever, he led it with 19 saves.

With the final pitch of the 1939 World Series, an era came to an end. The Yankees continued to play well but the teams of the 1940s, though great in their own right, were different than the ones of the late 1930s. In 1940, a season that saw the closest pennant race in more than a decade, the Yankees slipped to third place with a record of 88–66 but were just two games out of first. With a 101-win season in 1941, they reclaimed the throne that seemed rightfully theirs and went on to defeat their crosstown rivals, the Dodgers, in the World Series. Two more pennants followed and another World Series title in 1943. Still, without Gehrig, the heart of the Yankees for so many years, and Colonel Ruppert, without whom the club would never have reached the heights that it did, it just wasn't the same team.

1939–40
Cincinnati Reds

Much of the decade of the 1930s was not kind to the Cincinnati Reds; for four consecutive seasons, 1931–34, the club finished last in the National League. A new chapter in Reds history began, however, in 1937 with the hiring of Warren Giles as general manager. Backed by the money of radio tycoon Powell Crosley, who had bought the franchise in 1934 and was willing to spend to get good players, Giles quickly set about remedying the problem. One of his first big moves was the hiring of Bill McKechnie as manager in 1938. One of the best at inspiring players and molding young talent, McKechnie had led both the Cardinals and the Pirates to the pennant in the 1920s.

The 1938 season saw the Reds rise to fourth place. Perhaps as an omen of the great things to come, that season also saw a Reds' player turn in one of the greatest performances in the history of the game: In June a relatively unknown young lefthander named Johnny Vander Meer pitched back-to-back no-hit games. It was a feat never equaled in the years before or since.

Vander Meer was just one of the rising stars the Reds had going into the 1939 season. At first base, the team had 6'4" Frank McCormick. An All-Star in 1938, his first full season in the big leagues, McCormick played a large role in helping pull his team out of the cellar. Ernie Lombardi was the Reds' catcher. Nicknamed "The Schnozz" (due to his generously proportioned nose), he was big (6'3" and 230 lbs.) and slow as molasses but he made up for it with a powerful bat and a rifle for an arm. With the team since 1932, he had developed into one of the game's best hitting catchers — in 1938 he won the National League batting title with a .342 average.

To shore up some weaknesses, Giles brought in a few seasoned veterans. Well-traveled third baseman Billy Werber was signed from the Athletics after the 1938 season. A three-time stolen base champ in the AL, he added speed and a good glove to the infield. Pitcher Bucky Walters had been purchased from the Phillies in mid–1938. Walters, in the big leagues since 1934, had never had a winning season with the lowly Phillies but the move to a contending team helped him greatly: he was 4–8 with a 5.23 ERA for the Phillies in 1938, and 11–6 with a 3.69 ERA after joining the Reds. Also joining the Reds in mid–1938 was slugging outfielder Wally Berger. Brought over in a deal with the New York Giants, Berger had been a four-time All-Star for the Boston Braves in the early 1930s.

As 1939 spring training broke, things looked promising for the Reds. McKechnie's team had come together with the young players and new additions seeming to mesh well with those players who had been around since the club's last-place days. The season got off to an average start for the team but by late May the Reds had taken the league lead and they held on. At season's end their record stood at 97–57, four-and-a-half games ahead of the Cardinals.

Frank McCormick (.332, 18 HR) was the Reds' most powerful hitter, and he led the league with 209 hits and 128 RBI. Despite his size, he was also a wizard with the glove and the league's best fielding first baseman for three consecutive seasons beginning in 1939. Second baseman Lonnie Frey joined McCormick on the National League All-Star roster thanks to a season that was the best of his long career — he hit .291, drove in 55 runs and scored 95. The league's leading run scorer that season with 115 was Reds' third baseman Billy Werber (.289). Shortstop Billy Myers also had a good season and hit .281 with 56 runs driven in. Backing up in the middle infield was young Eddie Joost who batted .252 in 42 games.

Though his batting average dipped below .300 for the first time since 1933, Ernie Lombardi (.287, 20 home runs, 85 RBI) showed plenty of power and his defensive play was crucial to the Reds' success. Backing him up was Willard Hershberger (.345 in 63 games), also a good-hitting catcher.

Among the outfielders, All-Star Ival Goodman (.323, 84 RBI) was the leading hitter. The Reds also got a solid performance from Harry Craft who, in his second big league season, hit .257 and drove in 67 runs. Wally Berger, who had some injury trouble, never showed the power the Reds had hoped for but he managed a .258 average with 14 home runs and 44 RBI in 97 games. Often filling in for Berger, reserve Nino Bongiovanni played in 66 games and had an identical batting average. Late in the season, with a berth in the World Series seeming certain, the Reds secured the services of former All-Star Al Simmons. The two-time American League batting champ played a very small role for the Reds, however, and only appeared in nine regular season games and one World Series contest.

The Reds' pitching staff was the league's best in 1939. Bucky Walters (27–11, 2.29 ERA), who tied the franchise record for wins, was practically flourishing in his new environment and led the league with 319 innings pitched, 31 complete games, and 137 strikeouts. Veteran Paul Derringer, who had lost 25 games for the last-place Reds in 1933, had what would prove to be the best season of his outstanding career. In 35 starts he pitched 28 complete games, 301 innings, and his 25–7 record gave him the league's best winning percentage. The Reds' next most successful pitcher was rookie Junior Thompson who compiled an exceptional 13–5 record with a 2.54 ERA. Lefthander Lee Grissom won nine games as an occasional starter while Whitey Moore, who was used primarily in a relief role, finished the season with a 13–12 record. Johnny Vander Meer, who had won 15 games in 1938 and achieved baseball immortality with his no-hit games, had a surprisingly poor season and finished with a record of only 5–9.

The 1939 World Series promised to be a classic showdown between the superb pitching staff of the Reds and the power of the New York Yankees batters. In reality, though, it turned out to be rather disappointing.

Game One was the closest contest. Paul Derringer pitched a great game for the Reds as did Red Ruffing for the Yankees. With the score 1–1 in the ninth, New York rookie Charlie Keller tripled and then scored the game-winner on a single by Bill Dickey. In Game Two, Yankees pitcher Monte Pearson had a no-hitter going until he gave up a single to Ernie Lombardi with one out in the eighth. Bucky Walters didn't fare quite as well for the Reds and, after giving up nine hits including a home run to Babe Dahlgren, he took the 4–0 loss.

The Cincinnati bats finally came alive in Game Three and they outhit the Yankees 10–5. Unfortunately, all of the Reds' hits were singles while the Yankees answered with a pair of two-run homers from rookie Charlie Keller, another two-run shot from Joe DiMaggio and a solo blast from Bill Dickey. The final score read New York 7, Cincinnati 3.

Game Four was scoreless until the seventh when Dickey and Keller both hit home runs off Derringer. The Reds answered with three runs in the bottom of the inning and then added one more in the eighth for a 4–2 lead. An error by shortstop Billy Myers on a potential double-play ball allowed the Yankees to pull within one, and then Joe DiMaggio (who would have been out if not for Myers' error) tied the game up when Joe Gordon singled. The game went into the tenth and with runners on the corners and one out, DiMaggio singled to right, and broke the tie. The damage should have stopped there but Ival Goodman misplayed the ball and Keller headed home from first. Goodman threw to the plate but Lombardi, failing to hold the ball, was knocked senseless by the charging Keller. As a result, DiMaggio circled the bases while Lombardi lay stunned and unable to retrieve the ball. The play was dubbed "Schnozz's snooze" and, even though it was not terribly important to the outcome of the Series, it has become one of the more famous plays in the history of the Fall Classic. Despite getting runners on base in the bottom of the tenth, the Reds were unable to score. For the fourth consecutive year, the New York Yankees had won the World Series and for the second year in a row had done it by sweeping their opponent.

The Reds recovered from the humiliating end to their 1939 season and came out strong in 1940. With league-leading pitching and fielding, they made a steady run at the pennant. By late August they had essentially shaken off all challengers (the closest being the Dodgers at 12 games back) and went on to finish with the first 100-win season (100–53) in the history of the franchise.

Once again, Frank McCormick was the star performer for an offense that was otherwise very mediocre. He batted .309 with 19 HR and 127 RBI, and his 191 hits and 44 doubles were both league bests. Third baseman Werber (.277) scored 105 runs and was the league's best fielder at his position. Lonnie Frey (.266) also scored more than 100 runs and stole a league-leading 22 bases. The shortstop position was a definite weakness in the batting order for the Reds in 1940. Neither Billy Myers (.202 in 90 games) nor his backup Eddie Joost (.216 in 88 games) had any punch at all with the bat. Reserve third baseman Lew Riggs, who had been an All-Star for the Reds in 1936 but had barely played in 1939, came off the bench and hit .292 in 41 games.

Though they were great defensively, the outfield unit was probably the weakest hitting ever for a championship team. Right fielder Ival Goodman's (.258, 63 RBI) average dropped considerably from the previous season and Harry Craft, though the league's best fielder at his position, hit only .244. Rookie Mike McCormick hit .300 and was a solid fielder but with only one home run and 30 RBI, had little power. Seeing the need for more hitting, GM Warren Giles made some mid-season moves. He shipped Wally Berger to the Phillies and in return picked up Morrie Arnovitch. Giles also bought in lefthanded-hitting Jimmy Ripple from the Dodgers. Both players made big contributions down the stretch with Arnovitch hitting .284 and Ripple contributing a .307 average with 20 RBI in 32 games.

All-Star catcher Ernie Lombardi (.319, 74 RBI) had another of the great seasons that would eventually lead to his enshrinement in the Hall of Fame. For the third straight season Lombardi's more than able backup was Willard Hershberger. On August 3, however, Hershberger didn't show up for a game in Boston. McKechnie sent someone to his hotel room to check on him and only then was it discovered that the catcher had committed suicide. To this day no one is sure of the reasoning behind his act. Some say Hershberger was distraught over recent poor performances in games, but he was hitting well (.309 in 48 games) and contributing to what would be one of his club's greatest seasons ever. The loss of Hershberger forced the Reds to activate 40-year-old coach Jimmie Wilson to serve as backup catcher; he wound up playing 16 games.

The Reds pitching staff more than made up for the team's offensive shortcomings. Once again, Bucky Walters was brilliant and led the league in wins (22), ERA (2.48), complete games (29) and innings pitched (305). Paul Derringer (20–12) also repeated as a 20-game winner and got the victory in that summer's All-Star Game. Junior Thompson also had another standout season and finished at 16–9 with a 3.32 ERA. Whitey Moore wasn't quite as effective as he had been in 1939 but had several good starts and was an eight-game winner. Johnny Vander Meer (3–1), still struggling to regain his form, had injury problems and only appeared in 10 games.

Much like Bucky Walters had done, pitcher Jim Turner benefited by a move from a bad team to a really good one. The lefthander had won four games and lost 11 for the Boston Bees in 1939 but after being purchased by the Reds, he improved to 14–7 and his ERA dropped to 2.89. Another newcomer, Joe Beggs, had a phenomenal season. After playing part of the 1938 season with the Yankees he had been sent back to the minor leagues the following season. Acquired by the Reds he made the team in spring training and was given the role of the team's primary relief pitcher. Beggs didn't disappoint — he compiled a 12–3 record with an ERA of 2.00 and a league-leading seven saves. It would be the best season of a career that would eventually last nine.

In the 1940 World Series the Reds took on the Detroit Tigers. Though they had won ten more games than the Tigers, the Reds were not favored against a powerful lineup that included the likes of Hank Greenberg, Charlie Gehringer, and Schoolboy Rowe.

Game One was played in Cincinnati and the Reds sent Paul Derringer to the mound. The Tigers countered with Bobo Newsom, who, at 21–5, had enjoyed the best season of his 20-year career. The Tigers' bats drove Derringer from the game after he gave up five runs in the second inning and then added two more in the fifth. Newsom surrendered only single runs in the fourth and eighth innings and cruised to an easy win. In Game Two, Bucky Walters gave up two first inning runs. The Reds came back with two of their own in the second and then took the lead in the third thanks to Jimmy Ripple's two-run homer. Walters settled down and went on to take a 5–3 victory.

The Tigers took the series lead in Game Three with a 7–4 win as Reds pitchers surrendered 13 hits including a pair of two-run homers. With Derringer recovered from his Game One shelling, Cincinnati evened the Series the next day with a 5–2 win. Newsom picked up his second win of the series in Game Five when he pitched a three-hit shutout. Junior Thompson, meanwhile, gave up a three-run home run to Hank Greenberg in the third inning which accounted for the first three of the Tigers' eight runs in their lopsided win.

Down three games to two, the Reds had the home field advantage for the final two games but they had to win them both. Bucky Walters had an incredible Game Six, pitching a 4–0 shutout and driving in two runs, one with a solo home run. The deciding Game Seven saw a rematch of Newsom and Derringer, the pitchers from the Series' first game. In the third, the Tigers took a 1–0 lead and Newsom, pitching masterfully, held it through the sixth. In the seventh, however, doubles by Frank McCormick and Jimmy Ripple started a rally that led to two runs. It was all Derringer needed as he shut the Tigers down for the remaining two innings. Overall, the Tigers had both outpitched and outhit the Reds and even scored six more runs, but in the end, Cincinnati had won its first world championship since 1919. With two wins and an ERA of only 1.50, Walters was the hero of the Series. Offensively, Billy Werber led the team with a .370 average and four runs batted in. He was followed — surprisingly — by coach turned catcher Jimmie Wilson, who in six games hit .353 and even accounted for the Reds' only stolen base.

Despite more great pitching in 1941 the Reds dropped to third place and finished 12 games behind the Dodgers. Elmer Riddle (19–4, 2.24 ERA), a pitcher who only had one win in 1940, was the National League's best and Johnny Vander Meer struck out a league-leading 202 batters. But with the team's two biggest bats, Frank McCormick and Ernie Lombardi, having off-seasons, the offense just didn't have enough to make the Reds pennant contenders.

1942–46
St. Louis Cardinals

The 1941–46 St. Louis Cardinals have earned a place among baseball's all-time greatest teams because of their perseverance. Over the course of those five seasons, the club endured the loss of many top players to military service, the departure of the general manager who essentially built the team, and a change of field managers. Despite all of this, the Cardinals won three World Series and four National League pennants during that time.

In the early 1930s, the Cardinals and their "Gas House Gang" team had been great, winning the 1934 World Series, but by the latter part of the decade they had slipped into mediocrity. In 1941, fueled by a wealth of talented young players, the Cardinals again became contenders and finished only two-and-a-half games behind the Dodgers.

The man behind that seemingly endless stream of new talent was general manager Branch Rickey. With the club since 1916, Rickey had served many roles for the Cardinals including field manager and part owner but his greatest role was as a developer of young talent. Before the late 1920s, major league teams were built by purchasing up-and-coming players from the minor leagues. With the best young prospects going to the big league teams with the deepest pockets, the less-moneyed teams, a group which included the Cardinals at that time, were left with only mediocre players from which to choose. To save having to pay large sums to buy his players, Rickey came up with the idea of what is today known as the farm system. With an army of scouts working for him, he proceeded to find unknown young players and sign them to play for minor league teams which the Cardinals owned. Before this time, minor league teams were independent franchises who made a large part of their money by selling players. In Rickey's system, the Cardinals bought franchises in minor leagues of different levels of play. Just like players are developed today, he would start them out in a Cardinals-owned club at a lower level and then as their skills increased, move them up. Rickey knew that most players would never make it all of the way up the ladder to St. Louis but with so many players under contract, he could take his pick and then sell the rest. Though this new strategy changed baseball forever, it worked wonderfully for the Cardinals.

After his club's strong finish in 1941, Rickey surprised many people by selling first baseman Johnny Mize, the Cardinals' biggest star, to the Giants. Always the shrewd businessman, Rickey knew that with exciting players like Stan Musial waiting in the wings, there was no need to pay the sizable salary of an established star like Mize.

Leading the team on the field, the Cardinals had Billy Southworth. An above average outfielder during his 13-year big league playing career, Southworth was in his second stint as manager, having served in that capacity (rather unsuccessfully) while still a player for part of the 1929 season. After a decade of guiding minor league clubs in the Cardinals' chain he was ready to return to the majors, taking over in St. Louis during the 1940 season.

The pennant race was a close one in 1942 and the Cardinals chased the Dodgers for most of the season before finally overtaking them in mid–September. With 12 wins in their final 13 games to hold off the Brooklyn club, the Cardinals finished with a record of 106–48 and claimed their first pennant since 1934.

Much of the Cardinals' success that season was thanks to pitchers Mort Cooper (22–7, 1.77) and Johnny Beazley (21–6, 2.14), who finished one-two in the league in both wins and ERA. The club also got strong performances from Howie Krist (13–3) and lefthanders Max Lanier (13–8) and Ernie White (7–5), all three of whom had ERAs under 3.00. Harry Gumbert appeared in 38 games — half of them as a starter — and won nine times while Murry Dickson and Howie Pollet were the main men out of the bullpen.

Right fielder Enos Slaughter (.318) provided much of the team's offensive power with his 98 RBI and 100 runs scored. He was joined in the outfield by always-reliable veteran Terry Moore (.288) in center; both men were named to the National League All-Star team that season. Left fielder Stan Musial, who had debuted with the Cardinals in September of 1941, would develop into one of the game's greatest all-time players. Probably the greatest product ever of Branch Rickey's farm system, he batted .315, scored 87 runs, and drove in 72 in 1942. Another talented young outfielder for the Cardinals that season was Harry "The Hat" Walker. Playing in 74 games, he hit. 314.

At the infield corners, the Cardinals had third-year player Johnny Hopp (.258) at first and Whitey Kurowski (.254), who had made his big league debut the previous September, at third. Holding down shortstop was Marty Marion (.276), also in his third season, who would develop into one of the game's great fielders at his position. The outstanding play of veteran second baseman Jimmy Brown (.256, 71 RBI) earned him a spot on the league All-Star team. In the primary backup roles were Frank "Creepy" Crespi, who hit .243 while playing in the middle infield, and rookie Ray Sanders (.252), who saw a fair amount of playing time at first.

Behind the plate, the Cardinals had Walker Cooper, another great Branch Rickey discovery. The younger brother of Mort Cooper, the club's star pitcher, he hit .281 with 65 RBI in his first full big league season and was named a league All-Star.

Despite the Cardinals' great momentum going into the World Series, they were not favored to beat the New York Yankees. The defending world champions came out swinging in Game One and scored seven runs before the Cardinals even got on the board. With a loss at home to start the Series, things didn't look good for the Cardinals but they rallied to take Game Two with a narrow 4–3 victory. With the Series even at one, the two teams traveled to New York where the next three games would be played. Amazingly, the young Cardinals pulled off an upset by taking all three contests. In Game Three, Ernie White pitched a 2–0 shutout, but the following day it was the Cardinals offense that won the game as they scored nine runs to win by three. Game Four was close but home runs by Slaughter and Kurowski gave the Cardinals a 4–2 victory and the World Series title.

On October 29, while the Cardinals were still celebrating their World Series win, Branch Rickey left the team. After numerous disputes with owner Sam Breadon he moved on to become general manager of the Brooklyn Dodgers. It remains unknown if Rickey resigned or was actually fired, but either way, the man who created the Cardinals and made them the great team that they had become was gone. In the history of baseball, no "front office" has had a greater impact upon the game. Rickey's creation of the farm system was only one of great triumphs; with the Dodgers he would integrate baseball by signing Jackie Robinson and then in the late 1950s his threats to form a new league ultimately led to the expansion of the major leagues beyond the original 16 teams.

Entering the 1943 season, the loss of Branch Rickey was not the only one the world champions had to endure. Also gone were outfielders Enos Slaughter and Terry Moore and pitcher Johnny Beazley, each of whom would spend the next three seasons in the military. Still, the Cardinals had more than enough talent to run away with the league pennant; with a record of 105–49 they finished 18 games ahead of second place Cincinnati.

To help make up for some of the loss the Cardinals brought in veteran Debs Garms from the Pirates. A versatile player capable of playing in the outfield or on the left side of the infield, he hit .257 in 90 games for the Cardinals that season. The team also signed former Cubs All-Star Frank Demaree. Near the end of his career, he still was a threat at the plate and in 39 games batted .291. In mid-season the Cardinals acquired outfielder Danny Litwhiler from the Phillies; he hit .279 in 80 games. Among the outfield returnees, Harry Walker (.294) took over as a starter and played well enough to earn a spot on the All-Star team. With a performance that won him the league's Most Valuable Player Award, Stan Musial won the first of his seven batting titles with a .357 average and led the league with 220 hits, 48 doubles, and 20 triples.

Walker Cooper (.318, 81 RBI) continued to excel both at the plate and behind it, finishing second to Musial in voting for the league's MVP award. The infield core of Ray Sanders (.280), Marty Marion (.280) and Whitey Kurowski (.287) was consistently reliable but they did have to deal with the loss of second baseman Frank Crespi to military service (where a broken leg in an army ball game ended his promising career). His departure left second base to Lou Klein, who was promoted from the Cardinals' Columbus farm club. In somewhat of a surprise, Klein had an outstanding rookie season and batted .287 with 180 hits and scored 91 runs.

With a 21–8 record and an ERA of 2.30, Mort Cooper was once again the top pitcher in the National League. Lefty Max Lanier had a league-best 1.90 ERA to go with his 15–7 record, while the other regular starters, Howie Krist (11–5) and Harry Gumbert (10–5), came through with strong performances as well. The loss of Johnny Beazley forced the Cardinals to call up several young players from the minor leagues, namely lefthander Harry Brecheen and George "Red" Munger. Brecheen, who had a brief trial with the Cardinals in 1940, played a key role for the team as a reliever and occasional starter; in 29 games he compiled a 9–6 record with an ERA of 2.26. Munger (9–5) was used primarily as a reliever, though he did toss five complete games. Another rookie, lefthander Al Brazle, joined the team at the end of July. Giving the team a big boost down the stretch, he proceeded to compile an 8–2 record with an ERA of 1.53.

The 1943 World Series was a rematch of the 1942 October Classic but this time it was the Yankees who came out on top. Getting revenge for their upset defeat of the previous season they had little trouble with the Cardinals and took the Series, four games to one. Neither team hit well (the Yankees' team average was .224 while the Cardinals' was only .220) but the pitching was superb,

The 1944 St. Louis Cardinals

particularly by New York. Spud Chandler, the American League's best hurler that season, shut the Cardinals down and in his two complete-game wins had a minuscule ERA of 0.50. Only Game Two, in which Marty Marion and Ray Sanders both homered, proved to be a Cardinals' victory.

With even more players entering the service, manager Billy Southworth had to continue the constant alterations of his lineup card in 1944. Harry Walker was gone from the outfield, promising second baseman Lou Klein had also departed, and the pitching staff lost Al Brazle and Howie Krist. Still, the Cardinals didn't let these setbacks slow them down. The wealth of talent in the farm system, combined with trades for a few experienced players, was enough to sustain their high caliber of play and the club finished with a record of 105–49, identical to that of the previous season. And just as in 1943, the Cardinals faced no serious challengers to their throne with their closest rival, Pittsburgh, 14½ games back.

The Cardinal outfield that season was made up of Danny Litwhiler (.264, 82 RBI), Johnny Hopp and Stan Musial. Hopp, who had the best season of his career, batted .336 and scored 106 runs, while Musial, fast becoming the rock the team was built upon, hit .347, drove in 94 runs, and scored 112. Rookie Augie Bergamo became the team's top reserve and batted .286 in 80 games.

The lack of players led the Cardinals to bring former All-Star Pepper Martin back to the team. One of the original members of the "Gas House Gang,"

Martin had essentially retired from the major leagues in 1940 to serve as a player-manager in the minors. The 40-year-old outfielder gave the young team some needed veteran leadership as well as a good bat coming off the bench; in 40 games he hit .279.

Though none of its members were true offensive stars, the Cardinals infield that season is among the best ever. Shortstop Marty Marion (.267, 63 RBI) was the leader of the group. The winner of the National League MVP Award, he combined brilliant play in the field with a solid offensive performance. Ray Sanders (.295, 102 RBI), the league's best defensive first baseman that season, also had some power at the plate and was the only player on the team other than Musial to top the 100 RBI mark. Rookie second baseman Emil Verban (.257) took over for Lou Klein at second base and played well, while Whitey Kurowski (.270, 87 RBI), the league's leading fielder at third base, was named to the All-Star team.

Backstop Walker Cooper, named to the All-Star team for the third consecutive year, hit .317 and drove in 72 runs. Veteran Ken O'Dea backed him up and batted .249 in 85 games.

Just like the power of Musial and the all-around play of Marion, the consistency of Mort Cooper was a huge factor in the team's success; his record of 22–7 in 1942 was followed by a 21–8 mark in 1943 and another 22–7 performance in 1944. He was supported by the superb lefthanded duo of Brecheen (16–5, 2.85 ERA) and Lanier (17–12, 2.65 ERA), with second-year man Red Munger (11–3, 1.34 ERA) having a standout season as well. Two rookies also played a big role in the staff. After a 16–8 season at Columbus, righthander Ted Wilks got a call-up to the big leagues. He didn't disappoint and in 21 starts he tossed 16 complete games, compiled a 17–4 record, had an ERA of 2.64, and led the league with a .810 winning percentage. Reliever Freddy Schmidt also did well in his first big league season, winning seven games and saving five.

The 1944 World Series never left Sportsman's Park in St. Louis since the Cardinals were matched up against the St. Louis Browns, with whom they shared the stadium. Though the Cardinals were heavily favored in the Series, Game One went to the Browns. Mort Cooper gave up only two hits, though unfortunately a single was followed by a home run, giving the Browns a 2–0 lead. The Cardinals tried to rally in the ninth but came up a run short. The Series' second game was also decided by a one-run margin but this time it was the Cardinals who came out on top. The Browns again pitched well but four errors allowed the Cards to score two runs. With two runs in the sixth, the Browns tied it up but the Cardinals scored in the tenth to take the game. Errors also cost the Browns two runs in Game Three but their offense made up for the miscues by scoring six times and Jack Kramer allowed only two runs on seven hits.

With the Browns holding a two games to one advantage (which would have been 3–0 if not for errors) St. Louis' American Leaguers looked to be the better team. However, a home run by Musial in the first inning of Game Four ignited the Cardinals and they took an easy 5–1 win. They followed it up with a shutout from Mort Cooper, which was supported by solo home runs from Sanders and Litwhiler, to take the advantage in the Series. Game Six was close and the Browns held a 1–0 lead in the fourth but again an error cost them dearly. Shortstop Vern Stephens' wild throw allowed the Cardinals to score two of their three runs and with Lanier and Wilks combining to hold the Browns to one run and three hits, it was all Billy Southworth's team needed.

The loss of players to military service finally caught up with the Cardinals in 1945 when Stan Musial departed for the navy in January of that year. Walker Cooper was also gone (he played four games) as was Danny Litwhiler. Also missing from the lineup was Pepper Martin, who retired for the second time. During the previous two seasons, the Cardinals' depth had carried them despite the absence of key players but in 1945 the Chicago Cubs dethroned them in the National League. It was a close race and Southworth's team played well (95–59), but in the end the Cubs, led by batting champ Phil Cavarretta, took the pennant by three games.

With much of the team's power gone, it fell to third baseman Whitey Kurowski (.323, 21 HR, 102 RBI) and outfielder Buster Adams (.292, 20 HR, 101 RBI), who was acquired from the Phillies shortly after the start of the season, to lead the offense. They did an outstanding job but unfortunately the rest of the offense lacked scoring punch.

With nearly identical batting averages, Kurowski's infield mates — Marion (.277), Sanders (.276) and Verban (.278) — turned in solid performances. Johnny Hopp (.289) continued his strong play as did third baseman/outfielder Debs Garms who, in the final season of his career, batted .336 in 74 games. It would also prove to be the last season in the big leagues for outfielder Augie Bergamo (.316 in 94 games). With the absence of Walker Cooper, Ken O'Dea (.254) took over as starting catcher though rookie Del Rice (.261 in 83 games) saw nearly as much playing time.

The 1945 season saw a promising rookie named Albert "Red" Schoendienst arrive in St. Louis. The 1943 batting champion and MVP of the International League while with Rochester, the Cardinals' top farm club, he could play both in the outfield and at second base. In the first season of a career that would lead to the Hall of Fame, Schoendienst hit .278 and led the league with 26 stolen bases.

Among the pitchers, Harry Brecheen (15–4) continued to shine but Mort Cooper was traded to the Braves shortly after the start of the season. In return the Cardinals got underachieving veteran righthander Red Barrett. A pitcher who had finished the previous two seasons with records of 12–18 and 9–16, it appeared to be a risky move for the Cardinals. Instead, it paid off beautifully as Barrett had by far the best season of his career with a 21–9 record and league-leading numbers in complete games and innings pitched. Cooper, on the other hand, was 7–4 for the Braves. Barrett was the only surprise success on the pitching staff: rookie Ken Burkhart took a spot in the rotation and turned in an 18–8 record.

Though the players on the Cardinals' roster had often changed due to the war, the one thing that had remained constant was the guidance of manager Billy Southworth. After the 1945 season, however, Southworth decided to leave St. Louis for a job managing the Boston Braves. Like many of the team's players, the new manager was also a product of the Cardinals' farm system. After meeting with great success managing St. Louis farm teams in Houston and Columbus among others, Eddie Dyer, who had been a pitcher for the club in the 1920s, was hired as Southworth's replacement.

Fortunately for the Cardinals, they avoided the problems that often follow a change in management. Dyer did an outstanding job guiding his new charges, many of whom he had helped develop when they were minor leaguers, and the Cards continued their winning ways in 1946. Soon after the start of the season it became obvious that the pennant race would come down to two teams: the Cardinals and the Brooklyn Dodgers. When the season ended the clubs were tied, the first time that had ever happened in the major leagues. With identical 96–58 records, they were forced into a best-of-three playoff but the Cardinals prevailed by taking the first two games.

One big reason for the Cardinals' success that season was the return of players from military service. Enos Slaughter, back from three years in the Army Air Corps, picked up right where he left off and hit .300, scored 100 runs and drove in a career high 130. Terry Moore (.263) and Harry Walker (.237) also rejoined the team after long absences but the biggest returnee was Stan Musial. After earning his discharge from the military in March, "Stan the Man" seemed ready to take on the National League single-handedly. He took the batting title with a .365 average, drove in 103 runs and led the league in runs scored (124), hits (228), doubles (50) and triples (20). It was a performance that easily won Musial the National League MVP Award.

Walker Cooper did not return to the Cardinals when he got out of the military. In January, the team sold their star catcher to the Giants for $175,000, the largest amount ever paid for a single player. That left 20-year-old rookie Joe Garagiola to share the catching duties with Del Rice and newcomer Clyde Kluttz. Early in the season the Cardinals made a couple of other big roster moves, sending Emil Verban to the Phillies (in exchange for backup catcher Clyde Kluttz) and Danny Litwhiler, Ray Sanders and Johnny Hopp to the Braves.

Among the remaining Cardinals, second-year man Red Schoendienst (.281, 94 runs) continued to improve and joined shortstop Marty Marion (.233) and third baseman Whitey Kurowski (.301, 89 RBI) on the All-Star team. Versatile Erv Dusak, who had appeared in a few games back in 1942, rejoined the team. Appearing in 100 games at either second or third base as well as in the outfield, he batted .240. Rookie first baseman Dick Sisler, who had spent several seasons in the Cardinals' farm system before leaving for the military, made the big league roster in spring training and contributed with a .260 average in 83 games.

Lefthander Howie Pollet was the surprise star of the pitching staff that season. Just back from three years in the service, he had what would prove to be the best season of a long career with a 21–10 record and a league-leading 2.10 ERA and 266 innings pitched. Harry Brecheen and Murry Dickson each won 15 games while Al Brazle won 11 as the other members of the starting rotation. Ted Wilks contributed eight wins as the team's most frequently used member of the bullpen. Johnny Beazley, a 21-game winner in 1942, returned to the club after three years in the military but, unable to regain his prewar form, finished the season with only a 7–5 record.

The Cardinals' pitching depth suffered a blow when veteran Max Lanier, who had tossed six complete game victories with no losses and an ERA of 1.93, was lured to the independent Mexican League by the promise of a big paycheck (as was reserve second baseman Lou Klein). Lanier was greatly missed but the return of Red Munger, who rejoined the team in August after being released from the military, helped fill the void.

Propelled by the arm of Harry Brecheen, the Cardinals survived a tough battle with the heavily favored Boston Red Sox to take their third World Series title in five years. After dropping Game One by the score of 3–2, Breechen evened the Series by pitching a four-hit shutout in Game Two. Pitcher Dave Ferriss of Boston then returned the favor in Game Three by tossing a 4–0 shutout of his own. Four hits apiece by Slaughter, Garagiola and Kurowski led a 12-run Cardinal onslaught for an easy victory in the next game, but Boston recovered to take Game Five, 6–3. With the Series on the line, Brecheen pitched beautifully in Game Six, giving up just one run while his teammates supported him with four.

Game Seven was back and forth. Boston scored in the first but St. Louis tied it up an inning later. Two runs in the fifth gave the Cardinals a 3–1 lead but the Red Sox answered with two of their own in the top of the eighth to draw even. Enos Slaughter led off the bottom of the eighth with a single but remained stranded there two outs later. Harry Walker then came to the plate and proceeded to crack a hit just over the shortstop. In a play that will always be remembered as one of the greatest in World Series history, Slaughter took off from first and never slowed down until he slid across home plate. Beating the relay throw from Johnny Pesky, he scored what would prove to be the Series-winning run. The game wasn't over, though, and Harry Brecheen, who had come on in relief in the eighth — despite having pitched a complete game the evening before — worked himself into somewhat of a jam. But with runners on first and second and no outs, Brecheen retired the next three batters by forcing them to hit groundballs.

The heroes of Game Seven were the same ones who had carried the Cardinals throughout the exciting Series. Starting all seven games, Walker hit .412

and drove in six runs while Slaughter batted .320, scored five runs and was the only one to homer against the tough Boston pitchers. Brecheen, who earning his third win of the Series in Game Seven, equaled a feat that hadn't been accomplished since Stan Coveleski had done it for the Indians in 1920.

It is amazing that the Cardinals remained such a powerful team for those five seasons despite constant roster changes due to players entering the military, the departure of the general manager who was the architect of the team, and the departure of a field manager.

The Cardinals remained contenders for the next three years but each season they came up short and finished in second place; the closest race was in 1949 when they wound up only one game behind the Dodgers. Throughout the decade of 1950s the club usually posted a winning record, but they never really challenged for the pennant again until 1964.

1949–53
New York Yankees

The world had come to an end. The Yankees had not won the pennant. In fact, while they had contended until the final weekend of the 1948 season, they had finished third. Drastic measures were needed.

In fact, the staid Yankees had already undergone a good deal of change in the 1940s. The tempestuous Larry MacPhail, who had previously operated the Dodgers, had put together a small group to purchase the Yankees from the estate of their late owner, Jacob Ruppert. But MacPhail antagonized far too many people, including his legendary manager, Joe McCarthy, and in less than three years his two partners, Dan Topping and Del Webb, bought him out and promoted Farm Director George Weiss into the general manager's chair. Bucky Harris, the former "Boy Wonder," had been MacPhail's choice to lead the team and in truth he did defeat Brooklyn to win the 1947 World Series. But Weiss did not care for his style, specifically his indifference to controlling his players. However, he couldn't very well discharge a man who had won it all, so Harris was back in 1948. The Yankees spent the summer battling the Cleveland Indians and Boston Red Sox in a pennant race that went right down to the final weekend, but the Yankees lost their final two games in Fenway Park and wound up third; Cleveland won the pennant by defeating Boston in the American League's first-ever one-game playoff and then took the World Series by outplaying the other Boston club, the Braves, in six games. Weiss, meanwhile, now felt justified in firing Harris — he had *lost*, after all — and went looking for a new man.

The guy he had in mind had been a successful minor league manager but had failed to turn around losing situations in two previous attempts in a big-league dugout. Charles Dillon "Casey" Stengel had been a fine outfielder for five clubs back in the teens and twenties, though known as much for his sense of humor as his playing abilities. He had managed the Dodgers for three seasons in the 1930s and the NL's Boston Bees for six seasons, beginning in 1938, and only once in those nine years did his team finish above .500. But in (then) minor league cities like Milwaukee, Kansas City and Oakland, Stengel had been able to demonstrate his real managerial skills. He was a keen student of the game with a great memory for everything except players' names. He handled his men with the right blend of humor and discipline. He was a skilled teacher who refined the talents of a great many players, turning "diamonds in the rough" into jewels. And he was a firm believer in utilizing almost everyone on the roster. He would also prove to be popular with the press: garrulous, naturally funny and a born mimic, he was always "good copy," especially when he launched into one of his long, rambling, stream-of-consciousness monologues the media dubbed "Stengelese." He would move from one topic to another to another to yet another, scarcely taking a breath let alone inserting a comma, but if you were astute you would recognize that he had answered your question (in his own way) and imparted some other baseball wisdom in his meanderings.

Not all of this was recognized in 1948. Weiss had to persuade Topping (he already had Webb in his corner) to sign off on the deal. And when they did introduce Stengel as the new skipper, it was greeted with great skepticism by many. One Boston newspaper writer told its readers, "Well, sirs and ladies, the Yankees have now been mathematically eliminated from the 1949 pennant race. They eliminated themselves when they engaged Professor Casey Stengel to mismanage them for the next two years."

The team Stengel inherited was a mixture of veterans and youngsters. The team leader was unquestionably center fielder Joe DiMaggio, but "the great DiMaggio" (as Hemingway referred to him in The Old Man and the Sea) was now 34 years old and beset by leg injuries. Bone spurs in his right heel would force him to miss the first 65 games in 1949. "Old Reliable" Tommy Henrich was now 36 and better utilized, Stengel thought, at first base rather than in the outfield. He missed time due to fractured vertebrae, but still led the team with 24 home runs. Relief ace Joe Page was 31 and starting pitchers Allie Reynolds, Eddie Lopat and Vic Raschi were all beyond 30 while the fourth member of the group, Tommy Byrne, was 29. Even shortstop Phil Rizzuto, the team's most consistent player, was 31. But these graybeards were joined by some talented young athletes like catcher Yogi Berra, second baseman Jerry Coleman and outfielder Hank Bauer.

Stengel had two problems to overcome in 1949, one of which was injuries. DiMaggio's was the most obvious, of course, but the manager found it necessary to check with the trainer every day before making out his lineup. By the time the season ended the Yankees had suffered through 72 injuries. But as aggravating as they were, injuries could be fixed, or at least the wounded player could be replaced. The other problem, however, went deeper. The "old guard" on the Yankees, the ones who had played for McCarthy, did not like Stengel's style, and in some cases did not like him, period. The quiet leader of this faction was DiMaggio, who felt the new man was in over his head. Casey was no doubt aware of this and unquestionably understood that how he handled this group would go a long way towards determining his future in New York. Having failed in Brooklyn and Boston he resolved not to fail again. He probably worked harder in 1949 than in any other season.

Another hard worker was Berra. While no one questioned his abilities as a hitter, even if he did swing at pitches out of the strike zone, his talent behind the plate was debatable. Weiss hired Bill Dickey, the greatest catcher in Yankee history, as a coach, but specifically he was charged with refining Berra's skills. Berra took to Dickey's teachings and became an excellent receiver; in the two previous seasons Berra had logged a lot of time in the outfield, but in 1949 Stengel felt confident in leaving him behind the plate.

New York jumped off to a quick start and surprisingly pulled away from the league. Their rotation of Reynolds, Lopat, Raschi and Byrne was dominating (they would win 68 games between them), their hitting proved to be timely, and their defense was exceptional, especially around the keystone, where young Coleman was superb. More importantly, even with Stengel running players in and out of the lineup, they played smartly, never beating themselves with mental errors.

By June the Red Sox had shaken off their lethargy and made a run at the top. Always the Yankees' arch rivals, they were managed by Joe McCarthy, of all people, which simply intensified the rivalry. On the field they presented probably the best lineup in the league, led by the one and only Ted Williams in his prime. Williams wound up leading the league in virtually every hitting category except batting average, which he lost to Detroit's George Kell by the margin of .000157. Teddy Ballgame was ably supported by shortstop Vern Stephens, who matched Williams' 159 RBI; second baseman Bobby Doerr; third baseman Johnny Pesky; and center fielder Dom DiMaggio, Joe's younger brother and one of the best defensive outfielders of his time as well as a fine leadoff man. Boston also had two outstanding pitchers in lefty Mel Parnell and righty Ellis Kinder, who won 48 games between them. Unfortunately for the Sox, the other 15 pitchers they used that season also combined for 48 wins, an indication of Boston's primary weakness.

Late in June the Yankees went up to Fenway for a three-game series, and Stengel had a surprise for everyone: Joe DiMaggio was ready to play. He singled in his first at-bat of the season and homered later in the game. The next day Boston took a 7–1 lead until DiMaggio hit a three-run homer. The Yankees tied it in the seventh and took the lead in the eighth on a home run by

DiMaggio. And in the series finale, with New York holding a slim lead, Joltin' Joe blasted a ball that hit the light tower in left field, giving the Yanks a comfortable cushion. Four home runs and nine RBI in three days told the world that DiMaggio was back. The Red Sox lost a total of eight in a row and were seemingly out of the race.

When he led the Yankees McCarthy had been called a "push-button manager" because, many felt, his team had so much talent he didn't need to do anything more than push a button. In 1949 Joe McCarthy proved otherwise. He rallied his Red Sox players and led them back into the race. In August they played 32 games and won 24, and suddenly the Yankees were looking over their shoulders. In mid–September DiMaggio went down again, this time with viral pneumonia. The weight of the season seemed to be pressing down on the Yankees. With a week to go the two teams met and Boston swept three games to vault into first place. The final game had been won on a disputed call at home plate, which precipitated a huge argument and ultimately led to fines and a threatened suspension of Yankee reserve outfielder Cliff Mapes. The incident seemed to galvanize New York, but with just two games left they still found themselves trailing Boston by a game. However, the schedule-maker must have been prescient, because the Red Sox were coming to Yankee Stadium to close out the season.

Stengel started Reynolds, his money pitcher, but the "Superchief" didn't have his good stuff. Boston clipped him for two runs early and had the bases loaded in the third when Casey called for Joe Page, normally his late-inning relief man, to put the clamps on the Sox. Page, who saved 27 games that year and won another 13, promptly walked in not one but two runs, but then escaped further damage. Still, the Yankees trailed 4–0, and a loss would end their season. But DiMaggio, back in the lineup, got hits in both the fourth and fifth innings to help the Yankees tie the score. It was still tied in the eighth when outfielder Johnny Lindell, one of Casey's platoon players, blasted a home run; Page, who had settled down after his inauspicious start, set the Sox down in the ninth and the pennant race was tied. In Sunday's winner-take-all game, Raschi and Kinder were both at their best and the Yankees held a slim 1–0 lead in the eighth inning. But when Kinder came out for a pinch hitter, Boston's lack of pitching depth caught up with them. Henrich led off the inning with a home run and Coleman later unloaded the bases with a pop-fly double as the Yankees took a 5–0 lead into the ninth. Boston wasn't quite finished, however. Doerr drove in two with a double and scored on a two-out hit, and all at once the Red Sox had the tying run at the plate. But that's as far as they got, and the Yankees won the pennant in a memorable finish. Later, Ted Williams would call it the worst moment of his baseball career.

Just as they had two years earlier, the Yankees faced the Brooklyn Dodgers, one of their crosstown rivals, in the World Series. The Dodgers had a formidable lineup that had led the National League in both home runs and stolen bases. They also featured the most exciting player in the game in Jackie Robinson, the first black man to play in the major leagues in more than sixty years; two other black athletes also made significant contributions, powerful catcher Roy Campanella and rookie pitcher Don Newcombe.

Pitching was the story for the better part of the first three games. Newcombe and Allie Reynolds hooked up for a classic in the opener, with neither team mounting a threat through eight innings. Then Tommy Henrich led off the bottom of the ninth with a home run, allowing New York to draw first blood. But the Dodgers repaid the compliment the next day as Preacher Roe spaced out six hits for his own 1–0 victory, knotting the Series. In Game Three, Stengel repeated the maneuver he used in the penultimate game against the Red Sox, calling on Joe Page early (fourth inning this time) and the southpaw responded again, shutting them down until the ninth. The Dodgers hit a couple of homers in their last at-bat but it wasn't enough, as the Yankees took the Series lead with a 4–3 victory. Dodgers manager Burt Shotton hoped that Newcombe could repeat his opening game brilliance but instead had to lift him in the fourth. Brooklyn came back against the Yanks' Eddie Lopat, but Stengel brought in Reynolds from the bullpen and he stopped the Dodgers cold for a 6–4 New York victory. In the fifth game, New York pounded four Dodger pitchers, building up a 10–1 lead before Brooklyn began to solve Raschi in the seventh. This time Stengel called on Page, who slammed the door in a 10–6 win, ending the season. "Perfesser" Stengel "mismanaged" the team to a World Series championship.

The Yankees made a few small changes in the off-season and into the spring, cosmetic changes really but important because they primarily involved the "old guard," who was slowly being phased out. Replacing them, meanwhile, were young men eager to play for the Old Professor, like outfielder Gene Woodling and infielder Billy Martin. They also imported a couple of pitchers from the St. Louis Browns — Tom Ferrick and Joe Ostrowski — who helped to fill out the bullpen. The previous August the Yankees had picked up aging slugger John Mize from the Giants, but an injury had limited him to 23 at-bats. Now Stengel put the 37-year-old at first base in place of the retired Tommy Henrich, and "Big Jawn" responded with 25 home runs.

First base, in fact, was a bit of a revolving door for New York, as no fewer than seven players saw time there. One of them was a fellow named Joe DiMaggio. Stengel recognized that DiMaggio's skills were eroding, and thought a move to first might prolong his career and help the ballclub. Stengel didn't ask Joe DiMaggio to make the move, however, because the two rarely spoke; co-owner Topping brought it up to the superstar. Joe D played one game there, did not feel comfortable and let it be known he would not go back. Experiment over. It was not, however, Stengel's only run-in with the future Hall of Famer that year.

DiMaggio started slowly and so did the Yankees. So did the Red Sox, for that matter, as Detroit and Cleveland set the pace. The Tigers, managed by former Yankee third baseman Red Rolfe, were the real surprise, but they had a very balanced team that year. Four regulars batted .300 or better while two others came very close, and five pitchers won in double figures. The Indians offered a similar mix, although they had more power with Al Rosen, Luke Easter and Larry Doby in their lineup. But no one scored runs like the Red Sox: not since the 1936 Yankees had a major league team topped 1,000 runs for the year, but Boston plated 1,027, and batted .302 as a team, too. Four players hit 25 or more home runs and three of them had well over 100 RBI; the exception, ironically, was Ted Williams, who had an excuse: an elbow he fractured at the All-Star Game. He was able to play in only 19 games in the second half of the year and still drove home 97 runs. The Sox wound up third, just four games shy of first place.

New York's starting pitching continued to set them apart. The Big Four of Raschi, Lopat, Reynolds and Byrne won 70 games, and in mid-season they got even stronger when a youngster from Long Island joined them. Edward "Whitey" Ford was a lefthander with a smooth delivery and an assortment of pitches. After coming out of the bullpen a few times he got a chance to start and made the most of it, winning nine in a row (seven of them complete games) before losing for the only time that season.

The Yankees stayed close to Detroit all summer, with Boston and Cleveland never too far behind. The Bombers' sparkplug was shortstop Phil Rizzuto, enjoying by far the finest year of his career; in the fall he would be chosen as the league's Most Valuable Player. Berra and Bauer also were having fine years, as was Mize and reserve outfielder Cliff Mapes. But DiMaggio continued to struggle and Stengel decided to drop him from fourth to fifth in the batting order, and made the move without consulting the Yankee Clipper. Then in August Casey announced that his center fielder was being given a few days off for a rest, but everyone knew it was an old-fashioned benching, the first time DiMaggio had ever been removed from the lineup for a reason other than injury. The two hadn't talked about this in advance, either, and privately DiMaggio seethed at Stengel. When he returned from his enforced sabbatical he was like a raging bull, pounding the ball at a better than .370 clip, driving in runs and playing superb defense. Had the days off simply recharged his batteries, or did he see Casey's face on the ball as it came to the plate? We'll never know. But Joe D's bat proved to be what the Yankees needed to put them over the top; they passed Detroit in mid–September and took the flag by three games.* The American League was definitely a portrait in disparity that season: the top four teams all won at least 92 games and finished within six games of one another, while the bottom four finished well below .500.

---

*DiMaggio wound up leading the league in slugging percentage, with a .585, was third in home runs with 32 and fourth in RBI with 122.

The 1950 World Series was marked by the appearance of the Philadelphia Phillies for the first time since 1915. The "Whiz Kids" they were called, a collection of 20-somethings that had jelled under manager Eddie Sawyer. But the final three weeks of the season had not been kind to the young Philadelphians. Southpaw Curt Simmons and his 17 victories had to report to his National Guard unit, which was activated for Korean War duty. Two other Phillie pitchers were injured, and ace Robin Roberts was asked to start three of the last five games of the season, including the finale against the Dodgers, which the Phils needed to win in order to reach the postseason. So it was a weary team the Yankees saw in the other dugout, but in retrospect they played inspired ball. Sawyer, casting about for a fresh arm, started his bullpen ace Jim Konstanty in the opener against Vic Raschi. Konstanty, a 33-year-old veteran, put together a career year in 1950, winning 16 and saving 22 to earn the National League's Most Valuable Player award. Although he had not started a game since 1946 he took the ball and held the Yanks to four hits. One of them was a double by Bobby Brown in the fourth, and the future American League president came around to score the game's only run on a pair of fly balls. Philadelphia could only manage a couple of singles against Raschi.

Robin Roberts, pitching on just three days' rest, opposed Allie Reynolds in Game Two, and the righthanders were both tough. After nine innings the score was tied at one, but in the top of the tenth Joe DiMaggio blasted a home run off Roberts, giving the Bombers a 2–0 Series lead as they headed back to Yankee Stadium. Once again Sawyer had to dig deep to come up with a starter, this time choosing lefty Ken Heintzelman, a sub–.500 pitcher for his career who had won just three games all year. Again he got an exceptional effort: Heintzelman held the Yankees at bay for seven innings, the Phils actually had the lead and needed to only get six more outs for the win. It didn't happen. New York tied it in the eighth and, with two out in the ninth, parlayed hits by Woodling, Rizzuto and Coleman against Russ Meyer to claim their third straight one-run victory. By the fourth game, then, the Phillies must have been emotionally exhausted, and it was no contest. The Yankees took a 5–0 lead into the ninth inning before Philadelphia managed to score a pair. Allie Reynolds relieved Whitey Ford and nailed down the final out for the first World Series sweep since 1939. While the Yankees only scored 11 runs in the four games, the Phils managed just five as that age-old adage held true: good pitching stopped good hitting.

Although the 1951 Yankees were two-time defending world champions, their chances of returning to postseason play seemed remote at best, as this team had more question marks than exclamation points on their roster. The Bombers' foremost concern was Joe DiMaggio, who began talking retirement as early as spring training. Another spring concern was Allie Reynolds, who was suffering from bone chips in his pitching elbow. The Superchief would not take the mound until May 3. First base was still unsettled, with Mize and Joe Collins handling the bulk of the playing time. As the Korean War escalated, many ballplayers were trading in their baseball uniforms for military garb, and Whitey Ford was one, helping to muddle a pitching staff that would eventually audition 19 hurlers that season. Stengel found himself relying on several rookies and a few veteran castoffs as he attempted to remain competitive with Cleveland and Boston. Gil McDougald shuttled between second and third base (he could also play shortstop) and performed so well — 14 home runs, 68 RBI, 14 stolen bases and a .306 average — that he was chosen the American League Rookie of the Year. Righthander Tom Morgan came up in mid-season and gave the pitching staff a shot in the arm, winning nine games just as Ford had done the year before. The Yankees also gave a couple of trials to a young Oklahoman named Mickey Mantle.

Mantle had spent two years in the minors, where he exhibited a near-perfect blend of both power and speed. Seeing him in spring training, Stengel gasped, "The boy runs faster than Cobb." His ability to hit the long ball, from both sides of the plate, was awe-inspiring; Paul Richards, who managed the White Sox and the Orioles, once said that Mantle could hit the ball out of any park in the country, "including Yellowstone." But he was green, just 19 years old and no doubt in need of more playing time in the minors. He was a shortstop who was prone to making errors. Stengel, taking DiMaggio's retirement talk seriously, saw Mantle as a possible heir apparent to the Yankee Clipper, and talked George Weiss into letting him keep the youngster in the majors and teaching him how to play the outfield. Mantle proved to be a quick study and, with his speed and strong throwing arm, became an excellent flychaser. He did need to spend a short time in the minors in 1951, but after driving in 50 runs in 40 games he returned to New York for good.

The 1951 season is remembered today for the battle that took place in the National League, with the Giants spotting the Dodgers a 13-game lead before forcing a tie and then winning the playoff with Bobby Thomson's dramatic three-run homer in the ninth. Forgotten is that the American League also sported a pretty good race. The White Sox surprised everyone by jumping out in front early before being supplanted by Boston. But eventually Cleveland and New York rose to the top and slugged it out. Allie Reynolds returned and won 16 out of 21 decisions, including two no-hitters. He had a unique record that season: he led the league with seven shutouts, and led the team with seven saves. His no-hitters were thrown against the cream of the league, Cleveland and Boston. In the second, he had to face Ted Williams with two out in the ninth, and induced him to hit a foul ball behind the plate. Inexplicably Berra dropped the ball, giving Teddy Ballgame a new life. But Reynolds got him to hit another foul pop, this time Berra didn't miss, and Reynolds had his second no-hitter of the year.

The Indians came to the Bronx for a short series in mid–September, holding a slim one-game lead and throwing their aces, future Hall of Famers Bob

Feller and Bob Lemon. The Yankees took both to move into first. After soundly defeating Feller the Yankees found themselves in a tie game against Lemon. Loading the bases in the ninth, they scored in a most un–Yankee-like way as Phil Rizzuto laid down a squeeze bunt and DiMaggio raced home. The Tribe never recovered, losing five of their next eight while New York won nine of their final twelve to capture their third straight pennant.

Their sensational finish in the National League had propelled the Giants into the World Series. Like Stengel, manager Leo Durocher had brought up his own young *wunderkind*, Alabama-born Willie Mays, who was just a year older than Mantle. The 1951 World Series would be the only time that DiMaggio, Mantle and Mays actually met on the playing field. This phenomenon, however, only lasted into the second game. Mays hit a ball to right-center in the fifth inning and both Yankees sprinted for it. Suddenly Mantle went down — "I thought he had been shot," DiMaggio later remarked — and had to be carried off the field on a stretcher. In actuality he had tripped over a wooden sprinkler cover, but the result was torn ligaments in his right knee and an operation. Mantle already suffered from osteomyelitis in his left leg, a souvenir from a high school football game, and consequently he played the bulk of his career with pain in both legs.

Since his pitching staff was worn out from the three-game playoff with the Dodgers, which had ended just the day before, Durocher started veteran Dave Koslo in the opening game. Koslo had relieved in more games than he had started but against the Yankees and Reynolds he pitched like an All-Star, going the route for a 5–1 win. Eddie Lopat squared the Series with his own complete game, but the Giants came back to win Game Three as the Yankees played one of their poorest games of the year. Two errors led to five unearned runs, and they were barely able to cash in on the eight walks issued by Giants righthander Jim Hearn.

The turning point in the Series may have been a day of rain. Had Game Four been played on schedule, Stengel would probably have started Johnny Sain, the former Brave who had been acquired in an August deal. Given an unexpected day of rest, Casey chose Reynolds instead, and his workhorse evened things up with a 6–2 win. DiMaggio, hitless through the first three games, contributed two hits, including what proved to be the final home run of his career. The next day McDougald hit a grand slam while Rizzuto and DiMaggio each drove in three runs as the Bombers roughed up five Giant pitchers in a 13–1 slaughter. Needing just one more win, the Yankees got some two-way heroics from Hank Bauer. First, he tripled in the sixth inning with the bases loaded to break open a tie game. Then in the ninth inning the Giants loaded the bases with no one out. Monte Irvin and Bobby Thomson both hit sacrifice flies, making the score 4–3. Pinch-hitter Sal Yvars followed with a sinking line drive to right that could have tied the game, but Bauer made a great grab to preserve the Yankee win and give them another World Series triumph.

In December Joe DiMaggio retired. In his thirteen seasons he became the symbol of the All-American athlete, always performing with grace under pressure. He batted .325 for his career, and his 56-game hitting streak of 1941 remains one of baseball's all-time records. But perhaps his most amazing numbers were these: he hit 361 home runs in his career, but struck out only 369 times. He was a ballplayer's ballplayer.

The Korean War took Bobby Brown, Jerry Coleman and Tom Morgan away from the Yankees, joining Whitey Ford. Billy Martin broke an ankle in spring training, and Mickey Mantle was still limping following his knee surgery. In mid-season Lopat hurt his shoulder and missed about six weeks of action. If ever a team was ripe for the taking, it was the 1952 Yankees, and the Cleveland Indians seemed to be up to the task. Their lineup was the most potent in the league: Doby and Easter finished 1-2 in home runs; Rosen and Doby finished 1-2 in RBI; Doby, Bobby Avila and Rosen finished 1-2-3 in runs scored. In addition, the league produced five 20-game winners in 1952 and three of them wore Cleveland uniforms. Early Wynn, Mike Garcia and Bob Lemon started and relieved for manager Al Lopez and pitched 888 innings between them, about 63 percent of the Tribe's total for the year.

Stengel responded by doing his usual platooning. McDougald played second base until Martin was ready to return, then he moved to third. Mantle started the year in right field to reduce the stress on his knee, then moved over to center. Johnny Sain pitched as both a starter and reliever and won 11 games, backing up the reliable Reynolds and Raschi, and Lopat returned from the disabled list in August to reel off five straight wins. New York went into first place in June and stayed there until late August, when a brief slump put them behind Cleveland. But they didn't remain there for long and jumped back into the lead and stayed there, nosing out the Indians by two games. The only Yankee who led the league in any category was Reynolds, who had the most strikeouts and shutouts and the lowest ERA, but New York played as a team and won as a team. It may have also helped that only the White Sox committed fewer errors than the Yankees, while Cleveland proved to have the most porous defense in the league.

The World Series would once again be an all–New York City affair as the Yankees went down to Brooklyn for the opener. Reynolds had trouble keeping the ball in the small ballpark, as three Dodger homers supported a route-going performance by NL Rookie of the Year Joe Black. Raschi came back the next day and held the Brooks to just three hits in a 7–1 win, with a Billy Martin home run highlighting the key five-run sixth inning. Shifting venues to the Bronx, the Dodgers won Game Three when the Yankees made an uncharacteristic mistake. Holding a slim 3–2 lead in the ninth inning, Pee Wee Reese and Jackie Robinson singled and moved up 90 feet on a double steal. Then Yogi Berra committed a passed ball, and not only did Reese come home but the still-speedy Robinson, ever the daredevil even at age 33, tore around the bases to score as well. Reynolds and Black hooked up again in Game Four and both were even better than they had been in the opener. New York could manage just three hits and a run in seven innings against Black, but Reynolds was absolutely superb, blanking the Dodgers on four hits to even the Series.

Stengel's choice to start Game Five was a surprise: Ewell Blackwell. "The Whip" had once been one of the most feared pitchers in the National League but was coming to the end of the line. George Weiss had picked him up from Cincinnati in one of those late-season deals he liked so well, but Blackwell had only pitched in five games for New York. Nevertheless he got the nod against Carl Erskine, but left the game after five, trailing 4–0. The Bombers came back, however, with John Mize getting the big blow, a three-run home run, to give the Yanks the lead. Brooklyn tied it in the seventh and went ahead in the 11th, but Erskine — still pitching — would have to face Mize one more time. The big slugger hit the ball hard again, but just before it left the ballpark the Dodgers' right fielder, Carl Furillo, made a leaping grab to save the game.

The Yankees, without any room to maneuver, now faced the prospect of having to win twice in Ebbets Field. Dodger center fielder Duke Snider — who became part of the great three-part debate as to who was better, Willie, Mickey or The Duke — solved Raschi for a pair of home runs, giving him four in the Series. But they were solo shots, and the Yankees answered with their own blasts off the bats of Mantle and Berra. But in this game of long ball the key hit and RBI was ironically delivered by Raschi, a notoriously poor hitter. The Dodgers threatened in the eighth but Allie Reynolds came in to preserve the 3–2 win, setting up the climactic seventh game. Lopat started but the entire staff was on call to relieve, and both Reynolds and Raschi were used. New York had a slim 4–2 lead when the Dodgers loaded the bases with just one out in the seventh. Stengel then made a gutsy move, calling in lefthander Bob Kuzava to face the lefty-swinging Snider. While it was the right thing to do from a strategic standpoint, it had long been a truism that southpaws had trouble pitching in Ebbets Field, which had a short left field porch. But Kuzava, in his only appearance in the Series, got Snider to pop up. Then Stengel left him in to face the righthanded Robinson, and he got Jackie to pop up as well. Only this one proved to be a little trickier as the ball, hit between the mound and first base, seemed to get lost in the late afternoon sun. With all three runners moving the Yankees could ill afford to let it drop, and a hustling Billy Martin didn't, tearing in from his second base position to catch the ball at knee level. Brooklyn couldn't touch Kuzava in the eighth and ninth innings, and the Yankees won their fourth consecutive championship, matching the mark of Joe McCarthy's great club in the late 1930s.

In 1953 the Yankees celebrated the return of Whitey Ford from the military, and he made his presence felt immediately. As the only starting pitcher under the age of 34, he personally took charge of the rotation and led the team with 18 wins. He also allowed Stengel to utilize Reynolds and Sain as swing men, pitching primarily in relief but also occasionally as starters. This plan worked, as they combined for 27 wins and 22 saves.

Cleveland still trotted out the same powerful lineup and could rely on the same Big Three rotation, but no matter. New York exploded out of the gate in April, stumbled slightly in early May, and then just before Memorial Day launched into an 18-game winning streak, and a spell of 23 wins in 25 games. The good times, however, were followed by some bad as they lost nine in a row to end the month of June and come back to the pack. Stengel, chasing history, prowled the dugout like a caged tiger but his players stayed cool and soon enough the Yankees had the rest of the American League playing for next year's salary. They clinched the pennant with almost two weeks left in the regular season.

As good as the Yankees were in the summer of 1953, the Dodgers were better. They won more games (105–99), enjoyed a larger margin of victory over their nearest competitor (13–8), and even won their flag a few days earlier. Charley Dressen's team was loaded with speed, power and confidence that they could finally overtake the Yankees.

Doctor Long Ball was in the House That Ruth Built to open the Series. A couple of first-inning triples, by Bauer and Martin, gave the Yankees the early lead, but a pair of Dodger home runs brought them back into the game in the sixth. But Joe Collins untied the contest with a homer off Clem Labine, and then New York put the game out of reach in the eighth inning, highlighted by relief pitcher Johnny Sain's two-run double. The Doctor made another House call the next day, breaking up a soft-toss duel between Eddie Lopat and Preacher Roe. Trailing by a run, Martin got the Yankees even in the seventh, then Mantle untied it in the eighth for a 4–2 New York win, and the Bombers headed to Ebbets Field dreaming of a Series sweep.

New York took the early lead in Game Three, but the day belonged to Dodger pitcher Carl Erskine. Knocked out after one inning two days earlier, the Brooklyn righthander mixed a moving fastball with a sharp-breaking curve to strike out 14 Yankees, a new one-game World Series record. The Dodgers did not seal their first win in the Series, however, until an eighth inning home run by Campanella. The next day Brooklyn raked Ford and three successors, and suddenly the Dodgers, left for dead in Yankee Stadium, had made this World Series a best-of-three affair.

Stengel gave the ball to Jim McDonald for Game Five. McDonald was a spot starter who had won nine games in 1953, his career high, including two shutouts. While the Dodgers were able to touch him for 12 hits, he gave up only two runs through seven before tiring in the eighth inning; he proved to be the unsung hero of the Series. New York had seven extra-base hits in this game, including a grand slam home run by Mantle in the third, to give them a 10–2 lead. Brooklyn knocked out McDonald with their four-run eighth, but any further damage was blunted in the ninth by Reynolds, who induced Jackie

Robinson to hit into a double play, ending the game. Back in the Bronx the Yankees went for the kill. They nicked Erskine for three runs in the first two innings and Ford had a 3–1 lead after seven. Stengel asked Reynolds to close it out, but in the ninth inning Carl Furillo blasted a two-run homer, tying the game. It didn't stay tied for long. Hank Bauer walked against relief ace Clem Labine, and after an out Mantle beat out an infield single. Then Billy Martin got a clean hit up the middle, scoring Bauer to win the game and give the Yankees, and Stengel, their record-breaking fifth consecutive World Series victory. It was definitely Martin's Series, as the pugnacious infielder collected 12 hits, a record for a six-game affair, had five extra-base hits, knocked in eight runs and batted .500. While the Dodgers had more hits than the Yanks (64–56) and a higher team batting average, the Bombers more importantly scored more runs, 33–27. The Dodgers also helped to beat themselves, issuing 25 walks (Yankee pitchers walked just 15) and committing seven errors (the Yankees made just one).

Because Stengel's team made all the routine plays and rarely made mental errors, they seemed to be unbeatable. It would take a truly great club to prevent the Yankees from winning their sixth straight American League pennant and World Series, and that's exactly what happened. Though New York won 103 games in 1954, more than any other squad Stengel managed, the Yankees finished second to the Cleveland Indians, which set a new league mark with its 111 victories.* The streak was over.

The Yankees remained one of baseball's preeminent teams in the 1950s, but they were not quite as invincible in the Fall Classic, losing three times in five appearances before Stengel's surprising departure in the fall of 1960. Casey's true zenith as a manager came with his Yankee teams from 1949 through 1953.

Circumstances are different in baseball today. If they have the money, free agency will allow teams to fill holes quickly, and if they don't it can turn them from contenders to also-rans overnight as their stars defect to other clubs. Under these existing economic conditions, sustaining a dynasty is extremely difficult, at best. It is hard to imagine, therefore, that any team in the foreseeable future will challenge the Yankee mark of five consecutive pennants and five consecutive world championships, and what Stengel and his Bronx Bombers achieved in the early 1950s is to be admired.

The 1954 Cleveland Indians are detailed elsewhere in this book.

1949–56
Brooklyn Dodgers

They have been immortalized as "The Boys of Summer." Their ballpark, now just a memory, has become a symbol for classic, "old-time" baseball. Their lineup was historic and came to be seen as what was right about post–World War II America. And their very names, almost half a century later, are legendary.

And yet, in a decade in which they were one of two dominant teams, they managed to win only one World Series championship. And they lost perhaps the most famous game ever played. And in the end they left a community that worshipped them and wanted them to stay and moved 3,000 miles away, leaving a void that has never fully been filled.

They were the Brooklyn Dodgers.

They were a storied franchise, but for many years most of the stories were humorous ones, about three players occupying one base, or batted balls bouncing off players' heads or shoulders. They started off the 20th century in style, winning the National League pennant in 1900, then went 16 years before occupying the top spot again and playing in their first World Series. They went back to the Fall Classic four years later and then descended into darkness, not making another postseason appearance for 21 years, until 1941, just weeks before Pearl Harbor. The Giants' player-manager, Bill Terry, once asked jokingly, "Is Brooklyn still in the league?" Other people may have been wondering the same thing.

In September of 1942 a majority of Dodger stock was purchased by a trio made up of Branch Rickey, Walter O'Malley and John Smith. Rickey, while running the St. Louis Cardinals, had developed the farm system, which transformed player development and turned the Cardinals into one of baseball's powerhouses. But he and owner Sam Breadon were feuding, and he looked forward to not only running a team but to being (more or less) his own boss. O'Malley, an attorney, worked for the Brooklyn Trust Company, the local bank that had lent the Dodgers so much money over the years that they were, in a way, the real owners of the team. O'Malley handled legal matters for the team and jumped at the chance to purchase the stock. Smith was affiliated with the Pfizer Company, which was then riding high with its new wonder drug, penicillin. Rickey set out to rebuild and reform the Dodgers: rebuild because, despite their 1941 pennant, the roster was filled with over–30 veterans while the minor leagues were bereft of prospects; reform because a great many of those veterans were the hard-drinking, fast-living type, the antithesis of the clean-living, college-educated player Rickey preferred. So the Dodgers signed players like Ralph Branca from New York University, and Clyde King from the University of North Carolina, and Jackie Robinson from the University of California at Los Angeles.

Of course, the signing of Robinson was historic as well as significant. Baseball had had an unofficial "color line" for eight decades, refusing to allow black athletes to play in the majors and minors, forcing them to compete in their own leagues. Although both John McGraw and Bill Veeck had attempted to sign black players, they had been thwarted by the almost-dictatorial power of baseball's first commissioner, Judge Kenesaw Mountain Landis, who kept the game segregated for more than twenty years. With his death in 1944 and the election of former Kentucky governor and U.S. Senator A.B. "Happy" Chandler as the new commissioner, however, a new era was ushered in. Chandler felt that, if young black men were good enough to fight fascism in both the European and Pacific theaters during World War II, they should be good enough to play professional baseball. Rickey agreed, signed Robinson and followed up by signing a great many other talented black athletes, which helped to restock the farm system and to eventually fuel the Dodgers' climb back to the top of the National League. Robinson's signing has been well-chronicled elsewhere and won't be rehashed here; it must be said, however, that this act by Rickey, and the subsequent success of Jackie Robinson, overshadows baseball to rank as one of the most significant social turning points of the 20th century.*

Robinson was a star at Montreal in the International League in 1946, leading them to the title and a victory in the Little World Series against Louisville, the American Association champions. That was enough for Rickey, who brought Robinson up to the Dodgers in 1947. Despite incredible vilification from a great many fans and opposing players around the league, plus opposition from some of his own teammates — a few players even signed a petition, imploring Rickey not to bring Robinson up to the majors — Robinson proved to be the catalyst of the 1947 team. He led the league in stolen bases and finished second with his 125 runs scored, all the while playing the unfamiliar position of first base, where the Dodgers needed help but also where he was a little less liable to be spiked. Robinson won the Rookie of the Year Award as the Dodgers edged the St. Louis Cardinals for the NL crown. They lost the World Series to the Yankees in a seven-game classic that included the first pinch-hit home run (by Yogi Berra); the first television broadcast of baseball's annual showcase event; and a no-hit game, by the Yankees' Bill Bevens, broken up by a double with two out in the ninth inning that drove in the tying and winning runs for the Dodgers.

In the off-season the Dodgers traded longtime fan favorite Dixie Walker to the Pirates. Walker had been the instigator of the anti–Robinson petition,

---

*More thorough books about Robinson include his own I Never Had It Made; Red Barber's 1947: When All Hell Broke Loose in Baseball; and Jules Tygiel's Baseball's Great Experiment: Jackie Robinson and His Legacy.

and this was his payback. In exchange the Dodgers received pitcher Elwin "Preacher" Roe and third baseman Billy Cox. Then they sent second baseman Eddie Stanky to the Boston Braves, opening up the keystone for Robinson. They taught catcher Gil Hodges how to play first base, partly to get his bat into the lineup and partly to make room for another former Negro League star, catcher Roy Campanella, who was promoted from the minors in mid-season. The Dodgers, with Hodges, Robinson, shortstop Pee Wee Reese, Cox and Campanella, had put together an infield that would stay intact for the next five seasons.

But the Dodgers didn't win in 1948. They were Team Turmoil, with much of it stemming from their manager, Leo Durocher. The brash Durocher had been suspended for the entire 1947 season by Commissioner Chandler for hanging out with known gamblers and allowing "unsavory types" to come into the Dodgers' clubhouse. Calm, easygoing Burt Shotton had managed the team to the World Series, but Durocher was back in 1948, basically unchanged, and the team didn't seem to respond to him the way it had in previous seasons, or the way it had with Shotton the year before. Rickey finally determined that Durocher had to go, but "Lippy" wouldn't resign and Rickey wouldn't fire his old friend. So in July a deal was worked out: the New York Giants dismissed their manager, former star outfielder Mel Ott, and Durocher left the Dodgers to go over the East River and take charge at the Polo Grounds; Shotton came back to manage in Brooklyn. In New York City, where the rivalry between the Dodgers and Giants was so fierce that players literally hated one another and fistfights between loyal fans was common every year, Durocher's action was tantamount to treason (in the eyes of the Flatbush Faithful) and sleeping with the enemy (in the minds of Giants' supporters). Shotton had a calming influence on the Brooks and they rocketed from last place, where they had been just two weeks prior to Durocher's departure, to first at the end of August. They could not keep it up, however, and wound up the season in third place.

The Dodgers' dominance of the National League began for real in 1949. Shotton, who managed in street clothes à la Connie Mack, was in the dugout right from the beginning of spring training, continuing to serve as a calming influence. A young outfielder named Edwin Snider, who had impressed Shotton in the final few weeks of 1948, took over in center field and quickly became the Duke of Flatbush with his lefthanded power, perfectly complementing the righthanded bats of Campanella, Hodges, Robinson, Reese and right fielder Carl Furillo. And the team brought up another black player, a six-foot-four-inch righthanded pitcher named Don Newcombe, who wound up leading the staff with 17 wins and earning Rookie of the Year honors.*

As good as Brooklyn was in 1949, so were the St. Louis Cardinals. Led by

---

*In 1949 there were just seven black players in the majors and three of them were Dodgers. In fact, only two other teams employed black players: the Giants, with Monte Irvin and Hank Thompson; and the Cleveland Indians, with Larry Doby and Satchel Paige.

Stan Musial, probably the best player in the league, the double-play combination of Red Schoendienst and Marty Marion and outfielder Enos "Country" Slaughter, the hero of their 1946 World Series triumph, the Cards of Eddie Dyer were a smart aggregation of veteran players. After a slow start they made their move, finally landing in first place towards the end of June, where they stayed for three months. The relatively-young Dodgers were expected to wilt but remained close to St. Louis all summer. With just five games left the Cardinals held a one-game lead, then inexplicably lost four in a row while the Dodgers won two of three to move into first place. On the final day of the season the Cardinals snapped their losing streak; if the Dodgers lost to the Phillies they would be tied with the Cardinals and forced to play a best-of-three playoff for the National League pennant. (The same scenario had occurred in 1946 and St. Louis had been victorious.) Brooklyn jumped to a 5–0 lead but Newcombe couldn't hold it, and the teams went into extra innings tied at seven. In the top of the tenth inning, Reese singled, was sacrificed to second and scored on Snider's clutch hit. Moments later the Duke scored, the Phillies couldn't retaliate and the Dodgers were National League champions.

The race in the American League had been just as tight and just as exciting, with the Yankees beating the Red Sox in the final two games of the season to finish ahead of Boston by a single game. A seasoned team, New York was still led by Joe DiMaggio, who had batted .346. But Joe D was slowing down: he had missed half the season with a foot injury, and was in the World Series starting lineup despite battling a case of viral pneumonia. Pitching really won for the Yankees in 1949, as four starters won in double figures and lefty Joe Page turned in a phenomenal season, winning 13 games and saving another 27 out of the bullpen in Casey Stengel's first year at the helm in the Bronx.

And pitching was the story for the better part of the first three games. The two teams traded 1–0 victories at Yankee Stadium, and the Dodgers felt they were in good shape heading back to Ebbets Field. But they would not win again that season. All three games in Brooklyn followed the same pattern: the Yankees took the early lead, and then when the Dodgers would rally that good New York pitching would put the clamps on them. The Dodgers' fabulous season came to a sudden end with those three straight losses at home.

The Dodgers made no changes for the 1950 season, and their young lineup really blossomed into a fearsome group. They led the league in runs scored with a whopping 847, in home runs with 194, in hits, average and slugging percentage. But the pitching didn't keep up with the hitting. Newcombe and Roe won 19 games apiece and 22-year-old Erv Palica won 13 as both a starter and reliever, but Shotton had trouble putting together the rest of the pitching staff. Meanwhile, the Dodgers' competition came not from the Cardinals, who faded into fifth place, but from the Braves, Phillies and Leo Durocher's Giants. This quartet stayed bunched up until after the All-Star break, when the Phillies got hot and forged into the lead.

Philadelphia was even younger than the Dodgers and quickly picked up the nickname of "Whiz Kids." Led by pitchers Robin Roberts and Curt Simmons, outfielders Richie Ashburn and Del Ennis and shortstop Granny Hamner, they were attempting to win a pennant for the first time since 1915. Their chances looked pretty good when, on September 12, they led the Dodgers by 12 games. But then two of their pitchers were injured and Simmons had to join his National Guard unit, which was activated for Korean War duty. The Phils lost 8 of their next 11 while Brooklyn got hot and took 12 of 16. And as luck would have it, they were scheduled to close the season with a two-game series in Ebbets Field. Momentum carried the Dodgers to a win on Saturday, making a playoff a possibility for the second year in a row. In 1949 the Dodgers had won to avoid it; in 1950 they hoped to force it.

The pitching-shy Phils started their ace, Robin Roberts, for the third time in five days, while Brooklyn countered with Newcombe, and the two workhorses were up to the task. With the score tied at one, the season came down to two plays. In the bottom of the ninth the Dodgers' Cal Abrams tried to score from second on a Duke Snider hit but was thrown out at the plate by Richie Ashburn. Then, in the tenth inning, Dick Sisler (son of Hall of Famer George Sisler) sliced an opposite-field, three-run homer off Newcombe to win the game, and the pennant, for the Phillies.

Unlike the previous off-season, the Dodgers were busy in the fall of 1950. Walter O'Malley had maneuvered himself into the position of controlling stockholder, and he chose not to renew Rickey's contract as general manager and bought out his stock as well. He fired Burt Shotton, ostensibly for losing that final game to the Phils, hired Charley Dressen as the team's new manager, and brought in outfielder Andy Pafko in a June trade with the Cubs. The hard-hitting Pafko, a four-time All-Star, was seen as the answer to the long-standing mystery in left field, and the key to a World Series championship. With Newcombe and Roe on their way to 20-win seasons and, finally, stable secondary pitching with young righthanders Carl Erskine, Ralph Branca and Clyde King, the Dodgers looked unbeatable in 1951. On August 11, they led the Giants by 13 games.

Durocher felt he had a good club, but not so good that it couldn't use some new parts. In late May they made a move that was akin to putting a new engine into an old car — they brought up 20-year-old Willie Mays from the minors. Mays could simply do it all: hit for average, hit for power, field, throw and run. Especially run. Out in center field his territory seemed to be foul line to foul line. On the bases he ran with abandon. At the plate he went hitless in his first dozen at-bats, then cracked a home run off future Hall of Famer Warren Spahn for his first major league hit, which broke the ice. Mays wound up as the NL's Rookie of the Year, batting .274 with 20 homers and 68 RBI in just four months. His presence also allowed Durocher to make another change, shifting Bobby Thomson from center field to third base. The "Flying Scot" responded with 32 homers and 101 RBI. A couple of days before Mays arrived, Durocher allowed Whitey Lockman and Monte Irvin to switch positions. Both flourished, especially Irvin, who was more comfortable in left field than at first base and wound up leading the league in runs batted in.

The Giants finally seemed to put it all together in mid–August when they went on a 16-game winning streak. At the same time, the Dodgers lost Clyde King to a sore arm, while that powerful lineup began to slow down. The Giants cut the lead to single digits. The Dodgers brought up pitcher Clem Labine and he contributed five wins, but the Giants countered with Al Corwin, who matched those five. Sal Maglie and Larry Jansen were the equivalent of Newcombe and Roe, and Jim Hearn, unsuccessful early in the season, changed his delivery and went on to win 17 games for the Giants. Durocher's crew crept closer, but still trailed by four on September 20. They had only seven games left on their schedule, while the Dodgers had ten. If Brooklyn could just split those ten games, it wouldn't matter what the Giants did.

New York won all seven of its remaining games, while the Dodgers lost six of ten, and on the last day of the regular season, Brooklyn — incredibly — found itself having to beat the Phillies to force a tie with the Giants. Trailing 8–5, the Dodgers scored three in the eighth to tie, then the two teams settled in for a siege. In the 12th inning Philadelphia loaded the bases with two out. The Phils' Eddie Waitkus smashed a line drive to the right of second base, a sure base hit to end the Dodgers' season. But Jackie Robinson dove and somehow caught the ball, ending the inning. Then in the 14th Robinson homered off Robin Roberts, setting up the playoff.

Ralph Branca gave up only four hits in the first game but two of them were home runs, to Thomson and Irvin, and the Giants won at Ebbets Field, 3–1, behind Hearn's five-hitter. The next day, though, at the Polo Grounds, the Dodgers clobbered Giant pitching, 10–0, to set up the final, winner-take-all showdown. Newcombe and Maglie battled it out for seven innings but in the eighth Brooklyn scored three times for a 4–1 lead. And that was how it stood as the Giants came up to bat in the bottom of the ninth.

The first two New York hitters reached base before Newcombe retired Irvin; the Dodgers just needed to get two more outs. But Lockman doubled to left, scoring one run and convincing Dressen that his pitcher was tired. Both Branca and Erskine were warming up in the bullpen, and Dressen asked coach Clyde Sukeforth who was ready. There was no doubt in Sukeforth's mind: "Erskine got up and tried to throw … but … [h]e didn't have anything…. It was Branca all the way. Branca was really firing." So in came Branca, and the Dodgers chose to pitch to Thomson rather than walk him, which would put the potential winning run on base, and face the rookie Mays. It was a decision that is still second-guessed today. The first pitch was a called strike and the second pitch was hit into the seats for a three-run homer and a 5–4 New York win. "The Giants win the pennant!" screamed radio announcer Russ Hodges, over

The 1955 Brooklyn Dodgers

and over. Brooklyn, up by 13 games in mid–August, had squandered the big lead, had watched their hated rivals win 39 of their final 47 games, and had been unable to get the final two outs in the final game of the regular season. "The Giants win the pennant!" It is, perhaps, the most memorable moment in baseball history.

It was also a long fall and winter, but in the spring the Dodgers were back, intent on making everyone forget the previous year. Uncle Sam, however, wasn't going to make it easy on them: Don Newcombe and his 56 wins in three seasons was drafted into the army. Neither was Father Time, as 37-year-old Preacher Roe injured his arm and pitched 100 fewer innings than the year before. Branca and Labine also suffered injuries, making them unavailable for parts of the season. Dressen patched up his pitching staff with three minor league righthanders. Ben Wade had appeared in a couple of games with the Cubs a few years before but had spent the bulk of his career in the "bushes." Given a chance by the Dodgers, he won 11 games in 1952. Billy Loes, who was from the neighboring borough of Queens and only 22 years old, won 13 games. Joe Black was the biggest find of all. A Negro League veteran, he came in and anchored the bullpen, leading the team both in wins and saves (15 apiece) and giving the Dodgers their third Rookie of the Year award winner.

Things weren't a whole lot better over at Coogan's Bluff. Monte Irvin broke his ankle during an exhibition game and in late May Willie Mays joined Newcombe in the army. Larry Jansen, who had won 23 for the Giants in 1951, was limited to 11 wins in 1952 while battling a bad back. Like Dressen, Durocher was able to pick a plum from the minors, a 28-year-old knuckleballer from North Carolina named Hoyt Wilhelm, who matched Black's 15 wins out of the bullpen.

New York picked up where they had left off the previous season, winning 26 of their first 34 games. But then they fell into a slump and the Dodgers roared past them. At one point, around the All-Star Game, Brooklyn had a winning percentage of well over .700. They also sported a ten-game lead in late August, but three weeks later the Giants had crept to within three and it looked like fans might be in for a rerun of the previous season's frantic finish. It didn't happen. The Giants ran out of gas and the Dodgers won the National League crown; for the first time since 1948, the title wasn't decided on the final day of the season.

Despite having started just two games all season, Dressen chose Joe Black to open the World Series against the Yankees (who else?), and the big righty did not disappoint. The Yanks scored first but the Dodgers did the rest, bashing three home runs to support Black's six-hit, 4–2 victory, which made him the first black pitcher to win a World Series game. The series then seesawed back and forth. The Yankees won Game Two, the Dodgers, utilizing Robinson's speed, won Game Three. Black was back on the mound in Game Four and pitched even better than he had in the opener, but Allie Reynolds was superb, blanking the Dodgers on just four hits, as he evened the Series with his 2–0 win.

Carl Erskine pitched Game Five and took a 4–0 lead into the fifth inning, but the Yankees scratched for a couple of runs and then their first baseman, Johnny Mize, hit a long three-run homer to put New York on top. The Dodgers came back to tie it in the seventh and then a Snider double gave them the lead in the 11th inning. Meanwhile, Erskine was still pitching, having not given up a hit or walk after the Mize round-tripper. The two had to face each other in the 11th, and it looked like Big John had done it again when he cracked one to deep right. But Carl Furillo made a leaping catch — the defensive play of the Series — to preserve Brooklyn's 6–5 victory. After giving up those five runs in the fifth, Erskine retired 19 consecutive batters.

The Dodgers now went back to Ebbets Field needing to win just one game to claim their first World Series title, and they handed the ball to Billy Loes, who pitched well enough to win many games, but not this one. Particularly damaging was an RBI single collected by his mound opponent, Raschi, who also threw the better game and had the good fortune to be rescued by Reynolds in the eighth. With everything on the line the Dodgers once more called on Black, but this time he could only pitch into the sixth. New York had a slim 4–2 lead when the Dodgers loaded the bases with just one out in the seventh.

Casey Stengel made a surprising move, bringing in Bob Kuzava from the bullpen, and the lefthander did his job, inducing both Snider and Robinson to pop up to the infield. Jackie's ball proved to be a little tricky, and it took a hustling play by Yankee second baseman Billy Martin to retire the side. Kuzava then disposed of Brooklyn with ease in the eighth and ninth, making it another long winter for the Flatbush Faithful.

The traditional refrain in Brooklyn had been "wait 'til next year," and in 1953 it looked as if next year had finally arrived. A speedy young infielder, switch-hitting Jim "Junior" Gilliam, impressed enough in the spring to win the second base job and claim the leadoff spot; he would also extend the Dodgers' domination of the Rookie of the Year Award. This made Robinson a jack-of-all-trades as he spent time in left field (replacing the departed Andy Pafko) and third base (in a timeshare with Billy Cox). Robinson had one of his best seasons, batting .329 and driving home 95 runs, but he might have been overlooked because the 1953 Brooklyn Dodgers were, quite simply, one of the best hitting teams ever put together. Robinson's 95 RBI only placed him fourth on the club, behind Campanella's league-leading 142, Snider's 126 and Hodges' 122; Furillo was right behind Jackie with 92. Furillo led the league in batting, Gilliam led the league in triples, Snider led the league in runs scored; six Dodgers scored 100 or more runs, a major league record. As a team, Brooklyn scored 955 runs, the most in the National League in more than twenty years. They batted a collective .285, had a slugging percentage of .474 (50 points better than the Cardinals), and led the league in home runs and stolen bases. While they did repeat as National League pennant winners, becoming the first team to turn the trick in the Senior Circuit since St. Louis in 1942–44, they didn't blow the rest of the league away until the second half. Pitching, as always, was a concern, although Carl Erskine established himself as the ace with his first (and only) 20-win season. Russ Meyer, acquired from the Phillies, won 15 and Billy Loes came through with 14 victories. Dressen cobbled together the rest of the staff, which managed to survive due to the daily explosiveness of the offense.

Prior to the All-Star game, the big surprise in the league was the Braves. Relocation from Boston to Milwaukee had seemed to work wonders for the franchise, and they battled Brooklyn for first place. However, the Phillies, Cardinals and Giants were all within shouting distance of the top, and it seemed like a good race was brewing. But, as they might say in Flatbush, "fuhgedaboudit." The Dodgers won 16 of their first 19 games after the break, and 41 of 50 games until September 1 to leave all the other teams far behind. They clinched the pennant on September 12, the earliest date in NL history, won 105 games, a team record, and wound up 13 games ahead of the Braves. But in order to be recognized as the best you have to beat the best, and for the fourth time in the past seven years the road to the championship went through the Bronx. The Yankees had a pretty good club, too, winning 99 games, and they could also score runs, tallying 801 on a .273 average, both figures tops in the league. Young southpaw Whitey Ford had returned from the military to join the aging veterans Reynolds, Raschi, Lopat and Johnny Sain, giving Casey Stengel a pitching staff that posted a major league–best ERA of 3.20, nearly a full run better than the boys from Brooklyn.

The Series opener proved to be a slugfest. The Yankees pounded Erskine for four runs in the very first inning and held a 5–1 lead after five, but by the seventh the game was tied. New York's legendary "five o'clock lightning" struck again, however, as the Yankees scored in the seventh and eighth innings to put the game out of reach, 9–5. The next day, Preacher Roe held the Yankees to five hits, but two of them were home runs, by Martin and Mantle, and the Dodgers were down by two games.

Dressen asked Erskine to pitch on just one-day's rest, and "Oisk" made him look like a genius by striking out 14 Yankees, a new record for a World Series game. Not only that, but the Flatbush Faithful all went home happy as Erskine's batterymate, Campanella, hit an eighth inning home run off Raschi for a 3–2 victory. The next day Brooklyn touched Ford for three runs right away and never looked back, tying the Series with their 7–3 win. Maybe this *would* be the year!

In the first four games of the Series Dressen had not yet called on 15-game winner Russ Meyer, and he bypassed him again in Game Five, giving the start to 20-year-old lefty Johnny Podres. But by the third inning a nervous Podres had already given up two runs and had loaded the bases, causing Dressen to bring in Meyer. Remembering Erskine's success the day before, Dressen instructed Meyer to throw curveballs to Mickey Mantle, even though the "drop" wasn't Meyer's best pitch. Mantle deposited one into the seats for a grand slam, and by the time Brooklyn's bats came alive in the eighth inning the Yankees had a 10–2 lead on their way to an 11–7 win and the Series' lead. It looked like New York had it won when they took an early 3–0 lead in Game Six, but the Dodgers tied it up in the ninth inning on a two-run homer by Furillo. But in the bottom of the ninth Billy Martin, having the week of his life, collected his 12th hit, a World Series record, and drove in his eighth run, and just like that it was over. The Dodgers, once again, were bridesmaids.

Newcombe returned from the military in 1954. A fiery young third baseman named Don Hoak made his presence felt and wormed his way into a hot corner rotation that also included Robinson and Cox. The rest of the veterans were back, as expected, to try again for the world championship, with one glaring exception: Charley Dressen. The skipper had decided that, after two pennants and one near-miss, he deserved the security of a three-year contract. So did his wife, who wrote a letter to Walter O'Malley requesting the new agreement. The problem was that the Dodgers did not believe in multiyear pacts, even for successful managers. Dressen tried to compromise with a two-year deal but O'Malley wouldn't budge. In late November of 1953, O'Malley introduced Walter Alston as Brooklyn's new manager. Alston had played exactly one game in the major leagues, and had spent the past decade in the Dodgers system, managing a great many of the players now on Brooklyn's roster. He was a quiet man who, unlike Dressen, instituted numerous rules and demanded respect. The veterans had trouble with him, and he had trouble with many of them. As a result, the Dodgers never seemed to jell in 1954. Of course, it didn't help that Newcombe battled a sore arm, Podres had appendicitis, and Campanella missed time due to surgery for bone chips in his wrist. It also didn't help the Dodgers that Willie Mays had returned from the service as well and batted .345 with 41 home runs, 110 RBI and 119 runs scored to spark the Giants to the pennant.

Sandy Amoros claimed left field, and third base became a little less crowded when Cox was peddled to Baltimore, leaving Robinson and Hoak to platoon. This didn't set well with Jackie who, though he was 36 years old, knew he could still play and didn't like being pushed aside just because of his age. He and Alston quietly sniped at each other throughout the spring until just before the regular season opened. As they worked their way north from Florida the Dodgers played an exhibition game in Louisville. In the clubhouse Alston and Robinson finally exploded, and only the cooler head of Campanella prevented a fistfight. But, after a year of trying, this incident seemed to earn Alston some respect; at the very least, he had finally made it clear he was the boss.

Whether this confrontation had anything to do with it cannot be determined, but Brooklyn opened up the 1955 season with ten straight victories, a new major league mark. After losing two of three to the Giants, they then reeled off another 11 wins to find themselves already far ahead of the league with a 22–2 record. The National League race was over.

There was one other challenge to Alston's authority. Twice within a week Don Newcombe was asked to throw batting practice and refused. The first time the manager said nothing, the second time he told him to take off his uniform. Management backed Alston by fining and suspending their ace righty, who had to apologize before being allowed back in the clubhouse. There were no further confrontations that season.

The Dodgers officially clinched the pennant on September 8, four days earlier than in 1953, to establish a new standard. Once again their offense sizzled, as they led the league with 201 home runs, 857 runs scored, a .271 average and a .448 slugging percentage. Snider topped all hitters in runs scored and runs batted in, and Campanella and Hodges also drove in more than 100 runs, while Furillo just missed with 95. But perhaps the club's most remarkable achievement was leading the league in earned run average. Newcombe won 20, and Labine teamed up with rookie Ed Roebuck to give Alston two tough relievers to call on in close games. When injuries hobbled Erskine, Loes and Podres at different points in the season, minor league call-ups Don Bessent and Roger Craig helped to stabilize the staff as they combined for 13 wins. Brooklyn even let a local kid pitch a few games, a wild lefthander named Sandy Koufax, and he contributed two victories.

Once again, however, the Yankees loomed in front of the Dodgers like the specter of Marley's ghost. The Bombers could hit, too: Mickey Mantle had led the league in home runs, triples and slugging percentage, while a total of eight Yankees, including four part-time players, reached double figures in homers. The pitching staff was very different from the one that had limited the Dodgers to just two victories in the 1953 World Series, with Whitey Ford being the only familiar face, but they nevertheless turned in the best ERA in baseball, 3.23, and induced 180 double plays.

The World Series opened in Yankee Stadium, and the Bombers shelled Newcombe, who was suffering from a sore arm and would not appear again. The Dodgers mounted a comeback late in the game but the Yankees held on for a 6–5 win. The next day, Tommy Byrne became the first lefthander all season to beat the Dodgers with a complete game, giving the Yankees a 2–0 Series lead with his five-hitter, 4–2.

Alston gave the ball to Podres on the southpaw's 23rd birthday, and the Dodgers celebrated the occasion with an 8–3 win. Two Yankee runs scored on a Mickey Mantle home run, but the New York center fielder was only able to limp through three games in this Series due to leg injuries. He was joined on the disabled list by right fielder Hank Bauer, placing a strain on the Yankee bench. But the pitchers seemed to be the ones feeling the pinch, as they were touched for another eight runs in Game Four. Campanella, Snider and Hodges all homered as five New York hurlers gave up 14 hits and the lead in the Series.

The ball continued to fly out of Ebbets Field in Game Five. All told, there were 11 home runs hit in the three games played in Flatbush, seven of them by the Dodgers. Snider hit a pair and Sandy Amoros banged one for Brooklyn, offsetting two Yankee round-trippers, as the Dodgers won their third straight game, 5–3.

The Yankees, faced with possible elimination, handed the ball to Ford, and he responded with a four-hit triumph, 5–1. New York scored all their runs in the first inning, including three on a home run by first baseman Bill "Moose" Skowron. The season was down to its final game.

Lefthanders Podres and Byrne took the mound on October 4 for the deciding contest. Alston, playing the percentages, put righthanded batters Jim Gilliam in left and young Don Zimmer at second (Robinson could not play due to an injured heel). The Dodgers picked up a run in the fourth, then scored another in the sixth and had the bases loaded. Alston, hoping to break open the game, pinch hit for Zimmer, but the maneuver failed and in the bottom of the sixth he moved Gilliam back to second base, his natural position, and put Sandy Amoros in left field. Right away the first two Yankees reached base, bringing up the ever-dangerous Yogi Berra. The Yankee catcher hit a fly ball down the left field line, the perfect spot, because the Dodgers were shading him to hit towards right. It was a sure extra-base hit, and the two runners would certainly score to tie the game. But Amoros ran as hard as he could and, nearing the stands, lunged, stuck out his glove and caught the ball. If Gilliam had still been out there he would have had to backhand the ball, since his glove was on his left hand; Amoros, the southpaw, had a little easier time making the catch. Amoros then fired the ball to Reese who threw to Hodges to double up the Yanks' McDougald, trying to scamper back to the bag. The rally was aborted.

The game wasn't over, however. New York put two men on in the eighth, but Podres, perhaps getting his second wind, disposed of the next two hitters, including Berra. And in the ninth, despite the presence of three righthanded bats, Alston did not go to his bullpen and Podres rewarded him by retiring the Yankees in order. The Dodgers won, 2–0, and captured the World Series for the first and only time in their Brooklyn history. "Next year" had finally arrived.

The Dodgers' clubhouse was jubilant; so many of these players had been disappointed before. They had lived through the humiliation of 1951 and the tension of 1954, to say nothing of four losses to the Yankees since 1947. Why, Pee Wee Reese had even been in the lineup back in 1941, when the Yankees beat the Dodgers in five games! So this victory was sweet and long overdue. But for Brooklyn fans it was almost the equivalent of the Second Coming. The celebration in the streets was unrestrained, as if a war had ended, which, in a way, it had. Firecrackers exploded, ships in the harbor blew their whistles while cars on the borough's thoroughfares blew their horns. People danced in ecstasy far into the night. For once, the world was at Brooklyn's feet.

The euphoria lasted into the spring. The baseball writers overwhelmingly predicted the Dodgers would win the pennant again in 1956. But for the first three months of the season Brooklyn found itself battling for first place with four other teams, and at the All-Star break the Dodgers were looking up at the surprising Cincinnati Reds and the Milwaukee Braves.

All three teams could really hit the ball. The Reds, with the addition of rookie Frank Robinson, suddenly featured the most explosive lineup in the league; three players hit over 30 home runs and two more just missed, and the team as a whole tied the major league record with 221 four-baggers. The Braves had a lefty-righty slugging combination of Eddie Mathews and Joe Adcock, plus a 22-year-old outfielder named Henry Aaron who showed signs of being about as good as Willie Mays. And the Dodgers still were the Dodgers, with Snider, Campanella, Hodges, et al. So in the long run, as is generally the case, pitching would be the key. Cincinnati's hurlers were only adequate, but Milwaukee had a formidable Big Three in Warren Spahn, Lew Burdette and Bob Buhl, who would wind up winning 57 games between them. Brooklyn had Newcombe, enjoying his finest year, but Alston was having trouble backing him up. Podres had gone into the navy, and Erskine and Craig were having mediocre seasons. The Dodgers looked for pitching help and purchased Sal Maglie from Cleveland in May. Maglie was the "Barber," the hated former Giant. "It'll seem a little strange to see him come walking through that door," said Reese of his one-time nemesis. Maglie carried other baggage, too: he was 39 years old and had a bad back. It took him a couple of months to round into shape, but beginning in late July he fashioned a 10-2 record with a sparkling 1.88 ERA, and on September 25 he tossed a no-hitter. The Dodgers would not have come close without Maglie.

The three teams stayed within shouting distance throughout August, but in mid-September the Reds suffered a four-game losing streak. While not very long, it proved to be deadly for Cincinnati, which never could catch up to the Dodgers and Braves. Meanwhile, Milwaukee maneuvered themselves into a one-game lead with just three left to play, then lost two games to St. Louis, including a 2-1 heartbreaker in 12 innings. Brooklyn, meanwhile, was beating Pittsburgh, putting the Dodgers back in first place. With the pennant on the line, Duke Snider and Sandy Amoros both hit two home runs as the Dodgers swept the Pirates and moved into yet another World Series showdown with the Yankees.

The Yankees were once again the Bombers of yore, setting a new American League record for homers with 190. The Grand Marshal of this parade was Mickey Mantle, who challenged Babe Ruth's all-time single-season record before settling for 52 home runs. Mantle also led the league in batting (.353) and RBI (130), making him the first player to win the Triple Crown since Ted Williams in 1947. Mantle had ample support from Berra, Skowron, Bauer, et al., but he was clearly the foreman of this particular wrecking crew. Pitching, on the other hand, was a little different story. Aside from steady Whitey Ford, the Yankees found, in 1956, that they couldn't count on their usual starters and had to turn to a couple of young righthanders, Johnny Kucks and Tom Sturdivant, who both posted career years in contributing 34 victories. New York won seven of their first eight games in 1956 and cruised to Casey Stengel's seventh pennant by a nine-game margin over Cleveland.

Alston chose Maglie to open the Series and The Barber continued his miraculous year. Despite giving up homers to Mantle and Billy Martin, Maglie went the route in a 6-3 Dodger win, with Brooklyn knocking out Ford in the third. The second game was one of the highest-scoring games in Series history. The Bombers drove Newcombe from the mound in the second, with Berra cracking a grand slam to give them an early 6-0 lead. But the Dodgers came roaring back in the bottom of the inning, pounding starter Don Larsen and two relievers for six of their own. Brooklyn then kept up the attack, and when it was all over they had tagged seven Yankee pitchers for 12 hits, in addition to picking up a record 11 walks, in a 13-8 marathon.

The Dodgers found themselves in an unfamiliar position, leading the Series 2-0, and in the sixth inning of the third game they found themselves ahead again. But any dreams of a sweep were dashed by the oldest man on the field, former Cardinal star Enos Slaughter, who was part of Stengel's ever-present platoon system. "Country" blasted a three-run homer off fellow North Carolinian Roger Craig, putting the Yankees back in the Series. Whitey Ford pitched nine innings to give the beleaguered bullpen a rest. His effort was matched the next day by Sturdivant, who held the Dodgers to six hits in a 6–2 Yankee triumph. Brooklyn picked up a run in the ninth and had the bases loaded with just one out, but Stengel stayed with Sturdivant, who retired the last two batters without incident.

With the World Series now even, Alston came back with Maglie while Stengel sent Don Larsen to the mound, looking for a better effort than he had seen in Game Two. What he got has never been matched in postseason play. Throwing by far the game of his life that October 8, Larsen needed just 97 pitches to toss a perfect game. Brooklyn sent 27 men to the plate and all 27 returned without reaching base. There were a couple of close calls: Larsen had a 3–1 count on Reese in the first inning but came back to strike him out; a hot shot by Jackie Robinson in the second bounced off the third baseman's glove, but shortstop Gil McDougald grabbed it and threw Robinson out at first; a long drive by Hodges was run down by Mantle in the fifth. Larsen had to be good because Maglie only surrendered five hits, one of them a fourth inning homer to Mantle, which was all the Yankees would need. They did pick up another run in the sixth, and this historic 2–0 victory gave the Yankees the lead in the Series.

Whereas only days before Brooklyn seemed to be on the verge of repeating as champions, they now found themselves with their backs to the wall. They pinned their hopes on Labine, while the Yankees sent burly righthander Bob Turley out to finish the job. Both pitched magnificently, holding the opposition scoreless through nine. But with two on in the tenth, Robinson hit a ball to left that perhaps was catchable. Unfortunately for New York, their left fielder was the 40-year-old Slaughter, and it went over his head, driving home the only run of the game.

This was the sixth time since 1947 these two clubs had met in the World Series, and for the fourth time it would be decided by one game. In 1956, however, the Dodgers would not get the clutch pitching they had received the year before from Podres. Don Newcombe gave up five runs in less than four innings on a solo homer by Elston Howard and a pair of two-run shots onto Bedford Avenue by Yogi Berra. One more Yankee round-tripper — a grand slam by Bill Skowron — ended the scoring in a 9–0 romp. The Dodgers, meanwhile, could only solve Johnny Kucks for three singles that afternoon as the Yankee starters delivered their fifth straight complete game. In fact, after their heroics in the first two games of the Series, Brooklyn's bats went silent. They scored 19 runs in those first two games and only six thereafter — and only one in the final three games. Of the 15 home runs hit, 12 were by the aptly-named Bombers. While no one man can lose a World Series by himself, Don Newcombe had a particularly bad week, pitching just under five innings combined in his two games, giving up 11 hits and 11 runs and compiling an ERA of 21.21.

Dodger fans could not have realized it, but their era had come to a close.

Jackie Robinson retired after the season. The aging team made a brief run at the 1957 pennant but faded in the heat of the summer and finished third behind Milwaukee and St. Louis. And despite drawing a million fans again, O'Malley eventually broke off new stadium negotiations with the City of New York and bolted for California, taking Horace Stoneham and the Giants with him. After 70 years the intense rivalry between Brooklyn and New York, unmatched by any two major league franchises before or since, would now be transferred to Los Angeles and San Francisco.*

1954 Cleveland Indians

After winning the world championship in 1948, the Cleveland Indians assumed the unofficial role of bridesmaids in the American League. In 1949 they finished third behind the great New York–Boston battle that went down to the season's final game. In 1950 they were part of a four-team struggle that saw them win 92 games, but they still ended up behind the Yankees, Tigers and Red Sox, though they were just six games out of first. And in 1951–1953 they outlasted everyone except the Yankees, winning 93 games twice and 92 once, but were shut out of postseason play.

Lou Boudreau had led the team through most of the 1940s, serving not only as the team's All-Star shortstop but also, beginning in 1942 at the tender age of 24, as the playing manager. But he left after the 1950 season and the Tribe hired a new manager, Al Lopez, who had been an outstanding defensive catcher for 18 years, and who held the record (since broken) for the most games played by a catcher in the majors, nearly 2,000. Lopez knew that you needed strong pitching to win, and he had inherited a spectacular starting staff, the best in the league. Bob Feller, Mike Garcia, Bob Lemon and Early Wynn had been the Indians' backbone since 1949, when Garcia came up from the minors and Wynn came over from Washington. They were the primary reason that Cleveland was always a preseason threat to unseat the Yankees atop the American League. From 1949 through 1954, this quartet accounted for no fewer than 84.9 percent of the Indians' victories; in 1951, Lopez' first year at the helm, Cleveland won 93 games and this quartet won 79 of them, an astounding 84.9 percent.** But while the Tribe's starters were the envy of all baseball, they never

---

*The issues involved in the Dodgers' move to Los Angeles are far too complex to be discussed here. For an excellent treatment of the subject, see Neil J. Sullivan, The Dodgers Move West, New York: Oxford University Press, 1987.
**In fact, only three other pitchers won games for Cleveland that year.

had a Joe Page or Hoyt Wilhelm or Johnny Sain, a guy who could come in out of the bullpen and protect the lead in the late innings. In that same six-year period, Cleveland's Big Four threw about 900 more innings than Casey Stengel's top four starters, an indication that the Yankee skipper had more confidence in his bullpen than Lopez, and made frequent use of it.

Unlike, say, the Dodgers of the 1960s, the Indians weren't strictly a team that emphasized pitching. Beginning in 1950, they led the league in home runs five straight years and were always among the top scoring teams in the game; they led the league in runs scored and slugging percentage in 1952. Al Rosen was the prototype third baseman, a powerful righthanded batter who twice topped the AL in homers and RBI and was the Most Valuable Player in 1953. Larry Doby, the first black player in the American League, was a seven-time All-Star who could be counted on to hit at least 20 home runs per season while keeping his average around .300. Bobby Avila was one of the best second basemen in the game, another consistent .300 hitter who could make all the plays in the field. In addition, they needed a good catcher to complement their pitching and Cleveland had one of the best in Jim Hegan, who was not much of a hitter (a .228 lifetime average) but who was a defensive whiz and an acknowledged master at calling a game.

In 1953, even though only two other teams in baseball had won more games (the pennant-winning Yankees and Dodgers), the Tribe finished second again. It had to be frustrating for management, the players, and the fans as well. Lopez decided to make a few changes in an attempt to close the gap with the Yankees. Doby had been flanked by two aging outfielders, Dale Mitchell and Wally Westlake, and Lopez demoted both to reserve duty. In their place he inserted a veteran, Dave Philley, acquired from the A's in the off-season, and a youngster, Al Smith. Philley proved to be something of a disappointment — a .265 lifetime hitter who had batted over .300 in 1953, his average plummeted nearly 80 points to .226, though he did hit 12 homers and drive in 60 runs. Smith, on the other hand, batted .281 with 11 home runs and scored 101 runs at the top of the order.

The pitching also got tweaked a bit. Rookies Ray Narleski and Don Mossi made an effective righty-lefty combo out of the bullpen, winning nine and saving 20, and they received some help from a very unexpected source. After being given his release the previous summer, the world assumed that a sore arm had ended the career of Hal Newhouser. But Prince Hal, the premier lefthander of the war years (he won 80 games from 1944 through 1946), decided to give it another try with the Tribe. He proved to be effective in relief with seven wins and seven saves, while also serving as a mentor to the two youngsters in the bullpen. In another development, Lopez found it necessary to alter his Big Four. At age 35 Bullet Bob Feller was no longer the overpowering flame-thrower who had won 20 or more games six times and struck out a record 348 batters in 1946. The previous year the Tribe had picked up righty Art Houtteman from Detroit and had used him as both a starter and reliever; now, in 1954, Lopez decided to make Houtteman the number four starter and Feller number five. Both responded: Houtteman won 15 games and Feller contributed 13, his last season in double figures.

After having won five straight world championships, the Yankees were naturally favored to capture the American League flag again, and no one was concerned when they got off to their usual slow start. The White Sox, with a good solid pitching staff of their own, set the early pace, but Cleveland moved into first in mid–May. A couple of weeks later they made one final move to solidify their team, trading seldom-used pitcher Bob Chakales to Baltimore for Vic Wertz, a slugging outfielder who had twice been among the league leaders in RBI when he played for Detroit. Lopez immediately moved him to first base, where production had been poor for more than a year, or since age had caught up with former Negro League star Luke Easter after he had produced three big seasons in the majors. Wertz adapted to his new position and his new team, clouting 14 home runs and driving home 48. Meanwhile, the Yankees moved into second place, and at the All-Star break trailed the Tribe by just one half game. Even when Cleveland sizzled in August, winning 13 games in 14 starts, they couldn't shake New York, which won ten straight. But after Labor Day the Indians launched another winning streak, this time 11 in a row. Included was a sweep of a Sunday doubleheader from the Yankees in which more than 86,000 people, an all-time regular season record, cheered them on. They clinched the pennant a few days later and a week after that won their 111th game of the year, a new American League record and the second-best victory total in history, trailing only the 1906 Cubs. Ironically, in finishing second the Yankees won 103 games, the only time that Stengel managed a team to more than 100 wins. It was the fourth time in history that a team had reached the century mark in wins but had not won a pennant.*

Doby led the league in homers and RBI while Avila won the batting title with a .341 average. Eight players, including reserve outfielder Westlake, reached double digits in home runs. But aside from round-trippers, the Tribe did not top the AL in any offensive categories. Pitching, however, was another story. Wynn and Lemon's 23 wins apiece were the best in the circuit, and Garcia, Lemon and Wynn finished 1-2-3 in ERA. For the eighth time in the last nine years a Cleveland pitcher led in innings pitched (this time it was Wynn), Garcia led in shutouts, and in nearly every other category an Indians hurler finished in the top three, including winning percentage, complete games, strikeouts and saves (Narleski's 13). As a team, the Tribe gave up the fewest hits, the fewest walks, and had the best ERA in all of baseball; their 2.78 ERA, in fact, was a new league record.

---

*The others were the 1909 Cubs (104 wins), the 1915 Tigers (100), and the 1942 Dodgers (104). Since 1954, the 1961 Tigers (101), 1962 Dodgers (102), 1980 Orioles (100) and 1993 Giants (103) have also joined the club.

Their opponents in the World Series were the New York Giants, managed by the intrepid Leo Durocher. After their stunning stretch drive and playoff victory in 1951, the Giants had become mortal again, finishing second to the Dodgers in 1952 and a woeful fifth, 14 games under .500 and 35 games out of first, in 1953. Durocher did not panic, however, because he knew that, after two years of military duty, he would have Willie Mays back in the lineup. The 1951 Rookie of the Year did not disappoint, becoming the 1954 Most Valuable Player on the strength of his league-best .345 batting average, .667 slugging percentage and 13 triples, not to mention 41 home runs and 110 runs driven in. Mays was ably assisted by fellow outfielder Don Mueller, who just missed out on the batting title with his .342, shortstop Al Dark, third baseman Hank Thompson and outfielder Monte Irvin, and reserve outfielder and pinch-hitter deluxe Dusty Rhodes, who batted .341 with 15 homers and 50 RBI in only 164 at-bats. Off-season acquisition Johnny Antonelli won 21 games and led the league in shutouts and ERA, while relievers Marv Grissom and Hoyt Wilhelm won 22 and saved another 26. The Giants' 97 wins were 14 fewer than Cleveland had amassed, but it was good enough to bring them home five lengths in front of Brooklyn.

The Indians were favored to win, even though the Series would open in New York, and they started off as if they planned to make short work of the Giants, scoring two in the first against Sal Maglie. But the NL champs tied it up against Lemon in the third, and the two teams then stayed off the board for much of the rest of the afternoon, although Cleveland threatened frequently and wound up leaving 13 men on base.

The eighth inning proved to be the turning point. The first two Indians reached base, bringing up Wertz. Durocher called on southpaw Don Liddle to face the lefthanded hitter, but Wertz hit a drive to dead center that went well over 400 feet. In most ballparks it would have been a home run, or at least an extra-base hit, but center field in the Polo Grounds was nearly 500 feet from home plate, and the Giants employed a center fielder named Mays. In a performance that has been replayed a thousand times, Mays turned his back to everyone, raced straight back and caught the ball in full flight, like a wide receiver in football catching a long pass from his quarterback. And then came the truly magnificent part: Mays whirled and got the ball back to the infield quickly and accurately, preventing the runner on first from advancing at all and the runner on second from even thinking about trying to score on the long fly. It is one of the most memorable moments in World Series history, and still rated as the greatest catch made in postseason play. Grissom then came in and retired the side, preserving the tie. The Tribe got a runner to third in the tenth inning but could not plate him, and finally paid for all that futility. Lemon, still in the game for Cleveland, walked Mays with one out; Willie followed with a steal of second. Thompson was passed intentionally to set up the double play, and Rhodes was called upon to pinch hit. He hit a fly ball to right field that would be an out almost everywhere else, but the foul lines in the Polo Grounds were about as short as center field was deep, with right field only some 260 feet from home plate. Avila even went out from his second base position, thinking he had a chance on the ball, but it just dropped into the stands for a three-run homer and a 5–2 Giant win.

Al Smith led off Game Two with a homer off Antonelli, and again Indian rooters expected their heroes to assert themselves. It didn't happen. Though Antonelli walked six and was touched for eight hits, he refused to give up any more runs. Wynn, meanwhile, allowed only four hits, but the Giants took advantage of their only serious opportunity. In the fifth inning Mays walked and Thompson singled, and Durocher decided to send up Rhodes to pinch hit again. This time he settled for a single, driving in the tying run. Moments later Antonelli was called safe at first as Cleveland attempted to complete an inning-ending double play, and New York took a 2–1 lead. Rhodes stayed in the game and hit a seventh inning home run to end the scoring.

A change of scenery didn't help the Indians at all. Garcia started and looked nothing like the American League's ERA leader. He was out after three, having given up four Giant runs, two of which scored when Rhodes, pinch hitting yet again, drilled a two-run single in the third. New York led 6–0 before the Tribe could score; Cleveland only mustered four hits in their 6–2 defeat. With their backs to the wall Lopez asked Lemon to pitch with just two days' rest (there had been no off-day for travel). A couple of misplays helped the Giants score a pair in the second, then they pounded Lemon and Newhouser for four runs in the fifth. Trailing by seven the Indians attempted to play catch-up and got as close as 7–4, but when they threatened in the eighth Durocher brought Antonelli in from the bullpen and he slammed the door, bringing Cleveland's otherwise-magnificent season to a sad and unexpectedly quick conclusion. It was the first National League victory in the World Series since the Cardinals' 1946 triumph, and only the second time that an NL club had won in four straight (the 1914 Braves were the other). The Tribe batted just .190 against Durocher's hurlers (who had a 1.46 ERA), collecting just 26 hits and nine runs. In contrast, New York had only a few more hits than Cleveland (33), but scored 21 runs, an indication that they capitalized on many of their opportunities. Avila, Doby, Hegan and Philley all batted under .200, while shortstops George Strickland and Sam Dente went hitless in 12 at-bats. Rhodes was the obvious hero for the Giants, driving in seven runs with his two homers and two singles.

Nevertheless, despite their shocking defeat, the Indians' season — especially their record-setting .721 winning percentage during the regular season, still the best in American League history — qualifies them as one of the finest teams to ever take the field. Except for the Yankees and White Sox, their nearest competitors, they dominated the junior circuit in 1954, winning 89 of 110 games (an .809 winning percentage) against Baltimore, Boston, Detroit, Philadelphia and Washington.

Common folklore has the Tribe falling into a funk after the World Series sweep and, like Moses and the Israelites, wandering about the desert of the second division for 40 years. That's not quite accurate because it didn't happen quite that fast. Though the performances of many regulars slipped in 1955, the team still took part in a three-team battle for first, eventually finishing with 93 wins, three fewer than the Yankees. Smith led the league in runs scored (and was a close third in the MVP balloting), Lemon tied for the lead in wins, and Narleski's 19 saves marked him as the AL's top fireman. In addition, the Tribe had an exciting Rookie of the Year in lefthander Herb Score, who won 16 games and fanned a league-best 245 batters. The next year Score was even better, striking out 263 while winning 20, a feat repeated by Lemon and Wynn. Cleveland finished second again but this time were nine back of the Yankees, and now their era was over. Lopez left after the season to manage the White Sox, where he would win a pennant in 1959. Score nearly lost an eye when hit by a line drive in 1957, and never could regain his form, winning just 19 more games after capturing 36 in his first two years. In the next 37 years the Indians would register just nine winning seasons, contending for the pennant only in 1959. It was not until the John Hart/Mike Hargrove regime assembled a group of talented young players in the early 1990s that winning ballgames once more became a regular occurrence along the shores of Lake Erie, bringing back memories of that Summer of '54.

1960 Pittsburgh Pirates

Branch Rickey, one of baseball's foremost philosophers and theoreticians, said, "Luck is the residue of design." Since Mr. Rickey was one of the chief architects of the 1960 Pittsburgh Pirates, this statement is both ironic and apt: ironic because Rickey was long gone from Pittsburgh when they triumphed, apt because his grand design, and a dash of luck, helped make this team memorable.

Some may question the inclusion of the 1960 Pirates in an anthology of baseball's 25 greatest teams, but there was never any doubt in these writers' minds that they belonged. They were built in classic fashion, rising from the dregs to serve as a model for future franchises such as the New York Mets and Atlanta Braves. They featured several excellent athletes, including one future Hall of Famer, as well as a roster full of role players who each made their necessary contributions to the team's success. They were managed by a beloved, colorful skipper, and most of all they participated in perhaps the wildest World Series ever played. It all added up to an unforgettable team and one remarkable season, and thus their inclusion here.

In the final decade or so of the 20th century, in baseball's age of free agency, there was a great deal of discussion in the mass media over the disparity between clubs, alternately called the "Haves" and "Have Nots," or big market and small market teams. While this is certainly the prime economic issue facing the game today, it is by no means a new one. Consider this: in the 1930s and 1940s, two of the National League's eight clubs (Pittsburgh and Philadelphia) did not win any pennants, and one (Boston) won just once. St. Louis, on the other hand, captured seven flags in those twenty years. They signed more players for their elaborate minor league system than anyone else in baseball, which made them one of the major "Haves" of their time.

The man behind the Cardinals' success was Branch Rickey. The farm system was, in large part, his idea, and it was designed to provide a continuous flow of talent to the major league team. After leaving St. Louis, Mr. Rickey took his concept to Brooklyn, and laid the foundation for a team that would dominate the National League in the decade following World War II. And then he was hired to work his magic in Pittsburgh.

As mentioned above, the 1930s and 1940s were not kind to the Pittsburgh Pirates. While they would find a way to finish above .500 more often than not, it was generally by a margin of just a few games and, come September, they were rarely involved in the pennant race. When Rickey lost a power struggle with Walter O'Malley and left the Dodgers in 1950, he was snapped up by the Pirates, a club that had not won a pennant since the Waner brothers led the team to the World Series against the legendary 1927 Yankees. Rickey then initiated a five-year plan designed to bring the Pirates from the National League basement to its penthouse.

The team that Rickey inherited had just one legitimate star, perennial home-run king Ralph Kiner. The rest of the roster was dotted with fringe major leaguers, men who had generally always sat at the end of the bench or bullpen throughout their careers. These Pirates were loaded with players who had already passed 30, including a 40-year-old pitcher and a 38-year-old catcher. There were a few younger guys on the team, like 20-year-old righthander Vernon Law and 21-year-old outfielder Gus Bell, but for the most part this was an old, slow team that held up the National League with its 96 losses.

The 1951 team avoided the cellar by nosing out the Cubs, but they still lost 90 games. However, Rickey started bringing in the kids, importing them from the minor leagues (outfielder Frank Thomas and pitcher Bob Friend), the college ranks (shortstop Dick Groat came directly from the Duke campus to the Pirates in 1952), even from other teams (first baseman Rocky Nelson and catcher Joe Garagiola — the same Garagiola who would later gain fame as a sportscaster, humorist and television personality).

The nadir was reached with the 1952 team. Garagiola has written that the team "lost ten out of the first fourteen and then had a slump." They won only 42 times in the 154-game schedule, a winning percentage of just .273, and were

22½ games out of seventh place. When the New York Mets proved to be a little more inept ten years later, winning just 40 of 160 games (a .250 percentage), they became known as lovable losers and had a home attendance of almost one million people; the 1952 Pirates were just considered to be losers and didn't reap any financial bonanza. But at least they were losing with youth: while the pitching staff still contained some graybeards (including 35-year-old ace Murry Dickson, who won 14 of those 42 games), a majority of the position players were now in their twenties, and Bobby Del Greco captured the center field job at the age of 19.

The Buccos changed managers for the 1953 season, with Fred Haney replacing Billy Meyer, and continued to shuffle players in and out, even trading Kiner, their only drawing card, to the Cubs in a multiplayer deal. The team still lost 104 games and finished 55 games behind the pennant-winning Dodgers. The O'Brien twins, college basketball standouts, were the double-play combo that year (Groat was in the military), but neither could hit very well and both enjoyed only brief major league careers. The pitching staff did see the addition of diminutive righthander Elroy Face, who threw a tantalizing forkball as both a starter and reliever, while Frank Thomas was able to replace Kiner's power with 30 homers and 102 RBI. The 1954 squad lost over 100 games for the third consecutive season, though Thomas continued to hit the long ball and was joined in the lineup by rookie first baseman/outfielder Bob Skinner.

Even without Branch Rickey the Dodgers still had one of the deepest farm systems in the game. At the 1954 Winter Meetings the Pirates tapped into that system, drafting a 20-year-old outfielder from Puerto Rico named Roberto Clemente. He moved right into Pittsburgh's starting lineup and batted .255, displaying gap power and an ability to hit the ball to all fields. He also brought speed, great defensive skills and an incredible throwing arm to spacious Forbes Field. He didn't prevent another last-place finish, but for the first time since 1951 the Pirates did not lose 100 games. It was not enough to save Haney's job, however, and former Phillie and Dodger infielder and catcher Bobby Bragan took the helm. It was not Branch Rickey, though, who made the hire; frustrated by the failure of his five-year plan, Rickey gave up day-to-day control of the team three weeks after the end of the 1955 World Series. His assistant, Joe L. Brown — son of comedian and actor Joe E. Brown — became general manager.

While his dad may have known what was funny, the younger Brown knew that his Pirates weren't. He also knew talent when he saw it. The 1955 Rookie of the Year in the National League had been the Cardinals' Bill Virdon. When the bespectacled outfielder got off to a bad start the following spring, St. Louis unexpectedly gave up on him and Brown pounced, trading Del Greco (and pitcher Dick Littlefield) for him. Virdon wound up batting well over .300 in a Pirate uniform and finishing second in the NL batting race behind Hank Aaron. (Third on the list, by the way, was Roberto Clemente.) Another new addition was second baseman Bill Mazeroski, a steady fielder who was brilliant at turning the double play and who also added another good righthanded bat to the lineup. With three pitchers winning in double-figures for the first time since 1949 (including Face, who was now pitching almost exclusively out of the bullpen), the team finally escaped the cellar.

But 1957 proved to be a disappointment. Brown had expected the improvement to continue, but the team slid back to last place instead. With the team 31 games under .500 and on a pace to win only 54 games, Bobby Bragan was fired and replaced by one of his coaches, Danny Murtaugh. A former major league infielder who scrapped his way through seven full seasons and parts of two others, the Pennsylvania native changed the clubhouse atmosphere and the athletes responded, playing .500 ball the rest of the way to tie for seventh with the Cubs. Murtaugh proved to be the right man for the Pirates: he wound up managing over 2,000 games for Pittsburgh, the only team he ever led.

Not much was expected of the 1958 Pirates and, for the first half of the season, not much was delivered. While four members of the team were selected for the All-Star Game (Friend, Mazeroski, Skinner and Thomas), the Bucs were still dragging around near the bottom of the league. But shortly after the annual break, the club caught fire, triggered, in part, by Dick Stuart's promotion from the minor leagues. Stuart, a muscular righthanded first baseman, had electrified baseball two years before when he slugged 66 homers while playing at Lincoln in the Western League. In 67 second-half games in Pittsburgh he banged out 16 home runs and drove home 48. Perhaps, too, it was the leadership exuded by Groat, who had been named team captain by Murtaugh. Or perhaps it was the growing maturity of the young players who had suffered through so many losing seasons. Most likely it was a combination of all those factors, but it translated into a magnificent second half. Pittsburgh actually crept to within three games of the defending world champion Milwaukee Braves — managed by Fred Haney — before running out of gas in late September. However, their second-place finish was the franchise's best since 1944.

Sensing that the young team needed a few veterans to push it over the top, Brown swung a major off-season deal, sending Frank Thomas to Cincinnati for pitcher Harvey Haddix, catcher Smoky Burgess and third baseman Don Hoak. Haddix was a small lefthander who had won 20 games for the Cardinals in 1953. Burgess, a lefthanded-hitting catcher with some power, would be joining his fourth major league club. And Hoak, who came to the big leagues with the Dodgers, brought a fiery personality as well as a steady bat and glove at third base.

Attention was focused on Pittsburgh in 1959, but not because they made a real dash for the pennant. Compared to the teams that had inhabited Forbes Field earlier in the decade there was great improvement, but since much was expected of this club after their second-half charge the year before, there was general disappointment with the season. The Pirates never seemed to gain any momentum as they watched the Giants, Dodgers and Braves fight it out in a

National League race that had to be decided by a playoff, with the Dodgers, now in Los Angeles, winning two straight from Milwaukee to advance to a World Series triumph. The Pirates' 78–76 record left them in fourth place. The attention they drew, though, was because of two pitchers. Elroy Face established himself as unquestionably the top relief pitcher in the league by winning 17 consecutive games — 22 in a row going back to 1958 — and not suffering a defeat until September. His final record was 18–1, and his winning percentage of .947 is still baseball's all-time best. He also saved ten games. The other pitcher of note was newcomer Harvey Haddix. He won 12 games for the Bucs, but it was a game he lost that is still remembered. On May 26, playing against the Braves in Milwaukee, Haddix pitched a perfect game for 12 innings. Unfortunately, the Pirates could not score against Lew Burdette, and despite retiring all 36 batters he had faced, Haddix found the game still tied as he went out for the 13th inning. If "The Kitten" didn't have triskaidekaphobia before that night he could be pardoned for developing it afterwards, as the 13th proved to be his undoing. Don Hoak's throwing error gave the Braves their first baserunner of the night. After a sacrifice bunt, Hank Aaron was intentionally walked to set up the double play, but big first baseman Joe Adcock homered to end the game. Only one run scored, however, as a jubilant Adcock passed Aaron on the bases. No matter, the Braves still won and Haddix, in defeat, etched his name indelibly into baseball history.

The Pirates made no major changes in the off-season, and as a result little attention was paid to them in the preseason rankings. The Pirates were consigned to fourth place as the baseball writers favored the young and exciting San Francisco Giants. The Bucs split their first six games, and then did something they could never seem to do in 1959: they went on a winning streak. Their nine-game spurt was the most by the franchise since 1944, their 12–3 mark was the best since the 1938 club, and most importantly they jumped into the National League lead. The month of May saw the Pirates and Giants take turns at the top until Joe Brown made his move, sending minor league players to St. Louis for veteran lefty Wilmer "Vinegar Bend" Mizell. Having already won 69 games in the major leagues, Mizell brought balance to the starting rotation that included fellow southpaw Haddix and righties Vern Law and Bob Friend. This quartet would start 80 percent of the team's games in 1960.

After acquiring Mizell the Bucs went on a six-game win streak that put them back into first place. They would only relinquish it once over the next four months.

The race, however, was far from a cakewalk. At the All-Star break only nine games separated the first five teams in the league, with only the Reds, Phillies and Cubs not thinking about a second-half pennant battle. And when the Pirates lost seven of their first eleven games following the break, they saw their old nemesis, the Milwaukee Braves, move into first. But, as Dick Groat has written, this was a team of "25 Professionals," with everyone contributing to victories and a different hero emerging every day. Never was this more evident than in September. Team leader Groat, who had more hits than anyone else in the league and was battling for the batting title, had his wrist broken by a Lew Burdette pitch in the first week of the season's final month. With their captain out of action some expected the Pirates to fold, but Groat's replacement, Dick Schofield, led the final spurt to victory. A lifetime .227 hitter, Schofield batted over .400 in September as the Bucs pulled away from the Braves and Cardinals.

These 1960 Pirates won 23 games in their final at-bat, 12 of them when they were just one out away from defeat. Groat came back for the last three games of the season to win the batting crown with a .325 average; later he would be voted the National League's Most Valuable Player. Clemente batted over .300 for the second time in his career; except for a .291 in 1968, he would never fail to reach that magic mark for the rest of his Hall of Fame career, leading the league four times and winning his own MVP Award in 1966. While no Pirate drove in 100 runs, six players drove in at least 50 as Pittsburgh led the league in runs scored with 734. On the mound the Big Four dominated, led by Vern Law's 20–9 mark, which earned him the Cy Young Award. Bob Friend won 18, Haddix won 11 and Mizell was 13–5 in a Pirate uniform, while Face chipped in with ten victories and 24 saves.

The city of Pittsburgh celebrated the team's first flag in 33 years, but also felt some caution heading into the World Series. The last time they had appeared in the Fall Classic, 1927, their opponents were the New York Yankees, the "Murderers' Row" of Ruth and Gehrig. And with the Bambino clouting two home runs and driving home seven, the Yankees had swept the Pirates aside in four games, outscoring them by a 23–10 margin. Now, these many years later, the Pirates were back, and their opponents were none other than the New York Yankees, with a modern-day home run duo of Mickey Mantle and Roger Maris.

It is a common fallacy that the 1960 Yankees were a dominant club; they were not. They certainly could hit the long ball, clouting a league-record 193 home runs, and they scored 746 runs, best in the AL. But they had only one .300 hitter, first baseman Bill Skowron, and no speed aside from Mantle. Their pitchers were good enough, collectively, to tie Baltimore for the best team ERA with a 3.52 (Pittsburgh, by the way, led the NL with a 3.49) and to throw a league-leading 16 shutouts, but individually they were not very impressive, and 11 different pitchers started games that season for manager Casey Stengel. It had taken a 15-game winning streak in September to separate the Yankees from the Orioles and White Sox and carry them into the Fall Classic.

Nevertheless, it seemed to be Yankee mystique against Pirate magic as the World Series began in the Steel City. And when Roger Maris — who had clouted 39 home runs and drove in a league-leading 112 runs during the regular season on his way to the MVP Award — hit a home run in his first World Series at-bat, it seemed as if 1927 would be reprised. But the Bucs scored three in their half of the first, knocking out Art Ditmar, and Bill Mazeroski hit a two-run homer off Jim Coates to give the Pirates a solid lead. When the Yankees put two men on in the eighth, Face relieved Law and left them stranded. This proved to be significant as Elston Howard pinch hit a two-run homer in the ninth, but with the tying run at the plate Face threw a double-play ball to end the game in Pittsburgh's favor, 6–4, even though the Yankees outhit them, 13–8.

The next two games, however, were more on the order of what people had been expecting. With Mickey Mantle hitting two colossal home runs, the Yanks pounded six Pirate pitchers for 19 hits in a 16–3 runaway. One of Mantle's shots was estimated at having traveled 475 feet as he became the first righthanded batter to clear center field in Forbes Field. Then, with the Series relocating to Yankee Stadium, the Bombers did it again, bombarding another half-dozen hurlers in a 10–0 rout. Neither Mizell nor late-season pickup Clem Labine (who, as a Dodger, had won games against New York in both the 1955 and 1956 World Series) could get out of the first inning as the Yankees scored six times, four on a shocking grand slam by second baseman Bobby Richardson, who had hit only three homers in his major league career. This was more than enough for Whitey Ford, who surrendered just four hits, but the Yanks came back with four more in the fourth inning, as Mantle hit another 400-foot homer and Richardson delivered a bases-loaded single. His six runs batted in for the game is still a World Series record.

Having given up 30 runs and 48 hits in the first three games, it would have been easy for the Pirates to raise the flag and surrender. But the true character of this team, and the reason they are included in this volume, was just coming to the fore. Vern Law was given the task of stanching the bleeding but it looked like another massacre in the making as New York loaded the bases in the very first inning. But Law induced Yogi Berra to hit into a double play, ending the early threat. Then in the fifth inning, trailing 1–0, Pittsburgh broke through against young Ralph Terry. With two men on base and two out, Law cracked a double, tying the game, and Virdon singled to center, scoring two more. The Yankees drew to within one in the seventh and, with two men on, seemed poised to tie or go ahead. Murtaugh summoned Face, and the first man he saw, outfielder Bob Cerv, drove a pitch over 400 feet, but this time it would not leave the ballpark. Center fielder Virdon made a spectacular catch, probably preventing two runs from scoring. The Pirates won, 3–2, knotting up the Series at two games apiece.

Art Ditmar, knocked out in the first inning of the first game, only lasted into the second inning in Game Five, although a Yankee miscue did not help his cause. Usually sure-handed infielder Gil McDougald, playing third base, dropped an easy throw to allow one run to score, and then Mazeroski pounced on the mistake, driving in two more runs with a double. Haddix stymied the Yankees on just three hits through six, but when two men singled in the seventh in came Face, who ended the threat, then pitched scoreless ball in the eighth and ninth. Inexplicably, despite the two pastings, the Pirates went back to Pittsburgh just one victory away from the world championship.

Yankee bats awoke again in Game Six, and Murtaugh, for the third time in the Series, called on six pitchers in one game as New York evened things with a 12–0 win. Ford tossed his second straight shutout, Richardson drove in three more runs, and this World Series came down to one game, winner take all.

Had the seventh game been some conventional affair, the Series would still have been rated by historians as one of the better Fall Classics. But when you add the wild nature of that final contest to what had already transpired, you get a Series for the ages, perhaps the most memorable one ever played.

Bob Turley started for the Yankees but was knocked out in the second inning. Vern Law drew his third starting assignment for Pittsburgh and took a 4–1 lead into the sixth inning, but then he wilted. Face came on for the fourth time but the long season may have finally caught up with him. He gave up a run-scoring single to Mantle and then a three-run homer to Berra; in the eighth, the Yanks nicked him for two more runs and a 7–4 lead.

At the beginning of this chapter Branch Rickey was noted as saying, "Luck is the residue of design," and it was mentioned that the 1960 Pirates needed "a dash of luck"; it came in the bottom of the eighth inning. Veteran lefty Bobby Shantz had been in since the third and had kept the Yankees in the game, frustrating the Pirates with his off-speed pitches. He gave up only his second hit to a pinch hitter for Face leading off the eighth, but then induced Bill Virdon to hit a perfect double-play ball to short. Instead of bringing the Buccos to within four outs of elimination, however, the ball hit a rock and struck Yankee shortstop Tony Kubek in the throat. Kubek had to leave the game and Pittsburgh had two men on and no one out. Groat singled in a run, chasing Shantz, but then Jim Coates retired the next two batters and seemed to be out of the inning when Clemente hit a grounder to first. Coates, though, was slow getting to the bag, Clemente beat the throw, and another run scored, reducing the Yankee margin to 7–6.

The next batter was Hal Smith. Smith was a journeyman catcher — five teams in ten years — who had served as the righthanded complement to the lefty-swinging Smoky Burgess. This two-headed catching platoon had served Danny Murtaugh well during the season, collecting 18 home runs and driving home 84 runs, and Smith had entered the game after Shantz had become the pitcher. But now he was facing a righty in Coates, which should have given the Yankees the advantage. Not this time: Smith blasted a long three-run homer, "probably the most forgotten home run in World Series history," and suddenly the Pirates were on the verge of victory.

But nothing would come easy in this game. Bob Friend, pounded by New York in the second and sixth games, came on in relief, gave up hits to the first two men he faced, and was immediately removed for Haddix. After Maris went out Mantle singled for a run, putting men on first and third with just one out.

Berra then hit a sharp grounder to the right side. Pirate first baseman Rocky Nelson stepped on the bag, retiring Berra, then looked to get Mantle going into second. But the Yankee Hall of Famer alertly realized that he would never be able to beat a throw to second, and by stepping on the bag Nelson had eliminated the force play, giving Mantle possession of first. So The Mick dove back behind Nelson, avoiding the swipe tag and allowing the tying run to score.

After Smith's home run Ralph Terry had come on to get the third out, and he went out there for the ninth inning. Bill Mazeroski was the leadoff batter. Terry's first pitch was called a ball. Terry's second pitch was hit to left; Yogi Berra went back as far as he could and then just watched as the ball cleared the wall for a home run. With startling suddenness the game and the Series was over, and Pittsburgh was the improbable winner, 10–9. Forbes Field went berserk, with fans spilling out onto the field and escorting a jubilant Mazeroski around the bases. The city of Pittsburgh went wild, partying for days in a revelry that rivaled the end of World War II. And the baseball world marveled at what the Pirates had wrought.

The numbers, in this case, don't tell the true story. The Yankees batted a collective .338 against Pittsburgh pitching, scoring 55 runs on 91 hits, 27 of them for extra bases (including ten home runs), and 142 total bases — all World Series marks that still stand. The Pirates scored 27 runs on 60 hits, and had 15 extra-base hits. The Bucs hit just four homers in the Series, three of them coming in that final game. Pittsburgh's team ERA was an astounding 7.11, and in five of the seven games they allowed the Yankees ten or more hits. If you simply look at these statistics you would assume that New York had destroyed Pittsburgh, just as they had done in 1927. But the Pirates won because, in the crucial Games Four and Five, their hitters were the ones who delivered in clutch situations. The Pirates took advantage of many of their opportunities in this Series, much like a boxer who is knocked down several times but keeps getting back up, scores with his jab and wins the fight on points. Battered and bloodied, the Pittsburgh Pirates won baseball's version of the heavyweight championship of the world.

The Pirates, unfortunately, could not duplicate their miracle season in 1961. Vern Law hurt his arm early in the year and won only three games, while Vinegar Bend Mizell won just seven and would retire a year later. Roy Face and Bob Friend both had off-seasons, as did Dick Groat, whose average dropped 50 points. The Pirates fell to sixth, four games under .500. Although they rebounded in 1962 to win 93 games, management started to break up the Bucs, many of whom were now well beyond thirty. Throughout the rest of the 1960s the Pirates seemed to follow a good year with a bad year; they nearly won the pennant in 1966 but were not factors in the race again until 1970. By then only Clemente, Mazeroski and Murtaugh (who had twice tried to retire and twice been brought back) were left as reminders of 1960 and the unforgettable World Series that put an exclamation point on the Pirates' incredible season.

1960–64
New York Yankees

The headlines told the shocking story to a disbelieving public: the New York Yankees were in last place in the American League. It was late May in 1959 and few could remember the last time this had happened. *Last place!* This was essentially the same Yankee squad that had won the World Series just seven months earlier, the Bombers of Mickey Mantle, Yogi Berra and Whitey Ford. People wondered if they were getting old, or if perhaps too many late-night parties had finally caught up to them. There were whispers that manager Casey Stengel, approaching age 69, had run out of magic tricks at last. Or perhaps supernatural forces were at work, because what else would explain why the New York Yankees were in *last place*?

The answer turned out to be two-fold: other teams in the league, especially the Chicago White Sox, had improved themselves; and the Yankees, after having won four straight pennants and nine of the previous ten, were simply having a bad year. That same month the Yankees acquired versatile Hector Lopez and pitcher Ralph Terry from Kansas City and began a slow climb back to respectability, eventually finishing a distant third behind Chicago and Cleveland. However, their 79–75 record was the franchise's poorest mark since 1925.

Stengel was willing to forgive the poor years, but he also knew that some changes needed to be made. Lopez had proven to be a tough hitter but more suited to the outfield than third base, which was the Yankees' most pressing need. Berra and right fielder Hank Bauer were both well past 30 and showing definite signs of slowing down. Out in the bullpen, Ryne Duren threw the ball as hard as anyone in baseball, but often had no idea where it was headed; years later he admitted that his control problems were due to alcoholism.

Two weeks before Christmas New York swung a deal with Kansas City, their favorite trading partners in the 1950s. Bauer, starting left fielder Norm Siebern and two others went to the Athletics in exchange for three players, the most notable being outfielder Roger Maris. The quiet Midwesterner was a left-handed pull hitter, which meant he could take advantage of Yankee Stadium's short right field fence. He was also, however, an excellent baserunner and an outstanding outfielder with a terrific arm. The Cleveland Indians had probably not recognized what they had in Maris, and while the A's had not been anxious to give him up he was, as far as the Yankees were concerned, the key to the deal. The Yankees knew that Maris was, in fact, a complete ballplayer who was not flashy but did everything well.

Maris moved into right field and Lopez took over in left. Third base was shared more or less by veteran Gil McDougald — one of Stengel's favorite players because he was equally at home at second, third or short and was always productive at the plate — and young Clete Boyer. The younger brother of Cardinal star Ken, also a third baseman, Clete had been in the big leagues for parts of four seasons but had not even played 200 games. Stengel recognized that Boyer was not a great hitter (only once in his career would he bat higher than .251), but he was a magnificent fielder with a tremendous arm. Behind the plate Stengel went more and more with Elston Howard, although Berra, still dangerous with the bat, caught a couple of games a week and also played some in left field. Duren and diminutive southpaw Bobby Shantz continued to do an adequate job out of the bullpen, though neither could dominate a game the way Joe Page had done for Stengel a decade earlier.

Once again New York got off to a slow start, as the White Sox set out to defend their crown. Their nearest pursuers in the early going were the Baltimore Orioles, the former St. Louis Browns franchise which had never finished above .500 since moving east following the 1953 season. Managed by Paul Richards, the Orioles' starting lineup had just one player over the age of 30, and a starting rotation made up of three 21 year olds and one 22 year old. Then in June the Yankees caught fire, winning 23 games to move into first place. The race remained close for the next three months.

Shortly after the All-Star break General Manager George Weiss made the kind of move he was noted for, purchasing veteran pitcher Luis Arroyo from Cincinnati's Jersey City farm team in the International League. The 33-year-old southpaw had won 11 games as a Cardinal rookie but had since fallen on hard times. Weiss and Stengel thought that, if he could control his screwball, he could help out in the bullpen.

The Yankees and Orioles faced each other in Baltimore at the beginning of September and the Baby Birds reached their peak, sweeping the three-game series in convincing fashion. The Bombers couldn't score a run until late in the third game and left Maryland in second place. Two weeks later they met again, this time in New York and this time for four games, with the Yankees leading Baltimore by two percentage points and Chicago by two games. New York swept the series, launching them on a 15-game win streak that took them to the end of the season and broke open the pennant race. It was Stengel's tenth pennant in his 12 years in the Bronx.

The Yankees did it primarily with the long ball. Maris had a terrific year, hitting 39 home runs and driving in 112, which led the league and enabled him to win the Most Valuable Player Award, just edging Mantle and his league-leading 40 homers. First baseman Bill Skowron had 26 circuit clouts and drove home 91, while the team as a whole set a new American League record with their 193 home runs. Righthanders Art Ditmar and Jim Coates had career years, winning 15 and 13 games, respectively, while Whitey Ford, battling shoulder ailments, had one of his poorer seasons, logging just 12 victories. The real pitching star was Arroyo, who gave the entire pitching staff a boost with his seven saves and five wins in the season's final nine weeks.

The 1960 World Series is detailed in the previous chapter on the Pittsburgh Pirates, so all the particulars won't be repeated here, but what follows is an explanation of just why the Yankees lost.

No one can say that New York didn't hit against Pittsburgh: they batted .338, scored 55 runs on 91 hits, and hit ten home runs. They won three games by football-like scores, and five times they had ten or more hits in a game. But when they weren't treating Pirate hurlers like pitching machines, they were having trouble delivering in the clutch, and for that reason were defeated in seven games. In the opening game they outhit Pittsburgh by a 13–8 margin, but couldn't score after Lopez and Maris opened the eighth inning with hits, and didn't sustain a ninth-inning rally that brought the potential tying run to the plate. In Game Four they loaded the bases against Pirate ace Vern Law in the first inning but didn't score. They also failed to tie the game in the seventh with two on and one out, though a spectacular catch by center fielder Bill Virdon proved to be the key play in that game. And the next day, trailing 4–2, New York put two men on in the seventh inning and again failed to score.

Stengel, too, failed in a pivotal situation. In the seventh and final game the Yankees held a 5–4 lead going into the eighth inning, and were able to add two runs against the Pirates' tired bullpen ace Elroy Face. With runners on second and third and two out, pitcher Bobby Shantz was due to bat. Shantz had pitched very well, allowing just one hit in five innings, but this was a perfect opportunity to try and put the game out of reach. For some reason Stengel elected not to send up a pinch hitter, Shantz made the third out, and the Bucs went on to win the wildest game of the wildest World Series ever.

Five days later the Yankees fired Stengel. They tried to whitewash it and make it seem as if he had resigned or retired of his own accord, but Stengel himself told reporters gathered at the news conference, "They have paid me off in full and told me my services are not desired any longer by this club." Two weeks later Weiss was dismissed after 28 years with the organization as New York decided that their top management needed to get younger. Roy Hamey replaced Weiss, and Stengel's chief lieutenant, Ralph Houk, accepted the assignment of replacing the legend.

Houk had an undistinguished playing career, appearing in only 91 games over eight years as a reserve catcher, which included two World Series at-bats. But he was a student of the game, a successful minor league manager who was promoted to the Bronx to be one of Stengel's coaches and, ultimately, his successor. A major during World War II, Houk was tough and firm but a good leader who never criticized his men in public. He had learned a lot under the Old Professor, but brought his own ideas to his first major league managerial position.

Aside from Houk and Hamey New York had not made any major changes, but baseball as a whole had undergone a considerable facelift. Attempting to prevent Branch Rickey's Continental League from going into prime locations and becoming a third major league — and always wary that their precarious antitrust exemption could be snatched away by Congress — baseball approved an aggressive expansion program following the 1960 season. In the American League, Calvin Griffith and his Washington Senators were permitted to move to the Minneapolis–St. Paul area and become the Minnesota Twins, and brand new teams were added in Washington, D.C., and Los Angeles, all effective immediately. With a ten-team league, the schedule would be increased from 154 games to 162. The National League would also add two teams, in New York and Houston, but not until 1962. The existing clubs would be allowed to protect a cadre of players and the new teams would then be allowed to select those players who had not been safeguarded. Needless to say, the talent pool available to the new clubs was pretty slim, consisting primarily of third-string players, past-their-prime veterans and minor leaguers. In their first year of operation the new Senators lost 100 games and the Los Angeles Angels lost 91.

Also lost that season were baseballs, as American League hitters blasted home runs as never before. Over the previous five years teams in the junior circuit had averaged 133 round-trippers per season, but in 1961 they averaged 153, a 15 percent increase. Scoring as a whole was up by only 9 percent, which meant that the home run total was pronounced and therefore more dramatic, a story that demanded media attention. And the focal point for these inquiring minds was New York, as the Yankees were leading the assault on the bleacher seats, particularly Roger Maris and Mickey Mantle. Batting third and fourth in the order, they were driving baseballs out of ballparks at a record clip. Maris hit 12 homers in the first two months of the season, then he really found the range in June, belting 15 in that month alone. That was when newspapers began keeping track of the "home run race," as they called it, comparing the pace of Maris and Mantle with that of Babe Ruth when he set the single-season standard of 60 homers in 1927.

Fans who were solely enthralled by homer heroics were missing a pretty good pennant race. The Detroit Tigers had been primarily a .500 club since 1955, never challenging the Yankees for AL supremacy. The previous year they had made headlines when they actually traded managers, swapping Jimmy Dykes to Cleveland for Joe Gordon. The bizarre deal didn't help either team in the standings, especially Detroit, which finished in sixth place, 12 games under .500 (and five games behind Cleveland). In the off-season they brought in yet another manager, Bob Scheffing, who made a commitment to youth, starting rookies at both second and third, and using two more rookies in platoons at shortstop and catcher. He brought in an experienced center fielder from Milwaukee, Bill Bruton, and reaped the benefit of monster years from first baseman Norm Cash, outfielder Rocky Colavito, and pitcher Frank Lary. The result was a team that battled the Yankees right into September, when the two teams opened the month with a three-game showdown in the Bronx. Only one-and-a-half games separated them on Friday afternoon, but by Sunday night New York had a four-

and-a-half-game bulge after sweeping the series. As they had done the year before, the Yankees then blew the race apart, winning 13 straight while Detroit dropped eight in a row to end their pennant hopes, although they did finish the year with 101 wins, matching the previous franchise record.

With a World Series appearance assured, the only real contest in the American League, then, was the Maris-Mantle onslaught on Ruth's record. By the end of July they had matched their home run totals of 1960, and by hitting a pair in the Sunday game against the Tigers, Mantle joined Maris in the 50-homer club. The two were also combating time as well as opposing pitchers since Ford Frick, the commissioner of baseball, had ruled that any record broken after the 154th game of the year would go into the books with an asterisk to show that it was accomplished in a slightly longer season. A great stretch run didn't materialize, however, as Mantle was forced from the lineup with an abscessed hip. This left Maris alone with Ruth's ghost and the ever-present reporters, who hounded him day and night. Here he was, a small-town man, chasing the biggest legend in sports history, in the media capital of the world. What should have been the most thrilling time of his life turned into a personal nightmare.

The night the Yankees clinched the pennant was also the last game Maris could "officially" catch or surpass Ruth under Frick's edict, and he did hit a homer, number 59, but no more until a few days later, when he became the second man in major league history to reach 60. Then, on the final day of the season, he belted his 61st of the year, which also gave New York their 109th win for 1961. Roger Maris eclipsed Babe Ruth's 34-year-old record for home runs in a season, and it was his mark that would be assaulted 37 years later by Mark McGwire and Sammy Sosa in another two-man battle.

Maris led the league in runs batted in and total bases, Mantle led in slugging percentage and walks, and the two tied for the lead in runs scored while combining for 115 homers. The 1961 Yankees hit 240 home runs as a team, 47 more than the record they had set just the year before and 19 more than the NL high of 221. Six players had 20 or more homers, including Johnny Blanchard, a part-time catcher and outfielder and Houk's primary late-inning pinch hitter. Four other players in the league topped 40 homers; in contrast, the National League had just two.

This team was not just about power, however. Houk had instituted a regular four-man pitching rotation and Whitey Ford thrived as never before, winning 25 games and the Cy Young Award. Ralph Terry blossomed, winning 16 games, and two youngsters, sophomore Bill Stafford and freshman Rollie Sheldon, combined for another 25. Two other pitchers won in double figures for New York: Jim Coates, who was used as both a starter and reliever, and Luis Arroyo, who won 15 and saved a league-leading 29. Their team ERA of 3.46 was second-best in the league behind Baltimore. And the defense took a back seat to no one, committing just 124 errors and turning 180 double plays. The infield of first baseman Bill Skowron, second baseman Bobby Richardson, short-stop Tony Kubek and third baseman Clete Boyer was perhaps the best in the club's history. Elston Howard, now the full-time catcher, was one of the three best in the league, and Mantle and Maris could both catch and throw the ball about as well as they could hit it.

For the second straight year the National League had an unexpected pennant winner, the Cincinnati Reds. Sixth-place finishers in 1960, the Reds retooled their infield and made an off-season trade for righthanded pitcher Joey Jay, who was only a spot starter in Milwaukee but became the Reds' ace, winning 21 games. Jim O'Toole and Bob Purkey gave manager Fred Hutchinson two more solid starters, and he also had a fine bullpen tandem in righty Jim Brosnan and southpaw Bill Henry. The offense revolved around Frank Robinson, the league's Most Valuable Player with 37 homers and 124 RBI, and Vada Pinson, who batted .343 and led the league with 208 hits.

The World Series opened in New York. Whitey Ford was brilliant, limiting Cincinnati to just two singles. O'Toole pitched well for the Reds, but two of his serves left the yard (courtesy of Howard and Skowron), and the Yankees won, 2–0. But the next day Jay held the Bombers to only four hits in a 6–2 triumph, which allowed the Reds to go back to old Crosley Field with the Series tied. Game Three then proved to be the key match. Purkey and Stafford were both at their best but the Reds held the edge after six, 1–0, as the Yankees were only able to manage one hit. The two teams swapped runs in the seventh, and then the Bombers unleashed their power: Blanchard hit a pinch-homer to tie the game in the eighth, and Maris ripped his only home run of the Series in the ninth. Arroyo, meanwhile, blanked the Reds over the last two innings, and the Yankees had the lead.

For all intents and purposes, the Series was settled. Ford was brilliant again in Game Four, holding the Reds scoreless until he had to be removed in the sixth due to an ankle injury. Coates came in and completed the 7–0 triumph. Ford's 14 consecutive shutout innings, on top of the pair of whitewashings he had administered to Pittsburgh the year before, gave him a new World Series record of 32 consecutive scoreless frames. The old standard had been set by Babe Ruth, going back to the 1916 and 1918 World Series. Having had his home run record eclipsed just the week before, 1961 proved to be a rough year for the Bambino, deceased for 13 years. Houk needed to use his bench in Game Five. Mantle had already missed most of the Series due to his abscess, and Berra was unable to play this day, but Blanchard and Lopez were more than capable fill-ins. Both hit home runs while Lopez also contributed a triple and five RBI as the Yankees ripped Jay, Purkey and six other Cincinnati pitchers for a pair of five-run innings in a 13–5 cakewalk. The five-game Series was the shortest since 1954, and it made Ralph Houk only the third manager in history to win the World Series in his first year on the job.

While home run production rose slightly in 1962, the total number of runs scored actually decreased a bit, an indication that things were returning to normal in the baseball world. The Yankees' key decision in the spring centered around the shortstop position. Regular Tony Kubek had to do a six-month stint in the military, so rookies Tom Tresh and Phil Linz battled it out in training camp, with the switch-hitting Tresh — son of a former major league catcher — the ultimate winner. Otherwise the team was set.

The Cleveland Indians seemed to be the Bombers' prime threat that year. Under new manager Mel McGaha (who took over for the traded Jimmy Dykes), the Tribe had nine players who would reach double digits in home runs for the year. When they swept the Yankees in a four-game series in June, they seemed to be for real, but their bubble burst after the All-Star break as they lost 19 of their first 24 games and sank to sixth place. New York, meanwhile, played their best ball during the same stretch to take a comfortable lead over the Minnesota Twins and the second-year Los Angeles Angels. Those two surprising contenders were able to get to within two games in late August but never could catch up, and the Yankees coasted to the pennant by five games.

There was no home run chase this year but the team could still dent the plate, scoring just ten fewer runs than they had the year before. Maris had a fine year, hitting 33 homers and driving home 100, but he ceded the Most Valuable Player Award to Mantle, who, despite missing nearly 40 games due to leg injuries, batted .321 (second in the league), with 30 home runs. Tresh was the Rookie of the Year, partly due to his .286 average with 20 homers and 93 RBI, but primarily because, when Kubek returned from the military in August, he had been able to move to left field, and played the position as if he had been there all his life. Bobby Richardson batted .302 and collected 209 hits, the most by a Yankee since Red Rolfe in 1939. New York needed the offense because the pitching was not nearly as strong as it had been the year before. Ralph Terry turned in the only 20-win season of his career, going 23–12, while Ford contributed 17 victories and Stafford had another 14. But Houk never could find a reliable fourth or fifth starter, and his pitching woes were compounded by an arm injury suffered by Arroyo, which limited him to just one win and seven saves. The staff was rescued by lefthander Marshall Bridges, who had pitched in only a handful of games for Cincinnati the year before. Picked up in a minor deal during the off-season, Bridges stepped up when Arroyo went down and saved 18 games.

The National League had produced a spectacular pennant race in 1962, with the Reds, Dodgers, Pirates and Giants all involved. Los Angeles seemed to have it won with a week to go, but the Giants caught them on the final day of the regular season to force a playoff. In the third and final game, the Dodgers held the lead going into the ninth but, in an eerie reminiscence of their 1951 playoff, gave up four runs in the ninth to let San Francisco sneak into the World Series.

The Giants, managed by Alvin Dark, could hit: Willie Mays, Orlando

Cepeda and Willie McCovey, all future Hall of Famers, graced their lineup. They also got great production from outfielders Felipe Alou and Harvey Kuenn, third baseman Jim Davenport, and the catching tandem of Tom Haller and Ed Bailey. This group led the league in average, hits, runs and home runs. But they also featured a brilliant starting quartet: Jack Sanford, Juan Marichal (also a future Hall of Famer), Billy Pierce and Billy O'Dell were responsible for 77 of the Giants' 103 victories. They would be formidable opponents for the Yankees, and in fact the two teams played an excellent, well-balanced World Series.

Ford finally gave up a postseason run, ending his streak just shy of 34 innings, but otherwise held the Giants in check in winning the opener, but then Sanford blanked the Yankees on just three hits. Terry gave up only six hits but did surrender two runs, which was more than enough to tie the Series. Stafford and Pierce matched zeros for six innings in Game Three before Maris drove in two runs and later scored a third in the seventh inning. This was enough to offset Bailey's two-out, two-run ninth inning homer, and the Yankees took the lead. The fourth game was tied after six, but the Giants loaded the bases against Coates and Bridges. Second baseman Chuck Hiller, who had hit just three home runs all season, then became the first National Leaguer to hit a grand slam in World Series play, tying the Series once again. The winning pitcher in this game, by the way, was reliever Don Larsen — precisely six years to the day after he had pitched his famous perfect game against the Brooklyn Dodgers. Terry and Sanford then hooked up once more and again they dominated, but in the eighth Kubek and Richardson singled and Tresh followed with a three-run homer to move New York to within a game of the title.

It was raining in San Francisco, and everyone had to sit around for three days waiting for it to stop; since there had also been a one-day rain delay in New York, this became the soggiest Series on record. When play finally resumed the Giants pounded Ford in the fourth and fifth innings, and Pierce held the Yanks to just three hits as San Francisco forced a seventh game. It proved to be a memorable contest, as Terry and Sanford, both starting for the third time, were simply overpowering. The Yankees scored a run in the fifth when they loaded the bases and Kubek grounded into a double play. Meanwhile, no Giant reached base until the sixth inning, and going into the ninth they had solved Terry for just two hits. Felipe Alou's younger brother, Matty, led off with a bunt single as a pinch hitter. Terry retired the next two hitters, but then Willie Mays sliced a ball down the right field line. Maris made a great play, first in getting to the ball quickly and then in rifling it into the infield, holding the speedy Alou at third. This brought up the always-dangerous McCovey, and Terry chose to pitch to him rather than to Cepeda, who was on deck. McCovey ripped a vicious line drive, but right at Richardson, who snared it to end the game and the Giants' hopes. New York, which batted just .199 as a team, thus made Ralph Houk the only manager in history to win the World Series in his first two years at the helm.

The Yankees sent Skowron to the Dodgers in the winter to open up first base for a 22-year-old Brooklyn native, Joe Pepitone, but otherwise made no other changes. During the season, however, Houk found himself juggling the lineup much like Stengel used to do. A bad back and other ailments limited Maris to 90 games, and a broken foot in early June restricted Mantle to a career-low 65 games, many of them as just a pinch hitter. Maris and Mantle appeared together only 30 times, and combined for only 38 home runs and 88 RBI. As a result, Lopez, Blanchard and Linz saw a lot of action and drove in over 100 runs. Elston Howard produced an MVP season as he hit 28 homers and drove home 85, while Pepitone justified the Yankees' faith in him with 27 round-trippers and a team-leading 89 RBI. In addition, the pitching was much better than it had been the previous year. Ford led the league with his 24 wins, and young Jim Bouton, in only his second season, won 21. Terry won 17 and rookie left-hander Al Downing, recalled from Triple-A in June, was a lifesaver with his 13 triumphs. Neither Arroyo nor Bridges could repeat their previous successes out of the bullpen, but 25-year-old Hal Reniff took control of the late innings, saving 18. An early-season deal brought tall southpaw Steve Hamilton to the club, and he also proved to be valuable in the bullpen.

The only semblance of a pennant race took place in the first half. Several teams took turns at the top of the American League, with the White Sox the most persistent suitors. As June was winding down, Chicago drew to within two percentage points of the Bombers, but that would prove to be their high-water mark. The Yankees edged away, took a five-game lead into the All-Star break, and kept right on going in the second half, finishing the season with 104 wins and a 10½-game bulge over Chicago.

After losing the playoff to the Giants the year before, the Dodgers were determined to conquer the National League in 1963, and they succeeded after beating back a late-season challenge from the St. Louis Cardinals. Los Angeles won games primarily with pitching, speed and defense; five NL teams scored more runs and six hit more homers, but no team in baseball topped their 124 stolen bases, and no one could match their team ERA of 2.85. Brooklyn-born southpaw Sandy Koufax had a phenomenal season, leading the league with 25 wins, 306 strikeouts, 11 shutouts and an ERA of 1.88. He and righthander Don Drysdale, who won 19, were true workhorses, starting more than half of LA's games that year. Johnny Podres was the reliable third member of the rotation, and lefthander Ron Perranoski anchored the bullpen, winning 16 and saving another 21.

This was the first time these two franchises had met since 1956, one year before the Dodgers had left Brooklyn for the West Coast. In seven previous interborough wars the Yankees had won six times, but now the Dodgers made up for at least some of those tough losses by doing something that no other team had ever accomplished — they swept the Yankees out in four straight games. They did it with their pitching, holding the erstwhile Bombers to just four runs, 22 hits and a .171 average. New York's pitching was more than adequate, giving up just 12 runs, but you can't win if you can't score and the Yankees simply could not score against LA.

Koufax set the tone right at the beginning, striking out the first five batters he faced. Meanwhile, the Dodgers picked up four runs in the second inning against Ford, three of them coming on a home run by catcher John Roseboro. Afterwards, the only question was whether Koufax would break the single-game strikeout record and he did, fanning the last batter of the day for his 15th punchout. The next day the Dodgers plated two runs before many fans had been seated as Maris uncharacteristically misjudged a Willie Davis fly into an RBI double. Podres kept the Yankees off-balance until the ninth, when they picked up their only run, but Perranoski came in and slammed the door.

The two games in Los Angeles produced real pitching masterpieces. Bouton gave up just four hits and a run, but Drysdale was almost unhittable, giving up just three singles. The Dodgers scored the only run of the game in the first inning on a walk to Jim Gilliam, a wild pitch and a base hit by Tommy Davis. Ford and Koufax squared off again in Game Four and once more the hitters took the day off. Big Frank Howard was the only Dodger to solve Ford, picking up a single and a fifth inning home run. Mickey Mantle tied the score with a seventh inning blast, the only time in the entire Series that the Yankees didn't trail. Their hopes for a miraculous comeback, however, did not last very long. Gilliam led off the bottom of the seventh with a high bouncer to third. Boyer did a good job in leaping and gloving the ball, and he fired to first. But Pepitone lost the ball amidst a background of white-shirted spectators, and by the time the Yankees retrieved it the speedy Gilliam was on third; he scored a moment later on a sacrifice fly.

Despite the humiliating defeat in the World Series, the only major changes the Yankees made in the off-season were in their management team. Roy Hamey decided to retire and Ralph Houk was promoted out of the dugout to replace him.* Taking over as Yankee skipper was Yogi Berra, which proved to be a popular decision for the wrong reason. Since he had played with almost all the players on the roster, Yogi reportedly found it difficult to make the transition from being "one of the guys" to "the boss." The result was a lack of discipline that led to a lackluster performance for most of the season.

The Chicago White Sox and the resurgent Baltimore Orioles, managed by former Yankee Hank Bauer, set the pace in the American League. The Sox were much like the Dodgers, long on pitching (a phenomenal team ERA of 2.72) and short on hitting (seventh in the league in runs scored, ninth in home runs). The Orioles were powered by the left side of their infield — third baseman

---

*Houk would eventually return to manage the Yankees from 1966 through 1973, then later spent five years managing the Tigers and another five years with the Red Sox. He never, however, took another team to the World Series.

Brooks Robinson, the league MVP, and speedy shortstop Luis Aparicio— and rookie righthander Wally Bunker, who won 19 games. Those two took turns at the top spot, with the Yankees remaining close at hand and occasionally dropping by for a brief first-place visit.

Four players made key contributions to the Yankee stretch drive. In August the club brought pitcher Mel Stottlemyre up from Triple-A, and the righthanded sinkerballer stabilized the rotation as the solid fourth man behind Ford, Bouton and Downing. But the bullpen was unsteady as Reniff and rookie Pete Mikkelsen were inconsistent and several pitchers suffered from arm ailments. So the Yankees did what they always seemed to do and dealt for a veteran player from a noncontender; this time it was Pedro Ramos coming from Cleveland. Ramos had been a good starting pitcher for a number of years with a bad Washington ballclub, throwing what he called a "Cuban palmball," which acted suspiciously like a spitball. With the Yankees, however, he was asked to take charge in the bullpen and he did, saving eight and winning one in that final month. Mantle injured a knee in mid–August, but for perhaps the first time in his career demonstrated real leadership skills by coming back just a week later and putting up big numbers despite the pain. Mantle batted .303, with 35 home runs and 111 RBI in what would prove to be his last great season.

The fourth contributor was utility infielder Phil Linz. Though there is not complete agreement as to exactly what happened, apparently one night in August, after a loss, Linz pulled out a harmonica on the team bus and played "Mary Had a Little Lamb" numerous times, even though he was asked to stop. Finally a frustrated Berra knocked the instrument from his hand. Some observers later tied the Yankee revitalization to this incident, saying that the players finally felt that Berra had acted like a manager and showed some authority.

In mid–September the three teams were still taking turns bouncing in and out of first place when New York once more put on a finishing kick. The Yankees went on an 11-game win streak that gave them just enough breathing room to hold on for their fifth consecutive pennant, equaling Casey Stengel's 1949–1953 squads (detailed elsewhere in this volume). With 99 wins, the Yankees managed to finish one game in front of the White Sox and two ahead of the Orioles in one of the tightest races in years.

But the New York/Chicago/Baltimore battle was nothing compared to the NL race. For much of the summer it looked like the young Philadelphia Phillies, managed by Gene Mauch, would reach the World Series for the first time in 14 years. But in mid–September, with a six-and-a-half-game lead, the Phillies' pitching broke down and the team lost ten in a row. This allowed St. Louis, Cincinnati and San Francisco to get involved in a mad scramble for first, and it was only after the last game had been played that a winner emerged — the Cardinals, capturing their first flag in 18 years by a single-game margin over the Phillies and Reds.

St. Louis manager Johnny Keane had taken over a downtrodden team midway through the 1961 season and turned them into champions three years later. He had two future Hall of Famers in his clubhouse — ace righthander Bob Gibson and speedy outfielder Lou Brock — who had been picked up earlier that season in a lopsided trade with the Chicago Cubs. He boasted an All-Star infield of first baseman Bill White, second baseman Julian Javier, third baseman Ken Boyer, and shortstop Dick Groat. He also had Curt Flood, the best defensive outfielder not named Willie Mays; and an old knuckleballer named Barney Schultz, both of whom saved games for the Cardinals time and again in their own fashion. It had been a strange year in St. Louis, punctuated by the acquisition of Brock, the mid-season firing of General Manager Bing Devine, numerous rumors of Keane's own job being on the line, and that final mad dash to the top, but the Cards were in the World Series.

Berra tapped Ford, his old pro, to start the Series, while the Cardinals went with their 20-game winner, Ray Sadecki. Ford was staked to a 4–2 lead but was driven out in the sixth as St. Louis won, 9–5. The "Chairman of the Board" had battled arm woes much of the year, as well as a sore heel, and after his first-game failure it was discovered he had an arterial blockage that forced him out of the Series and eventually required surgery. But the Yankees rebounded to win the next day, 8–3, as Stottlemyre shut down the Cards and Gibson. Bouton battled veteran southpaw Curt Simmons in Game Three, and both were superb. With the score tied, Keane brought Schultz in for the ninth, but he threw just one pitch. Mantle deposited it deep into the right field stands for a 2–1 win; it was also his 16th career World Series home run, making him the Fall Classic's all-time leader in that category, a distinction he still holds.

The Series turned on Game Four. New York drove Sadecki from the mound in the first inning, scoring three runs. Former Dodger Roger Craig came in and stopped the bleeding, but the Yankees still led 3–0 with AL strikeout leader Downing on the mound. In the sixth, St. Louis put two men on with one out and Groat hit a routine grounder to second that should have been a double play. Richardson couldn't get the ball out of his glove, however, loading the bases. Ken Boyer then cleared the bases with a grand slam, giving St. Louis the lead. Craig pitched perhaps the game of his life, striking out eight and giving up just two hits, and Ron Taylor came in behind him and also shut the Yankees down, tying the Series. Gibson and Stottlemyre met again the next day, and St. Louis led, 2–0, in the ninth. Mantle reached on an error and Pepitone lined a ball off Gibson's leg. The former Harlem Globetrotter pounced off the mound, fired to first, and Pepitone was called out despite vehement protests by the Yankees.* Tresh followed with a homer that tied the game, magnifying the importance of Gibson's fielding play. It didn't stay knotted for long, though,

---

*Co-author Adesman met Pepitone fifteen years later and asked him about that play. Pepitone first said it was very, very close, but finally admitted that the umpire just may have made the right call.

as Cardinal catcher Tim McCarver belted a three-run homer off Mikkelsen to put St. Louis back in the driver's seat.

New York powered their way back in Game Six. Maris and Mantle hit back-to-back homers in the sixth inning, then Pepitone smashed a grand slam in the eighth to force a climactic game, with Gibson and Stottlemyre being asked to work with just two days' rest. The Cardinals had consecutive three-run innings off the Yankee starter and two relievers, though they were also aided by some shoddy New York fielding. Trailing 6–0, Mantle cut the lead in half with a sixth inning homer, but it wasn't quite enough as a weary Gibson gamely hung on for a 7–5 victory and a World Series triumph for St. Louis that, four weeks earlier, was completely unimaginable.

And the improbable became impossible, even bizarre, over the next several days. Keane, still upset over those rumors that he was going to be fired prior to the Cardinals' late-season surge, resigned as manager less than 24 hours after the final pitch had been thrown. The same day the Yankees fired Berra, citing the lack of discipline on the club preceding the Linz incident. And several days later the Yankees held a press conference to announce that their new manager would be Johnny Keane.

What Keane could not possibly know was that the Yankee domination of the American League was over. After 15 pennants in 18 years, New York dropped to sixth place in 1965, finishing eight games under .500 and 25 games behind the first-place Twins. Injuries to Mantle, Maris, Howard, Ford and Kubek made the Yankees old and vulnerable. The following year, sitting in last place with a 4–16 record, Houk dismissed Keane and returned to the dugout, but it didn't prevent them from finishing in the basement with the franchise's worst record since 1913. It would be another ten years before the Yankees would return to baseball prominence.

1967–68
St. Louis Cardinals

The St. Louis Cardinals were up and down for the first part of the 1960s. In 1962 they finished sixth, rose to second in 1963 and then took the world championship in 1964. The following season, with the departure of manager Johnny Keane, who left for a job with the Yankees, the team dropped back to seventh. New manager Red Schoendienst, a recently retired former All-Star second baseman for the club, soon had the Cardinals turned around, however, and in 1966 they rose one spot in the league standings to sixth place.

Not long after the start of the 1966 season, the Cardinals made a deal with the Giants for their six-time All-Star first baseman, Orlando Cepeda. He immediately injected some much-needed power into the batting order. After the season, another big bat was added to the lineup — that of former Yankees outfielder Roger Maris. Combined with the speed of Lou Brock and the overpowering pitching of Bob Gibson, these two sluggers gave the Cardinals exactly what they needed to return to the top.

Even before the season started it was apparent that the Cardinals were serious pennant contenders. With unmatched talent and depth the team soon rose to the top of the standings and by the season's closing day had stretched their lead over second place San Francisco to 10½ games. With Red Schoendienst brilliantly guiding his team, the Cardinals finished at 101–60, topping the 100-win mark for the first time since 1944.

The well-rounded Cardinal offense had both power and speed. Much of the power came from Orlando Cepeda (.325, 25 home runs) who led the league with 111 runs batted in. The first baseman and future Hall of Famer had one of his finest seasons and his performance won him the National League MVP Award. Providing the speed was left fielder and leadoff hitter Lou Brock, who had perhaps the greatest season of his Hall of Fame career. He hit .299, led the league with 113 runs scored, 52 stolen bases and had career highs in both home runs (21) and RBI (76).

Though Brock and Cepeda were the team's true offensive stars, every other nonpitcher contributed greatly, either defensively or with his bat. Catcher Tim McCarver, who was second to Cepeda in MVP voting, hit .295, drove in 69 runs, and was the league's best defensive catcher. Veteran Cardinals star Curt Flood, who patrolled center field, hit .335 and drove in 50 runs while outfield mate Roger Maris knocked in 55 runs and batted .261. Holding down second base was veteran Julian Javier. In his finest offensive season the 30-year-old Dominican batted .281 with 14 home runs and drove in 64 runs. Third baseman Mike Shannon (.245, 77 RBI) and shortstop Dal Maxvill (.227) had both broken into the big leagues with the Cardinals in 1962 and each was very capable at his position. Among the bench players, the Cardinals had speedy 21-year-old Bobby Tolan (.253), who filled in at first base and in the outfield, and catcher Dave Ricketts, who was defensively strong and hit .273 in 52 games.

The Cardinals pitching staff suffered a major blow in mid–July when ace righthander Bob Gibson (13–7, 2.98) suffered a broken leg. Hit by a line drive off the bat of Pittsburgh's Roberto Clemente, Gibson was sidelined for eight weeks. The rest of the pitching staff, however, picked up the slack beautifully and the Cardinals held on to their league lead. Nelson Briles, only 4–15 in 1966, completely reversed his record to 14–5 with a 2.43 ERA. The 24-year-old Briles, converted into a starter after the loss of Gibson, won his last nine decisions of the season. The Cardinals' other two young starters also pitched brilliantly. Lefthander Steve Carlton (14–9, 2.98 ERA), in his first full big league season, struck out 168 batters while Dick Hughes, who had made his big league debut the previous September, finished with a 16–6 record, 161 strikeouts, and an ERA of 2.67. Also posting winning records were lefthander Larry Jaster, who contributed nine wins, and Ray Washburn, who finished at 10–7.

With Gibson out for two months, the relief pitchers played an even more important role. Jack Lamabe, who joined the team late in the season, won three games and saved four. Ron Willis appeared in 65 games, won six and saved ten, but the most reliable member of the bullpen was lefty Joe Hoerner. Called on 57 times, he saved 15 games, won four and had an ERA of 2.59.

In the World Series, it looked as if the Cardinals would have little trouble with the Boston Red Sox. Game One was a pitching duel but Bob Gibson prevailed over Jose Santiago for a 2–1 win. Two home runs by Carl Yastrzemski gave the Red Sox the second game, 5–0, but the Cardinals came back for a 5–2 win in Game Three. Game Four also went to St. Louis as Bob Gibson's five-hit shutout was supported by six runs from his teammates. The Cardinals had a chance to take the Series at home in Game Five but Red Sox pitcher Jim Lonborg denied them. Pitching a three-hit, 3–1 shutout, the only run he gave up was a solo homer by Maris in the ninth. That loss sent the Series to Boston for the remaining two games and the Red Sox made the most of that advantage in Game Six. None of the eight different pitchers the Cardinals sent into the game were effective at stopping the 12-hit, four–home run attack of the Red Sox, and Boston evened the Series with an 8–4 win. In the Game Seven finale, the Cardinals sent Bob Gibson to the mound. He was really all they needed as he tossed a three-hit game and even hit a home run himself as St. Louis easily took the contest 7–2. Without a doubt, the Cardinals owed the world championship, the eighth in the history of the franchise, to two players: Brock and Gibson. The left fielder batted .414, stole seven bases, scored eight runs, and even hit a homer; with three wins and 26 strikeouts Gibson had an ERA for the Series of 1.00.

Nineteen sixty-eight was the year of the pitcher. In the American League batting champ Carl Yastrzemski only hit .301 while pitcher Denny McLain of Detroit won 31 games, making him the first in that league to top 30 wins since 1931. In the National League, the Cardinals' Bob Gibson was almost just as spectacular. At the peak of his fabulous career, Gibson (22–9) led the league with 268 strikeouts, 13 shutouts and a minuscule ERA of 1.12. Needless to say, he was the unanimous choice for the NL Cy Young Award as well as the NL Most Valuable Player Award.

Primarily on the strength of Gibson's arm, the Cardinals repeated as pennant winners in 1968. Though perhaps not as overpowering as they had been in 1967, nor as balanced and well-rounded, the Cardinals still coasted to a 97–65 record which put them nine games ahead of second place San Francisco.

In addition to Gibson, the Cardinals starting rotation had youngsters Steve Carlton (13–11, 2.99) and Nelson Briles (19–11, 2.81), both of whom turned in strong performances. Veteran Ray Washburn had what would prove to be the best season of his career and finished 14–8 with a 2.26 ERA while Larry Jaster contributed nine wins. Once again, lefty Joe Hoerner was the ace of the bullpen staff. In 47 games he won eight, lost two, saved 17, and had a 1.48 ERA. Supporting him was Ron Willis (four saves) and rookie Wayne Granger, who won four games and had an ERA of 2.25 in 34 relief appearances.

Offense was down all across the National League in 1968 and the Cardinals were no different; their combined .249 mark was only slightly better than the league average of .243. Lou Brock (.279) was again the Cardinals' most potent offensive weapon, scoring 92 runs and leading the league in doubles (46), triples (14) and stolen bases (62). Curt Flood, who won his sixth straight Gold Glove in the outfield, also had a good season and batted .301 with 186 hits.

Though the Cardinals were a threat on the base paths, the team lacked the punch to drive runs across the plate. Gone was the power of 1967. First baseman Orlando Cepeda (.248, 16 home runs, 73 RBI) merely had an average season and Roger Maris (.255), in the final season of his career, drove in just 45 runs. The rest of the team had solid but not exceptional seasons at the plate. Among the infielders, third baseman Mike Shannon (.266) was the team leader with 79 RBI, second baseman Julian Javier hit .260 and was named to the All-Star team, while shortstop Dal Maxvill, the Gold Glove winner, batted .253. At catcher, Tim McCarver was again one of the league's best defensive backstops but he hit only .253.

In what was sure to be a battle between the best pitchers in baseball that season, the Cardinals met the Detroit Tigers in the 1968 World Series. With a pitching staff led by Denny McLain and Mickey Lolich, and an offense that featured the bats of Al Kaline, Norm Cash, and Willie Horton, the Tigers had won 103 games and easily taken the AL pennant. In Game One, Gibson completely shut down the Tiger offense while Cardinal batters scored three runs on McLain in the fourth and went on to a 4–0 win. Behind home runs from Horton, Cash and Lolich, who was also the winning pitcher, Detroit took an easy 8–1 win in Game Two. Home runs, this time by McCarver and Cepeda, also played a big role in Game Three as the Cardinals came from behind to take a 7–3 victory. Gibson and McLain again squared off in Game Four and once again it was Gibson who outlasted his opponent. McLain was gone from the game by the third and with home runs by Brock and Gibson himself, the Cardinals crushed the Tigers 10–1.

Up three games to one, St. Louis had a chance to take the Series in Game Five but Mickey Lolich again proved better than Cardinal batters. He gave up three runs, including a homer to Cepeda, in the first inning but settled down to toss a shutout for the next eight and Detroit won the game 5–3. Seven different St. Louis pitchers couldn't shut the floodgates in Game Six as the Tigers handed the Cardinals a 13–1 walloping. With Bob Gibson on the mound for Game Seven, St. Louis had one last chance at taking the Series but even the sold out Busch Stadium crowd couldn't will the Cardinals to win. Pitching on two days rest, Lolich scattered five hits and didn't give up a run until Mike Shannon hit a solo homer in the bottom of the ninth. Gibson also pitched well and shut out the Tigers for six innings but surrendered three runs in the seventh and one more in the ninth. It was a disappointing end to such a spectacular season by the future Hall of Famer.

In 1969, the Cardinals' lack of offensive power caught up to them. Roger Maris had retired and Cepeda was traded to the Braves but the roster moves failed to create more runs. Gibson had another great season, but even he couldn't keep his team from dropping to a fourth place finish in the National League East with a record of 87–75. It would be 1982 before the Cardinals again made it to the World Series.

1969
New York Mets

The seeds of the 1969 season were planted years before on the shores of both the Atlantic and Pacific oceans. From the moment the fledgling American League moved its Baltimore franchise into New York following the 1902 season, the nation's largest city had supported three major league teams — the Yankees in the AL, the Dodgers and Giants in the NL. For more than half a century, New Yorkers grew up arguing over which team was better, whose players were better. Over a span of 36 years, beginning in 1921, the World Series was an all–New York affair 13 times, including an amazing seven times between 1947 and 1956.

But while those years may be seen as a "golden age" for New York baseball, there were undercurrents churning that would change the diamond landscape. In the post–World War II economic boom, Americans were on the move as never before, traveling all over the country in search of a better life. The desire for more automobiles meant more highways and greater mobility. The car also became the principal mode of individual transportation, surpassing the train, bus and trolley. Many baseball fans were now living in suburbs, rather than the inner city, or in burgeoning towns. The old ballparks, built in the early part of the 20th century, were too small and cramped, were not near the new highways and did not provide enough parking; in short, they were not convenient for this new, mobile society. And many of the small towns that were developing into larger cities were looking to trumpet their growth by becoming "major league," one way or another.

The owner of the Brooklyn Dodgers, Walter O'Malley, recognized these shifting patterns and attempted to convince the borough of Brooklyn to build a new ballpark. He saw larger facilities being filled on a regular basis and recognized that greater attendance meant higher revenues, which would allow a team to spend more money to sign the best high school players, or to trade for the best (and thus more expensive) major league players. Ebbets Field, he believed, was just too small to compete with these larger ballparks, and because it had been built for public transportation, with no highways planned for that area, he saw his fan base being lost to New York's flourishing suburbs. A new stadium in a new location was a necessity for the Dodgers, according to O'Malley, and he was even willing to build it if the city would give him some land. But he could not convince the proper officials, especially the powerful Robert Moses, who literally controlled traffic in New York and Long Island.

O'Malley cast about for an alternative and found a willing partner in the City of Los Angeles, which was willing to not only build him a ballpark but also give him the land. O'Malley then convinced Horace Stoneham, owner of the New York Giants, to move out to the West Coast with him. Stoneham, who was losing money (unlike O'Malley), had been planning to move his team to Minneapolis, where he already owned the Triple-A franchise and where a new stadium had been constructed. O'Malley recognized that his fellow National League owners would look more favorably on his move if he could offer them the economic benefits of a two-city road trip, and so, after much maneuvering, the Brooklyn Dodgers and New York Giants left the Big Apple following the 1957 season and moved to Los Angeles and San Francisco, respectively. After 75 years, there was no National League team in New York.

The mayor of New York, Robert Wagner, facing a reelection battle, joined forces with attorney William Shea to try to lure an existing franchise to the city. When that failed, they began developing the idea of a third major league to challenge the American and National. With former Dodgers president Branch Rickey as its head, the Continental League sought to go into Triple-A cities that, like Los Angeles, wanted that "major league" stamp. However, their real goal was to force the existing major leagues to add teams, especially a franchise in New York. They succeeded: The American League allowed the Washington Senators to move to Minneapolis and then placed a new team in Washington, in addition to one in Los Angeles; the National League added teams in New York and Houston.*

Taking the name of one of their 19th century predecessors, the New York Metropolitans (or Mets) instantly became one of baseball's most recognizable franchises. They hired Casey Stengel, by now 71 years old, as their manager, and drew nearly one million people to the venerable Polo Grounds as National League baseball returned to the city in 1962 after a four-year absence. But the other nine NL squads treated the newcomers rather rudely — the 1962 Mets lost 120 of their games, winning just 40 times in 160 attempts, to become fodder for comedians around the country. They lost, in fact, more than 100 games in

---

*Atlanta, Dallas–Fort Worth, Denver and Toronto were other Continental League franchises that have subsequently found places in the major leagues. Only Buffalo has remained in Triple-A.

five of their first seven seasons, finishing last in those five years and ninth (in the ten-team league) the other two times.

Following the 1968 season baseball expanded again. The American League, which had allowed the A's to move to Oakland the year before, bowed to political pressure and placed a new team in Kansas City, as well as one in Seattle. (The latter would wind up staying for only one year before moving to Milwaukee; the current Seattle franchise was a result of yet another expansion, this one coming after the 1976 season.) The NL added teams in Montreal and San Diego, and with 12 clubs apiece, each league decided to break tradition and split into six-team East and West divisions. Every team would play more games within its own division, and when the regular season was over the World Series would be preceded by a best-of-five series between division winners to determine the league champions.

When this new structure was devised, even the most ardent Mets fan would not have dreamt that his/her heroes would be participating in the league championship series or the World Series for a number of years. The 1968 squad had turned in the best record in franchise history and still lost 89 games. Their team batting average was an abysmal .228, and they averaged fewer than three runs per game. The reigning National League champion St. Louis Cardinals, who had won back-to-back pennants, were placed in their division along with two up-and-coming young squads in Chicago and Pittsburgh. A realistic preseason appraisal for 1969 would have given the team a chance at a .500 mark and perhaps as high as a third-place finish in the National League East. In fact, a *New York Times* article on the eve of the season openers headlined "Runaway Victory Likely for Cards" and "Yanks and Mets Are Not Regarded as Contenders."

That evaluation would have seemed optimistic when the team lost seven of its first ten games. But over the next two months the young Mets, buoyed by one of the strongest pitching staffs in the league, climbed into second place. There was no talk of a pennant, however, as the Chicago Cubs were setting a torrid pace. After the games of June 15, the Cubs had won 40 times and sported a winning percentage of .678. They led the Mets, with their 30–26 mark, by 8½ games, the largest lead in any of the four divisions.

June 15 was the traditional trading deadline, and that day Mets General Manager Johnny Murphy — the same Johnny Murphy who had been the ace reliever for the great Yankee teams of 1936–39 — completed an important deal. He sent four minor league players to Montreal for first baseman Donn Clendenon, a tall righthanded slugger who had had good years in Pittsburgh before being claimed by the Expos in the expansion draft a few months before.* Clendenon proved to be the missing link, hitting 12 home runs in a Met uniform that season and

---

The four players were infielder Kevin Collins and pitchers Steve Renko, Jay Carden and Dave Colon. Only Renko wound up having a decent career, winning 134 major league games in 15 seasons.

becoming the run-producer the relatively weak lineup needed.

Three weeks later the Cubs, still
enjoying a large lead, came to Shea
Stadium for a three-game set. The
Mets won the first two before dropping an error-filled finale. Asked after
that victory whether these were the
real Cubs, Chicago's ever-quotable
manager, Leo Durocher, snapped
"No, those were the real Mets."

Who were the real Mets? Where
did they come from? They were primarily a young group, with only six
players beyond the age of 30. They
were a homegrown group, with 15 of
them coming up through the Mets

Lefthanded pitching ace Jerry Koosman.

minor league system. Murphy and his predecessor, Bing Devine, both
believed in building with pitching, and so the 1969 squad was led from the
mound. Tom Seaver was the undisputed ace, a strong righthander with an
explosive fastball, outstanding slider and perfect pitching mechanics. He had
won 16 games, and the Rookie of the Year Award, for a 1967 team that won
only 61 times, and repeated with another 16 the following season. In 1968 he
was joined in the rotation by lefthander Jerry Koosman, who also mixed a
good fastball with a couple of different breaking pitches and won 19 games,
posted the third-lowest ERA in the league and lost in the Rookie of the Year
balloting to Cincinnati's Johnny Bench by just one vote. In 1969 this dynamic
duo became a terrific trio when, for the third year in a row, the Mets brought
up a starter from the minors, righty Gary Gentry. These three wound up
starting 63 percent of the team's games in 1969 and won 55 percent, topped
by Seaver's Cy Young Award–winning 25–7 mark. Two more youngsters—
Jim McAndrew and a 22-year-old Nolan Ryan, plus the experienced Don
Cardwell, rounded out the starting rotation. The bullpen was anchored by
dual closers: young lefty Tug McGraw, a converted starter, and eight-year
veteran Ron Taylor. They also received valuable innings from righthander
Cal Koonce.

The everyday lineup could really count on only four players. Left fielder
Cleon Jones, batting third, offered a strong righthanded bat that sprayed hits
to all fields. He had been the first of the young Mets to claim a starting spot in
the lineup, back in 1966. After just missing a .300 average the year before, he
spent all of 1969 battling Pete Rose and Roberto Clemente for the batting title,
eventually finishing third with his club-record .340. Jones also led the team
with 16 steals, was more than adequate defensively and had a strong (though

unpredictable) arm. Tommie Agee had come to the team after the 1967 season and two All-Star berths with the White Sox. He promptly had the worst year of his career, causing many to question the trade, but Agee silenced all critics in 1969 with a fine season, which included 26 home runs from the leadoff spot and outstanding defense in center field. Shortstop Bud Harrelson simply solidified the infield when he came up to stay in 1967. He was not an especially good hitter, but he made up for it with a solid glove, terrific range and an astonishing arm. On a club that relied so heavily on its pitching, a good case could be made for him as the team's most valuable player. Good pitching needs good catching, and the New Yorkers had one of the best in Jerry Grote. Twice a National League All-Star, he had a good glove and strong arm, and at the plate he had a knack for driving in important runs.

The rest of the lineup featured a lefty-righty rotation. When a lefthanded pitcher took the mound against the Mets, Clendenon played first, Al Weis was at second, the ebullient Ed Charles was at third and powerful Ron Swoboda played right field. When a righthander was scheduled to face them, they would counter at first base with Ed Kranepool — who had played for the team every year since their 1962 inception and was still only 25 years old — Ken Boswell at second, rookie Wayne Garrett at third and Art Shamsky in right.

The man who put this all together was Gil Hodges. The former Brooklyn Dodger icon had been managing the Washington Senators for nearly five years, but Murphy and his front-office staff had decided Hodges had the qualities that could help transform their perpetual losers into winners. They convinced the Senators to let Hodges out of his contract by sending them $100,000 and a young pitcher, righty Bill Denehy, who had won one game for the 1967 Mets and would never win another in the major leagues. Hodges, meanwhile, brought patience and quiet strength to the clubhouse. He was a good teacher, skilled in bringing out the best in his young players. He and pitching coach Rube Walker carefully nurtured their pitchers, recognizing them as the team's lifeblood, and were rewarded with a league-leading 28 shutouts and a 2.99 team ERA, just .05 behind Bob Gibson's St. Louis Cardinals.

Just prior to the All-Star break the Mets went into Chicago and once again won two of three from the Cubs. Perhaps a pennant race was brewing in the National League East after all. But that seemed to be just a pipe dream as the team dropped 12 of their first 21 games following the All-Star Game, including six straight to their fellow 1962 expansion mates, the Houston Astros. The surging Cardinals had dropped them into third place, and it appeared the preseason evaluation would prove to be correct.

And then the miracles began to happen.

Even thirty years later there really is no better way to describe it. Strange things happened to the Mets over the final seven weeks of the 1969 season, wonderful things. Willie Mays, perhaps the finest outfielder of his generation, charged a groundball single in an extra-inning game and watched in horror as it rolled under his glove, allowing the winning run to score. Steve Carlton, emerging as one of the finest pitchers in the game, struck out a record 19 batters one night, yet lost because Ron Swoboda hit a pair of two-run homers. Both games of a doubleheader at Pittsburgh were won 1–0, with both runs being driven in by starting pitchers Koosman and Cardwell. They were even no-hit, by the Pirates' Bob Moose, but by then nothing could derail a Mets Express that captured 38 of their final 49 games.

In early September the Cubs came to New York for a two-game series. Leo Durocher's crew had perhaps the best starting lineup in the league but little depth behind them (six players wound up the season with over 500 at-bats), and thus came into the stretch run somewhat fatigued. In the opener Koosman hooked up with 20-game winner Bill Hands in what proved to be the key match of the season. Tied at two in the sixth, Agee doubled and headed home on a Garrett single. A strong throw came to the plate, Agee slid ... and was called safe, despite a vehement protest from catcher Randy Hundley.* The final score was 3–2 Mets, and it seemed to break the back of the Cubs. The Mets pounded Chicago ace Ferguson Jenkins the next night, then moved into first place to stay. Two weeks later, on September 24, 1969, rookie Gentry shut out the Cardinals on four hits as the Mets clinched the first Eastern Division championship in National League history in front of more than 56,000 hysterical fans at Shea Stadium. (Destructive fans, too: in their delirium they spilled out of the stands after the final out and tore up the playing field, grabbing sod, bases, anything they could find. The next day Shea Stadium looked more like the moon's surface than a baseball diamond. Thankfully, that September 24 game was the last one scheduled at the ballpark ... until the playoffs.)

When the hysteria died down, the Mets had won 100 games, just two seasons after they had lost 100 games, and wound up with an eight-game bulge over the Cubs. But this wonderful fairy tale would now certainly succumb to reality. Their opponents in the league championship series were the Atlanta Braves, who had outlasted a balanced Western Division to capture their first title since moving to Atlanta from Milwaukee following the 1965 season. The Braves' hard-hitting lineup featured the one-and-only Hank Aaron, Orlando Cepeda, Rico Carty and Felipe Alou, among others. Their pitching staff boasted four solid starters, led by knuckleballer Phil Niekro and his 23 wins, and relief ace Cecil Upshaw, whose difficult sidearm motion helped him rack up 27 saves. In addition, the first two games in this best-of-five series would be played in Atlanta, although the Mets had won four of their six regular-season games in Georgia.

---

*Ten years later, co-author Adesman was assistant general manager of the Amarillo Gold Sox in the Texas League, and Hundley was manager of the rival Midland Cubs. Before a game one day Adesman asked Hundley about that play, and the years melted away as the former catcher angrily insisted that he had, indeed, tagged Agee out at the plate.

As expected, Seaver and Niekro squared off in the opener. Perhaps having pitched more than 500 innings between them took its toll as neither Cy Young contender was at his best. But in the eighth inning, trailing 5–4, the Mets combined four hits with some shoddy Braves defense to score five times for a 9–5 victory. The next day the Mets shelled 18-game winner Ron Reed, knocking him out of the game in the second inning. Having scored in each of the first five innings they led 9–1, and with Koosman pitching the game seemed to be over. It wasn't. Atlanta drove the lefty from the mound with a five-run fifth to narrow the gap. That, however, was as close as they would get. Ron Taylor, who had saved the game for Seaver the day before with two shutout innings, was called in again for a rare middle-relief role and shut the door. He then gave way to Tug McGraw, who allowed just two baserunners over the final three innings, and the Mets returned to the now-repaired Shea Stadium for their first-ever home playoff game. Gary Gentry started for the Mets but he, like Seaver and Koosman before him, did not have his best stuff. After giving up a home run to Hank Aaron in the first inning — Aaron wound up hitting a homer in each of the series' three games — Gentry was removed by Hodges in the third inning after putting the first two men on base and watching a tremendous Rico Carty drive just curve foul. Nolan Ryan was brought in, struck out Carty, and proceeded to retire the side and end the threat. The Mets took the lead in the fourth but the Braves regained it in the fifth when Ryan made his only mistake, giving up a two-run homer to Cepeda. The Mets immediately jumped back into the lead when Wayne Garrett — who had hit only one home run all season — reached the seats against Braves starter Pat Jarvis. Ryan made it stand up, and the New York Mets swept the Atlanta Braves to win the National League pennant. Amazingly, the Mets won this series with their offense: they outscored the Braves, 27–15, had a higher team batting average (.327 to .255), and even out-homered their opponents, 6–5. There could be no doubt that something strange was going on.

But now, surely, the bubble would be broken, because the Mets' World Series opponents were the Baltimore Orioles. Manager Earl Weaver, in his first full season at the helm, had put together a fearsome club, one that won 109 times and finished ahead of the second-place Detroit Tigers — the defending world champs! — by 19 games. They had scored 779 runs during the regular season and bashed 175 home runs; by comparison, the Mets had scored 632 and hit 109 four-baggers. They trotted out an All-Star infield of Boog Powell at first base, Davey Johnson at second, Mark Belanger at short and Brooks Robinson at third; in the outfield they featured two-time MVP Frank Robinson and the magnificent Paul Blair. On the mound they had 20-game winning lefties Mike Cuellar and Dave McNally, plus future Hall of Famer Jim Palmer, and in the bullpen they mirrored the Mets with a lefty-righty closing tandem of Pete Richert and Eddie Watt. In their own league championship series against the Minnesota Twins (led by Billy Martin), they eked out a pair of extra inning victories, then completed the sweep with a convincing 11–2 drubbing. Smart money made them prohibitive favorites to capture the World Series and be recognized as one of the best teams the American League had ever produced without an "NY" on their jerseys.

Sunny skies greeted the two clubs in Baltimore, and things immediately became even brighter for the Orioles when left fielder Don Buford hit Tom Seaver's second pitch over a leaping Ron Swoboda for a 1–0 lead. The O's picked up three more runs in the fourth, and that proved to be more than enough as Mike Cuellar's screwball mesmerized the Mets. Held

The Mets' All-Star outfielder Cleon Jones.

to just six hits by the Cuban-born southpaw, New York dropped the opener, 4–1, and the experts confidently predicted an end to Met magic.

One of baseball's oldest truisms is "good pitching stops good hitting." It can also stop experts right in their tracks. In the second game, Jerry Koosman held the Orioles hitless for six innings before yielding two singles, and the tying run, in the seventh. Those were the only safeties Baltimore managed, however, and in the ninth inning Dave McNally committed one of pitching's cardinal sins: after retiring the first two batters, he couldn't get the third out. Ed Charles, Jerry Grote and Al Weis, who hit just .215 in the regular season, each singled for what proved to be the winning run in the Mets' 2–1 victory, sending the Series back to New York all tied up.

The third game was simply The Tommie Agee Show. The Mets center fielder led off the bottom of the first with a home run off Jim Palmer, and then his glove took over as he made two spectacular catches to rob the Orioles of four or five runs. In the fourth inning, with two men on base, he raced into left-center field to make a backhanded grab of catcher Elrod Hendricks' bid for extra bases. Then in the seventh a tired Gary Gentry walked the bases loaded. Nolan Ryan came in to pitch and Paul Blair hit a screaming line drive to right-center. Agee raced to his left, dove, slid, and somehow caught the ball. Agee, somewhat akin to a goaltender in hockey, proved to be the Mets' last line of defense in their 5–0 victory.

Game Four proved to be the most exciting. A Clendenon homer had given the Mets a 1–0 lead that Seaver nursed into the ninth. The Orioles put two runners on, however, when Brooks Robinson hit a sinking line drive to right-center. In any other year, against any other opponent, it's a sure hit, but in 1969, against the Mets, the impossible was most likely to happen. From out of nowhere came Ron Swoboda, New York's right fielder and a man never known for his defense. He threw himself at the ball and backhanded it before it hit the ground; while Frank Robinson did tag up after the catch and score the tying run, Swoboda's mind-numbing, ground-jarring catch prevented the Orioles from doing any more damage. Then in the bottom of the tenth the Mets put their first two runners on base. Backup catcher J.C. Martin, sent up as a pinch hitter, bunted, and pitcher Pete Richert threw to first. The ball struck Martin's left wrist as he headed down the basepath, bounded away, and the winning run crossed the plate. The next day, photographs showed that Martin was out of the baseline and should have been called out, but at the time of the play no one on the Orioles bench was alert enough to catch the gaffe. Earl Weaver might have, but he was not on the field, having been ejected earlier in the game.

Down three games to one, the Orioles fought to get the Series back to Baltimore. Pitcher Dave McNally cracked a two-run homer in the third, and Frank Robinson added a solo shot later in the inning to give the Birds a 3–0 lead. But it couldn't last. In the sixth, a ball in the dirt made Cleon Jones dance, and the Mets dugout screamed that it had nicked Jones' shoe. Sure enough, an inspection of the ball discovered shoe polish, and Jones trotted off to first. Donn Clendenon then powered his third homer of the Series, pulling the Mets within one. That only lasted until the next inning when Al Weis, of all people, hit a home run to tie the game. In the eighth, the Mets picked up two runs on a couple of hits and a couple of Baltimore bobbles. Jerry Koosman, almost unhittable after the third inning, did not require any bullpen assistance in the ninth inning, finishing off the Orioles with a five-hitter for his second World Series win. To the chagrin of bookies everywhere, the New York Mets were champions of the world!

Met pitching had been the great equalizer. The powerful Orioles batted a paltry .146, scoring just nine runs and collecting just 23 hits (19 of them singles) in the five games. In the middle three games, the O's managed to dent the plate just twice. The Oriole pitching staff, especially Cuellar and McNally, was almost as good as their New York counterparts, allowing only 15 runs, but the Mets were able to score against Baltimore's bullpen whereas the O's could never solve Met relievers. In addition, the Mets were nearly flawless on defense, making only two errors to go along with the aforementioned acrobatics by Agee and Swoboda. Sound, fundamental baseball had won the series for New York, though perhaps nudged along by the puckish baseball gods.*

---

*In 1980, former Baltimore reliever Eddie Watt was named manager in Amarillo while co-author Adesman was still assistant general manager. One time Adesman brought up the 1969 World Series with Watt, and found that the fires still burned more than a decade after the fact. He just couldn't believe his Orioles had lost, he said, since they were far and away the better club, and he flat-out blamed cosmic forces for their defeat. Adesman never brought up the subject again.

The city of New York went wild over their Mets, throwing parties and ticker-tape parades for a week or more after the victory. Throughout the off-season, whenever a member of the team made a personal appearance anywhere in the metropolitan area, he was mobbed by hundreds of adoring fans. It was New York's Winter of Complete Contentment.

Miracles have a short shelf life, however, and the Mets used up theirs in 1969. Despite returning essentially the same cast in 1970 (Ed Charles retired and was replaced at third base by Joe Foy), the team did not seem to play with the same verve. Clendenon, Agee and Shamsky were the only regulars to have good years, Seaver dropped from 25 wins to 18 as the three primary starters went from 55 wins in 1969 to 39 wins in 1970. Still, the Mets stayed in contention in the National League East until the final two weeks in September, but their 83 wins (17 fewer than the year before) placed them third, six games behind Pittsburgh and a game behind the Cubs. Over the next couple of years many of the players who had been members of the Miracle Mets left the team so that by 1973, when they returned to the World Series, only 11 men remained from that astounding triumph of just four years earlier. They even lost their manager, Gil Hodges, who succumbed to a sudden heart attack just days before the 1973 season began.

The Mets were not a dynasty, like so many Yankee clubs had been, or like Connie Mack's Athletics or "The Boys of Summer" Dodgers. But they had been the ultimate success story, a true-life script too improbable even for Hollywood. People always identify with the underdog, and these dogs had been under so long — 737 losses in seven years — that they generated a special feeling, not just in New York but all over the country, that once in a while the runt of the litter can win Best in Show. Because of how bad they had been and how far they had to come in just one short summer, the memorable 1969 Mets are included in this book.

1969–71 Baltimore Orioles

In 1971, Baltimore Orioles manager Earl Weaver was quoted as saying, "My best game plan is to sit on the bench and call out specific instructions like, 'C'mon Boog,' 'Get hold of one, Frank' or 'Let's go, Brooks.'" With the talented team he had it's almost believable that was all the managing he was required to do.

Led by a hot-tempered manager, two unrelated Robinsons, a guy named Boog, and a dream of a pitching staff, the Orioles won three straight American League pennants from 1969 to 1971. Though they had won the World Series in 1966 with an upset victory over the Dodgers, the Orioles slipped back to sixth place the following season. They rose back to second in 1968, but it wasn't a close pennant race as they finished 12 games behind Detroit. In 1969, everything came together and the Orioles destroyed the competition with a 109-win season. They took the league lead on April 16 and never relinquished it, finishing 19 games ahead of second-place New York. The results of the 1970 season were nearly identical as the O's won 108 games and left the Yankees trailing by 15 games. Though they dropped to 101 wins in 1971, their record still put them in first by 12 games.

Though he never made it to the major leagues as a player, Earl Weaver became one of baseball's greatest managers. After more than a decade guiding teams in the Orioles minor league system he was promoted to the position of coach with the big league club in 1968. At the midpoint of that season he was appointed to replace Hank Bauer as manager, beginning what would eventually be 17 seasons at the helm of the Orioles.

With a fiery disposition, Weaver was quick to argue with umpires — a habit that resulted in him being the most frequently ejected manager of his day. He was also a gifted strategist who built an incredibly balanced team that excelled in every area of the game: power, speed, pitching, and defense. He did this by knowing each player's strengths and weaknesses and then using that knowledge (and his entire roster) to make sure his players were used in the most efficient way possible. Though his team would again top the 100-win mark in both 1979 and 1980, the Orioles of 1969–1971 were Weaver's greatest accomplishment.

A six-time All-Star with the Cincinnati Reds, right fielder Frank Robinson had been acquired by the Orioles in December of 1965. Though they had to give up a lot to get him (pitchers Milt Pappas and Jack Baldschun, outfielder Dick Simpson) the trade was well worth it as Robinson won the American League MVP Award and the Triple Crown in his first season in Baltimore. After a subpar season in 1968, in which he only hit 15 home runs with 52 RBI, Robinson reestablished himself as the Orioles' veteran leader in 1969. Perhaps the toughest out in the league that season, he batted .308, drove in an even 100 runs, scored 111 times, drew 88 walks, and slugged 32 balls out of the park. Always the consummate professional, Robinson's play inspired those around him and he continued to lead by example in both 1970 (.306, 78 RBI, 25 HR) and 1971 (.281, 99 RBI, 28 HR).

The other Robinson in the lineup, third baseman Brooks, had been with the team his entire career. After making his debut at the end of the 1955 season, the gifted fielder spent the next several seasons up and down between Baltimore and the minor leagues while working on his hitting. He finally stuck with the big league club in 1959 and within a couple of seasons had developed into a respected power hitter. But hitting was never his biggest strength; one of the greatest fielders at his position the game has ever seen, Robinson won 15 consecutive Gold Glove awards from 1961 to 1975. He was no slouch at the plate either, batting .234 with 23 home runs and 84 RBI in 1969. He raised his batting average considerably in 1970 to .276 while hitting 18 homers and driving in 94 runs, followed by a .272-20-92 performance in 1971.

The biggest Oriole at plate during this period (both literally and figuratively) was John "Boog" Powell. At 6'4" and 240 pounds, the lefthanded hitter was one of the most feared sluggers in the American League for more than a decade. Powell broke into the big leagues with Baltimore in the final week of the 1961 season as an outfielder but, not particularly blessed with speed, he was soon converted to first base. The 1969 season would be the best of his career; he hit .304 with 37 home runs and 121 runs driven in. Still, he finished second to Minnesota's Harmon Killebrew in voting for the American League MVP. In 1970, however, Powell won the prestigious award with a .297 batting average, 35 home runs, 114 RBI, 104 walks, and 82 runs. In 1971 his batting average dropped to .256 but he still hit 22 homers and drove in 92 runs.

Also figuring prominently into the Orioles' equation during those seasons was a cast of players who would each have been stars on a lesser team. Speedy outfielder Don Buford averaged 99 runs scored, 17 stolen bases, 16 home runs and a .284 batting mark over those three seasons. His fellow outfielder Merv Rettenmund had a .306 batting average over the same period and in 1970 hit 18 home runs in 106 games. Catcher Elrod Hendricks was one of the best defensive backstops in the game. Gold Glove winning center fielder Paul Blair had both power and speed; in 1969 he slugged 26 home runs, scored 102 times and stole 20 bases. Shortstop Mark Belanger was a wizard with the glove, winning Gold Gloves in both 1969 and 1971, and a better-than-average hitter. Second baseman Davey Johnson, an All-Star in 1970, was also strong defensively and a Gold Glove winner in each of the three seasons. A consistent hitter, his batting averages from 1969 to 1971 were .280, .281, and .282, respectively.

And that was just the offense.

The Orioles pitching staff was, without a doubt, the best in the league during those seasons and among the best all-time. With the two best lefthanders in the game and a young righty who was on his way to Cooperstown, the Orioles were able to stifle opposing offenses. In 1970 they had three 20-game winners in the starting rotation. As if that wasn't enough, they had four pitchers top that mark the following season.

Cuban-born Mike Cuellar spent a lot of time in the minor leagues and had unsuccessful stints with the Reds and the Cardinals before finally sticking in the big leagues with the Astros. Converted from a reliever to a starter at Houston, Cuellar finally began to thrive and in 1967 won 16 games and earned a spot on the NL All-Star team. Desperately in need of another starter, the Orioles worked a five-player deal that brought Cuellar to Baltimore in December of 1968. It turned out to be a brilliant trade as Cuellar (23-11, 2.38 ERA) proceeded to set a team record for wins in 1969 as well as win the Cy Young Award (he shared the award with Detroit's Denny McLain). He made an even more impressive showing in 1970 by leading the league in wins (24) and complete games (21). The 1971 season saw Cuellar reach the 20-win mark yet again. Amazingly consistent during those three seasons, he averaged 293 innings pitched, 19 complete games and 38 starts.

Jim Palmer made his Oriole debut as a 19-year-old in 1965. He won 15 games in 1966 but arm injuries kept him either on the bench or in the minor leagues for most of the 1967 season and all of 1968. Fully recovered in 1969, Palmer (16–4, 2.34) played a key role in the Orioles' success and was the team's number-one righthanded starter. Back-to-back 20 win seasons in 1970 and 1971 (with ERAs of 2.71 and 2.68, respectively) firmly established him as one of baseball's top young pitchers. The bigger the game, the better Palmer seemed to pitch and from 1969 to 1971 he was 5–1 in postseason play.

Called up to the Orioles at the end of the 1962 season, lefthander Dave McNally was a regular starter by the following season. After several solid but unmemorable seasons he finally had his big breakthrough in 1968 when he won 22, lost 10 and had an ERA of 1.95. In 1969 he won 15 games in a row on his way to a 20–7 record. McNally tied Cuellar for the league lead in wins in 1970 with a 24–9 record and then led the league in winning percentage with a 21–5 performance in 1971.

Right hander Tom Phoebus was the other regular member of the Orioles starting rotation in 1969 and 1970. After leading the International League in strikeouts while with Rochester in 1966, Phoebus was called up to the big leagues. He won 14 games in 1967, 15 the following year and showed great promise with a 14–7 season in 1969. In 1970, however, he lost his effectiveness and won only five games. The Orioles decided to trade him and worked out a deal with the San Diego Padres that sent Phoebus and some minor league prospects west. In return they got Pat Dobson, another righthanded starting pitcher, who, in three seasons with the Tigers and one with the Padres, had never posted a winning record. The Orioles apparently thought he had potential and were proved correct when Dobson posted a 20–8 record with a 2.90 ERA in 1971.

Though he had the baseball's best starting rotation from 1969 to 1971, Earl Weaver also had the luxury of being able to call on a great bullpen when one of those starters got into a jam. His three primary relief pitchers — Dick Hall, Pete Richert, and Eddie Watt — were among the best in the game during those seasons. Hall had a 1.92 ERA in 1969 and then a 10–5 record in 1970. He won a total of 21 games and saved ten over the three seasons. Watt was virtually unhittable, a fact attested to by his 1.65 ERA in 1969 and a 1.82 mark in 1971. He averaged 13 saves and five wins during the Orioles' reign at the top of the American League. Hard-throwing lefthander Richert was just as effective as Watt and in 1969 saved 12 games and had an ERA of 2.20. He was even better the following season and recorded 13 saves, a 1.98 ERA as well as a 7–2 record.

Due to injury Richert's performance dropped off in 1971 but he still contributed with three wins and four saves.

The 1969 season was the first for divisional play and as champions of the American League East, the Orioles had to face Minnesota, champions of the West, for the pennant. It was no contest as the Birds easily swept the Twins and advanced to meet the underdog New York Mets in the World Series. Behind a strong performance from Mike Cuellar and a home run by Don Buford, the Orioles easily took Game One. Three two-out singles in the ninth inning of Game Two allowed the Mets to score and take a 2–1 victory, evening the Series.

In Game Three, a 5–0 Mets victory, outfielder Tommie Agee nearly single-handedly defeated the Orioles. He hit a home run in the first inning and then made two spectacular catches that saved what would have been five Oriole runs. Cuellar had another strong outing in Game Four but Tom Seaver was better and the Mets took the game, 2–1. The Orioles jumped out to a three-run lead in Game Five thanks to home runs by Frank Robinson and Dave McNally but the Mets retaliated with two homers of their own, which combined with two Oriole errors gave the upstart Mets a 5–3 win and the Series. Much like the World Series of three years before when the Orioles had knocked off the Dodgers, the heavy favorite fell to an upstart. This time, though, it wasn't the Orioles that did the upsetting.

The Orioles were not to be denied in 1970. Again they met the Twins in the ALCS and again swept them in three games. In the World Series the Orioles' opponent was to be the Cincinnati Reds, a team that won 102 games during the regular season. The first two games were close and the Orioles had to come from behind and then hold on to take each by just one run. In Game Three, Dave McNally gave up three runs but hit a grand slam himself as the Orioles easily took the game by the score of 9–3. Game Four was another one-run contest but this time it was the Reds who came out on top. The Orioles held a 5–3 lead in the eighth but Lee May's three-run homer put the Reds ahead for good. With three runs in the first, the Reds came out swinging in Game Five but Mike Cuellar settled down and held them scoreless for the remainder of the game. Meanwhile, home runs by Merv Rettenmund and Frank Robinson highlighted a 15-hit and nine-run Oriole attack that brought Baltimore the world title. Unlike the previous season, the Orioles left no doubt as to who was the best team in baseball.

In 1971, the Orioles came agonizingly close to repeating as world champions but fell one game short. Against the Oakland Athletics in the ALCS (a team which also had 101 wins) the Orioles had little trouble. The power of Boog Powell, who slugged two home runs, helped the O's score five runs in each of the three games and sweep the series. Heavily favored over the Pirates in the World Series, the Orioles jumped out to a two-game lead and appeared to be cruising toward back-to-back titles. When the Series moved to Pittsburgh for Game Three, however, the Pirates recovered and stormed back to take all three home games.

Returning to Baltimore for Game Six, the Pirates took a 2–0 lead but Don Buford pulled the Birds within one with a solo shot in the sixth. The Orioles tied it up in the seventh and then won the game in the tenth when Frank Robinson scored on a sacrifice fly by Brooks Robinson. Game Seven was a pitching duel between Mike Cuellar and the Pirates' Steve Blass. Neither team scored for the first three innings but Roberto Clemente put the Pirates on the board with a two-out home run in the fourth. Each team scored one run in the eighth but Blass retired the Oriole batters in order in the ninth to preserve his slim lead and deny Baltimore another world championship.

After the 1971 season, Frank Robinson was traded along with Pete Richert to the Dodgers for pitchers Doyle Alexander and Bob O'Brien, catcher Sergio Robles and outfielder Royle Stillman. Though he was entering the twilight of his career, Robinson had been the heart of the team and his departure essentially spelled the end of the great Orioles squad. In addition, it was a rather bad trade: Stillman only appeared in 33 games over two seasons, Robles was a career 2 for 18 at the plate, O'Brien never pitched a single game for the team, and Alexander, though he went on to have a long career, never found much success during four-and-a-half seasons in Baltimore. Robinson, on the other hand, had several productive years left in him and Richert put in two strong seasons of relief work for the Dodgers.

After a third-place finish in the AL East with an 80–74 record in 1972, the Orioles lineup went through more changes when outfielder Don Buford retired and second baseman Davey Johnson was traded to Atlanta. The club continued to play well, however, and returned to the top of their division in 1973 but lost in the ALCS to the Oakland Athletics.

Interestingly, the 1969–71 Orioles left a lasting legacy by producing three future big league managers. Frank Robinson managed the Indians, Giants and Orioles, while Davey Johnson won the 1986 World Series with the Mets and found further success with the Reds. Backup catcher Johnny Oates, who would replace Robinson at the helm of the Orioles in 1991, took the Texas Rangers to the playoffs for the first time in their history in 1996.

1972–74
Oakland Athletics

There is a story that may or may not be true, but it perfectly describes the world champion Oakland A's of the 1970s. The team was on the road somewhere and, having just finished a game, was boarding the bus to go back to their hotel. One woman was desperately trying to get some autographs but was not having any success. She finally cornered Reggie Jackson and said, "Mr. Jackson, could you ask your friends on the bus...." The future Hall of Famer, never at a loss for words, cut her off in mid-sentence. "Lady," he said emphatically, "there are no friends on that bus."

The Oakland A's were a product of the boisterous 1960s, and of their ubiquitous owner, Charlie Finley. They defied the traditional definition of the word "team" except for the fact that, between the white lines, they won. They won division titles, they won American League championships, they won three consecutive World Series titles. Perhaps more than any other sports franchise they defined their decade, swaggering and bickering in multicolored polyester, but winning all the same. There has never been a team quite like them.

The A's, of course, had spent more than fifty years in Philadelphia, known more formally as the Athletics and owned and managed for the most part by the legendary Connie Mack. But Arnold Johnson purchased the team from the Mack family in 1954 and relocated them to Kansas City for the 1955 season, where they spent 13 years as one of the doormats of the American League. They were under .500 every single one of those years, finishing last five times. After the 1960 season, Johnson sold the club to a Chicago-based insurance executive named Charles O. Finley, who proved to be his own man at all times. He fired managers (ten in his first ten years), general managers and other front-office executives, scouts and even one player in the middle of a World Series; well, at least he tried to do the latter, which will be discussed a bit later. He feuded with fellow owners and with baseball's hierarchy, most notably Commissioner Bowie Kuhn. He tried some zany experiments: a short fence in right field in an attempt to replicate the friendly confines of Yankee Stadium (he was told to tear down his "pennant porch"); an automatic ball-dispensing machine, shaped like a rabbit, that gave the umpires a new ball (it never worked properly); a designated runner, Herb Washington (a noted sprinter who, over two seasons, appeared in 105 games, scored 33 runs, stole 31 bases in 48 attempts, but never had an at-bat or appeared in the field); and a mule named "Charlie O." (for no discernible reason). He also advocated playing World Series games at night, the designated hitter and colorful uniforms, all of which baseball grudgingly adopted. And after the 1967 season, following flirtations with Birmingham and Louisville, Finley received permission to move the team to Oakland, California.

Finley also proved to have a fine eye for talent, as he personally scouted and signed many young players who would form the backbone of his 1970s dynasty. In 1965, shortstop Bert "Campy" Campaneris and pitcher Jim "Catfish" Hunter were in the majors to stay; in the next six years they were joined by third baseman Sal Bando, outfielders Reggie Jackson and Joe Rudi, catcher Gene Tenace, and pitchers Johnny "Blue Moon" Odom, Rollie Fingers and Vida Blue.

In 1968, their first season in Oakland, the A's managed to do something for the first time since 1952 — they finished over .500. They were still sixth, though, in a now ten-team league. In the off-season baseball added four new teams, two in each league (including a new Kansas City franchise in the

American League as a way of staving off congressional threats to revoke baseball's antitrust exemption, a movement triggered by Finley's transference of the A's), and divided into six-team divisions. In the new American League West, the A's finished second behind the Minnesota Twins despite two managerial changes: Hank Bauer replaced Bob Kennedy after the 1968 season, then John McNamara took over for Bauer in the last two weeks of 1969. The following year the A's kept McNamara for the whole season but still finished behind the Twins by the same margin of nine games. Finley decided that McNamara was too easygoing with his players and let him go at season's end, replacing him with Montreal Expos coach (and former Red Sox manager) Dick Williams. Unbeknownst to anyone in baseball, no doubt including Finley, the final piece in the puzzle had just been put in place.

The A's started off the 1971 season hot, winning 17 of 25, and never let up. They won their 50th game of the year before June was over, making a mockery of the American League West pennant race. They were improbably led by a 21-year-old rookie pitcher, southpaw Vida Blue. Blue had given a hint of his abilities a few months earlier when, in a September call-up, he threw a no-hitter. Now he blazed through American League lineups with regularity, featuring an overpowering fastball that reminded his manager of no less a star than Sandy Koufax. With Catfish Hunter and Chuck Dobson also providing consistent quality starts and a deep bullpen anchored by converted starter Rollie Fingers, the A's clinched the division by mid–September and wound up with 101 victories. Blue won 24, led the league with a 1.82 ERA and eight shutouts, and was second in victories and strikeouts. In the fall the baseball writers selected him as both the league's Most Valuable Player and its Cy Young Award winner. Hunter won 21, his first 20-win season and the first of five consecutive years in the charmed circle. Offensively, the "Swingin' A's" (their marketing slogan for the year) did not have any dominant players but they managed to score almost 700 runs. Seven players hit ten or more home runs, led by Bando's 32 and Jackson's 24. Shortstop Campaneris provided speed with 34 stolen bases, and defensively they were one of the best in the league, playing fundamentally sound baseball and rarely beating themselves. In the playoffs, however, against the defending world champion Baltimore Orioles, their youth and postseason inexperience came to the fore as the Orioles swept them in three games to earn their third straight trip to the World Series. The A's scored just seven runs in three games against an Oriole pitching staff that used only one relief pitcher — Eddie Watt for two innings in the opening game — and didn't even call on Pat Dobson, who won 20 during the regular season.

But the loss to the Orioles in 1971 proved to be a motivating factor to the A's. Rick Monday, the center fielder, said that the experience "may have driven a ballclub that had a taste of post-season play … to come back and play even better."

Oakland made one significant change in the off-season, trading Monday to the Chicago Cubs for lefthander Ken Holtzman. This shored up a pitching rotation that would eventually lose Chuck Dobson all year to a bad elbow and Vida Blue all spring to a holdout, but placed an added strain on both the offense and defense. While the team ERA was a magnificent 2.58 for the season (and yet *still* finished second to the Orioles), the team batting average dropped from 1971's .252 to .240 and they scored 604 runs, a decline of 12.6 percent. This offensive falloff was most clearly displayed by the pennant race. Whereas in 1971 the A's were never challenged for the lead, in 1972 they played tag with the surprising Chicago White Sox, led by slugger Richie (or Dick) Allen. In late August, desperate for an outfielder who could hit, Finley picked up former National League batting champion Matty Alou from St. Louis. Though Alou was not a home run threat, he did provide some key hits, plus experience and stability, down the stretch. In September, Oakland showed their championship mettle by sprinting past the White Sox to capture their second straight Western Division crown. Despite the presence of Jackson, Bando, Rudi, Campaneris, et al., pitching proved to be the A's real strength. Hunter once again won 21 and Holtzman contributed 19 victories, while Fingers, Bob Locker, Darold Knowles and the rest of the bullpen allowed manager Williams to make frequent pitching moves. In 1971, for example, the A's staff registered 57 complete games, but the next year that figure dropped to 40 as Williams learned to rely more on his relievers.

This would prove to be especially important in the postseason. In a taut five-game series with Eastern Division champion Detroit Tigers, the A's — many of whom grew mustaches during the season to give the team something of an 1890s look — lost two everyday players, Campaneris and Jackson. The shortstop, consistently pitched inside by Tiger hurlers, was hit by a pitch in the seventh inning of the second game and responded by throwing his bat at pitcher Lerrin LaGrow, which "precipitated a near riot." Campaneris was suspended for the balance of the series by American League President Joe Cronin. Facing elimination, Detroit won the next two games in Tiger Stadium, including a heartstopping Game Four when they gave up two runs in the top of the tenth inning, only to come back and score three off the vaunted Oakland bullpen. An infield error, committed by a catcher (Gene Tenace) playing second base in a makeshift extra-inning lineup, proved to be the key play. With the season on the line, Oakland then lost Reggie Jackson in the second inning of the fifth and final game. Crashing into All-Star Tiger catcher Bill Freehan, Reggie scored the game's tying run but severely injured a hamstring and had to be helped into the clubhouse. But Odom and Blue combined to hold Detroit to just five singles and no runs after the first, and the A's won their first pennant since the franchise was in Philadelphia in 1931. They scored just 13 runs in the five games but were able to win because they held the Tigers to only ten runs, 32 hits and a .198 batting average, while Hunter, Odom, Blue and Fingers all posted minuscule ERAs.

Campaneris was allowed to return for the World Series against the Cincinnati Reds. Commissioner Kuhn, after negotiating with Finley and the Major League Baseball Players Association, ruled he could play but would be suspended for the first week of the 1973 season. Jackson, however, was lost for the entire series, and little-used George Hendrick and Angel Mangual divided up his outfield spot.

With Jackson out the A's seemed to be short of power, especially against a Cincinnati squad that featured Johnny Bench, Tony Perez and Joe Morgan. But Gene Tenace stepped up to fill the void. Having won the lion's share of the catching job in mid-season from defensive whiz Dave Duncan, Tenace batted just .225 in the regular season, with only five home runs. Against Detroit he managed just one single, though it drove in the winning run in the final game. Now against the Reds he exploded for home runs in his first two at-bats, and then swatted two more in the next four games. Oakland needed all of it as every game except the sixth was decided by just one run in one of the most tightly contested World Series ever played. Again, A's pitching dominated. Holtzman, Fingers and Blue (pitching out of the bullpen in the postseason) won the opener, 3–2, even though Reds pitchers gave up only four hits, then Hunter blanked Cincinnati until tiring in the ninth and giving way to Fingers, who recorded the final out. Joe Rudi also sparkled in the game, hitting a home run in the third and making a spectacular catch in the ninth. Odom performed brilliantly in Game Three but was outpitched by Jack Billingham as the Reds scored a 1–0 victory, but Oakland came back to tally two runs in the bottom of the ninth for a 3–2 win and a three games to one lead.

At this point, though, Cincinnati's hitters began to solve Oakland pitching. Trailing by a run after seven and facing the prospect of going home for the winter, the Reds tied it in the eighth and won it in the ninth, both runs coming against Fingers. Returning to Ohio, the Reds pounded Vida Blue and three Oakland relievers for ten hits in an 8–1 win, the only game not decided by one run. This brought the Series down to one game, winner-take-all, and the A's responded. Scoring two runs in the sixth inning and using both Catfish Hunter and Ken Holtzman out of the bullpen, Oakland beat Cincinnati 3–2 to capture their first World Series title.

Following the 1971 season, the A's had made just one deal, trading Ken Holtzman for Rick Monday. Upon ascending to the top of the baseball ladder, however, Oakland proved to be far more active in the trade mart as they attempted to maintain their supremacy. During the off-season they reacquired lefthanded reliever Paul Lindblad and picked up center fielder Bill North, pitcher Horacio Piña and catcher Ray Fosse. World Series hero Gene Tenace would move to first base, and the newly-acquired North would alternate between the outfield and baseball's most recent innovation, the designated hitter. Advocated for years by Finley, this new position recognized that pitching had become too dominant and thus was designed to give a boost to lagging

The 1973 Oakland Athletics

batting orders by allowing someone else to bat for the pitcher without having to remove that pitcher from the game. Perhaps the 1972 World Series, in which just 37 runs were scored in the seven games, convinced baseball's powers-that-be to take this drastic step. Well, not all of them: the National League refused to go along, and so the DH appeared just in the American League, creating a slightly different set of rules between the two leagues for the first time in anyone's memory. While the NL had agreed, at the outset, to study the value of adding the DH, they eventually hardened their position against it so that the final 28 seasons of the 20th century produced two leagues with two differing philosophies.

The DH provided the American League with the jolt they were seeking. In 1972, the AL's 12 teams batted an aggregate .239, scoring 6,441 runs on 14,751 hits, of which 3,751 went for extra bases, while the league's pitchers produced a 3.06 ERA. A year later the batting average soared to .259, with 8,314 runs scoring (a whopping 29 percent increase) on 17,193 hits, 4,580 of which were extra-base knocks. Though a record number of 20-game winners were produced (12), in general AL pitchers took their lumps, as the league's 3.82 ERA was the highest since 1962.

Ironically, even though Finley had championed the use of a DH for years, it took the A's a while to adapt to the new rule. Billy North was originally placed in that spot, but a lack of production from center field and a sub–.500 mark in early May prompted a deal with Philadelphia for veteran Deron Johnson. North took over in center and provided the A's with great speed (his 53 stolen bases were second-best in the league, just one behind Boston's Tommy Harper), a good bat (.285) and solid defense. Johnson filled the bill at DH, swatting 19 home runs and driving in 81. The team began to jell and moved up in the standings while the opposition crumbled. The White Sox, their primary adversaries in 1972, lost reigning MVP Dick Allen to a broken leg in late June, which effectively ended their championship hopes for the season. Despite 20-game winners Nolan Ryan and Bill Singer and future Hall of Famer Frank Robinson, the Angels didn't hit with any consistency, especially after losing young outfield star Bobby Valentine, also to a broken leg. The Kansas City Royals and Minnesota Twins were both young and inexperienced, which allowed the A's to capture their third straight American League West title.

Oakland overcame its own injury problems. Catfish Hunter suffered a hairline fracture to his right thumb during the All-Star Game, putting him out of commission for a month. Manager Dick Williams had his appendix removed. Reggie Jackson, on his way to an MVP selection, pulled a hamstring late in the season and missed two weeks. A variety of aches and pains sidelined Joe Rudi for 40 games throughout 1973. And even owner Charlie Finley went down after suffering a heart attack on August 7. Yet the A's won because of their balance, as well as their experience and talent. Jackson, Bando, Tenace and Johnson supplied the power while North and Campaneris provided the speed as the team led the league in runs scored. Hunter, Holtzman and Blue each won twenty games and anchored a staff that had no other pitchers win in double-figures and had only two others (one of them relief ace Rollie Fingers) throw more than 100 innings.

The A's also won in spite of themselves. Veteran observers could not remember any team that squabbled so much in the clubhouse yet still managed to play winning baseball. Players constantly criticized Williams' managerial moves, while everyone seemed to snipe at something Finley did or said, primarily when it came to money. No one was quite as tightfisted as Charles O. Finley, who operated with the smallest front-office staff in the major leagues, and the fewest number of full-time scouts. His penuriousness became legendary, and his talented ballclub became baseball's traveling soap opera.

But they knew how to put it all together when it counted. Yet another injury sidelined a starter, this time North, for the entire playoff series against Baltimore, and when the Orioles bombarded Vida Blue in the opening game, 6–0, the A's chances to go back to the World Series looked bleak. Whereas another team might have given up, Oakland simply reached for something extra. Sal Bando hit two home runs (and narrowly missed a third), and Hunter and Fingers combined to stop the Orioles and tie up the series. Then Ken Holtzman and Mike Cuellar matched serves for ten nail-biting innings, giving up just six hits between them. Bert Campaneris ended the suspense by leading off the bottom of the 11th inning with a home run, giving the A's the victory. And when they jumped all over Jim Palmer the next day to take a 4–0 lead into the seventh inning, it looked like the A's had another AL pennant wrapped up. But the Orioles managed to tie it up and then win with a Bobby Grich home run off the usually reliable Fingers, sending the series to a deciding fifth game. Dick Williams made two changes in his lineup, starting mid-season acquisitions Jesus Alou and Vic Davalillo, and they combined to fuel a fourth inning rally that carried the A's and Catfish Hunter to a 3–0 victory.

The 1973 World Series pitted the defending champions against a team with the worst record of any pennant winner in history. On August 30 the New York Mets were in last place in the National League East, but were still within striking distance of the leaders in a weak but very balanced division. Winning 21 of their final 28 games as several injured players returned to action, the Mets captured the division with a record of just 82–79. Yet against the heavily-favored Cincinnati Reds, winners of a major-league high 99 games, Met pitching overcame the Big Red offense (and a full-scale brawl in Game Three which also featured New York fans littering the field with anything they could throw) to advance to the World Series. Despite their pitiful won-loss record, the Mets had a strong pitching staff, led by future Hall of Famer Tom Seaver and three outstanding lefties: veteran Jerry Koosman, young Jon Matlack and relief ace (and emotional leader) Tug McGraw.

The Series proved to be a wild affair, yet the key play occurred in the opening game. Matlack allowed only three hits, but they all came in the third inning. With two out his mound opponent Ken Holtzman, who hadn't batted all year, doubled. Bert Campaneris hit a routine grounder to second but the normally surehanded Felix Millan let the ball go through his legs for an error and Holtzman scored. Campy then stole second and scored on Joe Rudi's hit. The Mets only managed one run off Holtzman and the Oakland bullpen, and the A's won the game. If Millan fielded that groundball the Mets might have won the game and, as the series played out, the world championship.

Game Two had more twists and turns than a mountain road. Starters Koosman and Blue were both knocked out, but the Mets were poised for victory until the A's scored two in the bottom of the ninth to tie it up. In the 12th, the Mets scored four runs, three of which were the direct result of errors by reserve second baseman Mike Andrews on back-to-back plays. Incredibly, the A's actually rebounded and had the tying run on base in the bottom of the inning but fell short, 10–7, and the Series moved to New York all knotted up.

The following day, Finley attempted to fire Mike Andrews, claiming the veteran infielder had a bad shoulder. Oakland's players united and threatened to boycott the rest of the Series unless Andrews was reinstated. Commissioner Kuhn stepped in and ordered Andrews' reinstatement, and admonished "the Oakland club" (read: Finley) for their handling of the matter. While much of the country chuckled over Finley's antics, Dick Williams seethed. He had had enough of his boss, and privately told his players he would resign following the World Series.

Game Three also went into extra innings, but Oakland prevailed, 3–2, on an RBI single by Campaneris. Then Met pitching took over: Matlack stymied the A's, 6–1, in Game Four, and Koosman and McGraw combined on a three-hitter in the fifth game, 2–0, giving the Mets a 3–2 Series lead as the two teams returned to Oakland.

With their backs to the wall, the A's responded yet again. The starters — Cooperstown-bound Hunter and Seaver — pitched equally well; the difference proved to be Reggie Jackson and Rusty Staub. Jackson had three hits, including two run-scoring doubles, to power the A's. Staub, the Mets' best all-around player, had been able to hide an injured shoulder all week but it finally proved costly in Game Six, as he was unable to make two key throws, resulting in Oakland's final two runs, the margin of victory.

Through six games and 57 innings the A's had not hit a single home run. But in the seventh and final game of the 1973 World Series, Campaneris and Jackson both hit two-run shots off a weary Jon Matlack, pitching on just two days' rest, and the Oakland A's became the first team since the 1961–62 New York Yankees to capture consecutive World Series crowns.

The off-season began just moments after the final out was made, as Dick Williams announced his resignation in the celebratory locker room on national television. After months of public bickering and much speculation, Finley finally realized Williams meant what he had said and hired Alvin Dark as his manager. For baseball lifer Dark this would be his second go-round with Finley, having managed the then–Kansas City A's in 1966 and much of 1967 before being fired.

Dark's return was the only major change the A's made in the off-season. Despite the continual soap opera of players criticizing their owner, manager and one another, the A's had only a little trouble winning the American League West once again. An August slump let the upstart Texas Rangers get back into the race, and they remained within striking distance of the A's until the two met in mid–September. The Rangers, led by fiery manager Billy Martin and MVP outfielder Jeff Burroughs, won the first two games to come within four lengths of Oakland, but couldn't supply the knockout blow. Team captain Sal Bando cracked a two-run homer, and Rollie Fingers pitched almost five innings of relief to stall the Ranger locomotive. While not playing spectacular baseball, the A's played well enough down the stretch to advance to the postseason once again.

Once again the A's won with their balance. Bando led the club with 103 RBI but Joe Rudi contributed 99 and Reggie Jackson knocked in 93. That trio, plus Gene Tenace, gave the club four players with 20 or more home runs, but Billy North, Bert Campaneris and Jackson propelled a running game that wound up leading the league in stolen bases. A significant addition was 19-year-old outfielder Claudell Washington, who was called up from Double-A in early July and added a steady bat and more speed to the team. On the mound, Hunter led the league with his 25 wins and 2.49 ERA, on his way to the Cy Young Award. Holtzman won 19 and Blue won 17 as once again all three pitching mainstays worked more than 250 innings. When they needed help, Rollie Fingers as always was the key man out of the bullpen.

For the third time in four years the A's faced the Baltimore Orioles in the playoffs. And the usual pattern held true to form as the O's won the opening game, hitting three home runs off Hunter to support Mike Cuellar. Unlike previous playoff series, however, the A's immediately took charge after this loss; specifically, the pitchers thoroughly throttled the Birds. Ken Holtzman threw a five-hit shutout, then Vida Blue outdueled Jim Palmer, 1–0, in Game Three. Palmer only gave up four hits, but one was a 4th inning homer to Bando. Blue, for his part, yielded just two singles.

Cuellar and Hunter were back in Game Four, and both were hard to hit. Cuellar, in fact, did not give up a single safety, but was removed in the fifth inning because he had walked nine batters, including four in a row in the fifth inning to produce the A's first run. In the seventh, Reggie Jackson doubled home Sal Bando for the A's second run but only their first hit, and they would get no more. But Hunter gave up just three singles during his seven innings, and Fingers, despite a shaky ninth, held on to close out the series. Not only had Oakland won its third straight flag, but Alvin Dark became only the third manager in history to win pennants in both leagues (Joe McCarthy, with the Cubs and Yankees; and Yogi Berra, with the Yankees and Mets, were the others).

The A's faced off against the Los Angeles Dodgers in the first-ever all–California World Series. Walter Alston's last pennant winner featured a powerful pitching staff, with five hurlers posting double-digit victory totals (including relief ace Mike Marshall). They also had some power in their lineup, with first baseman Steve Garvey, third baseman Ron Cey, outfielder Jimmy Wynn and catcher-outfielder Joe Ferguson. Their chances seemed to improve against the more experienced A's when, prior to the opening game, pitchers Rollie Fingers and Blue Moon Odom had a fistfight in the clubhouse. Pugilism was nothing new to these A's, however; Jackson and North had squared off earlier in the season, and it had not stopped the team from winning their division. The same would hold true in this World Series.

The teams traded 3–2 victories at Dodger Stadium. Fingers relieved Holtzman in the fifth inning of Game One, and when he seemed to tire in the ninth, Dark surprised many by calling on Catfish Hunter, who struck out Ferguson, representing the winning run. The next day, Don Sutton bested Vida Blue, but when he tired in the ninth Mike Marshall came in and preserved the win to tie up the Series.

Hunter was back in Game Three, this time in his more familiar role as a starter. He blanked the Dodgers through seven, but left after giving up a solo homer. Fingers relieved, as usual, and gave up his own solo shot in the ninth, but had enough to save the Series' third straight 3–2 game. Then the next day,

Ken Holtzman not only held the Dodgers in check, he also blasted a home run, giving the A's their first run of the day. In the Series, Holtzman had a double and a homer; the previous year against the Mets, he hit two doubles. After the Dodgers took the lead, Oakland came back with a four-run sixth inning to put the game on ice.

It was Blue versus Sutton again in Game Five, and the A's struck early, picking up runs in the first two innings. But Los Angeles nicked Blue for a pair in the sixth and the game was tied. Hoping to send the Series back to L.A., Alston called on Marshall early; Joe Rudi, however, hit one into the seats in the seventh inning, putting Oakland back on top. The Dodgers had a chance in the eighth, as Bill Buckner lined a single off the newly-arrived Fingers. The ball got past North and Buckner went to second, then decided to try for third. Reggie Jackson, backing up the play just the way it's practiced in spring training, threw to second baseman Dick Green, who relayed to Sal Bando, who put the tag on the sliding Buckner for the out. The Dodgers went quietly after that, and the A's won their third consecutive World Series.

Even while the 1974 World Series was being played, however, the Oakland A's dynasty was about to come to an end. Just prior to the opening game, Catfish Hunter charged Finley with breach of contract. Hunter said that Finley had promised, in writing, to pay a $50,000 installment on Hunter's life insurance policy, which amounted to half of the ace pitcher's annual salary. Hunter said he would declare himself a free agent after the Series if Finley refused to make the payment. Finley, of course, denied the charge.

The Major League Players Association filed grievances against Finley on behalf of Hunter, and the case went before arbitrator Peter Seitz. On December 13, 1974, Seitz ruled that Finley owed Hunter the $50,000, plus six percent interest, and that Hunter was, in accordance with baseball rules, a free agent, effective immediately. It was the first time in history that a player was allowed to leave his team on his own terms. A bidding war then ensued as teams stampeded to rural eastern North Carolina courting the 28-year-old Hunter. Less than three weeks later, he signed a five-year contract with the New York Yankees worth $3.75 million, making him the highest-paid player in the game. The wall of absolute control built up by owners and management for more than eighty years suffered its first significant crack, and the balance of power was about to change.

On the field, there was still more than enough talent for the 1975 A's to win their fifth straight American League West title. Gene Tenace moved back behind the plate so Joe Rudi could move to first base and Claudell Washington could play every day. Washington batted .308 with 40 stolen bases, justifying the move, and Tenace and Rudi combined with Reggie Jackson and longtime National League All-Star Billy Williams to produce another formidable lineup. Vida Blue took charge of the pitching staff, winning 22 games, and Ken Holtzman chipped in with another 18, while Rollie Fingers saved 24 games and Paul Lindblad and Jim Todd provided valuable innings out of the bullpen. A May trade brought pitcher Dick Bosman from Cleveland, and he proved to be a reliable third starter, winning 11. The A's won 98 games, their best regular-season mark since 1971, outdistancing the up-and-coming Kansas City Royals. But in the playoffs against the Boston Red Sox, the dynasty crumbled quickly, shockingly. A close opening game was blown open in the seventh inning by poor defense and a bullpen meltdown, as Luis Tiant and the Sox three-hit the A's, 7–1. In the second game, Boston spotted Oakland a three-run lead, then came back to tie it in the fourth and pull away with single runs in the six, seventh and eighth innings, all against Fingers. Finally, in the third game, Holtzman was called on with just two days' rest, a decision possibly mandated by Finley, who didn't trust Bosman. Holtzman was gone by the fifth, and the Red Sox withstood an eighth inning Oakland rally to win, 5–3, and sweep the A's into history.

The final act was partially played out at an arbitrator's table. In a case brought by pitchers Andy Messersmith and Dave McNally, Peter Seitz ruled that, if a player did not sign a new contract and played a full season under the terms of his old agreement, he was entitled to become a free agent. (Seitz was subsequently fired by major league owners.) Finley realized that under this new world order, small-market clubs like Oakland would consistently lose out as the best players would go to the larger, wealthier, more glamorous cities. Rather than lose Reggie Jackson and receive nothing, therefore, he traded him to Baltimore just before the 1976 season began; Ken Holtzman was also included in this deal, in which the A's received outfielder Don Baylor and pitcher Mike Torrez. During the season, Finley attempted to sell Joe Rudi and Rollie Fingers to the Red Sox for $2 million, and Vida Blue to the Yankees for $1.5 million. If he couldn't re-sign his star players — and he knew his unhappy campers would all leave when the 1976 season was over — Finley reasoned he would take the money and use it to sign new players. Commissioner Kuhn, however, long Finley's prime nemesis, stepped in and voided the deals, claiming they were not in the best interests of baseball. Finley sued Kuhn and baseball, but eventually lost in U.S. district court.

Even amidst all the unhappiness and turmoil — Finley had also fired manager Al Dark and replaced him with former White Sox manager Chuck Tanner — the team amazingly stayed in the pennant race all season. But the young Royals outlasted Oakland for the Western Division title, and the A's dynasty officially came to an end. After the 1976 season, players fled Oakland in droves; the 1977 squad had just a handful of familiar faces, and the team plunged to the bottom of the division, losing 98 games. It would take several years, and an eventual change in ownership, before the Oakland A's were once again a force to be reckoned with in the AL West.

1975–76
Cincinnati Reds

Cincinnati's "Big Red Machine" was developed like fine wine — slowly, carefully, over time. While today that team is remembered for its 1975 and 1976 World Series triumphs, the seeds were actually planted about a dozen years earlier.

In 1963, the Cincinnati Reds were just two years removed from a World Series appearance and were still a top pennant contender in the National League. That year a 22-year-old switch-hitting second baseman named Pete Rose made the jump from Double-A to become Rookie of the Year. Rose's all-out, hell-bent style earned him the nickname "Charlie Hustle" and later came to symbolize the Reds' type of play. He would eventually become an All-Star at five different positions, win three batting titles and collect more hits in his career than any other man who had ever played the game. Two years later he was joined by Cuban-born Tony Perez. A powerful righthanded slugger, Perez had an uncanny knack for driving in runs; from 1967 through 1977 he had over 100 RBI six times and more than 90 in five other seasons. He was also a consummate team player. A first baseman by trade, he learned to play third base and manned the position for five years so the Reds could get the big bat of Lee May into their lineup. Then in 1968 the Reds daringly entrusted their pitching staff to a 20-year-old catcher. Despite his youth, Johnny Bench displayed a maturity beyond his years, to say nothing of his skills behind the plate. His quick feet helped to revolutionize play behind the plate, and it didn't hurt that he also featured a cannon arm. And with a bat in his hands he became one of the most feared sluggers of his time, twice winning the Most Valuable Player Award. This trio became the cornerstone of the Big Red Machine.

After a disappointing 1969 season, Cincinnati hired George "Sparky" Anderson to be their manager. Anderson was not afraid to go with youth: he installed 22-year-old Dave Concepcion at short and featured a starting eight and four-man rotation comprised entirely of players under thirty. Concepcion would become the very model of the modern shortstop, influencing the generation that followed him after 19 seasons as a Red — tall and rangy, with a good glove, powerful arm and a potent bat as well. That young 1970 squad won 70 of their first 100 games and won the Western Division by 14½ games, making it to the World Series before bowing to the powerful Baltimore Orioles.

Anderson and Reds fans everywhere probably thought their team was primed to challenge for the pennant every year. If that was the case, then 1971 was a major disappointment as they tumbled to fourth place, four games under .500. This led to a major off-season deal with the Houston Astros, a trade that literally transformed Cincinnati from a good team into the dominant National

League club of the decade. The Astros were looking for a power hitter, so the Reds sent them Lee May, plus infielders Tommy Helms and Jimmy Stewart, and received in exchange second baseman Joe Morgan, pitcher Jack Billingham and a little-used young outfielder, Cesar Geronimo, in addition to a couple of other players. The effect on the Reds' lineup was electric. Perez was able to move back to first base, his natural position, while Morgan, a fine player in Houston, truly blossomed in a Reds uniform. He hit for average and power, stole bases, played an excellent second base and became not only a team leader but also eventually was recognized as one of the very best players in all of baseball. Geronimo, despite his limited major league experience, was installed in center field and soon unveiled his Gold Glove talents. Though never much of a power hitter (only once did he reach ten home runs for a season), he made himself into a respectable batter, one who contributed on offense as well as defense. Billingham, meanwhile, became one of Anderson's most reliable starters, winning in double figures every year he wore a Reds uniform.

Remembered primarily for their offense, and rightly so, this team also featured some better-than-average pitching. Billingham was a mainstay, as was little Freddie Norman, a soft-tossing lefty who came over from San Diego in a 1973 trade. So, too, was Don Gullett, who won nearly 70 percent of his career decisions but unfortunately missed a great many starts due to a variety of injuries that forced him to retire at the age of 27. In fact, Anderson seemed to have been plagued with talented young hurlers whose careers were cut short due to ailments — Wayne Simpson and Gary Nolan being others. It was not, however, because Anderson overworked his starters. In fact, he was given the nickname "Captain Hook" because of his penchant for making frequent use of his bullpen. And over the years the Reds brought some talented pitchers into the game in the middle and late innings, such as the lanky Wayne Granger, the reliable Clay Carroll, the hard-throwing and sometimes-volatile Pedro Borbon, rail-thin southpaw Tom Hall, and Rawly Eastwick, the National League's best in 1975 and 1976. In many ways, Anderson's deployment of a deep and talented bullpen was the key to the Reds' continued success.

Cincinnati's new-look lineup roared back to the World Series in 1972 and missed winning it all by a single run in the seventh and final game. The 1973 club won 99 games in the regular season but somehow lost the league championship series to a New York Mets squad that had been in last place in August and won their division despite finishing just three games above .500. In 1974 they spent the summer battling the Los Angeles Dodgers for supremacy in the National League West but eventually came out second-best to Walter Alston's last pennant winner.

Always with an eye for young talent, Anderson was intrigued with the batting potential of a couple of his young outfielders: sweet-swinging Ken Griffey and powerful George Foster. But how could he get both of their bats into the game at the same time? The answer came from Pete Rose, who volunteered to move from the outfield to third base, thus allowing Anderson to put Foster in left and Griffey in right on an everyday basis. That move, and the addition of Eastwick to the bullpen, paved the way for the next two seasons and the legend of the Big Red Machine.

Though obviously loaded with talent, the Reds stumbled out of the blocks as the 1975 season got underway. The Los Angeles Dodgers, the defending league champs, came out strong and had opened up a five-and-a-half game lead over Cincinnati before Sparky Anderson finally got his team organized. The Reds began to rally in late May and over a 50-game period, they won 41 times. As early as the All-Star break, there was little doubt as to who was going to win the Western Division. In the end, Anderson's Big Red Machine finished with an amazing 108–54 record that put them 20 games ahead of the second place Dodgers.

The Reds' starting eight position players that season comprised just as much a "Murderers' Row" as the 1927 Yankees had. With a lineup featuring players like catcher Johnny Bench (.283, 28 HR, 110 RBI), third baseman Pete Rose (.317, 112 runs), and first baseman Tony Perez (.282, 20 HR, 109 RBI), the Reds could strike fear into the heart of even the best opposing pitcher. And it didn't stop there. At second base, Joe Morgan was the league MVP and the epitome of the complete baseball player. He could hit for both power and average, steal bases and score runs with his great speed, and play stifling defense. In 1975 he put together a season in which he batted .327, hit 17 home runs, scored 107 runs, drove in 94, stole 67 bases, drew a league-leading 132 walks, and won the Gold Glove Award. Shortstop Dave Concepcion (.274) stole 33 bases and was also a brilliant fielder while the outfield was made up of George Foster (.300, 23 HR), Gold Glove center fielder Cesar Geronimo (.257), and Ken Griffey (.305, 95 runs).

The Reds set a National League record in 1975 for the fewest number of players used in a 162-game season with just 29. Anderson had a great knowledge of his players and he seemed to know exactly when and where each of them had the best chance to succeed (he made the bold but brilliant move of switching All-Star outfielder Rose to third base early in the season). He used his bench players often but since his reserves played their roles so well, there was never a real need to make mid-season trades or a lot of call-ups from the minor leagues. Each appearing in at least one-third of that season's games were first baseman Dan Driessen (.281, 7 HR), utility infielders Darrel Chaney and Doug Flynn, catcher Bill Plummer, and outfielders Merv Rettenmund, Ed Armbrister, and Terry Crowley.

The Reds of the mid–1970s will forever be famous for their offense but the pitchers deserve credit as well. Though it certainly wasn't a staff that could compare to that of teams like the late 1920s Yankees or the early 1970s Orioles, they won when it counted the most and kept other games close enough for the Reds batters to make up the difference. The six pitchers from which Anderson drew to make up his starting rotation all won at least ten games and three of

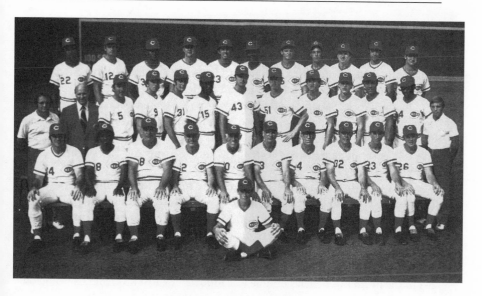

The 1976 Cincinnati Reds

them won 15. Lefty Don Gullett was the ace of the staff and his 15–4 record (with a 2.42 ERA) gave him a league-best .789 winning percentage. Gary Nolan (15–9, 3.16 ERA) and Jack Billingham (15–10, 4.11 ERA) both equaled Gullett's win total while Fred Norman won 12 games and lost only four. Pat Darcy finished at 11–5, and Clay Kirby contributed a 10–6 record.

The heavily-used Reds bullpen was led by a hard-throwing rookie named Rawly Eastwick. Called up to the big leagues the previous September, Eastwick earned the job of closer in spring training. Called on by Anderson 58 times during the course of the season, the righthander responded with a league-leading 22 saves, a 5–3 record and an ERA of 2.60. Appearing in 56 games, veteran Clay Carroll, who had been one of the best closers in the game during the late 1960s and early 1970s, saw just as much work as Eastwick. With an ERA of 2.62, he recorded seven saves and an equal number of wins. The team's lefthanded relief ace was second-year man Will McEnaney. Leading the team with seventy appearances, he saved 15 games, won five and had an ERA of 2.47. Completing the impressive relief corps was righthander Pedro Borbon; often used in middle relief he finished with a 9–5 record, a 2.95 ERA and five saves.

The Big Red Machine's first postseason victim in 1975 was the Pittsburgh Pirates. With 16 fewer wins than the Reds, the Pirates had taken the NL East with a 92–69 record. Though that team featured players like Willie Stargell, Dave Parker and Al Oliver, they couldn't slow the Reds' juggernaut. In the first game, Don Gullett allowed three runs over nine innings but drove in three runs himself with a home run and a single as the Reds took an 8–3 victory. The next day it was Tony Perez who homered as he led the Reds to an easy 6–1 win.

In the final game of the sweep the Pirates didn't roll over quite as easily. Cincinnati trailed in the eighth inning but Pete Rose put them ahead with a two-run homer. In the bottom of the ninth, however, Rawly Eastwick walked in the tying run. That forced extra innings but in the top of the tenth the Reds rallied for two runs and Pedro Borbon held the lead.

In the World Series, the Reds were heavily favored and expected to roll right over the Boston Red Sox. Instead, they had to fight down to the last inning of the last game to take what is arguably the greatest World Series ever played. Five of the seven games were decided by only one run and two of those went into extra innings.

Don Gullett got the start in Game One for the Reds while veteran Luis Tiant was on the mound for Boston. Both pitched well through six innings but in the seventh, the Red Sox bats came alive and they scored six runs. Meanwhile, the Reds' great hitters were never able to solve Tiant and he coasted to a complete-game, five-hit win. The Reds had to use four pitchers and a ninth-inning rally to even the Series with a 3–2 win in Game Two. Boston had led 2–1 in the ninth but Bench's double was followed by RBI hits from Concepcion and Griffey.

The Reds also took Game Three with a ninth-inning rally. In a game that featured three home runs by each team, the Red Sox scored first but the Reds stormed back to take a 5–1 lead at the end of five. The Red Sox didn't give up and tied the score in the eighth but Joe Morgan drove in the winning run in the bottom of the ninth. The following day the Red Sox evened the Series with a 5–4 win. Luis Tiant pitched his second complete game and, though he gave up four runs, Boston's five runs in the fourth inning gave him the run support he needed.

Tony Perez took it upon himself to single-handedly defeat the Red Sox in Game Five, essentially with two home runs and four RBI. The 6–2 win put the Reds only one game away from the title. Game Six may just be the most dramatic World Series contest ever played. Tiant was again on the mound for the Red Sox and got an early lead when Fred Lynn slugged a three-run homer in the bottom of the first. Tiant held the Reds scoreless through the fourth but key hits by Griffey and Bench allowed the Reds to tie it up in the top of the fifth. Adding two more runs in the seventh and one in the eighth (a solo home run by Geronimo), the Reds appeared to have the title wrapped up. In the bottom of the eighth, however, Boston sent pinch hitter Bernie Carbo to the plate with two men on and he responded with a game-tying home run over the center field wall. Neither team was able to score in the ninth and the game remained deadlocked after 11½ innings. In the bottom of the 12th, the Red Sox' first batter was catcher Carlton Fisk. On the first pitch thrown to him by Pat Darcy, the eighth pitcher the Reds had used, Fisk ended the game with a home run just barely inside the left field foul pole. The indelible image of Fisk frantically trying to wave the ball fair as he ran to first base is probably the most memorable baseball moment of the 1970s.

Boston had the momentum going into Game Seven and they had a 3–0 lead after three innings. Finally, in the top of the sixth, a two-run homer by Perez put the Reds on the board. They continued the rally in the seventh with a tying run and then pulled ahead with another score in the top of the ninth. The Red Sox had three outs left to stage another miracle but the magic was gone and reliever Will McEnaney retired the side to seal the title for the Reds.

Though hard to believe, the Reds were even better in 1976 than they had been in 1975. They won six games less than they had the previous season to finish with a 102–60 record but the competition was stronger (the winner of the NL East, the Phillies, also topped the 100-win mark). Still, the Reds managed to lead the major leagues in ten offensive categories — batting average, runs, hits, doubles, triples, home runs, walks, on-base percentage, and slugging percentage, as well as in fielding average. Seven of the eight Reds' starters made the All-Star team. The starting pitching rotation may have been unspectacular but they got the job done and were backed up by the league's best bullpen. In a word, the 1976 Reds were awesome.

For the second straight year, the offense was led by Joe Morgan and Pete Rose. Morgan had another spectacular season (.320, 111 RBI, 27 HR, 113 runs, 114 bases on balls, 60 stolen bases) and repeated as the winner of the league's Most Valuable Player Award. Rose (.323) showed why he was called "Charlie Hustle" by leading the league in hits (215), runs (130) and doubles (42). Rounding out the infield were Perez, who drove in more than 90 runs for the tenth straight season and hit 19 home runs, and Concepcion, who contributed a .281 batting average and 29 stolen bases.

Even if the infielders didn't beat opponents with their bats, they could do it with their gloves. If a ball coming through the middle was even close to being playable, Gold Glove winners Morgan and Concepcion stopped it. Rose was also a gifted fielder and had the league's best fielding percentage at his position (though the Phillies' Mike Schmidt took the Gold Glove) and, with a .996 fielding percentage, Perez's hands weren't exactly made of stone either.

Combining power, speed, and defense, the Reds outfield unit was nearly perfect. Right fielder Griffey led the team with a .336 batting average, scored 111 runs, and stole 34 bases. He also proved that it wasn't just Rose who hustled by beating out 37 infield hits. In left, Foster had a league-best .994 fielding percentage and his powerful swing had gotten even sweeter. He batted .306, slugged 29 home runs, led the league with 121 RBI and finished second to Joe Morgan in voting for the league MVP Award. In center field, Cesar Geronimo took his third straight Gold Glove Award, batted .307 and stole 22 bases.

After four years of 100-plus RBI and at least 25 home runs, Bench had an off-year in 1976 and batted only .234 with 16 homers and 74 runs batted in. It didn't matter, though, because what he lacked at the plate he made up for in defensive ability, leading all of the league's catchers with an incredible .997 fielding percentage.

Again, Anderson made good use of his bench players. Reserve first base-man/outfielder Dan Driessen (.247) saw considerable playing time and con-tributed seven home runs and 44 RBI (he also served as designated hitter in the World Series). Catcher Bill Plummer (.248), infielder Doug Flynn (.283), and outfielder Ed Armbrister (.295) were all capable backups, as were a cou-ple of veterans who had been picked up in trades before the season. Former Brave Mike Lum (.228), able to play in the outfield or at first, and third base-man/outfielder Bob Bailey (.298), who had been acquired from Montreal, were both versatile and experienced players.

The Reds pitching staff had to do without two of the key players from the previous season. Gone were both Clay Carroll (to the White Sox) and Clay Kirby (to Montreal) and to replace them the Reds were forced to rely on sev-eral rookies. Thrown into the starting rotation was a pair of 6'5" righthanders: Pat Zachry, who had had an outstanding 1975 season with the Reds' top farm club in Indianapolis, and 23-year-old Dominican Santo Alcala. The gamble paid off when Zachry posted a 14–7 record with a team-best 2.74 ERA, while Alcala finished the season at 11–4.

Six pitchers, used in various combinations, made up Sparky Anderson's starting rotation in 1976. Though none of them won more than 15 games, each had a winning record and at least 11 wins. In addition to Zachry and Alcala, the group included righthanders Gary Nolan (15–9, 3.46 ERA) and Jack Billing-ham (12–10, 4.32 ERA). Don Gullett (11–3, 3.00 ERA), the closest thing the Reds had to a true ace, and Fred Norman (12–7, 3.09 ERA) were the portsiders.

Just like the previous season, Anderson was quick to go to his bullpen but fortunately had the best one in baseball to call upon. In what would prove to be the best season of his career, Rawly Eastwick was again the Reds' ace reliever. Appearing in 71 games, he posted an 11–5 record with a 2.09 ERA and a league-leading 26 saves. Pedro Borbon (4–3, 8 saves, 69 games) and lefthander Will McEnaney (7 saves, 55 games) continued to excel while rookie Manny Sarmiento (5–1, 2.06 ERA), who was called up in late July, made a phenomenal debut.

The 1976 postseason wasn't nearly as exciting as the previous year's had been for the Reds. Once again in the NLCS, they swept their opponent in three straight games, though this time it was the other Pennsylvania team, the Phillies, who faced the wrath of the Big Red Machine. Though they trailed at some point during each of the games, the Reds offense could not be contained and the final scores read 6–3, 6–2, and 7–6.

The steamroller continued right on through the World Series matchup with the New York Yankees. With a team that included the likes of Catfish Hunter, Graig Nettles and Thurman Munson, the Bronx Bombers of manager Billy Martin had won 97 games during the regular season. They were no match, however, for Rose, Morgan, Bench and Company, who destroyed the Ameri-can Leaguers in a four-game sweep.

In Game One, Don Gullett and Pedro Borbon combined to surrender only five hits and one run while Morgan's first inning home run was the first of five Cincinnati runs. Game Two was actually close, and though the Reds scored three early runs, the Yankees fought back to tie it up in the sixth. In the bottom of the ninth with two outs, a throwing error by shortstop Fred Stanley allowed Griffey to reach second. He easily scored on a single by Perez to take the game.

Zachry got the start for the Reds in Game Three and pitched well, giving up only two runs on six hits before handing the ball off to McEnaney in the seventh. The offense, meanwhile, provided support to the tune of 13 hits (including a Dan Driessen homer) and six runs. The Yankees took a 1–0 lead in the first inning of Game Four but two home runs and five RBI by Johnny Bench, along with strong pitching by Nolan and McEnaney, shut the door. With the 7–2 win the Reds became the first National League team in 54 years to repeat as world champions.

After the season, it appeared that the Reds would have a shot at taking a third title but the trading of Tony Perez to the Expos and the loss of Don Gullett to free agency (he joined the Yankees) changed everything. Primarily because of age and the undeniable fact that the Reds needed pitching, general manager Bob Howsam decided to deal the 34-year-old Perez and make 25-year-old Dan Driessen the starting first baseman. The change at first base seemed to be the right one since Driessen was a very capable player, and he picked up right where Perez left off by batting .300 and driving in 91 runs in 1977. However, the pitchers the Reds picked up in the trade, ones they so desperately needed, never panned out. The part of the deal that Howsam didn't count on was how the loss of a popular veteran leader, one who had been with Cincinnati since 1964, would affect the overall character of the team.

The Reds still played outstanding baseball in 1977 but lacked the fire they had had the year before; at the end of the season they were left in second place, trailing the Dodgers by 10 games. (This was despite a monster season by MVP George Foster, in which he batted .320 and lead the league with 52 home runs, 149 RBI, and 124 runs scored.) The Reds improved by a few games in 1978 but still lost the division to Dodgers. After the 1978 season, the Big Red Machine era came completely to an end when Sparky Anderson was replaced as manager by John McNamara. Anderson went on to join the Detroit Tigers where he would build another great team and win the 1984 World Series.

1976–78 New York Yankees

No franchise has ever dominated a sport the way the New York Yankees dominated major league baseball. For a period of 44 years, from 1921 through

1964, they won no fewer than 29 pennants and 20 world championships. Only hockey's Montreal Canadiens, with 24 Stanley Cup championships in 78 years, could challenge this claim. Professional basketball's Boston Celtics, in the 1950s and early 1960s, and the UCLA Bruins in college basketball in the 1960s and early 1970s, were definitely dynasties but their time span was much shorter. The Yankees' reign lasted nearly two generations, through the terms of eight presidents of the United States (Warren Harding through Lyndon Johnson), from shortly after the end of World War I until shortly before the escalation of the conflict in Vietnam. The New York Yankees, to paraphrase William Shakespeare, did bestride their narrow world like a Colossus.

And then, suddenly, it was over. After years of staying ahead of the competition and replacing aging players with young talent, the magic touch deserted them. Beginning in 1965, just a year after taking St. Louis to a seventh game in the World Series, the Yankees dropped to the nether reaches of the American League, hardly factoring in the pennant race for nearly a decade. In 1966 they finished in last place for the first time since 1912.

While the team floundered in the second division, they did manage to produce a few good players. Pitcher Mel Stottlemyre was the undisputed ace and the last link to Yankee greatness. The righthander had been a 22-year-old rookie when he was summoned from the minor leagues in August of 1964; he proceeded to win nine games and helped propel New York into the World Series, where he won another game. After that, he never failed to win in double figures until his final season in the majors, three times reaching 20, and he was durable, averaging 242 innings per season. A five-time All-Star, he was complemented by Roy White and Bobby Murcer. White had been a second baseman in the minors but was found to be lacking at the keystone and shifted to the outfield. Although he did not have a very good throwing arm he proved to have great instincts for the game and quickly established himself as a solid, steady ballplayer, much in the mold of Tommy Henrich. He could drive in a run with either a single or a home run or a sacrifice fly (which seemed to be a specialty); he could steal a base when it was needed (233 in his career); he almost always walked more than he struck out; and he played Yankee Stadium's tricky left field as if it had been designed around him. Murcer, like White, had been an infielder in the minors but was quickly found to be better suited for center field when he came up to stay in 1969. That, coupled with his power-speed combination and his Oklahoma lineage, drew unfair comparisons to Mickey Mantle. Though not a classic power hitter, Murcer assumed the role as New York's chief home run and RBI threat in those discouraging seasons.

Thurman Munson was soon added to this trio. The gruff Munson became the best catcher to wear a Yankee uniform since the heyday of Elston Howard, and almost immediately became the team leader. He was also the American League Rookie of the Year in 1970. After the 1971 season, the Yankees completed a rare trade with their arch rivals, the Boston Red Sox, sending infielder Danny

Cater to New England in exchange for lefthanded pitcher Sparky Lyle. The Pennsylvania native reinforced the stereotype that all lefties are more that a little crazy; he was known, for instance, to leap naked onto birthday cakes that were brought into the clubhouse. But he possessed a wicked slider that broke sharply down and in to a righthanded batter, making it extremely difficult to hit. (Steve Carlton would later add a similarly-thrown pitch to his arsenal.) In the strike-shortened 1972 season, behind Lyle's 35 saves* and Murcer's 33 home runs, the Yankees actually made a run at the division title, battling with Detroit, Boston and Baltimore before fading in September. Lacking a solid third baseman and seeking more sock in the lineup, New York made an off-season deal with Cleveland, sending some young talent to the Indians for lefthanded slugger Graig Nettles. His swing was tailor-made for Yankee Stadium, and he wound up topping 20 homers in a season 11 times, leading the league in 1976 and producing 252 round-trippers in the 1970s, second in the AL only to Reggie Jackson. The added bonus proved to be his glove, as he anchored the left side of the infield with the finest defense seen in the Bronx since Clete Boyer. Yet despite the increased run production the Yankees never really challenged for first.

That season was the first under new ownership. Media giant CBS had purchased the team back in August of 1964 and had presided over the poorest decade of Yankee baseball since before Babe Ruth wore pinstripes. In the fall of 1971 CBS began looking for a buyer and more than a year later found one, a group put together by Cleveland Indians General Manager Gabe Paul that included a Cleveland shipbuilder, George Steinbrenner. A former football coach at Purdue University, Steinbrenner told the press that Gabe Paul would be coming to New York to run things as team president because "[W]e're not baseball people ... I'm going to be an absentee owner." One change the new proprietors insisted on was a renovation to fifty-year-old Yankee Stadium. After the 1973 season the Bombers moved to Queens to share Shea Stadium with the Mets for two years while the House That Ruth Built was gutted, redesigned and modernized. Since the Stadium was owned by the City of New York, the cost to the taxpayers topped $100 million, twice what was originally projected.

The 1973 season also proved to be Ralph Houk's last in a Yankee uniform. As previously mentioned, "The Major" won the pennant and World Series in 1961 and 1962 and the AL crown alone in 1963 before becoming the team's general manager. But when the team plunged to the cellar in April of 1966, he dismissed Johnny Keane and returned to the dugout himself, where he remained until his resignation after the 1973 season, leaving behind some thirty years with the organization. The new manager was Bill Virdon, the former Pirate player

*For his efforts Lyle would wind up third in the voting for the Most Valuable Player award, the highest finish for any Yankee since Mickey Mantle and Elston Howard were second and third, respectively, in the 1964 balloting.

and manager who had been dismissed in Pittsburgh in September even though his team was fighting for first place in the National League East.

Virdon and Paul set about to solidify the Yankees' lineup. They strengthened the team's defense by bringing over shortstop Jim Mason and center fielder Elliott Maddox from Texas; Maddox also proved to be a .300 hitter until an injury ruined his career. They picked up another former Rookie of the Year, corner outfielder Lou Piniella, from the Kansas City Royals, and acquired second baseman Sandy Alomar, Sr., and pitcher Rudy May from the Angels. Then on April 26 they stunned the baseball world — as well as their own players — by swapping five pitchers to Cleveland for first baseman Chris Chambliss and pitcher Dick Tidrow. Once they got over the shock of losing their friends, the revamped team charged into the lead in the American League East, only to run into an even greater effort by the Baltimore Orioles. Earl Weaver's veteran squad put on a drive of their own, winning 28 of their final 34 games, including 15 by a single run, to nose out the Yankees by just two games. But the baseball world was put on notice that the Yankees were back.

The Oakland A's capped off the 1974 season with their third straight World Series victory, and one of the key reasons for their success was righthander Jim "Catfish" Hunter. But as detailed earlier, Hunter charged Oakland owner Charlie Finley with breach of contract for failing to pay, as promised, a $50,000 installment on Hunter's life insurance policy. In December an arbitrator ruled in Hunter's favor and declared him to be a free agent, with the power to negotiate with every team in baseball. Every team wanted the control artist who had just won the Cy Young Award, had topped 20 wins in each of the past four seasons and owned 161 major league victories in his ten-year career. But Steinbrenner got him by giving him a bonus and five-year contract worth $3.75 million. The team seemed to be intent on collecting superstars that winter: in one of those trades that gets people to forget about football and basketball and talk baseball during the winter, they swapped Bobby Murcer straight up to the San Francisco Giants for All-Star outfielder Bobby Bonds.

The Yankees were the preseason favorites to win their division, but they never could put together a sustained run. On August 1, with the team just two games over .500, Steinbrenner overruled Paul and fired the mild-mannered Virdon, replacing him with former Yankee infielder Billy Martin. The tempestuous Martin had already managed the Twins, Tigers and Rangers, and while he was an extremely sharp skipper who seemed to be able to extract almost superhuman efforts from his players, he had also proven to be very difficult for ownership to live with and thus had been fired by the Twins, Tigers and Rangers after very short tenures. The Texas Rangers were a case in point. A franchise distinguished by failure since their expansion beginnings as the Washington Senators, they had finished over .500 just once in their first 13 years and had never challenged for a title. In the last month of the 1973 season they hired Martin, who had been let go in Detroit despite having won a division title just the year before. And in 1974 Martin almost achieved the impossible as the heretofore woebegone Texas Rangers stayed neck-and-neck with the two-time defending world champion Oakland A's until fading in late September. Martin was practically deified in Texas (a status previously reserved for football coaches), but by July of 1975 he had worn out his welcome with management and was dismissed. Yet, although he had played for seven teams in an 11-year career, he was a Yankee at heart, having come up through their farm system and starred in a couple of World Series with them, and his dream was to follow in Casey Stengel's footsteps. So shortly after being bounced in Texas, Billy Martin landed in the Bronx. Unfortunately, he didn't make a difference in 1975, as the Yankees finished third, 12 games behind the surprising Boston Red Sox.

Both Hunter and Bonds had terrific years, the former with his league-leading 23 wins, the latter with 32 homers and 30 stolen bases. But Martin identified three areas that needed improvement: pitching, and defense in the outfield and second base. Behind Hunter, the Yanks had serviceable pitchers like George "Doc" Medich, Rudy May and Pat Dobson, but they were looking for something a little better. At second base, Sandy Alomar was slowing down a bit and was perhaps more suited for spot starts. And in center, the injury to Maddox (and the earlier trade of Murcer) had left the team without a true man in the middle. The Yankees addressed these needs with two off-season deals, made in one stunning day. On December 11, 1975, they sent Medich to Pittsburgh for outspoken pitcher Dock Ellis and a 21-year-old Brooklyn resident, second baseman Willie Randolph. And they swapped Bonds to the Angels for center fielder Mickey Rivers and righthanded pitcher Ed Figueroa.

The response was spectacular. Martin favored an aggressive running game, and with Rivers and Randolph at the top of the order New York could play "Billy Ball." The newcomers responded with 80 steals between them, and the style met with favor throughout the lineup: Roy White stole 31 bases, a career high and as many as he had swiped in the previous two years combined; even Munson stole 14. Rivers was not a great outfielder but with his blazing speed he could simply outrun the ball and track it down. Randolph, meanwhile, made plays at the keystone that no Yankee had been able to make since Bobby Richardson had been in his prime. Figueroa won 19 games and Ellis won 17 games (as did Hunter) to give the team a solid starting threesome. And Lyle, who led the league with 23 saves, was ably set up by Tidrow, who saved ten himself.

New York jumped off to a big lead and stayed there. But Steinbrenner, feeling that the club needed more pitching, swung a massive June deal with the Orioles. Over the objection of Gabe Paul he brought in pitchers Ken Holtzman, Doyle Alexander and Grant Jackson in exchange for Rudy May and several highly-regarded young players. While the deal helped the Yankees in the short run — Alexander won ten, Holtzman won nine and Jackson won six out of the bullpen — it cost the Bombers in the long run, as they lost pitchers Scott McGregor, Tippy Martinez and catcher Rick Dempsey, all of whom would have excellent careers in Baltimore.* But in 1976 it was all about winning now, and this the Yankees did, finishing on top for the first time since 1964.

Their opponents in the league championship series were the young Kansas City Royals. An expansion team born after the 1968 season, they emphasized speed even more than the Yankees — no fewer than eight players had double-digit stolen base totals for the season. Their star was third baseman George Brett, who led the league in batting average, hits, triples and total bases. He nosed out teammate Hal McRae by just one point for the batting title, while ex–Met Amos Otis led the league in doubles. The Royals could offer up a fine young second baseman of their own in Frank White, and their pitching staff featured four men with ten or more victories, led by native New Yorker Dennis Leonard. With the Royals managed by Martin's old friend and teammate Whitey Herzog, the series promised to be an aggressive and hard-fought affair; thus no one was surprised when it went down to the wire.

The Yankees drew first blood, scoring two runs in the top of the first against former teammate Larry Gura. Although the southpaw settled down to pitch very well until the ninth, that was all New York needed as Catfish Hunter limited the Royals to five hits in a 4–1 triumph that was marred by a leg injury to Otis, which would force him out of the rest of the series. But the next day KC bounced back. Trailing 3–2 in the sixth, they drove Figueroa from the box with a pair of runs, then cemented their first-ever postseason win with a three-run eighth against Tidrow. Soft-tossing lefty Paul Splittorff was the Royals' hero in relief, holding the Yankees scoreless for nearly six innings. Momentum seemed to stay with Kansas City when the series shifted back to New York, as the Royals rocked Dock Ellis for three runs in the first inning. But Ellis got tough and the Yankees came back to score a 5–3 victory, with Chris Chambliss supplying a big two-run homer. The Bombers went for the kill in Game Four, sending Hunter to the mound. The Royals tallied three times in the third inning but the Yankees came right back with two of their own. More than 56,000 fans expected KC to wilt, but Doug Bird relieved starter Larry Gura and put the clamps on the Yanks. Kansas City then drove Hunter from the mound in the fourth and never looked back, knotting the series with a 7–4 win.

The season was down to one game for these two clubs, which by now resembled two tired prizefighters going for a last-round knockout. Figueroa and Leonard started but neither had their best stuff; Leonard only faced three batters before being lifted by Herzog. After seven innings, though, New York held a 6–3 lead and seemed to be headed for the World Series. After putting

---

*McGregor would win 138 games for the Orioles, Martinez would save 105, and Dempsey, one of the most popular players ever to wear a Baltimore uniform, was the MVP of the 1983 World Series. In contrast, Holtzman won just nine major league games after 1976, while Alexander, never quite fulfilling the great promise he had shown as a Dodger farmhand, was gone from New York the next year and bounced around to play for seven more clubs in his career.

the leadoff man on base, Martin felt Figueroa had gone far enough and replaced him with southpaw Grant Jackson. By the time George Brett came to the plate the Royals had two men on, and the lefthanded batter promptly tied the game with a three-run blast. Now in the bottom of the ninth the sometimes raucous New York fans got into the act. It began raining beer bottles out in right field, causing a delay as the grounds crew cleaned up the mess. Meanwhile, the Royals' new pitcher, hard-throwing Mark Littell, completed his allotted warmup tosses, then stopped to watch the show. After five minutes or so the game resumed, Littell delivered a fastball and Chambliss deposited it into the seats in right, ending the game, the series and Kansas City's season. Hundreds of fans poured out onto the field to "escort" Chambliss around the bases. The big first baseman was tripped at second base, almost had his helmet stolen right off his head at third, knocked one fan down as he headed towards home, and after reaching the clubhouse had to be escorted back onto the field by teammates and police so he could be sure he touched home plate.

New York would be facing the defending champion Cincinnati Reds, which had won 102 times to win their division by a comfortable ten-game margin, then had blitzed Philadelphia in a three-game playoff sweep. The Reds, as detailed elsewhere, were loaded with future Hall of Famers and a lineup that led the National League in most major offensive categories. Though New York had the better pitching staff, the Reds were simply too strong for the Yankees, which may have also been emotionally drained after the tough series with Kansas City.

Cincinnati opened with lefty Don Gullett and the Yankees countered with Doyle Alexander. Both teams scored early, but after their second-inning run the Bombers were unable to dent the plate again and only collected five hits. Meanwhile, the Reds chipped away at Alexander and knocked him out in the seventh as they took home a 5–1 victory. Hunter, who had defeated Cincinnati twice in the 1972 World Series (when he pitched for Oakland), tried to square things in Game Two. The Reds came up with three in the second inning, but the Yankees tied it up in the seventh, and the game was still knotted in the bottom of the ninth. Hunter got the first two men and the two teams seemed to be headed for extra innings when Ken Griffey, Sr., hit a grounder to shortstop Fred Stanley. The usually-reliable Stanley threw the ball away, Griffey reached second, and Tony Perez followed with a single, giving the Reds a 4–3 win.

The Yankees may have felt they would have an edge when they got back to the Bronx, but the Reds had a goal in sight and were not to be denied. Cincinnati pounded three Yankee pitchers for 13 hits, and National League co–Rookie of the Year Pat Zachry pitched well enough for a 6–2 triumph. In the fourth game the Yankees scored first — the only time in the Series they would have a lead — but Johnny Bench cracked a two-run homer in the fourth to put the Reds in front, 3–1. The Yankees got one back in the next inning and it was still a one-run game going into the ninth. Bench took matters into his own hands, however, launching a three-run homer to seal Cincinnati's four-game sweep.

Bench was the outstanding player with four extra-base hits and eight hits overall in 15 at-bats (a .533 average), six RBI and four runs scored. The Reds as a team batted .313, with 17 extra-base hits in just four games, and they outscored the Yankees 22–8. Lost in the debris was the Series enjoyed by Thurman Munson: nine hits and a .529 average.

While everyone in the Yankee family was happy to have won a pennant for the first time in a dozen years, no one was pleased at the quick exit in the World Series, even at the hands of the powerful Reds. Some changes needed to be made, and now there was a new way to do it: the re-entry draft. This was baseball's first attempt at allowing players to become free agents, though restrictions did place a limit on player movement. Steinbrenner wanted a shortstop (he had been very vocal in his opinion that his ballclub could not win it all with Fred Stanley at short) and everyone else wanted pitching. Under the theory, perhaps, that if you can't beat 'em, sign 'em, the Yankees brought the Reds' Don Gullett to the Bronx. They then set their sights on Baltimore's Bobby Grich, a record-setting second baseman who had been a star shortstop in the minors, but Grich signed with the California Angels. Seeking an All-Star at every position, Steinbrenner then went after dynamic slugger Reggie Jackson and, despite the objections of both Gabe Paul and Billy Martin, signed him to a five-year contract. Jackson, never one to shun the spotlight, called himself "the straw that stirs the drink," which didn't set well with Munson, the Yankee captain. The Bronx Zoo was born.

By the way, they did finally pick up that shortstop they needed, sending outfielder Oscar Gamble, a couple of minor league players and money to the Chicago White Sox for Bucky Dent in a spring training deal. And shortly after the season began, they swapped pitchers with Oakland, receiving Mike Torrez in exchange for Dock Ellis (plus more spare parts and more cash).

It was truly a team of stars, but all was not well within the not-so-friendly confines of Yankee Stadium. Having won without him the year before, there was some clubhouse resentment of Jackson and his ego. Martin was under daily pressure from Steinbrenner, who called repeatedly to offer "advice." On the playing field, Hunter seemed to be the same old Catfish when he limited the Brewers to just three hits on opening day, but late in the game he was struck on the foot by a line drive and wound up missing a month. Later he would hurt his shoulder, perhaps trying to ease the pressure on his foot, and he won just nine games, his lowest total in 11 years. Jackson's presence also meant that the bulk of the Yankees' power, except for Munson and Piniella, came from the left side, and they stumbled through the spring.

Gabe Paul knew he needed to address the need for a righthanded bat, and on the June 15 trading deadline he did just that, obtaining slugger Cliff Johnson from Houston for three minor league prospects. Johnson helped to balance out the lineup: of his 42 base hits in a Yankee uniform in 1977, 20 went for extra bases, including 12 home runs, and he drove home 31 runs. He proved to be yet another key acquisition.

A tight three-way race had developed with the Boston Red Sox and Baltimore Orioles. In mid–June the Yankees went up to Boston and were blown out of three straight games, giving up 16 home runs and getting outscored by a 30–9 margin. During the Saturday afternoon game, televised nationally by NBC, the Yankees' dirty laundry was aired out for the whole world. Jackson seemed to be less than enthusiastic in chasing down a ball hit to right (it became a double) and then in getting it back into the infield. Martin felt he was loafing and immediately removed him from the game. When Jackson came back to the dugout he asked Martin why he had been embarrassed in front of a national audience and the two nearly came to blows with the TV cameras recording all the action. Afterwards there were meetings, interviews, more meetings, and much speculation: Would Martin be fired? Were the Yankees unraveling? In the end Martin remained because Paul convinced Steinbrenner that firing Martin would be a sign to the other players that Jackson was, ultimately, calling the shots. So a truce was arranged, accommodations were made. Eventually Martin agreed to bat Jackson in the cleanup spot and play Piniella more often. Eventually Steinbrenner agreed to bring Martin's buddy Art Fowler back as pitching coach. Eventually Team Turmoil went back to the business of trying to win ballgames.

It all finally clicked in August. They won seven of eight at home, went on the road and promptly won six of seven. In a 23 game stretch, the Bombers won 20 to climb back into first place. The lineup finally exploded — Jackson, Nettles and Munson all drove in 100 or more runs while Chambliss had 90 — and Torrez won seven starts in a row to join Figueroa, the oft-injured Gullett and a young southpaw named Ron Guidry to finally establish a solid rotation. The bullpen, anchored as always by Lyle and Tidrow, was often spectacular; between them they won 24 games and saved another 31. Down the stretch the team would not be denied, and though Baltimore and Boston both had outstanding years, winning 97 games, New York repeated as AL East champions with 100 victories, the first Yankee squad to reach the century mark in 14 years.

The Royals provided the opposition once again in the league championship series. Kansas City, playing their home games on artificial turf, continued to feature an aggressive running game but this year also had more punch in their lineup and had added an 18-game winner, Jim Colborn, to their pitching staff. And, as if to seek revenge over their 1976 defeat, the Royals came out roaring in the opening game, pasting Gullett for two in the first and two in the second, then throwing in two more in the third against Tidrow before calming down. As he had the year before, Paul Splittorff proved to have the Yankees' number, and he coasted to a 7-2 triumph. The next day, however, Guidry was overpowering, limiting KC to just three hits as New York squared the series. The series moved to Kansas City and Dennis Leonard — who had had an ERA of

19.29 in the 1976 LCS — stymied the Yankees on just four hits to move the Royals to within one win of their first World Series appearance.

Figueroa started Game Four against former Yankee Larry Gura, but neither pitcher was very sharp. New York knocked out Gura in the third inning and handed "Figgy" a 4–0 lead, which he attempted to hand right back. With the Royals having shaved the lead to just 5–4, Martin took the extraordinary step of calling on Lyle in the fourth inning, far earlier than usual. The southpaw, who would win the American League Cy Young Award a month later, stopped the Royals' momentum and delivered the victory to New York, setting up an all-or-nothing fifth game for the second year in a row.

With both Gullett and Hunter ailing, Martin called on Guidry with just two days' rest, but "Louisiana Lightning" wasn't up to the task, and the Yankees found themselves down early, 3–1. Short rest, however, didn't seem to bother Torrez. Called on in relief just two days after losing Game Three, Mike blanked Kansas City into the eighth. But the Yankees still trailed because Splittorff once again was almost unhittable. Then in the top of the eighth, Royals manager Whitey Herzog made a crucial tactical blunder. Willie Randolph led off with a single and Herzog decided to go to his bullpen. Randolph eventually scored on a hit by Jackson, but most importantly, Splittorff was out of the game. In the ninth inning, now down just 3–2, New York combined a couple of hits, a sacrifice fly, and a key error by George Brett to ring up three runs and once again send the Royals home after a hard-fought, nail-biting five-game series.

There would be no revenge against the Reds, however. Despite adding Tom Seaver to their pitching staff, Cincinnati had not been able to catch the Los Angeles Dodgers, who began the season with 17 wins in their first 20 games and never looked back. In the off-season the Dodgers had changed managers for the first time in 23 years, replacing the retiring Walter Alston with ebullient Tommy Lasorda, and he directed a team with considerable firepower. Four players — first baseman Steve Garvey, third baseman Ron Cey, and outfielders Dusty Baker and Reggie Smith — reached the 30-homer mark in 1977. Their five-man pitching staff of Tommy John, Don Sutton, Rick Rhoden, Burt Hooton and Doug Rau had been steady and durable, starting 158 of the team's 162 games, and pitching a full 75 percent of the innings the team played that year. In their own league championship series against the Phillies, they had dropped the opener and then won three straight.

The Yankees had a problem: Hunter wasn't very healthy for this World Series, and Guidry, Torrez and Lyle had all pitched just two days before in the Kansas City finale. Martin opened with Gullett, hoping for the best, and got a pretty good effort from the lefthander. The Dodgers nicked him for a pair in the very first inning, but he kept them off-balance until the ninth. By then New York had come back to take the lead but LA tied it, and the opening game of the 1977 World Series went into extra innings. Finally in the bottom of the 12th inning, Willie Randolph doubled and reserve outfielder Paul Blair, who had gone in as a defensive replacement for Jackson, drove him in with a single for a Yankee win.

Hunter decided to give it a try in Game Two, but while his heart was in the right place, his pitches weren't. The Dodgers rocked him for five runs in less than three innings, and Burt Hooton's knuckle curve baffled the Yankees, as the Series shifted to California all tied up. With sufficient rest, Torrez and Guidry vaulted the Yanks into the lead. Except for a three-run homer to Baker, Torrez handcuffed the Dodgers in Game Three, then Guidry went him one better the next day, allowing just four hits and two runs (via a four-bagger by second baseman Davey Lopes), as New York was poised to capture the Series. Reggie Jackson helped the cause with his own home run. Facing elimination, the Dodgers pounded Gullett and the New York bullpen in Game Five. By the time the Yankees scored in the seventh, Los Angeles had a 10–0 lead and their plane reservations set for New York.

Torrez was tapped to face Hooton in Game Six; if it came down to a seventh game, Guidry would go on just three days' rest. Garvey tripled in two runs in the first inning, but Chambliss tied it up in the second with a home run. Reggie Smith hit his third circuit clout of the Series in the third inning, but that's when Reggie Jackson grabbed the spotlight and staged perhaps the greatest one-man show in World Series history. He put New York back on top in the fourth, belting Hooton's first delivery for a two-run homer. An inning later he drove reliever Elias Sosa's first pitch even further into the seats, giving the Yankees a 7–3 lead. And in the eighth he cracked Charlie Hough's first knuckleball into the center field bleachers, a monumental blast of close to 500 feet. Reggie pyrotechnics propelled the Yankees to their 21st championship but their first since 1962.

Jackson hit five home runs in the Series, a new record, drove in eight and scored ten. It was a good thing for New York that he succeeded when he did because the Dodgers otherwise played them very evenly. Los Angeles scored more runs (28–26) and actually hit more home runs (9–8); the Yankees had more hits (50–48), more extra-base hits (18–17), and a slightly lower team ERA (4.02 vs. 4.09). Had the Series gone to a seventh game, there is no telling what might have happened. Instead, the 1977 World Series will always be remembered for Jackson's Game Six heroics.

Well, if you liked 1977, you'll positively love 1978! One player who didn't was Mike Torrez. Given the opportunity to escape via free agency, the man who had solidified the starting rotation, especially in the second half of the year, fled the Bronx Zoo. Where he chose to go was significant — to the Yanks' arch rivals in Boston. Mike Torrez wound up having a fine year, winning 16 games, but his last appearance of the season would, ironically, put him back in the middle of the Yankee soap opera.

Gabe Paul resigned in December. He had seen his authority overruled by

Steinbrenner too many times, and he returned to Cleveland to try again and bring a winner to Lake Erie. Former Indian star Al Rosen was hired to replace him.

There was one notable, though surprising, addition: relief ace Rich "Goose" Gossage. A three-time All-Star, the hard-throwing righthander had come to prominence with the White Sox before being traded to Pittsburgh the previous winter. After one season there he opted for free agency and signed with the Yankees. What made the move questionable was that the Bombers already had one of the majors' best relief pitchers in Sparky Lyle, who had just won the Cy Young Award. Naturally Lyle was not pleased, grumbled about being traded, and insured that 1978 would prove to be another interesting year.

In the first two months of the season the Yankees played well enough, even though they suffered through a spate of injuries that limited their effectiveness. At one point, five Yankee pitchers were hurt, Willie Randolph's leg was in a splint and Mickey Rivers' hand was broken. Their primary problem was that the Red Sox were playing spectacular ball. They had a lineup of mashers, led by outfielder Jim Rice, that wound up featuring seven players with 12 or more home runs on the year. They had five pitchers win in double figures, including young Dennis Eckersley, who won 20 after being acquired from Cleveland, and relief star Bob Stanley, who won 15. They won early and often and jumped into the lead in the AL East, and by the All-Star break they could barely see the Yankees, or the rest of the division, in their rearview mirror. It looked like Boston's year.

On July 17, in a tie game against Kansas City, Munson singled to start the ninth, and Martin gave Jackson the bunt sign. After two pitches (and a 1–1 count), Martin took the bunt off; third base coach Dick Howser even came down the line and personally delivered the message. Jackson continued to attempt to bunt, striking out. Martin was livid at Jackson's defiance and suspended him indefinitely; later it was defined by Steinbrenner as five days. For Martin, however, this was not enough. The incident gnawed at him, as did everything else that had happened with Reggie, and with George. Managing the Yankees was the one job Martin always wanted, and now it was killing him. He looked bad, was not eating enough and was drinking way too much. Although the team had won five straight games Martin was not in a good frame of mind, and in a conversation with two New York reporters while in Chicago he kept coming back to Jackson. Finally he said, referring to Jackson and Steinbrenner, "The two of them deserve each other. One is a born liar and the other's convicted." While it was true that the Yankee owner had been convicted of an election violation and suborning perjury a few years before, for George Steinbrenner this public statement was the ultimate act of insubordination, and perhaps the death wish of an overwrought man. He demanded Martin's resignation and received it on July 24 with surprisingly little resistance. Martin was replaced by Bob Lemon, the Hall of Fame pitcher who had been fired as White Sox skipper just three weeks earlier.

End of story? Hardly, not with these Yankees. The fans were behind Billy and they let team officials know it. Martin had always been a fan favorite, ever since his playing days and exploits as Casey's Bad Boy. His hard-nosed, aggressive style had struck a chord with the people in the stands and they had made him one of their own. Now they were telling Steinbrenner they didn't like the way Billy had been treated, and the owner paid attention. He was also cognizant of the rumors that Martin might resurface with the crosstown Mets, a public relations disaster he simply couldn't let happen.

Five days after Martin's resignation was the Yankee's Old-Timer's Day, a major event every year. Amidst utmost secrecy that was worthy of the CIA, a new settlement was negotiated and Billy Martin trotted onto the playing field of Yankee Stadium with the announcement that he would be returning as manager for the 1979 season. Jaws dropped around the country as Yankee fans roared in delight.

Meanwhile, the 1978 season still had to be completed, and with Lemon at the helm a calm came over the New York clubhouse. They began to play the way they had the previous two seasons, which was just what Lemon asked them to do. They were finally healthy, too, which was more than could be said for the Red Sox. Three of Boston's four starting infielders and two of their three starting outfielders sustained injuries that either forced them to miss games or reduced their effectiveness when they played. All of New England discovered the need for an effective bench, something New York had known for a long time. They began to lose as the Yankees began to win.

The Bombers also cashed in on a small miracle. Catfish Hunter had been suffering from that bad shoulder for a year or more, and it looked as if his sterling career might be over at age 32. But somewhere he found a little more life in his right arm and reeled off six straight wins to give the Yankees the third starter they so desperately needed. All season long they had been relying on Guidry and Figueroa, and had not been disappointed. Guidry simply turned in a season for the ages: he wound up 25–3 with a league-leading ERA of 1.74, a Yankee record nine shutouts, and 248 strikeouts. In just his second full season in the majors, he was the undisputed ace of the pitching staff. Figueroa was not far behind, as his 20–9 record made him the first Puerto Rican–born pitcher to win 20 games in a single season. With the resurrection of Hunter and the powerful bullpen tandem of Gossage and Lyle, New York had sufficient pitching for the stretch drive.

The Red Sox, which had once led by 14 games, still enjoyed a four-game margin when the two teams met in Boston for an early–September series; when it was over they were separated by just percentage points. In what has become known as "The Boston Massacre," the Yankees annihilated Red Sox pitching to the tune of 42 runs and 49 hits in the four games. Boston scored only nine runs, and didn't help their cause by committing 11 errors. In the rematch the next weekend the Yankees won two of three and zoomed into the lead. But at a time when it would have been easy to fold, Boston didn't. They battled back, won their final eight games of the season, then watched Hunter pitch his first bad game in two months on the final day of the regular season, putting the two teams in a flat-footed tie for first and making a playoff game necessary.

Guidry volunteered to pitch on just three days' rest and was not his normal, overpowering self. His opponent was Mike Torrez and last season's Yankee hero was sharp in front of the Fenway Faithful, leading 2–0 after six. New York put a couple of men on in the seventh, bringing up Bucky Dent. The shortstop was only a .240 hitter and had swatted just four home runs all season, and after agonizingly fouling a ball off his foot he seemed less likely to become a hero. But following a short delay while the Yankee trainer numbed the pain, Torrez threw a pitch that caught too much of the plate and Dent hit it over the Green Monster in left field for a three-run homer, putting New York ahead. Later, when the Red Sox were rallying, a heady defensive play by Piniella helped the Yankees protect their lead, and with a 5–4 win the Bombers completed one of the great in-season comebacks in baseball history. Winning 48 of their final 68 propelled New York again into the postseason, where their opponents were — all together now — the Kansas City Royals.

After two straight frustrating losses to the Yankees, the Royals undoubtedly thought that 1978 would be their year. They even had their ace, 21-game winner Dennis Leonard, rested and ready to start the playoffs; Lemon could only call on rookie Jim Beattie, who had won just six games during the season. New York was also hurting physically, with Willie Randolph out for the postseason with a leg injury. So needless to say the Bombers cuffed around Royal pitching for a 7–1 win in the series opener. Beattie only gave up two hits, but when he loaded the bases in the sixth another rookie righthander, Ken Clay, came out of the bullpen to shut down KC the rest of the way, and Jackson put the game out of reach with a three-run homer in the eighth. The Royals came back to crush Figueroa and the New York bullpen the next day, and then Game Three proved to be the pivotal contest. The Royals' George Brett hit three home runs off Catfish Hunter, but they were all solo shots. Reggie Jackson, meanwhile, hit a two-run homer and then, after KC had taken a 5–4 lead, Thurman Munson hit a long two-run homer in the eighth inning to give New York a 6–5 victory. Guidry was finally ready to pitch in Game Four, and he was opposed by Leonard. Brett led off the game with a triple and Hal McRae singled him home, but Guidry then settled down. Leonard was extremely tough, yielding just four hits, but two of them reached the seats, the culprits being Nettles in the second inning and Roy White in the sixth. Guidry went into the ninth with the slim 2–1 lead, then gave up a leadoff double to Amos Otis. With the tying run in scoring position, Lemon called on Gossage, who retired three straight, ending the game and the series. For the third straight year, New York had dispatched Kansas City for the right to play in the World Series.

Once again it was Lasorda's Dodgers in the other dugout, and they came out with their bats blazing. They drove Figueroa from the mound in the second inning and built up a 7–0 lead before the Yankees could score (on a Jackson homer) in the seventh. There would be no New York rally today as Los Angeles won the opener, 11–5. The Yankees took a 2–0 lead in Game Two against Burt Hooton, but Dodger third baseman Ron Cey hit a three-run homer off Hunter in the sixth to put LA in front, 4–2. The Yanks got one back but, still trailing in the ninth, put two on with just one out and Munson and Jackson due to hit. Lasorda called on a fireballing 21-year-old righthander named Bob Welch to face the two veterans. Munson lined out, bringing up Jackson and a classic confrontation: fastball pitcher against fastball hitter. Reggie fouled off three heaters and then, on a full count, struck out in the style of The Mighty Casey. The Dodgers won to give them a 2–0 lead in the Series.

Guidry was on the mound when the action shifted to New York, but he was not the same pitcher he had been for most of the season, as the strain of nearly 300 innings were taking their toll. Los Angeles picked up eight hits, and Guidry issued seven walks, but the Dodgers could only manage one run. The reason was Graig Nettles, who made spectacular defensive plays in both the fifth and sixth innings, blunting bases-loaded rallies both times. Nettles saved at least four runs, maybe more, in New York's 5–1 victory; his heroic defense was the turning point of this World Series.

Game Four produced some controversy. Yankee nemesis Reggie Smith hit a three-run homer off Figueroa to give LA a 3–0 lead, but New York clawed its way back in the sixth. One run had scored and the Yankees had Munson at second base and Jackson at first with one out when Piniella hit a liner towards shortstop Bill Russell. Russell knocked the ball down, stepped on second for the force out and threw to first for what he assumed would be an inning-ending double play. But Jackson froze in the basepath and, instead of ducking out of the way, moved his hip towards the ball, which bounded into right field as Munson scored. Lasorda and crew argued interference but the umpires disagreed. The Yankees tied the game in the eighth, then won in the tenth on a hit by Piniella. The Series was all even.

The Bombers reciprocated LA's first game blowout with one of their own in Game Five. Collecting a record 16 singles, the Yankees spotted the Dodgers a 2–0 lead before starting the wipeout. Munson drove home five runs and White three to support Jim Beattie, who pitched the first complete game of his career. Back in California the Dodgers needed a victory to force a seventh game, and took an early 1–0 lead. But Don Sutton couldn't hold it, and Hunter once more summoned the old magic, retiring 11 straight hitters in the middle innings. Bucky Dent and Brian Doyle (subbing for the injured Randolph) spearheaded rallies in the second and sixth innings, and Jackson settled the score with Welch, cracking a long home run in the seventh, as New York won their second straight World Series. In the process they became the first club to capture the title after having lost the first two games of the Series. Jackson, by the way, cemented his reputation as "Mr. October" by once again crushing Dodger pitching with a .391 average and 8 RBI. Munson batted .320 with 7 RBI, while Dent batted .417 with 10 hits and 7 RBI. As a team the Yankees hit .306.

There was every reason to believe the dynasty would continue for the 1979 season as the Yankees brought pitchers Tommy John and Luis Tiant to New York to team with Guidry and Figueroa. And in truth the two newcomers held up their part of the bargain, winning 34 games between them. But not much else went right in the Bronx. Lemon's youngest son had been killed in an auto accident shortly after the World Series, and something seemed to die in the old pitcher as well. Gossage injured his thumb in some clubhouse horseplay and missed three months, and having traded Lyle in the off-season the Yankees suddenly were left without a closer in the bullpen. Rivers was traded in mid-season, and Figueroa suffered an elbow injury, limiting him to four wins. Billy Martin was brought back as manager to inject some spirit into the club, but everything came crashing down on August 2. Although it was a day off, the Yankees suffered their biggest loss of the year when Thurman Munson, piloting a small plane to his home in Ohio, crashed attempting to land the aircraft and was killed at age 32. If there had been any chance of a comeback it was now gone; Ed Linn has written that it "took the heart out of the club and cut the heart out of Billy." The Yankees finished fourth in the AL East, Martin was fired after an off-season fight with a marshmallow salesman, and the Yankees set out to regroup. While they won their division the next two seasons and even returned to the World Series in 1981 (this time losing to the Dodgers), it was not the same club, and they spent the bulk of the 1980s attempting in vain to recapture the magic of 1976–1978.

1984
Detroit Tigers

Their names are legendary in Detroit, and throughout the state of Michigan: Kaline, McLain, Horton, Lolich, Cash, Freehan, Northrup. The stars who brought the Tigers the 1968 world championship. The heroes who fell behind the St. Louis Cardinals, three games to one, then came back to win it all, even defeating the seemingly-invincible Bob Gibson in the seventh and final game.

For 16 long years the Ghosts of '68 haunted venerable Tiger Stadium. Detroit fielded good teams in 1969 and 1971, and in strike-shortened 1972 a scrappy club edged the Boston Red Sox by .003 to bring another Eastern Division crown to the corner of Michigan and Trumbull. That team, in fact, also came from behind; down to their last three outs in the tenth inning of Game Four against the Oakland A's of Reggie Jackson, Catfish Hunter, et al., they scored three runs to force a deciding game in the American League Championship Series, only to lose a 2–1 pitching duel and a chance to go to the World Series. It was the Tigers' last hurrah — two years later they wound up last, and the 1975 club finished with the worst record in the majors.

After four consecutive years below .500, the 1978 team showed marked improvement with their 86 wins, although they still finished fifth in the AL East and were never a factor in the pennant race. But that squad is historically significant because of its change in personnel. Building with youth, the Tigers turned the middle of their infield over to a couple of kids, 21-year-old Lou Whitaker at second base and 20-year-old Alan Trammell at shortstop, both of whom acquitted themselves very nicely in their first full year in the majors. Behind the plate, 22-year-old Lance Parrish split the backstopping duties with veteran Milt May, and though he caught fewer games and had fewer at-bats, Parrish had more homers, RBI and runs scored than his counterpart. And on the mound, a burly 23-year-old righthander named Jack Morris made 28 appearances for the year, seven of them starts. The comeback had begun.

Morris moved up to the head of the class in 1979, winning 17 games, one of only seven American League pitchers to win that many. He was joined in the rotation by another righthander, Dan Petry, as well as journeyman Milt Wilcox, who was blossoming in a Detroit uniform. And the bullpen picked up an anchor in Aurelio Lopez, a hard-thrower from Mexico who earned the nickname "Señor Smoke" with his riding fastball and 21 saves. The year's most notable achievement, however, was undoubtedly the change in managers. Longtime skipper Ralph Houk had retired following the 1978 season,* and veteran coach Les Moss was given the reins. One-third of the way through the year, however, the team dismissed Moss, even though their record was right around .500. The reason was the availability of George "Sparky" Anderson. The former Cincinnati manager, winner of four National League pennants and two World Series, had been let go just weeks before the start of spring training in a move that shocked all of baseball. Anderson, one of the most widely-respected men in the business, had his pick of job offers and chose the Tigers, taking over on June 12. But once again they finished fifth.

Former college football star and high-profile draft pick Kirk Gibson began to make his presence felt in 1980, appearing in 51 games and hitting nine home runs. The Tigers were respectable, finishing over .500 for the third straight season, but also ending up in fifth place for the third straight season as the AL East continued to be the most competitive division in the majors. And for the next two years that pattern held fast: the Tigers were able to hold their heads above water but just barely, a creditable team but not much of a factor in the pennant race, even with the importation of two fine outfielders, Chet Lemon and Larry Herndon.

*Houk would later un-retire to manage the Boston Red Sox from 1981 through 1984.

Here's how tough things were in the American League's Eastern Division: In 1982 the Milwaukee Brewers won their only championship, capturing 95 games. A year later they won 87, certainly a solid achievement, yet tumbled down to fifth place. The Orioles replaced them as division champs but were challenged most persistently by the Tigers, who turned it up a notch and won 92 games. A fine season, for sure, but Sparky Anderson and General Manager Bill Lajoie recognized what steps needed to be taken to move the club to the next level. They needed Kirk Gibson to be either a full-time outfielder or full-time designated hitter and not shuttle between the two roles. They needed to solidify third base, which had been manned primarily by light-hitting Tom Brookens for the past four years. And they needed a lefthanded relief pitcher to deal with such power hitters as Milwaukee's Cecil Cooper and Ben Oglivie, the Yankees' Don Mattingly, and Toronto's Willie Upshaw and Lloyd Moseby, to say nothing of Reggie Jackson (now with the Angels), Kansas City's George Brett, Minnesota's Kent Hrbek, Oakland's Dwayne Murphy, Seattle's Alvin Davis and Ken Phelps, and the White Sox' Harold Baines over in the Western Division.

In the winter they signed free agent Darrell Evans to serve as their designated hitter. In 13 full seasons with Atlanta and San Francisco in the National League, Evans had hit 262 home runs and had just come off a 30-homer year with the Giants. He also had experience at both first and third base, giving the Tigers an insurance policy at those positions. In the spring they decided they liked what they saw of 23-year-old Howard Johnson and anointed the switch hitter as their starting third baseman. And while they were still tuning up in Florida, Lajoie made a deal for a lefty in the bullpen, picking up Willie Hernandez and first baseman Dave Bergman from the Phillies for a couple of fan favorites, rifle-armed outfielder Glenn Wilson and catcher-utilityman John Wockenfuss. Bergman was installed at first (primarily against righthanded pitchers), Gibson was given the right field job, and Hernandez joined Lopez out in the bullpen. Anderson was now confident his Tigers would be competitive in the major's toughest division.

Competitive? The team won their first five games, all on the road. Darrell Evans hit a home run in his first regular-season game in a Tiger uniform. Jack Morris no-hit the White Sox, the first Tiger pitcher to accomplish that feat since Jim Bunning in 1958. They then came home to a Tiger Stadium that had been spiffed up with a fresh coat of paint and new siding in the off-season and proceeded to win their next four before tasting defeat for the first time in 1984. Right away the fans caught the fever; pitching coach Roger Craig, whose career as a player, coach and manager had spanned nearly thirty years, wrote, "I believe this is the most enthusiastic baseball town I've been in. Detroit reminds me a lot of Brooklyn."

Some of those old Yankee juggernauts were often accused of wrapping up the pennant by Mother's Day; the 1984 Tigers came close. By late May they had played 40 games and won 35 of them, by far the best start in baseball history.

Needless to say they cooled off after that — had they maintained that pace they would have won 141 games — but they easily outdistanced the rest of the division. The traditional competition in the AL East proved to be for second place, a spot won by the young Toronto Blue Jays, who nosed out the Yankees, Red Sox and Orioles.

The components Anderson and Lajoie had been putting together for nearly a decade came together and made this 104-victory season a reality. Homegrown products Trammell, Whitaker, Gibson, Parrish and Johnson combined with imports Evans, Lemon, Herndon and Bergman to produce the most potent lineup in the league, one that scored 829 runs and hit 187 home runs; eight players, including reserve outfielder Rupert Jones, reached double-figures in homers. Gibson, with his fiery personality and gridiron mentality, was the emotional leader, while Trammell and Whitaker provided steady leadership, and Evans' presence stabilized the lineup. On the mound the Big Three of Morris, Petry and Wilcox won 54 games; for the 34-year-old Wilcox, often beset with injuries, his 17 wins proved to be a career high. Morris, of course, was the staff workhorse; over a two-year stretch of 32 starts, he pitched at least seven innings 31 times. But the rebuilt bullpen proved to be the real key. Hernandez, acquired to face lefthanded hitters and to complement Lopez, took control of the late innings and wound up saving 32 games and only blowing one save chance all season. He also won nine games. Three times the Tigers endured four-game losing streaks, and three times Willie Hernandez stopped the downslide with a clutch save. In the off-season, his yearlong magnificence was recognized by the Baseball Writers Association of America, which selected him as both the Cy Young Award winner, emblematic of the league's best pitcher, and the Most Valuable Player. Lopez contributed his fair share as well, saving 14 games and winning another ten, while Doug Bair proved to be an unsung hero with his 94 innings in middle relief.

The Tigers led the league every day of the year, from beginning to end, becoming only the fourth wire-to-wire champion in history, while Sparky Anderson became the first manager to ever win 100 games in a season in both leagues. More than 2.7 million fans poured into Tiger Stadium throughout the season, a team record, and another 2.1 million came out to see them when they toured the rest of the American League. It was a magical summer in Michigan.

But other teams have had the sweet taste of victory turn sour with post-season defeats. In order for the Tigers to be truly classified as a great club they needed to go through the Kansas City Royals in the league championship series and then defeat the National League representative in the World Series.

Except for off years in 1974 and 1983, the Kansas City Royals had been one of the American League's elite teams for more than a decade. They had been the AL representatives in the 1980 World Series, losing in six games to the Philadelphia Phillies. Their Western Division title in 1984, after a hard-fought battle against the California Angels and Minnesota Twins, was the fifth in club

Kirk Gibson slugs one of his two home runs during Game Five of the 1984 World Series. (Courtesy of Ruta Zemaitis Bloomfield.)

history, impressive for a team whose first season was 1969. Their everyday lineup was led by the game-breaking speed of center fielder Willie Wilson, the steady hitting and spectacular fielding of second baseman Frank White, and the all-around excellence of future Hall of Famer George Brett. Their pitching featured a crafty veteran, Larry Gura, four youngsters in Bret Saberhagen, Bud Black, Mark Gubicza and Charlie Leibrandt, and the league's top closer, Dan Quisenberry, whose practically-underhanded delivery had accounted for 180 saves in six seasons, including 89 in 1983 and 1984 combined. While they had won 20 fewer games than the Tigers that year, Detroit's darlings knew they could not take them lightly.

Prior to the beginning of both league championship series, major league umpires announced they would not work the games in a contract dispute with the commissioner's office. Rather than cave in to the umpires' demands, baseball recruited retired umpires and amateur arbiters to work the games, which went off without incident. In the Tigers-Royals series, retired ump Bill Deegan worked behind the plate for all three games.

The opening game, and perhaps the entire series, turned in the third inning. The Tigers had a 2–0 lead but the Royals loaded the bases against Jack

Morris with two out. George Brett then hit a vicious line drive to right that looked like a sure hit, guaranteed at least to tie the game and perhaps put KC in front. But Kirk Gibson, who had spent long hours with former Tiger great Al Kaline to make himself a better defensive outfielder, made a diving catch to end the inning. By the time the Royals finally did score they were trailing 5–0 in a game that ended up 8–1.

The second game produced a rarity of sorts. Leading 3–2 after seven, Sparky Anderson removed starter Dan Petry in favor of Willie Hernandez. Nothing strange there, but then Hernandez, who had coughed up only one lead all season, promptly gave up the tying run on a pinch-double by Hal McRae. Perhaps fearing that Hernandez was feeling the effects of appearing in his 82nd game of the year, Anderson brought in Lopez to pitch the ninth. The Royals had a chance to win the game in the tenth when they put two men on base in front of slugger Steve Balboni, but the big first baseman flied out to end the threat. The Tigers then touched Quisenberry for a pair on a double off the bat of DH Johnny Grubb. Lopez almost gave it right back in the bottom of the 11th inning, putting the tying runs on base, but he rewarded Anderson's faith in him by getting the final out in the 5–3 victory.

Game Three, played in Detroit, proved to be an old-fashioned pitching duel between Wilcox and Leibrandt, who gave up just five hits between them. The Tigers scored in the second inning on a couple of singles and an infield out, and Wilcox made it stand up. Tiring in the eighth, he gave up only his second hit, then saw Willie Wilson smash a ball towards right field. But Darrell Evans, playing first base, made a diving stop of the ball and then beat the speedy Wilson to the bag to end the Royals' last threat of the season. Hernandez pitched a scoreless ninth inning to sweep the series and send Detroit into the Fall Classic for the first time in 16 years. The victory by Wilcox, by the way, made him the first pitcher in history to win the deciding game in both the American League and National League Championship Series; as a 20-year-old Cincinnati relief pitcher, he had been credited with the victory in the Reds' 1970 triumph over Pittsburgh.

Perhaps the only real surprise in the series was how hard the Royals fought and how Detroit had to work for their pennant. The National League series, however, did produce an unexpected winner: the San Diego Padres. Another 1969 expansion club, the young Padres, managed by former Boston and Oakland skipper Dick Williams, had adopted a get-rich-quick approach for the 1984 season. A .500 club the previous two years, they imported third baseman Graig Nettles and ace reliever Rich "Goose" Gossage from the Yankees, plus first baseman Steve Garvey from the Dodgers. These veterans had all played with prior World Series champions and could give their younger teammates that championship leadership so vital over the long haul. The Padres also got great production out of some of those young players: 70 stolen bases from second baseman Alan Wiggins, 20 home runs from outfielder Kevin McReynolds, and a league-leading 213 hits and a .351 batting average from outfielder Tony Gwynn. They also saw all four starters win in double figures as the Padres became the only team in the NL West to finish above .500.

But the delight of both the fans and the media that summer had been the Chicago Cubs. The perennial losers, who had not finished above .500 since 1972, shocked the baseball world even more than the Tigers by making an early dash to the top of the NL's Eastern Division and then staying there throughout the summer. With just the right blend of youth and experience, the Cubs seemed to be a team touched by the baseball gods in 1984. When they soundly defeated the Padres in the first two games of the LCS in Wrigley Field, it appeared as if a matchup of the 1945 World Series combatants — the last time any Cub franchise had made it to the Fall Classic — was about to unfold.

The Padres, though, had a different idea. They avoided the sweep with a win in Game Three, then broke a ninth-inning tie in the fourth game when Garvey cracked a two-run, opposite-field home run against the Cubs' ace reliever, Lee Smith, to tie the series. With a World Series appearance on the line, the Cubs took the early lead and, with eventual Cy Young Award winner Rick Sutcliffe on the mound, looked like they could get the 12 outs they needed. It didn't happen. The Padres picked up two runs in the sixth inning, and then Cubs first baseman Leon "Bull" Durham let a routine grounder go through his legs in the seventh, opening the floodgates for San Diego. When the dust had cleared, four runners scored in that frame and the Padres, not the Cubs, won the honor of hosting the first two games of the 1984 World Series.

Once again the Tigers were favored but knew they could not take their opponents lightly. Confident that they were the better club, they sought to prove it by starting ace Jack Morris in the series opener. The Padres rattled that confidence right away, reaching Morris for three hits and two runs in the very first inning, much to the delight of nearly 58,000 fans. But Larry Herndon put Detroit ahead with a two-run homer off Padre starter Mark Thurmond in the fifth inning, and Morris made it stand up. He was helped along by Padre DH Kurt Bevacqua, who led off the seventh with a double, stumbled rounding second base but attempted to go to third anyway and was thrown out, killing a great chance for San Diego to tie the game. Detroit won, 3–2, and Morris became the first pitcher Sparky Anderson ever let go all the way in a World Series game.*

Detroit's four-game postseason win streak came to a close the next day as the Padres spotted the Tigers a three-run lead, then came back to claim a 5–3 victory. The game's big blow was struck by Bevacqua, who atoned for the previous day's baserunning error with a three-run home run off Dan Petry in the fifth inning. The Padre bullpen also shone this day, as Andy Hawkins checked the Tigers for five-plus innings after they had chased starter Ed Whitson with

---

*Anderson had managed Cincinnati in the 1970, 1972, 1975 and 1976 World Series.

three in the opening frame, and lefty Craig Lefferts earned the save with three scoreless innings. The series was tied as they headed back to Detroit.

Tiger Stadium saw a walkathon in Game Three. Padre starter Tim Lollar walked four batters in less than two innings, and his replacement, Greg Booker, also walked four men in his inning of work. The Tigers utilized these free passes, along with a couple of timely hits (including a surprise home run by utility-man Marty Castillo, playing third base), to build a 4–1 lead. After Booker walked the bases loaded in the third, new pitcher Greg Harris promptly hit a batter, allowing Detroit to score a run without even putting a bat on the ball. Harris settled down and finished the game, although he did walk three to give Padre hurlers an unenviable World Series record: 11 walks in a single game. Milt Wilcox was the winning pitcher, with the unofficial save going to center fielder Chet Lemon, who robbed Padre catcher Terry Kennedy of an extra-base hit with a spectacular catch to end the seventh inning. A run would have scored had he not caught the ball, and the potential tying run would then have come to the plate. Instead, the Tigers "walked" away with a 5–2 victory and the lead in the series.

Jack was back in Game Four, with more-than-able support from Alan Trammell. While the Padres outhit the Tigers, 10–7, Morris made sure that only two of those hits — a second inning Kennedy home run and a ninth inning Garvey double — were responsible for runs. He was tough throughout the game and, in something of a surprise, was allowed to go the route. Detroit's offense, meanwhile, revolved around the double play duo of Trammell and Whitaker. Sweet Lou reached in the first inning on an Alan Wiggins error, and Trammell followed with a long homer to left. Two innings later Whitaker singled and his keystone partner reached the seats again. Detroit didn't dent the plate again but Morris made sure they didn't need to as the Tigers now took a command-ing lead in the Series.

The Tigers had made it a postseason habit to score first in every contest (including the series with Kansas City), and Game Five was no exception. Kirk Gibson followed a Whitaker hit with an upper-deck blast, and when three more hits plated another run Padre starter Mark Thurmond's day was done. But a Tiger rout didn't materialize and San Diego fought back to tie the score. Gib-son put Detroit back in front in the fifth, not with his power but with his speed. After collecting a base hit, he tagged up on a fly ball and moved to second. After a pair of walks loaded the bases, Gibson tagged up once again and scored, this time on a pop into short right that second baseman Wiggins had to catch with his back to the infield. The teams traded runs, making the score 5–4 Tigers, until the eighth inning. Detroit put two men on base against Goose Gossage, bringing Gibson to the plate with just one out. Most of America assumed the lefty-swinging Gibson would be walked intentionally so the Padres would have a better chance at a double play against the righthanded — and slower — Lance Parrish. But Gossage, the former Yankee, recalled past successes against Gibson and persuaded Dick Williams that he could get the out. The Ghost of At-Bats

Past was crushed by present-day reality: Gibson reached the upper deck again, and Detroit, with Willie Hernandez on in relief, finished off the Padres.

Indeed, while they certainly presented a strong lineup, pitching was the key for Detroit, as it had been all year long. Dan Petry was the only Tiger pitcher to have a poor World Series, and he, of course, had been a solid 18-game-winner during the regular season and had also contributed a win in the playoff series against the Royals. When Petry faltered in Game Five against San Diego, Aurelio Lopez came in and shut the door, as he had done so many times that year. Including their eight postseason games, the Tigers had an incredible mark of 98–0 in games they led entering the ninth inning, a true testimony to the overpowering bullpen of Hernandez and Lopez. In contrast, San Diego only had one starter — Mark Thurmond in the opening game — give them at least five innings. The Padre bullpen matched their Tiger counterparts, but they were almost constantly pitching from behind and trying to prevent further Detroit uprisings.

Detroit's triumph capped a magnificent season, one that saw them dominate their difficult division, the rest of their league, and then the best the Senior Circuit could offer. In the process, they made Sparky Anderson the first manager in history to win a World Series in both leagues, and they established themselves as one of the great clubs of the 20th century.

But if there was any talk of a dynasty that winter in the Upper Midwest, it proved to be without foundation. The AL East went back to being a black-and-blue division, with several good teams beating each other and vying for the top. The Tigers had a respectable year in 1985 but watched the race from afar as Toronto and New York staged the primary battle. Almost everyone got into the act in 1986 before Boston advanced to the postseason and its now-legendary date with destiny.* Detroit was back in 1987, sweeping the final three games of the year in a showdown against Toronto to advance to the postseason, but this time around the baseball gods were not smiling on the Tigers; the Minnesota Twins defeated Detroit and went on to capture their first World Series. In 1988, the Tigers participated in a five-team battle that featured one of the tightest races in years, but lost out by just one game to the Red Sox. And that, essentially, was it for Sparky Anderson's troops. But for one year — 1984 — Detroit was about as dominant as a baseball team could ever hope to be.

---

*The 1986 Red Sox are not chronicled in this volume, but they provided two memorable postseason highlights. In the league championship series against the Angels they lost three of the first four games and were down in the ninth inning of Game Five when they rallied to go ahead, then won in extra innings. Spurred on by this miraculous victory they won the next two games to advance to the World Series against the New York Mets. There it seemed that almost seven decades of frustration would end, as they had the edge after five games and scored twice in the tenth inning of Game Six. They still had that lead after getting the first two men out, but would never record the third. The Mets tied the game on a wild pitch and won the game on Bill Buckner's infamous error, and captured Game Seven to continue the curse that seems to hang over Boston baseball.

1990s
Atlanta Braves

"So the last shall be first…" — Matthew 20:16

In baseball history there have been a few examples of traditionally down-trodden teams that experienced miracle years and contended for a pennant, per-haps even won: the 1969 Mets, detailed in this book, immediately come to mind, as do the 1944 St. Louis Browns. Rarely, however, do these miracles last for more than one season. The Mets were no more than a .500 club for several years after they astounded the world, while the Browns went back to their nor-mal doormat status in the American League just two years after playing for the world championship. Baseball teams — successful baseball teams — are built slowly, over time, as you would a business, with care, from the ground up, and constructed (ideally) for long-term success.

This is what makes the Atlanta Braves so unique, and so deserving of recognition here. While they were, indeed, designed for the long haul, their transformation from tailenders to champions seemed to occur overnight. And having reached the mountaintop, they were able to stay there throughout the final decade of the 20th century.

The Braves were historically a franchise with more valleys than peaks. Dur-ing their long tenure in Boston they were a power in the 1890s, had their own incredible year in 1914 (winning the World Series after being in last place in July), and won the pennant in 1948. In most other years they were also-rans in the National League. They moved to Milwaukee in 1953, just as their young players were starting to mature, and were contenders through 1960 (winning it all in 1957), respectable for several years thereafter. They moved again, this time to Atlanta, after the 1965 season, won the first National League West title in 1969 (losing to those Mets in the league championship series), then spent the bulk of the 1970s as spectators to the pennant races going on around them. But in 1982 they won their division and contended again in 1983 and the first half of 1984 before tumbling in 1985. And there they stayed throughout the 1980s, the butt of jokes and an embarrassment to the region in which they were the major leagues' only representatives, the Southeast.

Cable television tycoon Ted Turner had purchased the team in 1976, and proved time and again that he knew far more about TV than he did about base-ball. He was constantly getting into hot water with the Commissioner's Office or with his fellow owners, either for making some rash decision (he actually managed the team for a day in 1977 before being informed it was against the rules; he lost the game, by the way), or for spending money wildly and fool-ishly, or for remarks he made in public. He also signed off on some terrible base-ball deals, such as the trade for pitcher Len Barker, who wound up winning just ten games for the Braves while the young prospects they gave up, Brett Butler and Brook Jacoby, enjoyed excellent careers.

In 1978 the Braves hired a former Yankee infielder, Bobby Cox, to manage the team. Cox stayed four seasons, finished below .500 three times, and was dismissed following the strike-marred year of 1981. The team he had nurtured came of age in 1982 and won the division for Joe Torre, while Cox resurfaced in Toronto and built a contender there, highlighted by a division title in 1985.

Then Ted Turner, admitting that firing Cox was the worst mistake he had ever made as a baseball owner, brought him back as the Braves' general manager. Perhaps somewhere in their negotiations was an agreement that the bombastic owner would finally let the baseball people run the baseball club. The rebirth of the Atlanta Braves had begun.

It was, however, a slow gestation period. Cox and farm director Paul Snyder worked hard to restock their minor league system with talented prospects and slowly brought the youngsters up to the majors, first for a taste of big-league life, then for permanent residence. From 1987 through 1990, infielders Ron Gant, Jeff Blauser and Mark Lemke; outfielder David Justice; and pitchers Steve Avery, Tom Glavine and John Smoltz made their major league debuts. They were not, however, instant hits: during the first four years that Cox served as GM, the Braves finished last three times and next-to-last the other year.

Nineteen-ninety proved to be a watershed year for the Braves. Ron Gant's powerful righthanded bat needed to be in the lineup, but finding a defensive position for him was something of a challenge. Although he played second base in the minors and during his rookie year of 1988, it was deemed he lacked the range for the keystone and he was shifted to third. His discomfort at the hot corner was apparent after some fifty games, and the Braves took the unusual step of sending him back to the minors to learn to play the outfield. Gant returned in 1990 and claimed his position on the strength of 32 home runs, 84 RBI, 107 runs scored, 33 stolen bases and a .303 average. Another strong bat was being wielded by rookie Dave Justice. The lefthanded hitter was an outfielder by trade, but moved to first base to fill an Atlanta need. He was not, however, the second coming of Gil Hodges around the bag, so the Braves made a bold move to break up their outfield logjam. In early August they traded their franchise player, Dale Murphy, to Philadelphia. Murphy was an icon in Atlanta, a legitimate superstar who had won back-to-back Most Valuable Player Awards in the National League (1982 and 1983), a slugger who was also superb defensively and a quiet, clean-living, church-going family man to boot. But Murphy's skills were also declining rapidly: after hitting 44 home runs and driving home 105 in 1987, he hit just 44 round-trippers over the next two years combined. And though he sported a .279 lifetime average through 1987, he batted just .226 and .228 the next two seasons. So when Murphy continued to slide in 1990, the Braves decided to deal him and put Justice in right field. The youngster responded to the pressure of replacing a hero by swatting 20 homers, driving home fifty runners over the last two months and capturing the Rookie of the Year Award.

Trading Murphy wasn't the team's only headline-grabbing event that summer. Just weeks prior to the Murphy deal, Cox fired manager Russ Nixon, in his third season at the helm, and went into the dugout himself to get a first-hand look at the club in action and to determine how best to improve their plight. Because in spite of the slugging of Gant and Justice, the pitching efforts of youngsters John Smoltz and Tom Glavine, and the change in managers, the Braves finished in last place yet again.

Cox had a sartorial decision to make: wear a suit to work every day, or a uniform. He chose the latter, and the Braves lured John Schuerholz to Atlanta to serve as general manager. Schuerholz had been the GM in Kansas City, where he had successfully built that club into a perennial contender and the 1985 World Series champion. Schuerholz and Cox then planned their strategy for moving the team up in the National League West. They determined that the pitchers needed a better defensive infield behind them. Jeff Treadway, at second base, was adequate, but young Jeff Blauser was probably not yet ready for the daily grind of being a starting shortstop in the majors. The corner spots, meanwhile, needed a complete overhaul. The pitchers could also benefit from having a great glove man in center field, giving them the kind of defense Murphy had once supplied. The starting rotation needed another arm or two, and someone needed to take control in the bullpen. It seemed to be a long-term renovation.

Except that, in the late 20th century World of Baseball, anything was possible with a bit of shrewd management and a lot of cash. Getting Turner's blessing to spend some money on free agents, Schuerholz was able to revamp the infield. Sid Bream and Rafael Belliard were "mid-priced" free agents who came over from Pittsburgh to take over first base and shortstop, respectively. A more expensive acquisition was third baseman Terry Pendleton, who had had some good years in St. Louis, where he played in the 1985 and 1987 World Series. Also imported to Atlanta was Otis Nixon, a veteran outfielder who, despite a good glove and incredible speed, was unable to secure a starting spot in Montreal; Bobby Cox planned to play him every day and have him bat leadoff.

Hard-throwing lefthander Mike Stanton made an impression in the spring and became a workhorse in the bullpen. He was joined by a couple of other youngsters from the farm system: southpaw Kent Mercker (who had been with the team in 1990) and rookie righthander Mark Wohlers, whose fastball was occasionally clocked at 100 MPH, and the veteran Juan Berenguer, who was putting on his seventh big-league uniform. Many others also passed through the Atlanta bullpen in 1991, as relief pitching proved to be the team's biggest trouble spot.

Nothing much was expected of a team that had finished either fifth or sixth in the previous six seasons. Plus, the Braves resided in a division — the

National League West — that had produced two of the past three world champions, so it was assumed they would simply be content with vacating the cellar. In the season's first half that was undoubtedly correct. Atlanta was definitely improved as they made a run at a .500 mark, and the newcomers were all blending in with the budding young stars. Pendleton was especially impressive, consistently knocking in key runs, playing a heady third base and providing steady leadership in the clubhouse. He would lead the league in batting, hits and total bases and be selected as the league's Most Valuable Player. Belliard was not much of a hitter but he furnished eye-popping defense at short, gobbling groundballs with such regularity that he picked up the nickname "Pac-Man," an allusion to a popular video game in which the hero eats everything in sight. Nixon also proved to be better than advertised, keeping his average near .300 while battling his former Montreal teammate Marquis Grissom for the stolen base title.

And then there was the pitching. Glavine emerged as the stopper, turning in winning efforts every time the Braves seemed to need one. He became Atlanta's first 20-game winner since Phil Niekro in 1979, and won the Cy Young Award. Steve Avery, who had won just three times the year before, put it all together to win 18 games, while fellow lefty Charlie Leibrandt won 15 and John Smoltz, the only righthander in the rotation, chipped in with 14 wins. This quartet wound up starting 141 of the Braves' 162 games.

With the collapse of the previous two pennant winners, Cincinnati and San Francisco, the Los Angeles Dodgers seemed to have clear sailing to the division title, and enjoyed a comfortable lead at the All-Star break. Once the players returned from the mid-summer showcase in Toronto, however, something strange happened: the Braves caught fire, winning nine of eleven, and shaved seven games off the Dodgers' lead in twelve days. Suddenly trailing by just two-and-a-half games, Atlanta was in its first pennant race in years.

Berenguer had assumed the role of closer, but in August he injured his arm and was lost for the season. Realizing the need for a veteran presence in the bullpen, Schuerholz picked up Alejandro Peña from the New York Mets. Peña, who had ironically achieved some early success with the Dodgers, stepped right into the breach, saving 11 games.

The city of Atlanta went bonkers over their Braves, coming out to Atlanta–Fulton County Stadium in record numbers. The rest of the nation also caught the fever, as Turner's cable superstation, WTBS, broadcast Braves games to fans all around the country. America's traditional sympathy for the underdog made everyone a Braves fan in the summer of 1991.

The two teams marched in lockstep down the stretch until Atlanta provided a finishing kick. They swept three-game series in both Houston and Cincinnati to move into first place, then came home to defeat Houston on Friday night and Saturday afternoon; coupled with Dodger defeats, the Atlanta Braves were champions of the National League West.

The league championship series opened in Pittsburgh, and the Pirates cuffed Glavine for a 5–1 win. But Steve Avery was overpowering in outdueling former Brave Zane Smith for a 1–0 victory. Mark Lemke shared star billing in this game, driving home the only run and preventing a potential RBI single from getting out of the infield in the eighth inning. The teams headed south and the Braves cracked three home runs in routing Pittsburgh, 10–3. But the Bucs captured the next two games. First they eked out a 3–2 win in the tenth inning of Game Four, then took their own 1–0 game the next day. Smith again pitched well against his ex-mates, and he and reliever Roger Mason blunted the Braves every time they threatened to score.

Back in Pittsburgh with their backs to the wall, Avery hooked up with Doug Drabek, the 1990 Cy Young Award winner, for a pitching duel extraordinaire. Scoreless after eight, the Braves finally plated a run — their first in 26 innings — on a double by catcher Greg Olson. Then Peña allowed the potential tying run to reach third base, but struck out center fielder Andy Van Slyke — looking — to end the game. With a World Series appearance now riding on just one game, rookie Brian Hunter, who had become the first baseman against left-handed pitching, hit a two-run homer in the first and John Smoltz threw a six-hitter for a 4–0 victory. For the first time since they were in Milwaukee in 1958, the Braves would be playing on baseball's biggest stage.

Atlanta's opponents were the Minnesota Twins, and writers all around the country had a field day with this fairy-tale matchup, since the Twins, like the Braves, had finished in last place the year before. They were led by irrepressible outfielder Kirby Puckett, hard-hitting first baseman Kent Hrbek, designated hitter Chili Davis, outfielder Shane Mack, and Rookie of the Year second baseman Chuck Knoblauch. Former Detroit Tiger ace Jack Morris headed a pitching staff that also featured youngsters Scott Erickson and Kevin Tapani, and bullpen ace Rick Aguilera.

The first two games were held indoors at the Metrodome, and the Twins feasted on home cooking. Morris stymied the Braves, and shortstop Greg Gagne hit a three-run homer off Charlie Leibrandt for a 5–2 victory in the opener. Glavine gave up just four hits in Game Two, but two of them left the park, including an eighth inning shot by third baseman Scott Leius that untied the contest and gave Minnesota a 3–2 win.

Game Three, in Atlanta, was a four-hour marathon that featured 13 pitchers. The Braves took a 4–2 lead into the eighth, but Chili Davis tied it up with a homer against Peña, who had relieved Avery. Cox and Twins manager Tom Kelly matched wits until the 12th inning, when Justice singled, stole second, and was driven home by Lemke. The little second baseman was also the hero the next day. Morris had held the Braves at bay again, but Lonnie Smith homered against reliever Carl Willis to tie the game. Then in the ninth Lemke tripled and scored on a sacrifice fly by pinch-hitter Jerry Willard. Although the Twins argued that Lemke had been tagged out, the run counted and the Series was tied. Then the Braves put their hitting shoes on in Game Five, pounding out 17 hits, eight for extra bases. A close, 5–3 game was blown open by a six-run seventh inning as Atlanta swept all three games at home to move to within one win of a world championship. Lemke, by the way, continued his hot hitting, cracking two more triples.

Now it was the Twins who needed a win, and they got it because of Kirby Puckett. The Twins' undisputed leader drove home three runs and saved one with a leaping catch of a Ron Gant drive. With the score tied in the 11th inning, Cox brought Leibrandt into the game for his first relief appearance since 1989. Puckett drove the lefthander's fourth pitch over the fence for a home run, sending the Series to sudden death. John Smoltz and Jack Morris were their managers' choices for the finale, and they produced one of the most talked-about games of recent times. Both righties were at their best, setting down hitters inning after inning. The Braves squandered a chance to score in the eighth, however, and lived to regret it as Minnesota broke through with a run in the tenth inning to win this heart-pounding World Series.

It is still considered to be the finest Fall Classic played in the 1990s. Three games, including the final two, went extra innings, while four were decided by the final swing of the bat. Both teams played like champions, but in the end the Twins prevailed.

Mark Lemke was rewarded for his World Series heroics by becoming the starting second baseman, and Cox discovered a successful platoon behind the plate as switch-hitting Damon Berryhill alternated with Greg Olson. Otherwise the Braves started 1992 as essentially the same club. They got off to a slow start, but in late May they went on a tear, winning 41 of 56 games to move into first place to stay, proving that the previous season had not been a fluke. Pendleton and Glavine continued to lead by example. The third baseman once again led the league in hits and was second with his 105 RBI while batting over .300 again; he finished second in the MVP voting. Glavine won 20 games again and led the league in shutouts; he finished behind the Cubs' Greg Maddux in the Cy Young balloting. Two other players made notable contributions. Former football star Deion Sanders, serving as the fourth outfielder, used his great speed to lead the league in triples with 14 and to steal 26 bases while batting .304. Jeff Blauser reclaimed the shortstop position from Belliard and contributed 14 home runs while forming an effective double-play partnership with Lemke.

This time the Braves won the division by a comfortable eight games, and again faced off against Pittsburgh. They were at a bit of a disadvantage, however, as they had lost two key performers to injuries in the second half. About a year after his acquisition, closer Peña injured his elbow, ending his season. The Braves picked up an aging Jeff Reardon to replace him. Then in mid–September catcher Olson broke a leg in a collision at the plate, leaving Berryhill as the primary receiver.

The series opened in Atlanta and it was all Braves. Smoltz gave up just four hits and the Braves KO'd Drabek, last year's nemesis, in the fifth inning on their way to a 5–1 win. The next day just about everyone contributed as Atlanta used three big innings to dispose of Pittsburgh by a 13–5 score. Any thoughts of a sweep, however, went dancing out of their heads in Game Three. Playing at home, Pittsburgh started rookie righthander Tim Wakefield, a knuckleballer who had won eight of nine decisions after a mid–season promotion. Though the Braves managed solo home runs by Bream and Gant, they were only able to manage three other hits against Wakefield, while the Bucs nicked Glavine for three runs and their first win. Smoltz and Drabek came back on just three days' rest, and while neither was at his best Smoltz proved to be a little better. Pittsburgh took the early lead but the Braves drove Drabek from the mound and solidified it against reliever Randy Tomlin in a 6–4 triumph which brought them to within one win of the National League pennant. They handed the ball to Steve Avery, but the hero of the 1991 league championship series was only able to retire one batter. With a 4–0 lead the Pirates coasted the rest of the way as the two teams headed back to Atlanta.

Almost 52,000 Braves fans came for a party and instead attended a wake, administered by Mr. Wakefield. Once again the Braves could do nothing with the knuckler, and for the second straight game one of Atlanta's vaunted starters was shelled early. This time it was Glavine, who couldn't retire anyone in the second inning. Barry Bonds had two hits in the second as the Bucs scored eight times to effectively end the game. Having come back from the brink to force a seventh game, the Pirates seemed to have momentum on their side and clipped Smoltz for a run in the first and another in the sixth for a 2–0 lead. Meanwhile, Drabek was pitching like a true ace and had the Braves shut out on five hits as they came up for their last licks in the ninth. Pendleton doubled, then Pirate second baseman Jose Lind bobbled Justice's routine grounder. Bream walked, loading the bases as Stan Belinda replaced Drabek on the mound. Gant drove in Pendleton with a fly ball and Berryhill walked to fill the bases once more. Hunter popped out, and with two out Cox called on Francisco Cabrera, a catcher who had been added to the roster due to Olson's injury. Cabrera had just ten at-bats in the majors in 1992, but he forever etched his name in Atlanta baseball lore by lining a single to left field. Justice scored the tying run and Sid Bream, one of the slowest runners on the team, came chugging around third as fast as he could and slid in just ahead of Bonds' throw, giving the Braves the most dramatic victory of the series and their second consecutive pennant.

The 1993 World Series was an historic one even before the first pitch was thrown. The American League representatives were the Toronto Blue Jays, making it the first time the Fall Classic was played outside of the United States. That would happen in Game Three; meanwhile, the Braves recognized a familiar face out on the mound in the opener. During the off-season Toronto had signed Minnesota's Jack Morris as a free agent, and now the man who had thwarted

Atlanta in the final game of the 1991 World Series was toeing the rubber to begin the 1992 Series. Tom Glavine opposed him and allowed a Joe Carter home run in the fourth inning, but batterymate Damon Berryhill got it all back, and more, when he lined a three-run shot off Morris in the sixth, and that was all the scoring for the game. The Braves roughed up Toronto's David Cone for four runs in less than five innings, but the Jays' bullpen proved to be true stoppers as they held Atlanta without a hit the rest of the way. Still, the Braves led 4–3 in the ninth when pinch-hitter Ed Sprague whacked Jeff Reardon's first pitch for a two-run homer, and Toronto closer Tom Henke retired Pendleton with the tying and winning runs on base. The competition remained fierce as the action moved north of the border. Avery and Toronto starter Juan Guzman matched serves for eight innings. In the bottom of the ninth, however, Cox and his Toronto counterpart, Cito Gaston, changed pitchers and hitters in an attempt to create the most favorable situation, which ultimately boiled down to Jeff Reardon pitching against outfielder Candy Maldonado with the bases loaded and one out. Maldonado ended the chess match with a base hit for a 3–2 Toronto victory. Game Four proved to be another nail-biter. Glavine only gave up two runs, but the Braves could not solve the off-speed slants of left-hander Jimmy Key until the eighth inning. The Jays' bullpen then did its job once again, and Toronto's 2–1 win moved it to the brink of the championship. Jack Morris and John Smoltz opposed each other for the first time since their classic matchup of the year before, but the Braves' Lonnie Smith stole the spotlight. Serving as the designated hitter, Smith unloaded a grand slam homer in the fifth inning to break open a close game and send the Series back to Atlanta, where Braves fans witnessed another nip-and-tuck ballgame. Trailing 2–1 in the ninth, Otis Nixon sent it into overtime with a single. In the 11th inning Cox, remembering Reardon's failures in Games Two and Three, stayed with Charlie Leibrandt and watched Dave Winfield drive home a pair of runs with a double. But it wasn't over quite yet, as Atlanta fought back with one run and had the tying run on third base. Nixon thought a surprise bunt would drive in the run, but Blue Jay pitcher Mike Timlin quickly fielded the ball and threw him out. For the second straight year the Braves came up short in the World Series.

The Braves made front-page news with a major free agent addition in the off-season. Greg Maddux had won 20 games and the Cy Young Award for the Chicago Cubs in 1992. A two-time All-Star, he had won 87 games during the previous five years for a team that had finished over .500 just once. Though he had decided to test the open market as a free agent, most observers thought the Cubs would pay a premium price to keep their ace. But John Schuerholz had a plan and, making Maddux an offer he couldn't refuse, gave the Braves a dominant starting rotation that included Glavine, Smoltz and Avery. A great many people thought the Braves had guaranteed themselves a permanent place in the World Series.

Nothing comes easy, however, and this time the difficulty came from San

Francisco. The Giants had picked up their own high-profile free agent in Barry Bonds, but just as significantly they had hired former Braves outfielder Dusty Baker as their manager. Baker proved to be one of the most effective leaders in the game, getting maximum effort from his players. That Bonds would lead the league in home runs, RBI, total bases and slugging percentage was not a great surprise; that Billy Swift would go from 10 wins to 21 and John Burkett from 13 wins to 22 could be attributed in large part to Baker's deft handling.

San Francisco got off to a great start and took a huge lead. The Braves were doing okay, getting great production from the usual crew, plus a couple of surprises. On offense, shortstop Jeff Blauser was hitting for a higher average and driving in more runs than ever before; he wound up sixth in the league in total hits. On the mound, rookie righthander Greg McMichael, who had been released out of Cleveland's minor league system two years earlier, began the season in middle relief but soon was tried as a closer by Bobby Cox and made the most of his first major league opportunity. His tantalizing changeup baffled National League hitters and brought some stability to the Atlanta bullpen.

About 500 miles south of San Francisco, the San Diego Padres were having a rough year. Their ownership, woefully underfinanced, had decided to sell off many of their higher-salaried players to make the team more attractive (that is, less top-heavy) to potential buyers. The Braves became one of the most ardent suitors of first baseman Fred McGriff, and in mid–July they swapped three top minor league prospects to the Padres for the lefthanded slugger.

McGriff was one of the most underrated players in the game. A power hitter who also knew how to do the little things that help to win ballgames, he brought a quiet leadership to a team. A product of the Yankee farm system, he had been swapped to the Blue Jays and immediately blossomed; in his second full season in Toronto, he reached the 30-homer plateau, and then stayed there for the next seven years. He led the American League in home runs in 1989, but a year later was traded to San Diego (along with All-Star shortstop Tony Fernandez) in a blockbuster deal that brought second baseman Roberto Alomar and outfielder–first baseman Joe Carter north of the border. It proved to be the cornerstone of Toronto's two consecutive world championships, but did nothing for the Padres. A year after leading the National League in home runs, McGriff was packaged off to the Braves, where he became the focal point of the offense.

In his first game McGriff whacked a two-run home run, helping Atlanta turn a 5–0 deficit into an 8–5 win over St. Louis. The Braves were playing well, 12 games over .500, but still far behind the Giants. McGriff's presence energized the team and they played incredible .750 ball the rest of the way. They needed every win, too, because San Francisco did not give an inch. Never separated by more than one-and-a-half games in the last nine days of the regular season and dead even on the final day, Atlanta beat Colorado* while the Giants were pounded by the Dodgers to finally settle this great race. Dusty Baker's crew had won 103 games, more than any other team in baseball — except for the Braves. Atlanta advanced to the postseason while San Francisco stayed home.

This looked like the Braves' year. They had power: Justice hit 40 homers and Gant had 36 as the team led the league. They had speed: four players were threats on the basepaths, led by Nixon's 47 steals. And they certainly had the pitching: Glavine and Maddux both won 20 (Glavine actually reached 22), while Avery and Smoltz combined for another 33 wins. Maddux led the league in innings pitched, complete games and earned run average, and would capture his second consecutive Cy Young trophy, while Glavine finished third in the voting. As a team, the Braves had the best ERA in all of baseball.

But Atlanta did not win the World Series in 1993; Atlanta, in fact, did not even reach the World Series in 1993. The Braves were upset in the league championship series by the Philadelphia Phillies, the surprise winners in the NL East. Atlanta constantly squandered opportunities in the series, beginning with the very first game. After tying it up in the ninth inning, they put runners on second and third in the tenth but couldn't score, then gave up the game-winning hit to a reserve infielder. After blasting Philadelphia pitching for 23 runs and 28 hits in the next two games to take the series lead, though, Atlanta simply forgot how to score runs. They outhit the Phillies in the next three games, 22–21, but stranded 23 baserunners, many of them at crucial times. In Game Four they left two men on in both the eighth and ninth innings and lost, 2–1. The next day they trailed by a 3–0 score going into the bottom of the ninth, then rallied against Phils' ace Curt Schilling to tie the game. With two men on and just one out another hit would have given them the win and the series lead, but they failed to deliver, and Philadelphia centerfielder Lenny Dykstra made them pay with a game-winning homer in the tenth. Then relying on Maddux to even things up and force a seventh game, the Braves were shocked when their righthanded ace had an atypical poor outing, giving up six runs in less than six innings, and preventing a World Series rematch with Toronto. Throughout the series, and especially in the final three games, it appeared that the Phillies wanted to win more than the Braves, and they worked harder to make it happen. They were rewarded with a berth in the Fall Classic.

The Braves didn't advance to the postseason in 1994, but through no fault of their own. There was no postseason in 1994. There was only shame, the blackest mark on the game since a group of Chicago players conspired to throw the 1919 World Series. The less said about that year the better, but a brief explanation is in order.

---

*The National League had added teams in Denver (the Colorado Rockies) and Miami (the Florida Marlins) for the 1993 season.

Major league owners claimed that 19 of the 28 teams were losing money, although they refused to allow their books to be examined to verify that statement. What was obvious to everyone, however, was that player salaries were spiraling up higher, and the gap between richer and poorer clubs was growing wider. A team like the Braves, for instance, could count on revenue from Ted Turner's successful television ventures; many other franchises, located in large metropolitan areas, had more opportunities to sell sponsorships or tickets or radio and TV spots than others and could thus bring in more money. The clubs that had access to rivers of cash could afford to pay the higher salaries, either for free agents or for their own young stars, while the teams that didn't were losing their best players, losing games, losing fans, losing money. And the circle seemed unbroken, as the rich could do what needed to be done to get richer while the poor could do little but get poorer.

More than thirty years earlier, the young commissioner of the National Football League, Pete Rozelle, had reminded his owners that Benjamin Franklin was right when he said "we must all hang together, or assuredly we shall all hang separately." Rozelle convinced NFL moguls to share television rights equally, which allowed smaller-market clubs to compete financially with their larger-market brethren and created a semblance of parity in football. Baseball owners now decided to implement something similar, but predicated any new revenue-sharing agreement on the players accepting a salary cap. The Players Association refused to consider this restriction, arguing that the athletes shouldn't be penalized for the owners' profligacy. Negotiations to break this impasse were fruitless and the players went out on strike on August 12. Further negotiations went nowhere, even with the help of federal mediators, as the owners saw an opportunity to weaken the powerful Players Association and strengthen themselves in the process. With the hard-liners firmly in command, baseball suffered the ultimate indignity when, in September, the balance of the season and any hope for postseason action were summarily canceled. The World Series had survived two world wars, numerous other American interventions abroad, a global depression and the aforementioned scandal of 1919, but could not get past a fight between millionaires.

Too bad, because enough excitement had been generated up through August 11 to hold out the promise of a great stretch run to conclude the 1994 season. The Braves found themselves in another pennant race but in a different division and with some different faces in the lineup.

The owners and players had agreed to a geographic realignment prior to the season, creating three divisions rather than two, and this put Atlanta into the new National League East along with Florida, Montreal, New York and Philadelphia. While the Phillies couldn't sustain any momentum generated by their improbable 1993 season and were not a factor in the race, the young Montreal Expos established themselves as more than Atlanta's equal. Led by an All-Star outfield of Moises Alou, Marquis Grissom and Larry Walker, and a pitching

staff that featured starters Pedro Martinez and Ken Hill and dominant relievers John Wetteland, Mel Rojas and Jeff Shaw, the Expos spotted the Braves an
early lead and then roared past them to hold a six-game bulge at the time of
the work stoppage. Had a postseason been played, however, Atlanta might have
participated anyway, because the three-division setup also allowed for a wild
card team — the club with the best winning percentage among the also-rans —
to make the playoffs, and the Braves had a better mark than Houston over in
the Central Division.

In the off-season the Braves had signed Ron Gant to a contract worth some
$5.5 million for the 1994 season. Then Gant severely injured his leg in a bik-
ing accident, and the prognosis was that he would miss at least the first half of
the year, maybe more. (In fact, he would sit out the entire season.) Under the
rules the Braves would have been obligated to pay him the full salary if he
remained on their disabled list after March 15, so they took the drastic and
shocking action of releasing Gant, thus saving more than $4 million. Rookie
Ryan Klesko, a first baseman throughout his minor league career, was converted into an outfielder during spring training. He often looked like a first
baseman in the outfield, but he did hit 17 home runs and show great potential.

Neither member of the catching tandem of the previous two seasons, Greg
Olson and Damon Berryhill, were offered new contracts, as the Braves were
committed to going with young prospect Javier Lopez behind the plate, and to
help him along they signed veteran Charlie O'Brien. Lopez contributed 13 home
runs as he learned the vagaries of catching in the big leagues from O'Brien, a
defensive master who surprised with his eight home runs and 28 RBI in just
34 games. Atlanta also made a change in center field, trading Deion Sanders to
Cincinnati on May 29 for the solid but well-traveled Roberto Kelly.

The offense, perhaps missing Gant, was not as potent as the year before.
McGriff stood out, however, batting .318, mashing 34 homers and driving home
94 runs before the work stoppage. On the mound, Maddux and Glavine continued to shine. While the latter won 13 games, third-best in the league, he was
completely overshadowed by his colleague, who by now was drawing comparisons to some of the great pitchers of the past. Maddux led the league in wins,
innings pitched, complete games, shutouts and posted an unbelievable ERA of
1.56. While there was no postseason play baseball did permit postseason awards,
and Maddux took home his third straight Cy Young Award. Avery and Smoltz,
however, had disappointing years, although Kent Mercker stepped up to claim
a spot in the rotation.

The strike officially ended on March 31, 1995. After the owners brought
some minor leaguers, recently retireds and "wannabees" to spring training as
"replacement players," a U.S. district court ruled that the owners could not
unilaterally implement their new financial plan — in other words, no salary cap
unless agreed to by the Players Association. After a devastating impasse of
nearly eight months, absolutely nothing had changed, which was bad news for

those smaller-market franchises. And perhaps no team in baseball suffered more from the fallout than the Montreal Expos. Realizing they would be unable to pay fair market value for all of their fine young players, the Expos systematically disposed of many of the men who had carried them to the best record in the majors at the time of the work stoppage; within two years, no fewer than ten key players were wearing other uniforms. The Braves were one of the first teams to benefit, swapping Kelly, two other players and cash for center fielder Marquis Grissom, a Georgia native and perhaps the best defensive outfielder in the league.

There had been one other casualty in 1994, though unrelated to the labor strife. During spring training the Braves' best minor league player, Larry "Chipper" Jones, had sustained a season-ending injury. A shortstop throughout his career, the switch-hitting Jones was acknowledged to be a surefire major leaguer, and so the Braves needed to determine where he would play once he returned in 1995. The decision was ultimately made to allow Terry Pendleton to leave and move Jones over to third base. While the leadership of Pendleton, the nominal team captain, would be missed, his skills on the field were declining; Jones, meanwhile, would contribute 23 home runs and 86 RBI in his rookie season.

Due to the lateness of the court decision the season was pushed back three weeks and would encompass 144 games, 18 fewer than normal. The Phillies got off to a fast start but faded, partially due to a series of injuries. The dismantled Expos, who had been 34 games above .500 the year before, were never a factor and finished 12 games under .500 in 1995. In fact, the Braves were the only club in the National League East above .500 for the season, and won the division by 21 games. Every member of the starting lineup except for Mark Lemke reached double-figures in home runs. Maddux, incredibly, was even better than ever: his record was 19-2, his ERA was 1.63, and he also led the league in several other categories, which of course brought him yet another Cy Young Award, his fourth in a row. Glavine won 16 and Smoltz 12, but Avery and Mercker both had losing records, bringing the otherworldly rotation back down to earth.

Under the new postseason format the Braves were matched against the third-year Colorado Rockies, who claimed the wild card spot. The Rockies had a built-in advantage in their ballpark because of Denver's mile-high elevation, which made the ball travel farther and also reduced the "bite" on a pitcher's breaking ball. The Rockies led the league in runs, hits, home runs and batting average and gave the Braves all they could handle. It took a ninth inning Chipper Jones home run and a bases-loaded strikeout by Mark Wohlers to win the opening game, and a four-run rally—keyed by reserve infielder Mike Mordecai's pinch-hit single that knocked in two—to capture Game Two. Back in Atlanta, however, the barrage continued. Colorado had the game won in the ninth, but reserve outfielder Luis Polonia delivered a pinch-single to tie it up.

The Rockies, however, solved Wohlers for two runs in the tenth to keep the series alive, but only until the next day, when Maddux, though not at his best, restored order with a 10–4 victory. McGriff hit two home runs in this game, and since Jones (first game) and Grissom (second game) had done the same thing earlier in the series, it made Atlanta the first team to have three players contribute multihomer games in the postseason since the Yankees (Babe Ruth, Lou Gehrig, Tony Lazzeri) in the 1932 World Series.

The Braves now took on the Cincinnati Reds, the Central Division champions. The Reds had the league's Most Valuable Player in shortstop Barry Larkin and the Cy Young runner-up in southpaw Pete Schourek, but they could do nothing against Atlanta's pitching staff, scoring just five runs and batting a mere .103 with runners in scoring position. The first game might have been the key. Schourek led Glavine, 1–0, through eight but the Braves finally broke through to tie it in the ninth and then won it in the 11th when another bench player, Mike Devereaux, delivered a hit. The next day provided another pitching duel and another extra-inning affair, broken up this time by Javy Lopez' three-run homer in the tenth. The long ball, in fact, was the chief support of the pitching staff: O'Brien's three-run homer and Jones' two-run shot scored all of Atlanta's runs in Game Three; and Devereaux, the surprise series MVP, had a three-run clout in a big seventh inning to finish off the first sweep of a postseason series since 1982. The Braves were back in the World Series, against an opponent that would truly test their pitchers.

The Cleveland Indians were a modern-day Murderers' Row. Seven regulars hit .300 or more for the season; the same number reached double-digits in home runs. They were led by Albert Belle, who had become the first man in history to collect fifty doubles and fifty homers in one season. Even in the abbreviated season they hit over 200 homers as a team, averaged nearly six runs per game, and batted .291. They won exactly 100 games for an amazing winning percentage of .694, then rolled over Boston and Seattle to reach the World Series for the first time since 1954.

The Series opened in Atlanta and the fans were treated to yet another pitching duel as Maddux and Cleveland's Orel Hershiser gave up just five hits between them. The Braves untied a 1–1 game without a hit in the seventh inning, using three walks, an RBI grounder by Polonia and a squeeze bunt by Rafael Belliard — starting in place of injured Jeff Blauser — to draw first blood. Maddux needed just 95 pitches for his two-hit win. Glavine continued the thread the next night, giving up just three hits in six innings. Lopez hit a two-run homer in the sixth and then, with Atlanta holding a 4–3 lead in the eighth, picked off Manny Ramirez after the Indian outfielder had singled. But the string of great pitching ended when the Series moved to Ohio. Smoltz was battered for six hits and four runs in less than three innings, and the bullpen was less than sterling in Game Three. Still, the Braves had a chance to take a commanding lead in the Series when they battled back and forged ahead in the eighth, only to see Cleveland come back to tie it right away and then win it in the 11th. Cox then made a calculated gamble for Game Four, opting to pitch Steve Avery rather than Maddux. Although Avery had had his first losing record since his rookie season, he had been brilliant against Cincinnati in that series' finale, and Cox was speculating he would get the same kind of effort against the Tribe. The Braves hit the jackpot: Avery allowed just three hits (one of them a Belle home run) in his six innings; Dave Justice drove home two runs against south-paw reliever (and former Brave) Paul Assenmacher; and Pedro Borbon came in to bail out a tired Wohlers in the ninth to give Atlanta a commanding 3–1 Series lead. With Maddux scheduled to pitch in Game Five it looked like the Braves would finally capture the brass ring. The Indians, however, had other ideas as Belle cracked a two-run homer in the first inning on their way to a 5–4 victory. The Series went back to Atlanta.

On the off-day, Justice made some caustic comments about the hometown fans. "If we get down 1–0," he said for publication, "they will probably boo us out of the stadium." He had other uncomplimentary things to say, which made him Public Enemy Number One in his own park for Game Six. Sometimes, however, things have a way of working out. With the game scoreless in the sixth, Justice drove a pitch from reliever Jim Poole deep into the seats for a 1–0 lead. And that was all Tom Glavine would need as the Braves' southpaw (with a perfect ninth inning from Wohlers) threw the first one-hitter in the World Series since 1967 to close out the Tribe. Winning by a 1–0 score was ironic since that was also the heartbreaking score in the final game of the 1991 World Series. The Braves' victory marked the first championship for any professional sports franchise in Atlanta, and they did it by holding Cleveland to a .179 average. The Indians only managed 35 hits and 19 runs in the six games.

Basking in the glory of their world championship, the Braves did not tin-ker with their core group of players, although there were a few new faces on the bench, including three rookies who made their presence felt in 1996. When a dislocated shoulder ended Justice's season on May 15, Jermaine Dye came on to claim right field, displaying a rocket arm and batting .281 with 12 homers. Eddie Perez displaced Charlie O'Brien as the backup catcher, and in August the Braves promoted Andruw Jones to the majors. Jones, a native of the island of Curaçao, had begun the year in Class A Durham, but after tearing up the Car-olina League in the first half was promoted to Double-A, then again to Triple-A before finally landing in Atlanta. Cox knew his 19-year-old *wunderkind* was not ready for big-league pitching (although he did hit five home runs in 106 at-bats), but recognized that Jones' glove, which he likened to Willie Mays, would help the team in the postseason.

There was little doubt they would be playing in October once again. The only opposition came from Montreal, where manager Felipe Alou (another for-mer Braves player) had taken a new group of young players and molded them into contenders. But they still finished eight games out. Jones and McGriff topped 100 RBI, Klesko came close with 93 (to go along with 34 homers), and Grissom had a wonderful year, reaching double-figures in doubles, triples, homers and stolen bases while batting .308 and collecting 207 hits. The pitchers were led, for once, by Smoltz, who was the NL's only 20-game winner and led the league in innings pitched and strikeouts. In November he would break the Greg Maddux stranglehold on the Cy Young Award. Maddux and Glavine each won 15 and finished among the top five in ERA (as did Smoltz). But Avery had another losing season, and on August 28 the Braves traded their top young pitcher, 23-year-old Jason Schmidt, plus a minor leaguer to Pittsburgh for the Pirates' best hurler, lefthander Denny Neagle.

The Dodgers were the National League wild card this year and the first two games produced great pitching battles. Smoltz was touched for just four hits and a run in the opener, but Ramon Martinez gave up only three hits and a run as the two teams went to extra innings. Javy Lopez settled the debate, however, with a home run in the tenth. The next night Maddux battled Ismael Valdes, and two Atlanta errors gave the Mexican righthander a 2–1 lead after six. But McGriff and Dye both homered in the seventh, and when a hamstring injury forced Maddux out of the game, McMichael and Wohlers finished up the 3–2 triumph. The Braves then used a four-run fourth inning to complete the sweep in Atlanta.

The St. Louis Cardinals had also swept their series, against San Diego. The Central Division champions had a strong four-man starting rotation and a balanced offense led by former Brave Ron Gant. It looked like Atlanta's momentum was continuing when Smoltz opened the series with a 4–2 win, but then the Cardinals shocked the world by running off three straight victories. They broke open a tied Game Two by getting to Maddux for five runs in the seventh inning, four of them on a Gary Gaetti grand slam. The Braves could only manage five hits against Todd Stottlemyre and three relievers. Gant clipped Glavine for a pair of homers and drove in all three runs in a 3–2 victory the next night, but the Braves seemed to have the series tied when they took a 3–0 lead into the seventh inning of Game Four. But the Cardinals tied it against Neagle and McMichael, and then former Atlanta Falcon football star Brian Jordan brought the Cards to within one game of the World Series with an eighth inning home run.

No team in league championship series history had ever been down three games to one and come back to win. Compounding the uphill fight was the fact that they were still in St. Louis. But the Braves, outscored by a 17–12 margin in the first four games, rediscovered the joys of hitting in Game Five. They blasted Stottlemyre for five in the first and two more in the second and never looked back. Smoltz breezed with the big lead and the 14–0 win gave the Braves some hope as they returned to Atlanta. Maddux then gave the shifting momentum a boost with a 3–1 triumph, setting up a seventh game that had seemed improbable only days before. The storybook ending became complete when

Atlanta rocked the Cards for six runs in the very first inning, including a bases-clearing triple by Glavine, in a mind-numbing 15–0 victory. In those final three games, the Braves outscored St. Louis 32–1.

Although Cleveland had won their division handily once again, they did not advance to the World Series in 1996; in fact, they didn't even get past the first round. Instead, the Braves found themselves pitted against the New York Yankees, returning to the Fall Classic for the first time in 15 years and managed by former Brave player and skipper Joe Torre. The Yanks offense was geared around outfielders Bernie Williams and Paul O'Neill, first baseman Tino Martinez and Rookie of the Year shortstop Derek Jeter. The always-tough David Cone and a pair of lefthanders — young Andy Pettitte and veteran Jimmy Key — headed the starting staff, but the bullpen had been the real secret to New York's success that season. Several pitchers had done well in middle relief, flame-throwing Mariano Rivera had positively owned the seventh and eighth innings, and former Montreal closer John Wetteland led the league with his 43 saves.

Relief, however, was the least of New York's concerns in the first two games. Andruw Jones became the youngest player to hit a World Series home run, then became the second man in history to have circuit clouts in his first two at-bats, as the Braves and Smoltz destroyed Pettitte and two successors in a 12–1 romp. The next night Maddux and Wohlers shut out the erstwhile Bombers, and McGriff drove in three runs for a 4–0 triumph. The two teams headed down to Atlanta with the Braves sporting a two game lead and a streak of five straight postseason wins in which they had outscored their opponents by a 48–2 margin. Many newspaper writers were saying the Series was over, the Yankees were overmatched, and that the Braves had to be compared with the greatest teams of all time.

The Yankees apparently didn't read the papers. Cone and his bullpen proved to be better than Glavine and his bullpen, and New York won, 5–2. The Braves took a 6–0 lead in Game Four before the Yankees began to score, and Cox called on Wohlers in the eighth inning. But the usually surehanded Belliard misplayed a groundball, then Wohlers tried to fool Jim Leyritz with an off-speed pitch and watched it sail out of the park for a game-tying home run. The Yankees then scored twice in the tenth inning for an 8–6 win, and the Series was suddenly tied.

Smoltz and Pettitte hooked up again in Game Five, with far different results. Both pitchers were at their best, displaying the kind of stuff in which one run would be enough. The Yankees got that run, then held off a ninth inning Atlanta rally to head back to New York with the lead. But the Braves felt they were in the same position they had been in against St. Louis, trailing their opponent but sending Maddux out to the mound. And the Professor pitched well, but had one bad inning, the third, when the Yankees clipped him for three runs. Jimmy Key pitched into the sixth and then handed the ball to his bullpen, and as they had all season they came through for a 3–2 victory. The Braves, after outscoring the Yankees by a 16–1 margin in capturing the first two games, dropped four straight and lost their chance to win back-to-back world titles.

Cox and Schuerholz felt that one reason for the defeat was the inadequacy of their bench; in contrast, the Yankees received several key hits from their secondary players. So in the off-season Atlanta sent Jermaine Dye (plus a minor league player) to Kansas City for infielder Keith Lockhart and outfielder Michael Tucker, who were both projected to beef up the bench. Then in the spring, just days before the season's opener, the Braves pulled the trigger on a blockbuster deal, sending Grissom and Justice to Cleveland for center fielder Kenny Lofton and pitcher Alan Embree. The Indians were afraid they would not be able to re-sign Lofton, in the final year of his contract, while the Braves saw him as a better leadoff hitter than Grissom. While Lofton's .333 average wound up third in the league, he also was disabled for six weeks, and his replacement, Andruw Jones, proved that, at least defensively, he was the equal to any other outfielder in the game. Lofton, perhaps eyeing free agency, also never seemed to fit in with the team. Tucker, on the other hand, proved to be a smart and reliable player, batting .283 with 14 home runs as he upset the preseason plan for him and became the regular right fielder. Lockhart did his job, becoming one of the league's premier pinch hitters, and when torn ligaments ended Lemke's season in August, he platooned effectively at second base with young Tony Graffanino.

In addition to a couple of new players, the Braves had a new ballpark to play in. After 30 years in Atlanta–Fulton County Stadium, Turner Field opened to rave reviews, and proved itself to be a little more pitcher-friendly than the old ballpark, which had been known as "The Launching Pad." McGriff, Klesko, Lopez and Chipper Jones continued to lead the attack, but more than ever the team centered around the starting four. In 1997 it was Denny Neagle stepping up, becoming the only 20-game winner in the league. Maddux was 19–4 with a 2.20 ERA, while Glavine and Smoltz won 29 games between them. Wohlers saved 33 games but the rest of the bullpen was inconsistent.

The Braves won the division again, taking an early lead, building it up just before the All-Star break and maintaining the comfortable margin for the rest of the year. Their main opposition this year came from the Florida Marlins, who had spent the off-season buying up free agents like Moises Alou, Alex Fernandez and Bobby Bonilla in an effort to bring an instant contender to South Florida. They won 92 games, nine fewer than Atlanta, and went into the postseason as the wild card.

The Braves hosted Central Division champion Houston Astros in the first round of the playoffs, with Maddux facing fellow 19-game winner Darryl Kile in the opener. Kile's big-bending curveball limited the Braves to just two hits, but they made the most of them: Lofton doubled and scored on a fly ball, and Klesko homered. The Astros collected seven hits off Maddux but only one run. The second game was tied in the fifth, but then the Braves erupted for eight runs in the next two innings to win in a romp. Moving to Houston didn't help the Astros at all, as Smoltz limited them to three hits and struck out 11 to quickly finish off the series. The Awesome Threesome pitched 24 of the series' 27 innings, holding Houston hitters to 16 hits (only two for extra bases), five runs and a .167 average. Neagle, the 20-game winner, never got close to the mound.

The Marlins won their series and the two East Division teams played for the right to advance to the World Series, and the tone was set in the first inning of the first game. McGriff made an error on a routine groundball and Chipper Jones did not come up with another grounder, all of which led to three unearned Florida runs. Two more runs scored due to a Lofton error, and Florida won, 5–3, with all the runs against Maddux being unearned. But the Braves rebounded the next day, with Klesko and Chipper Jones going deep to support Glavine. Andruw Jones misjudged a line drive in the sixth inning of Game Three and that proved to be the key play of the game. Instead of ending the inning with the lead, the Braves gave up four runs and lost, 5–2. Neagle then tied the series with a four-hit shutout, but the series turned on the fifth game. Home plate umpire Eric Gregg seemed to expand the strike zone for Marlin starter Livan Hernandez, who struck out 15 Braves — many of them looking — to outduel Maddux, 2–1. Back in Atlanta, the Braves asked Glavine to get them to a seventh game, but for once their ace lefty failed. He gave up four runs in the first inning, and then when the Braves drew to within a run, he was knocked out in the sixth. The Marlins' 7–4 victory ended the series and launched them to an improbable World Series title, while the Braves went home again for the winter.

And a memorable winter it was, as the team completely revamped the infield. Deciding it needed more of a righthanded presence, Atlanta signed free agent first baseman Andres Galarraga, who, while playing for Colorado, had led the league in RBI the previous two seasons. This made Fred McGriff expendable, and the Braves sold him to the expansion Tampa Bay Devil Rays so he could close out his career in his home area. They also signed another former Rockie, shortstop Walt Weiss, which meant saying goodbye to Jeff Blauser. By not offering a new contract to Mark Lemke, the Braves were closing the books on a combo that had handled the team's middle infield defense since 1992. Atlanta also chose not to resign Kenny Lofton, turning center field exclusively over to Andruw Jones; Lofton wound up going back to Cleveland.

On the face of it, the Braves had an easy time in 1998, winning a franchise-best 106 games and finishing 18 lengths ahead of the New York Mets. But the sailing wasn't all that smooth. Weiss had injury and personal problems off and on all season, limiting him to 96 games. Luckily, the Braves had picked up former White Sox shortstop Ozzie Guillen in the spring, and he filled in extremely well, batting .277 and keeping everyone loose with his upbeat personality. Graffanino proved unable to handle major league pitching, batting just .211, which forced Cox to use Lockhart as the starter more often than he had hoped.

Relief ace Mark Wohlers, after going on the disabled list in May, came back and inexplicably could no longer throw strikes. His wildness became a season-long soap opera as the Braves tried all sorts of cures in both the majors and minors to get him untracked. Kerry Ligtenberg, who had been discovered while pitching in an independent minor league, stepped into the closer's role and became the first rookie since Todd Worrell of the 1986 Cardinals to save 30 games in a season. Galarraga, however, proved that the thin air in Denver had not been the cause of his offensive pyrotechnics, as he batted .305 with 44 home runs and 121 RBI while serving as a real cheerleader on the bench and a wise counsel in the locker room. Javy Lopez and the Jones boys, Andruw and Chipper, all topped 30 homers for the year as the team exploded for 215 round-trippers, an all-time club record.

On the pitching front, Glavine became the league's only 20-game winner and consequently won his second Cy Young Award; Maddux won 18, Smoltz 17 (despite time on the disabled list), Neagle 16 and young Kevin Millwood, in his first full season in the big leagues, exceeded all expectations by winning 17 games as the number five starter!

Back in 1991, when they first took part in postseason play, the Braves were "the people's choice" because they had been so bad for so long before suddenly getting good. Now in 1998 they found themselves on the other side of that coin: their opponents in the first round of playoff action were the Chicago Cubs, the National League wild card, which had finished above .500 for just the fourth time in the past decade. Outfielder Sammy Sosa had garnered national publicity all season as he had battled the Cardinals' Mark McGwire — and the ghosts of Babe Ruth and Roger Maris — in the Great Home Run Chase. Despite hitting 66 round-trippers, Sosa did not get the record as McGwire bashed an incredible 70 to set a new standard. Sosa did league the majors with 158 RBI, won the Most Valuable Player Award, and had the ultimate satisfaction of taking his team into postseason play; for all of McGwire's long-ball heroics, the Cardinals finished just four games over .500.

But Atlanta's pitching staff made short work of Sosa and the Cubs. Backed by a two-run homer by Tucker and a grand slam from Klesko, Smoltz dispatched Chicago in the opening game. Glavine and Kevin Tapani hooked up for a classic duel in the second game, and the Cubs actually led, 1–0, in the ninth inning. But with one out Javy Lopez homered for the tie, and a Chipper Jones single won it in the tenth. And then, after Rookie of the Year Kerry Wood stymied them for five innings, the Braves erupted against Chicago's bullpen in a five-run eighth, with Eddie Perez's grand slam the key blow. The Cubs scored just four runs in the three games, and Sosa had just two hits, a single and double in the first game.

The San Diego Padres, having defeated the Houston Astros in their series, came into Atlanta and beat the Braves at their own game — pitching. Andy Ashby outperformed Smoltz in the opener and a tenth inning home run by Ken

Caminiti allowed the Padres to break out on top, then ace Kevin Brown (who had been with the Marlins the year before) limited Atlanta to three singles to take a 2–0 lead as the two teams headed for California. The Padres continued to pitch like, well, the Braves, as lefthander Sterling Hitchcock, who won just nine games during the season, and four relievers shut down Atlanta's hitters yet again. Three times the Braves loaded the bases in the third game, and three times they failed to score, leaving a total of 12 men on base. Trying not to be swept, the Braves found themselves facing imminent elimination when they trailed, 3–2, going into the seventh inning of Game Four. Suddenly their bats awoke as Lopez tied the game with a homer, Guillen singled for the lead and Galarraga put the game out of reach with a grand slam. The next night proved to be very similar, with one engaging twist. Again Ashby got the better of Smoltz, leading 4–2 after six. But in the seventh Padre manager Bruce Bochy went for the kill, bringing in Kevin Brown in relief when the Braves threatened. Brown got through that inning but not the eighth, as Michael Tucker bashed a three-run homer to put Atlanta in front. Then in the ninth inning, trailing by three, the Padres rallied against Ligtenberg and Cox made his own surprise move, bringing Maddux out of the bullpen to subdue San Diego and send the series back to Atlanta. The Padres' Wally Joyner, a veteran of 13 seasons, called it "the best game I've been a part of." Momentum seemed to be on their side, but the Braves saw it all end in one horrible inning. Scoreless after five, the wheels came off in the sixth as Glavine couldn't get the third out, and left fielder Danny Bautista made a crucial error that allowed two runs to score. Atlanta could only muster two singles against Hitchcock and his successors, and the Braves' 1998 season ended in disappointment.

The final year of the 20th century began in horrible fashion for the Braves. Andres Galarraga was diagnosed with lymphoma and was immediately disabled for the entire season to fight this life-threatening disease.* Only a few weeks later Kerry Ligtenberg went down with an arm injury that required season-ending surgery, which meant that even before Opening Day the team had lost two key members.

It went downhill from there.

After a spring full of guarded optimism, former relief ace Mark Wohlers still could not locate home plate and was sent first to the minor leagues, then to Cincinnati in a trade. Otis Nixon, brought back to inject some speed into the lineup, was not up to being the regular left fielder at age 40, batting just .205. In a three-day span in July, the Braves lost rookie southpaw Odalis Perez and catcher Javy Lopez for the balance of the season. John Smoltz found himself on the disabled list not once but twice. Outfielder Brian Jordan, signed as

---

*Doctors fortunately think they caught it in time, and the prognosis for Galarraga's recovery, as well as the continuation of his baseball career, is good. In fact, as this volume goes to press, he is playing first base nearly every day.

a free agent in the off-season and carrying the club offensively in the first half, had his hand broken by a pitch in June; although he didn't miss much playing time, his power was severely curtailed. Maddux and Glavine had very atypical years. They both got off to terrible starts and, while Maddux won 19, his ERA was higher than it had been in a dozen seasons. Glavine won 14 but struggled all year; between them he and Maddux gave up more than 500 hits.

And yet, somehow, the Atlanta Braves won 103 games and captured their division for the eighth straight time, a major league record. The key to the 1999 season was undoubtedly Bobby Cox, who turned in one of the finest managerial jobs in recent history. With his calm and quiet demeanor he continually rallied his battered troops, keeping them focused on the games at hand and refusing to let them get down when faced with all the adversity. He also made a key move, replacing Nixon with veteran Gerald Williams in left field. Though not a traditional leadoff hitter, Williams batted .275 and hit 17 home runs to jump-start the Braves offense. Cox also benefited from Chipper Jones' breakthrough season, as the third baseman took over the offense with his 45 home runs, 41 doubles and 110 RBI, numbers which led to the National League Most Valuable Player Award. On the mound Kevin Millwood became the team's most reliable starter, winning 18 and finishing second in the league in ERA. Hard-throwing lefthander John Rocker took over for the injured Ligtenberg and saved 38 games.

The Phillies and Mets battled the Braves in the first half, and when Philadelphia dropped out of the race after the All-Star break it became a two-team war. Jones sealed his MVP trophy by personally destroying Met pitching in two memorable weekend series, leading Atlanta to five wins in six games. The Braves' final margin of victory over New York was six games, but the Mets made the postseason for the first time in 11 years, going in as the wild card.

The Braves took on the Houston Astros in the first round of the playoffs, and visions of the previous season had to be dancing in their heads. Shane Reynolds held Atlanta to a single run, while Ken Caminiti, a nemesis the year before in a Padre uniform, broke up a close game with a three-run homer in the ninth to give Houston the win. But Kevin Millwood turned the series around the next day. Caminiti hit another homer, but that was Millwood's only gaffe as he one-hit the Astros to even the series. Game Three went 12 innings before the Braves prevailed, 5–3. Jordan doubled home two runs, and Millwood surprisingly came out of the bullpen to pitch a perfect final inning and record the save. In Game Four the Braves built up a 7–0 lead, then saw Caminiti hit another three-run shot in the eighth, requiring Rocker to come in and put out the fire, sending Atlanta on to the next round — against the Mets.

New York was led in 1999 by one of the finest infields of all time. First baseman John Olerud, second baseman Edgardo Alfonzo, shortstop Rey Ordoñez and third baseman Robin Ventura were all Gold Glove candidates at their positions and led the team to a record-low 68 errors for the season. They could also hit: Alfonzo and Ventura both batted over .300 with more than twenty homers and over 100 RBI while Olerud just missed in all three categories. Former Dodger Mike Piazza, in his first full year as the Mets' catcher, led the team in homers and RBI, and off-season pickup Roger Cedeño finished second in the league in stolen bases. They also featured an excellent bullpen and a fiery manager in Bobby Valentine.

But the Braves' September success against the Mets carried over into mid–October. Maddux pitched like Maddux as he won the opener, 4–2. Atlanta spotted the Mets a two-run lead in Game Two, then wiped it out when Jordan and Perez both hit two-run homers against late-season acquisition Kenny Rogers in the sixth inning. When the series moved to New York, the Mets' great defense betrayed them as two errors allowed the Braves to score in the first inning without the benefit of a hit. Atlanta could only manage three singles against Met starter Al Leiter, but Glavine was brilliant, striking out eight in giving the Braves a 3–0 lead in the series.

Poised for the sweep, the Braves watched the series take some strange twists. Jordan and Klesko hit back-to-back homers in the eighth inning of Game Four, giving Atlanta the lead, but Olerud singled just past Guillen's outstretched glove for two runs as the Mets won, 3–2. Game Five, played in a steady rain, saw a record 46 players used, with Valentine employing nine pitchers. The Mets scored a pair in the first and Atlanta countered with two in the fourth, and then, as if W.P. Kinsella's *The Iowa Baseball Confederacy* had come to life, neither team could dent home plate again, until a Lockhart triple gave the Braves the lead in the 15th inning. But having already used Rocker, Cox was left with rookie Kevin McGlinchy, who was unequal to the task. He walked in the tying run and then, completely unnerved, gave up what appeared to be a grand slam homer to Ventura. However, the third baseman never was able to circle the bases as his teammates mobbed him and he only got credit for a single and one RBI. It was enough, however, for a 4–3 victory. Then, after a much-needed day off to return to Atlanta, the two resumed their trench warfare once more as Game Six went 11 grueling innings. The Braves jumped all over Leiter, pitching on just three days' rest, for five in the first and held a 7–3 lead after six. But Cox called on Smoltz to make a rare relief appearance and the Mets lit him up for four runs, including Piazza's game-tying home run. Both clubs scored in the eighth, and repeated the parlay in the tenth. Finally in the 11th inning, Gerald Williams led off with a double against Kenny Rogers and was sacrificed to third. Two intentional walks loaded the bases, creating the possibility of a force at home. It didn't happen, though, as Rogers walked Andruw Jones unintentionally to force home the winning run.

Perhaps it was the travails of the year, followed by the exhausting series against the Mets that finally unraveled the Braves' great season. Or maybe they just met the better team when they got to the World Series; in any event, they were set down in four straight games by the New York Yankees. A Chipper Jones homer had given the Braves the early lead in Game One, but that was the only hit they could manage against Yankee starter Orlando Hernandez. Maddux was just as tough for seven innings, but wilted in the eighth and was clipped for all New York's runs in a 4–1 defeat. The next night the Yanks jumped all over Millwood and reliever Terry Mulholland, taking the Braves out of the game early. Atlanta played their best, ironically, in the Bronx in Game Three. They ripped lefthander Andy Pettitte for ten hits and five runs in less than four innings and held a 5–3 lead in the eighth inning. But Cox made a mistake by leaving Glavine in to pitch and the tired southpaw gave up the tying runs. Then Mike Remlinger, who had had a marvelous season in winning ten games out of the bullpen, was summoned in the tenth inning and gave up a leadoff home run to Chad Curtis, and the Braves' coffin was almost finished. The final nail was driven in the next night, as one bad inning — a three-run third — undid Smoltz, and Roger Clemens was finally able to taste World Series champagne after holding the Braves at bay. Atlanta scored a mere nine runs in the four games (New York scored 21), batted just .200 and in general looked nothing like the team that had overcome so many obstacles to get to the Fall Classic.

Despite winning just one World Series in the decade, the Atlanta Braves' accomplishment of eight division titles and five National League pennants in the 1990s is a feat unsurpassed by any club in the 20th century except for Casey Stengel's 1949–1960 Yankees. It is all the more remarkable when one considers that Smoltz, Glavine and Nixon were the only players to appear in both the 1991 and 1999 World Series. Cox and Schuerholz were able to continually replace players with either free agents or fresh young talent from the minor leagues while maintaining the team's lofty status as one of baseball's elite clubs, which is how the Atlanta Braves head into the 21st century.

1996–99
New York Yankees

The best team of the 1990s started out the decade with the worst record in the league.

That would be the New York Yankees. After the success of the 1976–1978 team, the Bronx Bombers fell into a spell of mediocrity, fielding a representative team that often teased their fans but was ultimately never good enough to win their division. They changed managers as frequently as a mother changes diapers on her infant. In an 11-year period, from 1982 through 1992, they had ten different managers, with Billy Martin serving three different terms and Lou Piniella two. Not surprising, therefore, that the 1980s were a Lost Decade for the Yankees.

By 1990 they had sunk to the bottom, winning just 67 games. Their best all-around player, first baseman Don Mattingly — the 1984 batting champion and 1985 Most Valuable Player — had seen both his average and power numbers drop significantly due to a bad back. The top winner on the pitching staff was a journeyman relief pitcher named Lee Guetterman. If anyone had suggested that this team would dominate baseball just a few years later, they would have been laughed out of the building.

The renaissance began after the 1991 season, when third base coach William "Buck" Showalter was chosen as the new manager. Showalter had played in the Yankees farm system, but when he saw he wasn't going to play his way to the majors he chose to become a manager, successfully piloting several teams before he was named to the coaching staff. His first Yankee squad showed a very modest improvement, and then he and General Manager Gene Michael went to work. They engineered a trade with Cincinnati, giving up starting center fielder Roberto Kelly in exchange for right fielder Paul O'Neill. They admired O'Neill's line-drive bat and his hustle in the outfield, and Showalter was confident they could replace Kelly with another product of the farm system, 24-year-old switch hitter Bernie Williams. They signed a couple of free agents: pitcher Jimmy Key and third baseman Wade Boggs. Key, the prototypical crafty lefthander, had reached double-figures in wins for eight straight years with Toronto, and his addition automatically gave the sad New York pitching staff an ace. Boggs was one of the game's legitimate superstars. In his 11 years with Boston he had won five batting titles, collected 200 or more hits in seven consecutive seasons, and had been an All-Star eight times. Having failed to hit .300 for the first time ever, the Red Sox determined that the 34-year-old Boggs had begun his decline and decided not to re-sign him; the Yankees snapped him right up. Boggs was no doubt satisfied, then, with the results of the 1993 season, as he not only returned to the .300 circle, but was able to help his new club finish eight games ahead of his old club. O'Neill also topped .300 and Key won 18 as Showalter led the Bombers to 88 wins and second place, their best finish since 1986.

In the previous chapter on the Atlanta Braves the details of the 1994 season are discussed in depth, specifically the reason the players went on strike in August, and the owners' cancellation of all postseason play. These writers speculate that no team in baseball suffered more from the walkout, and its aftermath, than the Montreal Expos, but the New York Yankees and their fans were also severely victimized. That is because Buck Showalter had his team in first place at the time of the work stoppage, with the best record in the American League and the second best in the majors (behind those Expos). For Yankee fans, it not only meant no postseason play for the 13th consecutive season, it also meant no postseason play for Mattingly, their long-suffering captain. On the plus side, O'Neill won the batting title with a .359 mark (and Boggs finished fifth with his .342), Key led the majors in wins with 17, and the team as a whole batted .290, the highest batting average in the majors and the team's best since

1936. But it was all for naught — nothing good came out of this strike, and nobody really won anything.

Dipping into the free agent pool again, the Yankees signed former Cy Young Award winner Jack McDowell to team with Key at the top of the rotation. They followed that with a move just before Opening Day that dealt a minor league prospect to Montreal — which was paring payroll in the wake of the strike — for relief ace John Wetteland. The best-laid plans, however, often get ambushed by shoulder injuries, which limited Key's season to just five games. Helping to step into the breach were a pair of young lefthanders, Sterling Hitchcock and rookie Andy Pettitte, who won 23 games between them. In July, as they battled for a playoff spot, they swung a major deal, sending three minor league pitchers to Toronto for veteran righthander David Cone. Winner of the Cy Young Award the previous season, Cone already owned 120 major league victories and had a reputation as a big-game pitcher. Despite the retooled pitching staff and Bernie Williams joining Boggs and O'Neill as .300 hitters, New York still finished behind Boston in the American League East, but they made the playoffs anyway as the first wild card in baseball's new postseason structure.

The Yankees were pitted against the Seattle Mariners, a club that had won the West Division for the first time; in fact, this was just the third winning season in its 19-year history. The Mariners had a tough lineup, featuring outfielders Ken Griffey, Jr., and Jay Buhner, designated hitter Edgar Martinez and first baseman Tino Martinez, while also boasting the league's most overpowering pitcher, 6-foot-10-inch southpaw Randy Johnson, who averaged more than 12 strikeouts for every nine innings he pitched. But New York won the first two games at home, including a spine-tingling Game Two marathon that concluded when catcher Jim Leyritz hit a two-run homer in the 15th inning. The Mariners regrouped back in the Kingdome and won Game Three, then broke open a tie game (one that the Yankees had once led by five) in the eighth with five runs, including an Edgar Martinez grand slam, to send the series to a fifth and final game. New York seemed poised to advance to the next round as they led, 4–2, in the eighth, but Showalter stayed with Cone a little too long and Seattle tied it up. Then, after the Yankees pulled ahead in the 11th, Seattle staged a furious rally to win, 6–5. The ecstatic Mariners advanced to the league championship series while the Yankees glumly went home.

And then came a curious cat-and-mouse game with Showalter. First, Steinbrenner relieved Gene Michael of his duties as general manager, then offered his manager a two-year contract, rather than a longer pact. He was also rumored to have asked for the dismissal of at least one coach, perhaps more. For his part, Showalter seemed to waffle over whether he wanted to return to the team. In typical Steinbrenner-era Yankee fashion, it is hard to distinguish fact from fiction, but the end result was a new management team in the Bronx: former player and Houston General Manager Bob Watson moved into the front office, while former All-Star and one-time Mets manager Joe Torre took Showalter's seat in the dugout.

These weren't the only major changes during the misnomered off-season. After rapping Seattle pitching for ten hits and a .417 average in the division series, Mattingly announced his retirement, causing the Yankees to search for a new first baseman. They found one, ironically, in the Pacific Northwest as they traded Hitchcock and top minor league prospect Russ Davis to the Mariners for Tino Martinez and two relief pitchers. They also swapped a couple of young pitchers to Colorado for catcher Joe Girardi, picked up veteran infielder Mariano Duncan and lefthanded pitcher Kenny Rogers as free agents, and signed — at Steinbrenner's insistence — former Met and one-time Cy Young Award winner Dwight Gooden, who had missed much of the previous two years due to drug problems.

The Yankees of the 1970s, with Billy Martin, Reggie Jackson, Thurman Munson and others, were often accused of being a soap opera in double-knits. The 1996 team was also something like that, except that the story lines were all much more positive. Gooden, responding to the second chance, won 11 games, including the only no-hitter of his career in just his seventh start in pinstripes. Another one-time Met star, outfielder Darryl Strawberry, was also given an opportunity to redeem himself after battling drugs and, after some time in Triple-A, returned to the majors to share the designated hitter job with mid-season acquisition Cecil Fielder; together they produced 24 homers and 73 RBI. David Cone, counted on to be the ace of the pitching staff, went on the disabled list early in the season with an aneurysm in his shoulder that was potentially life-threatening, but he returned for the last month or so of the season and gave the rotation a major boost with his gritty performances. But Joe Torre was perhaps the major contributor to this feel-good Yankee team. Generally considered to be a mediocre major league manager, he brought a quiet demeanor to the often-volatile clubhouse, serving as much as father-confessor to his players as their boss. He also brought an exciting brand of baseball to the Bronx, as the team bunted, hit-and-ran and stole 96 bases, nearly double their total from the year before. Torre also managed through pain: one brother was lost to a June heart attack while another, former Milwaukee Brave first baseman Frank, was hospitalized while waiting and hoping for a new heart.

New York jumped out in front early and kept on going, faltering only briefly in September, which allowed the Orioles to close the gap from double-digits to the final four-game margin. The hitters seemed to practice a share-the-wealth philosophy, as five starters batted over .300 and two more missed by just a few points. Martinez and Williams both drove in over 100 runs, while 22-year-old Derek Jeter gave the team their best shortstop play since Tony Kubek and proved to be an igniter of the offense as he garnered Rookie of the Year honors. On the mound, Pettitte led the league with his 21 victories while Key returned from an injury-plagued 1995 to win a dozen more, but it was the bullpen that really propelled this team. If the starters faltered, Torre could call on several middle relievers to guide the club into the seventh inning before young Mariano Rivera would take over. The 26-year-old Panamanian righthander, all of 170 pounds, blossomed in his second season in the Bronx, striking out 130 men in just 107 innings; American League hitters batted a mere .189 against him. Then Wetteland would come in to pitch the ninth and earn the save, which he did a league-best 43 times. The Rivera-Wetteland combination had the effect of shortening the game for the opposition to just six innings.

This year the Yankees were pitted against the West Division champion Texas Rangers, the one-time Washington Senators franchise making their first-ever postseason appearance. Led by outfielder Juan Gonzalez, whose 47 homers and 144 RBI would earn him the Most Valuable Player Award, they featured a powerful lineup that included eight players with double-digit home run totals and six players with over 80 RBI. Manager Johnny Oates had a solid if unspectacular starting staff but a weak bullpen. They made their first game a memorable one by winning in the Bronx by a 6–2 score, with Gonzalez and third baseman Dean Palmer both blasting home runs off Cone in a five-run fourth inning. Gonzalez hit two more the next day as the Rangers took an early lead, but the Yankees eventually tied it up and the game went into overtime. Torre wound up using four pitchers in the 12th but it paid off, as first the Rangers failed to score and then Palmer made a crucial throwing error to give New York the victory. Moving to the new Ballpark in Arlington, the Rangers took a 2–1 lead into the ninth but the Yanks scored twice for the win. In Game Four Texas took the early lead again — they were in front in all four games — but once more their bullpen couldn't hold it. Bernie Williams hit two home runs (Gonzalez, by the way, reaching the seats in every game, hit five in the series), and the relief corps gave up just one hit in the final six innings in a 6–4 New York wrap-up. The sterling Yankee bullpen was the series' showpiece, allowing just one earned run during their nearly twenty innings of work.

This brought on a showdown with Baltimore, which had scored a mild upset in defeating the Cleveland Indians. In a year in which seven American League teams hit more than 200 home runs and three of them topped the 1961 Yankees' old record of 240, the Orioles were kings, blasting 257 out of the park. Seven members of Davey Johnson's wrecking crew had at least 20 homers, with the ringleader being Brady Anderson, their leadoff man, who swatted 50 even though his previous career high had been only 21. Needless to say, the home run proved to be the major weapon in the series, with 19 balls being launched into the seats. A controversial solo shot by Jeter tied the opening game in the eighth inning, then Williams won it with an 11th-inning blast. But the Orioles rebounded to win Game Two, 5–3, as Todd Zeile and Rafael Palmeiro both hit two-run homers and hard-throwing Armando Benitez shut down a ninth inning New York threat.

They moved to Maryland for the balance of the series, and 19-game winner Mike Mussina was brilliant through seven, holding the Yanks to just four hits. But a pair of doubles, a weird error by Zeile (the ball dribbled out of his hand as he faked a throw to second base), and a home run by Fielder plated four runs and a 5–2 victory. After giving up a pair in the first Jimmy Key kept the O's off the scoreboard, yielding just three hits. Neither Game Four starter, Kenny Rogers and rookie Rocky Coppinger, was particularly effective, but when Baltimore cut the Yankee lead to 5–4 in the fourth the bullpen got tough and prevented further scoring, while Strawberry's second homer of the game capped a three-run eighth inning that gave New York the win. In the fifth and final game, slick-fielding second baseman Roberto Alomar made a crucial error in the third, and three Yankee home runs in that inning gave them a 6–0 lead on their way to a 6–4 win and their first World Series date in 15 years.

That rendezvous would be against the defending world champions, the Atlanta Braves, a team that seemed to have the perfect blend of pitching and power. John Smoltz had won a career-high 24 games but the other two starters, Greg Maddux and Tom Glavine, had only combined to win the previous *five* Cy Young awards. On those occasions when they faltered, Bobby Cox could call on flame-throwing Mark Wohlers to come in out of the bullpen. Atlanta hit 197 home runs, second in the league to Colorado, and presented a formidable lineup that included first baseman Fred McGriff, third baseman Chipper Jones, catcher Javier Lopez and outfielders Marquis Grissom and Ryan Klesko. The Braves were favored to repeat, and the odds skyrocketed after Atlanta thoroughly throttled New York in the first two games of the Series. A nervous Pettitte was rocked in the third, and the Yankee bullpen mystique was also shattered when Brian Boehringer was hit just as hard in a 12–1 Atlanta romp. The next night McGriff drove in runs in the first, third and fifth innings off Key, and Maddux mesmerized the Yanks for a 4–0 triumph. Momentum was all in Atlanta's favor: having outscored St. Louis and the Yankees 48–2 in the last five games they had played, and heading back to Fulton County Stadium, it seemed to be only a matter of time before the Braves would wear the crown once more.

David Cone had other ideas. He gave up just four hits through six innings and left with a 2–1 lead. Tom Glavine was tough but Bernie Williams broke the game open with a two-run homer in the eighth off reliever Greg McMichael as the Yankees won, 5–2, to snap Atlanta's five-game winning streak. But the Series really turned on Game Four. For the third straight time in this postseason Kenny Rogers was driven from the mound before the fourth inning. Limited to just two hits by southpaw Denny Neagle through the first five innings, the Yankees received some inadvertent help from an umpire. Jeter led off the sixth with a fly down the right field line that was foul but catchable. But umpire Tim Welke, trying to get out of the way of Jermaine Dye, instead slowed the Braves' outfielder down, and Dye couldn't reach the ball. Given new life, Jeter lined a base hit that ignited a three-run rally. Then in the eighth Cox brought in Wohlers, hoping he could get two strong innings from his ace. The first two men reached base but then Duncan hit a routine grounder to short. It should have been a double play but Rafael Belliard, one of the best glovemen in the business, didn't handle it cleanly and had to settle for a force at second. The impact of this misplay was felt moments later when backup catcher Jim Leyritz, unable to catch up to Wohlers' fastball, inexplicably saw a hanging slider and drove it out of the park for a game-tying, three-run homer. Had the Braves executed the double play, the Leyritz blast would have only brought the Yanks to within one. Once Wohlers left the game, Cox had merely secondary pitchers left in his bullpen, and in the tenth former starter Steve Avery gave up two hits, two walks and two runs as New York tied the Series with its comeback win, 8–6.

That fickle damsel, momentum, was now smiling on the Yankees, and Andy Pettitte made sure her head wasn't turned. He was brilliant, totally shutting the Braves down for better than eight innings. He had to be tough because Smoltz was equally uncompromising, yielding just four hits. But the Yankees scored in the fourth when Grissom and Dye didn't communicate on a fly ball hit by third baseman Charlie Hayes. Dye cut in front of Grissom and the ball bounded off the center fielder's glove, then minutes later Fielder delivered him with a hit. That's the way it stood until the ninth, when the Braves put Chipper Jones on third with just one out. Wetteland relieved Pettitte and got Lopez to bounce to third as Jones held his ground. Then Paul O'Neill, running as hard as he could (despite an injured hamstring) and extending himself as far as he could, caught up with a long drive to end the thrilling 1–0 game. Seemingly whipped when they left New York, the Yankees now returned home with the Series lead.

On the travel day preceding Game Six, Frank Torre received his new heart. The Braves should have saved themselves the trip, but tried to defy the fairytale finish by starting Maddux, who pitched well but gave up three runs in the third inning, including a key triple to Girardi, his initial hit of the Series, directly accounting for the first two runs. Key wasn't overpowering but the bullpen bailed him out, with a tired Wetteland, making his fifth appearance, giving up a run in the ninth but getting the final out for his fourth save.

It was the Yankees' first World Series triumph since 1978, but it was sweetest of all for Joe Torre. He had been an excellent player for 17 years, an All-Star nine times, a batting champion and an MVP. He had then managed for 14 years, but in more than three decades he had never made a single World Series appearance, until 1996. In the end, the emotional and human aspects of this story captured the nation's heart and remained a lasting memory, long after the specific details of the games had faded away.

The Yankees didn't stand pat in the off-season. Deciding that Mariano Rivera ought to be their closer, they allowed World Series MVP John Wetteland to join the Texas Rangers as a free agent. They allowed Jimmy Key to depart the same way, but signed stout southpaw David Wells as a replacement; ironically, Key hooked on with Baltimore, Wells' previous club, which meant the two rivals had simply traded over-30 lefthanders. And after weeks of talks, New York took a real gamble, trading two of their top minor league prospects to San Diego for the rights to Japanese pitcher Hideki Irabu.

New York actually won 96 games in 1997, four more than they had the preceding year. But the Orioles had another phenomenal season (although they hit 61 fewer homers) and edged the Bombers by two games. Tino Martinez had a great year in the Bronx, clouting 44 homers and driving home 141. O'Neill topped .300 for the fifth straight year and Williams for the third, and they both reached the century-mark in RBI as well. Chad Curtis, picked up in a June trade with Cleveland, played very well in left field (and in center, too, when Williams missed 33 games due to injury), batting .291 with 12 home runs. Pettitte had another fine season on the mound, winning 18, while Wells won 16 and became a fan favorite with his boisterous personality and historical interest in the persona of Babe Ruth. Cone won 12 despite a month on the disabled list with tendonitis, and Rivera easily adapted to the closer's role, saving 43 and fashioning a 1.88 ERA. But there were some disappointments, too. Irabu won only five games, had an ERA of 7.09, displayed less of a fastball than advertised, and seemed to be able to pitch competitively only against weaker teams. The third base platoon of Wade Boggs and Charlie Hayes was noticeably slowing down, especially on defense. Second base became a revolving door, especially after a mid-season trade of Mariano Duncan to Toronto. Luis Sojo, a reliable infielder when used in a backup role, found himself more-or-less the regular there, which reduced his effectiveness and weakened the Yankee bench.

Still, the Yankees had the second-best record in the American League (and the third-best in all of baseball), and entered the postseason as the wild card, matched up against the Cleveland Indians, the Central Division champs. The powerful Tribe had bashed 220 home runs during the season and had five players contribute 20 or more round-trippers, although the Yankees actually scored more runs. Cleveland's pitching was weak, however, with a team ERA uncomfortably close to 5.00. In the opening game they rocked David Cone for five runs in the first and had a 6–1 lead in the fourth, but Ramiro Mendoza shut them down on just one hit in his three-plus innings, and the rest of the New York bullpen followed suit. Then in the sixth, Tim Raines, Derek Jeter and Paul O'Neill blasted consecutive home runs to give the Bombers an 8–6 victory. When the Yankees clipped Jaret Wright, Cleveland's 21-year-old Game Two starter, for three runs in the first, they seemed to be well on their way to easily winning the best-of-five series. But Wright got over his jitters and shut New York down, while Cleveland nailed Pettitte for seven runs in the middle innings as they completed a 7–5 triumph. The Yankees only picked up four hits in Game Three, but O'Neill provided two of them and the victory. He singled home a run in the first and then, after Indian starter Charles Nagy walked the bases loaded in the fourth, unloaded a grand slam off reliever Chad Ogea. Wells went the route, giving up just five hits for the 6–1 win. Needing just one more triumph to advance in the playoffs, the Yankees clipped Orel Hershiser for a pair in the first inning, then Gooden and the bullpen made it stand up until Torre called on Rivera in the eighth. This time, though, the "Panamanian Express" failed to deliver. Cleveland catcher Sandy Alomar, Jr., tied the game with a home run, and the Tribe won it in the ninth with a run off Mendoza. This set up a winner-take-all fifth game, and for the second time Pettitte was ineffective, giving Cleveland a 4–0 cushion. The Yankees got back to within one, but this time the much-maligned Indian bullpen came through and stopped New York. Although the Yankees outhit the Tribe, 12–7, they could not deliver with men on base and were eliminated.

The weaknesses in the infield needed to be addressed. In the winter the Yankees sent Kenny Rogers and a chunk of cash to Oakland for third baseman Scott Brosius, whose average had plummeted 101 points in 1997 and was therefore deemed expendable. Then shortly before spring training they sent four minor leaguers, including highly-rated pitcher Eric Milton and shortstop Cristian Guzman, to Minnesota for All-Star second baseman Chuck Knoblauch. They also added a Duke to their family by signing Cuban refugee Orlando "El Duque" Hernandez. A righthanded pitcher with a baffling delivery and great control, Hernandez spent two months in the minor leagues to get used to American culture and umpires, then made his Bronx debut in June and contributed 12 wins, one of six pitchers in double-figures for the Yankees in 1998.

It was the year of the home run, as Mark McGwire of St. Louis and Sammy Sosa of the Cubs waged a two-man battle against Roger Maris' 1961 single-season record of 61 homers. While the nation became fascinated with their friendly rivalry, won by McGwire with an incredible 70 home runs (Sosa finished with a not-too-shabby 66), the Yankees quietly went about their business of winning ballgames. After losing four of the season's first five, they then won 16 of their remaining 18 April games to jump into the lead. In May they were treated to a perfect game from David Wells, the first one in franchise history since Don Larsen stopped the Brooklyn Dodgers in the 1956 World Series, and they were 20–7 that month. They had nearly identical records in June and July, to give them an incredible record of 76 wins against just 27 losses, a .738 winning percentage, going into August. The world finally realized there was another race going on besides McGwire-Sosa: the Yankees were chasing the 1906 Cubs' seemingly invincible marks of 116 victories and .763 winning percentage.

They didn't make it, but they still dominated, winning 114 games (a new single season record in the American League) and finishing a mere 22 games ahead of Boston in the East Division. They did it with a complete team effort. Bernie Williams, despite spending more time on the disabled list, won the batting championship with a .339 average; Derek Jeter led the league in runs scored; Wells tossed the most shutouts; and Cone was one of three 20-game winners in the AL. Aside from that, no Yankee led in any other category as they played unselfishly, as a team, dedicated only to winning. Still, Martinez and O'Neill drove in over 100 runs, while Brosius, batting *ninth*, and Williams just missed with 98 and 97, respectively. Strawberry, in only 295 at-bats, hit 24 home runs as the lefthanded DH, while Shane Spencer, after nine years in the minors, played his way onto the postseason roster by hitting ten home runs (including three grand slams) following his September call-up. Another youngster, Jorge Posada, wrested the catching job from Joe Girardi by hitting 17 home runs and driving home 63. The pitching was so solid that Irabu, with a 13–9 record, was merely the fifth starter.

But the overwhelming year also brought postseason pressure. The 1906 Cubs and 1954 Indians are recognized for their great years but are also tagged with the caveat that they didn't win the World Series. The Yankees, to a man, knew their season would be incomplete without capturing the Fall Classic.

They would also have to go forward without Darryl Strawberry. He finally decided to have a constant irritation in his stomach checked out, and it turned out to be colon cancer. Strawberry underwent surgery which, naturally, sidelined him for the entire postseason.

With those things in mind they literally wiped out the Texas Rangers in the first round. Juan Gonzalez had put together another MVP season, with 45 homers and 157 RBI, for a team that was one of six (the Yankees were another) to top 200 homers for the year. The Rangers also scored more than 900 runs for the second time in three seasons, but they barely sniffed home plate against Yankee pitching. Wells, Pettitte and Cone, plus the bullpen, allowed just one run in the three-game sweep. As a team New York didn't exactly pound the Rangers but Spencer did, cracking a couple of homers and driving in four of the Yanks' nine runs in the series as they quickly moved on to face Cleveland. The Indians continued to feature an exciting, explosive lineup, but backed it up with suspect pitching. Jaret Wright, so successful the year before against the Yankees, drew the first game assignment and was gone after 36 pitches. The first four batters singled for New York, and by the time Wells went out to pitch the second inning he had a 5–0 lead on his way to a 7–2 victory. The next two games, however, proved to be much more interesting. Hitters on both sides could do nothing in Game Two, which was tied going into the 12th inning. Cleveland first baseman Jim Thome singled and then third baseman Travis Fryman bunted. Tino Martinez fielded the ball but his throw hit Fryman, who was clearly running outside the baseline. The ball bounded away and Knoblauch, rather than chase the ball down, chose to argue his case for interference while the play was still going on. One run scored, Fryman went all the way to third and eventually came home as the Tribe evened the series. Then 23-year-old righthander Bartolo Colon demonstrated why the Indians viewed him as their staff ace of the future. After giving up a run to New York in the first inning, he stifled the Bombers on two hits the rest of the way for a 6–1 victory. Thome clubbed two homers off Andy Pettitte, who gave up three long balls in the fifth, all after two were out.

The Yankees' worst fear — failure in the postseason after their 114 wins — seemed to be coming true. But they handed the ball to Hernandez who, having lived in Cuba and escaped Castro's dictatorship, understood that being down in a playoff game wasn't real pressure. He calmly tossed a 4–0 shutout to knot the series and blunt the Indians' momentum. The next night Wells wasn't nearly as unhittable as he had been in his first two appearances, but his teammates staked him to a 3–0 lead in the very first inning, and Rivera came in to get the final five outs in the 5–3 New York victory. And in Game Five the Bombers took an early 6–0 lead, saw Cleveland close the gap on a Thome grand slam, then salted the game away on a sixth inning Jeter triple. The Yankees were heading back to the World Series.

They would be facing the San Diego Padres, the somewhat-surprising National League pennant winners. The Padres, as always, were led by a future Hall of Famer, Tony Gwynn, who had won eight batting titles in his illustrious career. Slowed a bit by injuries he "only" batted .321 in 1998. Big Greg Vaughn supplied the muscle with 50 home runs and 119 RBI, Kevin Brown and Andy Ashby led the young pitching staff, and Trevor Hoffman was the league's top reliever, having saved 53 games during the regular season.

Wells drew the opening game nod for the third straight series and had trouble with Vaughn, who hit two home runs. Gwynn also hit one out, and as the Yankees came up to bat in the seventh they trailed 5–2. But then their bats began to stir, and when Brown was replaced the Bombers really erupted. Knoblauch first tied the game with a three-run homer, then they loaded the bases for Tino Martinez, who greeted former Angel Mark Langston with an upper-deck grand slam. Rivera nailed down the final four outs for a 9–6 victory. New York duplicated that run total the next night, sending Ashby to a third inning shower. Everyone in the starting lineup collected at least one hit as Hernandez coasted to a 9–3 win.

Former Yankee Sterling Hitchcock matched serves with Cone for five innings before the Padres broke through for three runs in the sixth. The Yankees, however, didn't waste any time coming back, getting a solo homer from Brosius and another seventh inning run to cut the deficit to one. Then in the eighth, with Hoffman on the mound, Brosius put another ball into the seats, sending New York ahead. When the Padres crept to within a run in their half of the inning Rivera came in and secured the 5–4 win. It was a shock to the Padre faithful, who had seen Hoffman blow only one save opportunity all season. Now hoping to avoid the sweep, San Diego manager Bruce Bochy sent Brown back out for Game Four while Torre countered with Pettitte, his fourth different starter. After five scoreless innings Williams drove home a run, then the Yankees picked up two more in the eighth to cinch their first four-game wipeout since they ran over Philadelphia's Whiz Kids in 1950. Adding their 11 postseason wins to their summertime total, New York wound up with a 1998 record of 125 wins and just 50 losses, for a .714 winning percentage.

With media debate now comparing the Yankees with some of the great teams of the past, there didn't seem to be any need to tinker with the roster. But an opportunity arose before spring training and the Bombers took advantage of it. When five-time Cy Young Award winner Roger Clemens told Toronto management he wanted to be traded, the Yankees put together a package that included David Wells, lefthanded reliever Graeme Lloyd and infielder Homer Bush, who eventually claimed the Jays' second base job.

But early complaints about the rich getting richer dissolved just three weeks later as Joe Torre was diagnosed with prostate cancer. Bench coach Don Zimmer, who had been a major league player and manager for almost half a century, took over until Torre was able to return two months later. The announcement of his illness came just two days after all-time Yankee great Joe DiMaggio passed away at age 84. In many ways this was just the beginning of a very long year for the Yankees' extended family.

No one expected the Bombers to duplicate their phenomenal 1998, but the team had trouble sustaining even a small winning streak in the early going. Torre's return seemed to settle the team down and, with Jeter and designated hitter Chili Davis leading the way, the Yankees nosed in front of their arch rivals, the Boston Red Sox. New York would widen its lead during the summer but could never quite shake the Sox, who were receiving MVP-caliber seasons from shortstop Nomar Garciaparra and pitcher Pedro Martinez. For their part, the Yankees were getting the usual offensive numbers from Tino Martinez, Williams and O'Neill, who would all drive home more than 100 runs, as would Jeter. In fact, Jeter and Williams both topped 200 hits, the first time a pair of Yankees had accomplished that feat in the same season since Lou Gehrig and Joe DiMaggio in 1936. The pitching, however, was a little shaky. Hernandez moved his game up a notch to become the staff ace, but Clemens struggled with arm problems all year. Cone had ailments that limited him to pitching about once a week in the season's second half, and Pettitte got off to such a poor start that he was almost traded to Philadelphia until Torre pleaded his case. Nevertheless, Cone tossed a perfect game in July and was able to contribute a dozen victories, and Pettitte rebounded in the second half to win 14, the same number as Clemens, who saved his best for the very end. And Rivera was Rivera, saving a league-high 45 games with a 1.83 ERA. New York won 98 games, best in the league and four games better than Boston.

For the second straight year (and third time in four seasons) New York took on Texas in the first round of the playoffs, and for the second straight year the Yankees knocked them off easily. Hernandez was almost unhittable in the opener, giving up just a single and double to catcher (and AL MVP) Ivan Rodriguez, as he breezed to an 8–0 win. The Rangers actually took the lead in Game Two, on a Juan Gonzalez home run, but the Yankees pecked away and, with Pettitte pitching a strong game into the eighth, came out with a 3–1 triumph. Then Clemens limited the Rangers to just three hits as the Yankees once again limited the Rangers to just one run in the three games.

In a series that at times resembled a slow-pitch softball tournament, the Red Sox outslugged Cleveland to move into the league championship series. Boston was primed as they scored three times in the first two innings. But the Sox only had one reliable starter, Martinez, and he had pitched in the last game against Cleveland and would therefore not be available until Game Three. Brosius, then, brought New York to within one with a two-run homer in the second, a Jeter hit tied it in the seventh, and Williams won it with a leadoff homer in the tenth. Pedro's brother Ramon baffled the Yankees for six innings in Game Two and had a 2–1 lead, courtesy of a Garciaparra home run off Cone. But in the seventh Knoblauch doubled home the tying run and scored the lead run on an O'Neill hit, and Torre used four pitchers in the eighth before calling on Rivera in the ninth to sew up the 3–2 win. Game Three was supposed to be the marquee matchup of former Red Sox ace Clemens versus current Red Sox ace Martinez, but it didn't materialize. Boston pounded Clemens and Irabu for 19 hits and 13 runs, while Pedro gave up just two singles in seven innings as Boston handed New York perhaps their worst postseason defeat ever, 13–1. The Yankees rebounded the next day, however, getting some unexpected help from an umpire. Trailing by just a 3–2 margin, Boston beefed long and loud when the Yankees were credited with an eighth inning double play, claiming their runner had beaten the throw to second. Later umpire Tim Tschida admitted he may have made a mistake, but it didn't help Boston at all, especially in the ninth when the Bombers broke it open with six runs, four on a Ricky Ledee grand slam. Needing just one more win and attempting to avoid facing Pedro Martinez again, New York took it to the Sox right away as Jeter hit a two-run homer in the first inning. Hernandez made it stand up until the seventh, when two Boston errors helped the Yankees widen their lead and pretty much put the game out of reach.

The last World Series of the 20th century pitted the two best teams of the 1990s: the Yankees and Atlanta Braves. That the Braves made it that far was something of a miracle: first baseman Andres Galarraga, one of the best RBI men in the game, missed all season after being diagnosed with lymphoma in the spring; closer Kerry Ligtenberg was also disabled in the spring with an arm injury; catcher Javier Lopez went out in July with a damaged knee; and pitchers Rudy Seanez and Odalis Perez were also lost about that time. But the pitching of Greg Maddux, Tom Glavine, John Smoltz and Kevin Millwood kept them in most games, and the bats of third baseman Chipper Jones (the National League's Most Valuable Player) and outfielders Brian Jordan and (ex–Yankee) Gerald Williams gave the Braves just enough offense to win.

Hernandez and Maddux drew the opening assignments and dueled through seven, with Jones' fourth inning homer the only tally. But in the eighth the Yankees finally broke through against Maddux. Aided by two errors by reserve first baseman Brian Hunter, clutch singles by Jeter and O'Neill and a bases-loaded walk, New York scored four times. Rivera, as usual, finished up as the Yankees held Atlanta to just two hits in the 4–1 triumph. Young Millwood had won 18 games in the regular season and his 2.68 ERA was second-best in the league, but he had nothing in Game Two as New York clipped him for three runs in the first and two more in the third. Cone gave up just one hit in his seven innings as the Yanks cruised to a 7–2 win.

The handwriting seemed to be on the wall as play moved to the Bronx, but the Braves gave it their best shot in Game Three. Atlanta scored three times in the third and, when they drove Pettitte from the mound in the fourth, held a 5–1 lead behind ace lefty Glavine. The Yankees scored in the fifth and seventh on home runs by Chad Curtis and Tino Martinez, but still trailed by two. Braves manager Bobby Cox, however, made a tactical error at this point, allowing a tiring Glavine to pitch the eighth. Knoblauch made him pay with a game-tying home run, and it was now obvious that the sand was running out of Atlanta's hourglass. Curtis ended it in the tenth when, leading off the inning, he ripped the third pitch he saw from southpaw Mike Remlinger for a game-winning homer. New York then kept their date with history by completing the sweep, 4–1. They nicked Smoltz for three runs in the third and Clemens, given that opportunity to close out a World Series he had always craved, was up to the task, yielding just four hits. "I finally know what it feels like to be a Yankee," he said afterwards.

The Yankees had won back-to-back World Series, and the way they did it put them in select company. After losing Game Two to Atlanta in 1996, they won 12 straight games in the Fall Classic, tying a record. They became only the third team in history (the 1927–28 Yankees and 1938–39 Yankees were the others) to sweep consecutive Series. Their postseason record in 1998 and 1999 combined was 22–3. In addition, they accomplished all this with heavy hearts. Former Yankee great Jim "Catfish" Hunter passed away in September, a victim of Lou Gehrig's Disease. Scott Brosius' father succumbed to cancer in September, Luis Sojo's father died just before the World Series began, and Paul O'Neill played in Game Four even though his father lost his battle to lung and kidney failure the night before. If nothing else, this Yankee team knew how to persevere.

The New York Yankees began the decade as perhaps the worst team in the majors, but they completed it by being compared to the very greatest teams of all time. Perhaps the success of this selfless team is the most fitting way for baseball to close out one century and begin a new one.

THE RANKINGS

As we mentioned in the preface, we are closing with our rankings of these teams. They are highly subjective, of course, and you are free to disagree with any or all.

In fact, we disagree with each other, and when we discovered that fact we decided — in the interest of continuing our friendship! — to submit two separate lists.

Marshall's Rankings

1. 1936–39 Yankees
2. 1949–56 Dodgers
3. 1926–28 Yankees
4. 1929–31 A's
5. 1972–74 A's
6. 1921–24 Giants
7. 1949–53 Yankees
8. 1975–76 Reds
9. 1996–99 Yankees
10. 1984 Tigers
11. 1942–46 Cardinals
12. 1910–14 A's
13. 1960–64 Yankees
14. 1990s Braves
15. 1954 Indians
16. 1976–78 Yankees
17. 1906–08 Cubs
18. 1939–40 Reds
19. 1969–71 Orioles
20. 1960 Pirates
21. 1969 Mets
22. 1921–23 Yankees
23. 1967–68 Cardinals
24. 1934–35 Tigers
25. 1912 Red Sox

Chris' Rankings

1. 1929–31 A's
2. 1975–76 Reds
3. 1926–28 Yankees
4. 1936–39 Yankees
5. 1921–24 Giants
6. 1949–56 Dodgers
7. 1972–74 A's
8. 1949–53 Yankees

9. 1942–46 Cardinals
10. 1996–99 Yankees
11. 1910–14 A's
12. 1954 Indians
13. 1990s Braves
14. 1906–08 Cubs
15. 1939–40 Reds
16. 1912 Red Sox
17. 1984 Tigers

18. 1960–64 Yankees
19. 1969 Mets
20. 1934–35 Tigers
21. 1976–78 Yankees
22. 1967–68 Cardinals
23. 1921–23 Yankees
24. 1960 Pirates
25. 1969–71 Orioles

BIBLIOGRAPHY

Ballew, Bill. "Familiar Ending Haunts Braves Despite Record 106 Wins." *Baseball America's 1999 Almanac*, Allan Simpson, ed. Durham, NC: Baseball America, 1999.

Balzer, Howard. "Comeback Yanks Added to Storied History." *Official Baseball Guide*. St. Louis, MO: The Sporting News, 1979.

_____. "Royals Plans Were Short-Circuited by Yanks." *Official Baseball Guide*. St. Louis, MO: The Sporting News, 1979.

"Brooks Won 3-Club N.L. Race on Final Day." *Baseball Guide and Record Book*. St. Louis, MO: The Sporting News, 1957.

Carter, Craig, ed. *The Sporting News Baseball Guide*. St. Louis, MO: The Sporting News, 1992–1998 editions.

"Casey's Au Revoir with His 10th Yank Flag." *Baseball Guide and Record Book*. St. Louis, MO: The Sporting News, 1961.

Craig, Roger, and Vern Plagenhoef. *Inside Pitch: Roger Craig's '84 Tiger Journal*. Grand Rapids, MI: William B. Eerdmans Publishing, 1984.

Creamer, Robert W. *Stengel: His Life and Times*. New York: Simon and Schuster, 1984.

"Dodgers First N.L. Repeaters Since '44." *Baseball Guide and Record Book*. St. Louis, MO: The Sporting News, 1954.

"Dodgers' Greatest Year — Flag, World Title." *Baseball Guide and Record Book*. St. Louis, MO: The Sporting News, 1956.

Enright, James E. "World Champion Cubs of 1907." *Chicago Cubs 1876–1976: A Century of Diamond Memories*. Chicago, IL: Chicago National League Ball Club, 1976.

Fishman, Lew. *New York's Mets: Miracle at Shea*. Englewood Cliffs, NJ: Prentice Hall, 1974.

Fraley, Gerry. "Bobby Cox Returning as Braves' GM." *Atlanta Constitution*, October 22, 1985.

Gage, Tom. "Tigers Enjoy a Dream Season." *Official Baseball Guide, 1985 Edition*. St. Louis, MO: The Sporting News, 1985.

Garagiola, Joe. *Baseball Is a Funny Game*. Philadelphia, PA: J.B. Lippincott, 1960.

Golenbock, Peter. *Bums: An Oral History of the Brooklyn Dodgers*. New York: G.P. Putnam's Sons, 1984.

_____. *Wrigleyville: A Magical History Tour of the Chicago Cubs*. New York: St. Martin's, 1996.

Groat, Dick, and Frank Dascenzo. *Groat: I Hit and Ran*. Durham, NC: Moore Publishing, 1978.

Halberstam, David. *Summer of '49*. New York: William Morrow and Company, Inc., 1989.

Henkey, Ben. *Official Baseball Guide for 1970*. St. Louis, MO: The Sporting News, 1970.
Honig, Donald. *Baseball America*. New York: Galahad Books, 1985.
_____. *Baseball's 10 Greatest Teams*. New York: Macmillan, 1982.
"Indians Won Flag with Record 111 Victories." *Baseball Guide and Record Book*. St. Louis, MO: The Sporting News, 1955.
Jordan, David M. *The Athletics of Philadelphia: Connie Mack's White Elephants, 1901–1954*. Jefferson, NC: McFarland, 1999.
Kahn, Roger. *The Boys of Summer*. New York: Harper and Row, 1971.
Koppett, Leonard. "Close Races Expected in Three of Four Divisions." *New York Times*, April 6, 1969, Section 5.
Lang, Jack. "Simply Fantabulous, Those Mets." *Official Baseball Guide for 1970*. St. Louis, MO: The Sporting News, 1970.
Lieb, Frederick G. "Review of Series." *Official Baseball Guide*. St. Louis, MO: The Sporting News, Editions 1954–65.
Linn, Ed. *Steinbrenner's Yankees*. New York: Holt, Rinehart and Winston, 1982.
Lusk, Lacy. "Padres Hold Off Braves to Win First Pennant Since '84." *Baseball America's 1999 Almanac*, Allan Simpson, ed. Durham, NC: Baseball America, 1999.
Manuel, John. "Braves Continue Decade of Dominance, at Least in NL." *Baseball America 2000 Almanac*, Allan Simpson, ed. Durham, NC: Baseball America, 2000.
Marcin, Joe. *Official Baseball Guide, 1975*. St. Louis, MO: The Sporting News, 1975.
Markusen, Bruce. *Baseball's Last Dynasty: Charlie Finley's Oakland A's*. Indianapolis, IN: Masters Press, 1998.
Mead, William B. *Low and Outside: Baseball in the Depression, 1930–1939*. Alexandria, VA: Redefinition, 1990.
Neft, David S., Richard M. Cohen and Michael L. Neft, eds. *The Sports Encyclopedia: Baseball*, 18th edition. New York: St. Martin's, 1998.
Oakley, J. Ronald. *Baseball's Last Golden Age, 1946–1960*. Jefferson, NC: McFarland, 1994.
Okrent, Daniel, and Harris Lewine, eds. *The Ultimate Baseball Book*. Boston: Houghton Mifflin, 1981.
Perrotto, John. "Yankees Leave No Doubt About Team of Decade — Or Century." *Baseball America 2000 Almanac*, Allan Simpson, ed. Durham, NC: Baseball America, 2000.
"Pirates Pennant First in 33 Years." *Baseball Guide and Record Book*. St. Louis, MO: The Sporting News, 1961.
"Poetic Justice." *Burlington, N.C. Times-News*, October 29, 1995.
Ray, Ralph. "A's Top Tigers in Boisterous Series." *Official Baseball Guide, 1973*. St. Louis, MO: The Sporting News, 1973.
"Reds Dead, Baby, Reds Dead." *Burlington, N.C. Times-News*, October 15, 1995.
Reidenbaugh, Lowell. "Mets Fracture Form, Wipe Out Braves." *Official Baseball Guide for 1970*. St. Louis, MO: The Sporting News, 1970.
_____. *Official Baseball Guide, 1974*. St. Louis, MO: The Sporting News, 1974.
_____. "Yanks' 18th Flag, Third for Stengel." *Baseball Guide and Record Book*. St. Louis, MO: The Sporting News, 1952.
Robinson, Ray, and Christopher Jennison. *Yankee Stadium: 75 Years of Drama, Glamor and Glory*. New York: Penguin Studio, 1998.
Ryan, Jeff. "The Comeback." *The Yankees, George Steinbrenner's 25*. St. Louis, MO: The Sporting News (online), 1999.
_____. "World Series-bound." *New York Yankees, Century of Champions — 1973–1979: Return to Glory*. St. Louis, MO: The Sporting News (online), 1999.
"Star-Studded Yankees Shake Early Woes to Repeat as AL East Champs." *World Series 1977*, Clifford Kachline, ed. New York: Office of the Commissioner, 1977.

Stinson, Thomas. "Bad News Braves." *Atlanta Journal-Constitution*, October 11, 1998.
"Story of the Braves: The Team of the '90s." The Official Online Home of the Atlanta Braves (*www.atlantabraves.com*), 1999.
Sullivan, Neil J. *The Dodgers Move West*. New York: Oxford University Press, 1987.
Tenbarge, Lawrence. "Kings of the Hill." *The National Pastime: A Review of Baseball History*. Cleveland, OH: The Society for American Baseball Research, 1995.
Thorn, John, et al., eds. *Total Baseball*, 5th edition. New York: Penguin, 1997.
Von Borries, Philip. "Yesteryear: 1907 — What a Year!" *Chicago Cubs Official Souvenir Program Magazine*. Chicago, IL: Chicago National League Ball Club, 1983.
Wigge, Larry. "Tigers Complete Dream Season." *Official Baseball Guide, 1985 Edition*. St. Louis, MO: The Sporting News, 1985.
_____. "Tigers Sweep Royals Aside." *Official Baseball Guide, 1985 Edition*. St. Louis, MO: The Sporting News, 1985.
Williams, Pete. "McGriff Unleashed in Game Four Pounding." *USA Today Baseball Weekly*. October 11–17, 1995.
"With Mantle, Maris Hurt, Yanks Still Won." *Official Baseball Guide*. St. Louis, MO: The Sporting News, 1964.
"Yankees Edged White Sox, Orioles at Wire." *Official Baseball Guide*. St. Louis, MO: The Sporting News, 1965.
"Yanks Had Off Year, but Won Flag Anyway." *Official Baseball Guide*. St. Louis, MO: The Sporting News, 1963.
"Yanks Repeated Old Script Under New Pilot." *Baseball Guide and Record Book*. St. Louis, MO: The Sporting News, 1962.

INDEX